The Hollywood Social Problem Film

The
Hollywood Social
Problem Film

Madness, Despair,
and Politics from the
Depression to the Fifties

Peter Roffman and Jim Purdy

Indiana University Press • Bloomington

Dedicated to our parents,
without whose support, moral and
otherwise, this book would not
have been possible.

Chapter 4 appeared in slightly revised form in Take One, March 1977
(Vol. 5, No. 8), pp. 20–25, as "Hollywood Turns to the Right."
Chapter 7 appeared in slightly revised form in Cineaste, Fall 1978
(Vol. IX, No. 1), pp. 8–13, as "The Worker and Hollywood."

Library of Congress Cataloging in Publication Data
Roffman, Peter, 1950–
The Hollywood social problem film.
Bibliography: p.
Filmography: p.
1. Moving-picture plays—Criticism and interpreta-
tion. 2. Moving-pictures—Social aspects—United
States. I. Purdy, Jim, joint author. II. Title.
PN1995.R63 791.43'09'09355 80–8100
ISBN 0–253–12707–6 1 2 3 4 5 85 84 83 82 81
ISBN 0–253–20261–2 pbk.

CONTENTS

Preface   vii
Introduction   1

PART I: The System Breaks Down:
          The Individual as Victim, 1930–1933

    1. Prototypes: Gangsters, Fallen Women,
        and Convicts   15
    2. The Shysters   31
    3. The Populists—Or, Who's Afraid
        of the Big Bad Wolf?   46
    4. Desperation—Hollywood Turns to the Right   65
    5. From Despair to Recovery: Warner
        Brothers and FDR   78

PART II: The System Upheld:
          The Individual Redeemed, 1933–1941

    6. Unemployment—Doing Your Part   91
    7. Hollywood and the Worker   104
    8. Rural Problems   121
    9. The Juvenile Delinquent and Society   135
   10. The Ex-Con and Society   146
   11. Different Problems, Same Solutions   155

PART III: Fascism and War

12.	Native Fascists—Lynching and Legions	165
13.	Frank Capra's Super-Shysters and Little People	179
14.	More Plutocrats and Would-Be Dictators	190
15.	International Fascism—From Pacifism to War	200

PART IV: The Postwar World

16.	Readjustment—"Nervous from the Service"	227
17.	The Minorities	235
18.	More Neuroses—Alcoholism and Insanity	257
19.	Postwar Labor Problems	262
20.	The Individual and Society: Darker Views of the Postwar World	268
21.	HUAC and the End of an Era	284

Conclusion: Sullivan's Travels—
                  Hollywood Goes Slumming   300

Notes	307
Selected Bibliography	319
Selected Filmography	331
Index	353

Preface

In Preston Sturges' wonderfully caustic *Sullivan's Travels* (1941), big-time Hollywood director John L. Sullivan (Joel McCrea) argues that he's tired of making frivolous entertainments like "Ants in Your Pants of 1939" and "Hey Hey in the Hayloft." Instead, he wants to shoot "Oh Brother Where Art Thou?" because it will "realize the potentialities of FILM as the sociological and artistic medium it is." Sullivan's crassly commercial producers are, of course, outraged. They rant and rave, trying to convince their star director that it will "die in Pittsburgh" and that a picture's got to have a little sex in it to make it at the box office. But John L. will not be deterred from his apparently quixotic endeavor and he goes out into the "real world" to learn first-hand about poverty and suffering. What he finds is that the public just doesn't appreciate such a "deep-dish" movie. As his worldly butler haughtily remarks, "The subject is not an interesting one. The poor know all about poverty and only the morbid rich would find the topic glamorous." In short, to quote that old Hollywood rubric, "If you've got a message, send it Western Union."

Despite such conventional wisdom, Hollywood did in fact send a lot of messages and not via Western Union. Movies with a point of view and a sense of social commitment were not as rare as liberal critics of the thirties and forties lamented. And while a large number of these films proved to be as uninspiring as John L. Sullivan's would-be "Oh Brother Where Art Thou?" there are among them some of the finest films Hollywood ever produced. As a whole, the Hollywood social problem film represents a significant social and artistic achievement, marshalling the resources of film to provide a vivid commentary on the times.

John L. is expressing a genuine liberal concern, a need to say something "significant . . . to hold a mirror up to reality." Such concern required in the studios of Hollywood that he make a picture separate from the standard fare of trivial entertainment. His "Oh Brother" falls within a special genre, the social problem film. This was the genre reserved for making "statements" and is thereby characterized by a self-conscious approach to theme and topic. John L. is out to "teach a moral lesson of social significance" in a didactic fashion by calling attention to a contemporary social condition (in his case, the struggle between labor and capital). The focus of the genre is very specific: the central dramatic conflict revolves around the interaction of the individual with social institutions (such as government, business, political movements, etc.). While the genre places great importance on the surface mechanisms of society, there is only an indirect concern with broader social values (those of the family, sexuality, religion, etc.), the values that function behind the mechanisms. As such, the genre often seemed glib in its social analysis, viewing America as a series of social agencies that from time to time experience "problems" which must be corrected. For the most part, the films attack such problems in order to inspire limited social change or reinforce the status quo.

Thus, the problem film combines social analysis and dramatic conflict within a coherent narrative structure. Social content is transformed into dramatic events and movie narrative adapted to accommodate social issues as story material through a particular set of movie conventions. These conventions distinguish the social problem film as a genre. This book is an analysis of those conventions and the manner in which they influenced how social issues were promulgated to a mass audience.

Paradoxically, there is extensive crossing of genres, since many problem films also fall into other movie categories. Certain musical numbers that address social injustice, crime films where criminality is viewed in direct relation to social institutions, women's pictures that chart the heroine's plight as a result of economic conditions, and comedies that zero in on the paradoxes of political and economic structures are all self-consciously dealing with social conditions even while they retain the features of their basic genre forms. On the other hand, we have excluded for the purpose of this book the large roster of films which address themselves to similar issues but not within a contemporary context. These include historical "message" pictures such as Warners' Paul Muni biography cycle (*The Life of Emile Zola*, 1937, and *Juarez*, 1939) and *Viva Zapata* (1952).

The important distinguishing feature of the genre is its didacticism. It deals with social themes very much on the surface of the dramatic action. The vast majority of films whose political viewpoints are implied beneath the action cannot thus be counted as problem films. Films such as Shirley Temple musicals and Andy Hardy comedies connote establishment values while the Marx Brothers and *High Noon* (1952) imply subversive outlooks, but none of them draw explicit attention to their politics in the manner of the problem film genre.

That John L. should express such socially conscious sentiments ("How can I do a musical at a time like this?") was natural to the period. From the advent of the Depression to the rise of McCarthyism, a strong sensibility of social concern was given play in America. In politics, FDR and the New Deal functioned as the focal point of this sensibility, and in the arts, agitprop drama, proletarian literature, documentary photography represented a major strain of cultural expression. The economic breakdown of the Depression, the rise of fascism and the war against it, and the idealistic vigor of the postwar years all fostered a concern with social conditions, an impulse toward political change. The theater of Odets, the novels of Steinbeck, the songs of Guthrie all found a large public responsive to their criticism of social structures. But between the death of Roosevelt and the censure of McCarthy, this sensibility faded, partly due to McCarthyism itself and largely due to the changed social perspectives of the prosperous fifties.

The other major influence on John L.'s work would be Hollywood itself, for the social problem film emerged from the specific context of the Movies. From 1930 to the mid-fifties was the "golden era" of the Hollywood sound film and the studio system. A basic set of film conventions and a consistent ideological framework were imposed on almost all movie products. Familiar conventions of plot and character repeated themselves in infinite variations in westerns and musicals and thrillers. However, during the 1950s, this era gradually came to an end. With the rise of television, Hollywood began to lose its central prominence as a force in popular culture and, with the gradual breakup of the studios and the rise of the independents, it began to lose its control over the narrative and ideological conventions of movies. The Production Code, long Hollywood's arbiter of taste, in fact the studios' official ideological scripture, was regularly loosened throughout the fifties and entirely dispensed with during the early sixties. New film styles and new areas of subject matter emerged.

These two parallel elements—the era of social consciousness and Hollywood's studio formula—are the dominant forces behind the Hollywood social problem film. For this reason, the period from 1930 to the mid-fifties represents a distinct approach to social criticism. The problem film of this era constitutes a self-contained body of work with its own unique evolution and a consistent overall political viewpoint. While subsequent political films certainly grew out of these movies and often appear very similar in form and content, they are part of a different era, function within a different cultural framework, and serve a somewhat different social purpose.

Finally, it is important to appreciate the cultural force that the problem film represented. The Hollywood movie in its prime reached an immense audience. The weekly trip to the movies was not just a double bill of well-packaged entertainment but a forum where social values were played out in a very attractive and stimulating fashion. While all films have something to say, the social problem film functions to more directly influence the attitudes of the public. What its message was and what impact it had on either reinforcing or discouraging certain social values is a major question this book seeks to explore.

The purpose of this study is to provide a comprehensive overview of the cycles and patterns of the genre, examining the relationship between political issues and movie conventions, between what happened in American society and what appeared on its screens. Although we have endeavored to cover the full body of the problem film, it is inevitable that some films have been omitted. Still, we are confident that despite the absence of individual pictures, the following captures the prominent contours of the genre as a whole.

Acknowledgments are due to many who helped us in the various stages of research and writing. Particular thanks are due to Gerald Pratley and the staff of the Ontario Film Institute for allowing us to camp out in their film research library for so many years and to Joe Medjuck of *Take One* and Gary Crowdus of *Cineaste*. For the screenings of the films we gratefully acknowledge the Wisconsin Center for Theater Research at the University of Wisconsin; the Motion Picture Section of the Library of Congress; George Eastman House in Rochester, New York; the Film Study Center of the Museum of Modern Art; plus several distributors who generously extended us access to their prints; and to Ian Miller who kept the car in operation so we could travel to all of the above. For their perseverance and patience at typing the various drafts of the manuscript, we express our appreciation to Mildred Vitale, Hannah Shostack, and D. A. Nathan. And a special nod to Robin Wood for his comments on our manuscript.

INTRODUCTION

The Hollywood Formula

A "Hollywood movie" means more than just a film made in a studio in Southern California. Rather, it implies a whole style of film, a particular approach to film narrative, a peculiar set of cultural and social values. The character of the Hollywood movie is a given in terms of the social problem film, for the genre inherits the core qualities of the Hollywood film as well as its place in the cultural structure of America. It is important, then, to summarize the basic nature of the Hollywood movie in general before analyzing the social problem film specifically. To do this, one must understand the basis of film production within the Hollywood studio. How a movie is made and how it is consumed largely determine the shape of the final product and its impact on the public. The economic structure of the industry thoroughly influenced the process of moviemaking and movie-consuming, imposing certain variables on filmmaking and fostering certain expectations in audiences.

By the early thirties, power in American feature films rested with eight major firms—MGM, Warner Brothers, Paramount, Twentieth Century-Fox, Universal, RKO, Columbia, and United Artists—which had consolidated production, distribution, and exhibition into a monolithic corporate structure monopolizing the industry. The key element in the structure was exhibition. As long as they owned all the first-run theaters, the Big Eight had control over the market and could close it to any non-affiliated producer.[1] They managed to extend this structure more or less throughout the world, until foreign countries began imposing quotas and in 1947 their own country began dismantling the monopoly. But over the period from 1930 to the fifties, the Big Eight could determine entirely what the public could see, and therefore what pictures were made and

1

who made them. And obviously, it was their own production companies, the studios in Hollywood, which did all the moviemaking.

It is also important to realize that 90 percent of the industry's capital investment lay in the theaters, not the studios,[2] so that production of motion pictures was important only as an arm of the larger functions of distribution and exhibition. What was needed was a steady turnover of product for the theaters since revenue was tied in with the regular attendance at many theaters on a continual basis, not on high attendance for any one movie during a single run. From an industry point of view, then, making good pictures was secondary to making a lot of pictures.

This is not to say that production heads were not concerned with making good films. On the contrary, they worked very hard not just to turn out the quantity, but also to ensure a high level of quality. For all its limitations and drawbacks, the studio production system accomplished this twin purpose to a remarkable degree. The studios operated by and large on an assembly-line basis, with writers and directors usually assigned projects to be started Monday morning and with various departments concentrating solely on their specific spheres of activity from picture to picture.

The production heads—Mayer, Jack Warner, Zanuck, Cohn—were the ones with the creative power. They approved all projects and scripts; they chose or at least approved the choice of director and cast for each project; they required that scenes be rewritten or reshot or recut; and they oversaw in a very real sense every frame of film produced on their respective lots. Of course, variations within this framework were frequent, depending on the nature of the picture and the relationship between production head and the individual producer or director or writer. As long as Frank Capra continued to turn out hits and fight for the right to make films his way, Columbia's Harry Cohn was content to give the director artistic freedom.

The assembly-line method was essential to getting the quantity of product into the theaters, but unlike most assembly lines, the studios were not mass-producing exactly the same product over and over. While each car off the assembly line is no different from all the others, each movie was unique. Means were quickly developed for the mass production of different products. A series of basic conventions—character, narrative, thematic, stylistic—was established as a standard mode of expression. This formula was broad enough to be applied in a wide variety of ways and flexible enough to shift with changing times and tastes, yet fixed enough to serve as a pattern for production and marketing.

The other half of the equation lay with the public. If the pattern of production did not create movies audiences wanted, then the whole purpose was defeated. Just as movies were mass-produced so were they mass-consumed, and the public responded to them as they did to other consumer goods. Audiences required elements with which they were familiar from week to week, for the continuity of well-known ingredients reassured them why they were buying their tickets. This need of the public dovetailed with that of the studios and the result was production and consumption according to the Hollywood Formula.

This Formula had no impact on the quality of the films as film. It certainly determined the kind of films that could be made, but as the body of Hollywood movies attests, the requirements of the great commercial machine did not necessarily frustrate artistic expression but rather defined the nature of that expression. Considering the wit, charm, and energy of so many Hollywood films, it is not unreasonable to view the studio assembly line as a giant workshop in which many talents combined to create within an already established set of artistic conventions.[3]

The Formula was based on certain elements readily recognizable to a public that had to know in general terms what to expect every week at the picture show. It was also predicated on the fact that mass entertainment involved wish fulfillment, the presentation of things as we would like them to be. The primary ingredient in the Formula was the star who acted as an ideal for audience identification and who embodied a constant personality from film to film. Over a period of several films, the public came to know a star very well, so much so that it became difficult for actors to deviate very far beyond their normal range. Everyone knew more or less what was in store for them when they went to see a Clark Gable or a Bette Davis or a Jimmy Cagney picture, and the studios protected the stars' screen personae by tailoring films to enhance the qualities of each star. And because the stars were the projections of the public's own fantasies, they embodied most of the elements of wish fulfillment. They did all the things their public yearned to do and always came out on top. For this reason, the star system was the most important factor in marketing movies. Not only were character, storyline, and style built around the star, so was all the hype from ads to magazines to press coverage about the glamorous world of Hollywood.

The genre film was the second most important means of categorizing and marketing a movie. If the public knew the picture was a western or a musical, a screwball comedy or a horror movie, a gangster film or a woman's picture, then it knew what ingredients to expect; it was simply a question of how the ingredients would be mixed this time around.[4] Familiar genre forms provide variations on familiar movie experiences and made moviegoing a kind of ritual. Repetition meant a relatively effortless participation by the audience in the familiar screen experience. There was absolute trust that the hero would prevail and get the girl. It was just a matter of how and when.

Each genre had its own conventions of plot and style, but by and large they all conformed to an even more basic set of standards. This broad-based Formula of conventions was absolutely simplistic and many Hollywood films used it only as a starting point, developing beyond the conventions to a more sophisticated and often personalized approach to film. Still, the Formula was the mandatory starting point, for, as we have seen, it was imposed on the filmmaker by both the studio system and audience expectations. The Hollywood plot and character conventions grew out of the nineteenth-century melodrama, with a more sophisticated veneer applied as movies matured. Visual style was the manufactured studio realism which can be traced to Belasco's turn-of-the-century stage naturalism. These conventions only began to lose their complete dominance during the fifties when the studios began to lose their dominance over production and when television inherited both the movies' cultural function of serving entertainment to a mass public and many of the movies' conventions themselves.

The first convention was that the form be conventional, a linear narrative with the straightest line of action. A film had to tell a story, and do so as clearly and enjoyably as possible. Nonlinear elements could only function within the narrative in a form that did not distract from the narrative line, such as a musical number or a documentary montage that commented on the main action. The narrative must also be centered on the individual with whom the audience could identify. No Hollywood filmmaker could, as Eisenstein did, have the masses as hero.

The dramatic conflict was always structured around two opposing poles definitively representing good and evil, with a readily identifiable hero and villain. But since the hero was also the star, his goodness must conform to the star's personality. Absolute virtue, however, is generally unexciting and inhibits many of the star's qualities of illicit wish fulfillment. Thus the hero often embodied slightly tainted moral traits. As long as there was no doubt as to the hero's ultimate allegiance to the side of good, the audience could indulge in his minor transgressions. By subtly combining moral uprightness with an endearing toughness, the star was made more provocative and the hero a more effective combatant of villainy. He had the air of having been everywhere and seen everything. He was the Indian fighter who was raised by the Indians, the marshall who used to be an outlaw gunfighter, the police agent who was once one of the mob, and the ultimate good bad guy, the private eye who skirts between the world of law and the underworld of crime. This helped rationalize the hero's use of violent, even immoral means to achieve righteous ends. In the same way (though not nearly as often) sympathy could be extended to the criminal without ever upholding his criminality.

Conflict and emotion were generally expressed in terms of violent action. Violence allowed for straightforward visualization of feelings, crystallizing the issues in terms of physical combat. Language, too, adhered to this mode of expression, avoiding any indication of complex and hence confusing emotion.

An essential factor of wish fulfillment was romance and true love. This was presented as an elaboration on the good–evil conflict. Womanhood encompassed two poles, the purity of the virgin-heroine and the sexuality of the vamp-seductress, between which the hero must choose. He had to resist the vamp and the temptation of illicit, destructive sex and he must, when required, protect the heroine's virtue from the lecherous villain. His reward, the proper motivating force for all action, was the true love of a good woman and the promise of procreation and family.

Overt discussion of sexuality was avoided. At the same time, an essential component of many stars' appeal was their sexual allure and the audience fantasies constructed around it. The result was a sexual ambivalence in the films where the professed values of goodness were upheld while the supposedly rejected sensuality was indulged. The hero was often a rogue who at least temporarily delighted in the vamp's temptations. The ambivalence also emerged in the "good bad girl" of the 1940s. She combined the apparent experience and eroticism of the vamp with the actual virginal domesticity of the pure heroine.[5]

The good–evil morality called for a clear-cut, gratifying plot resolution —the Happy Ending, in which evil was destroyed and good rewarded. The ending left no doubt in the audience's mind that virtue was a positive force and that their fantasies could come true.

Along with the narrative went certain stylistic conventions. These varied from studio to studio, depending on management's taste and the corporation's economic status, and helped determine the nature of the films. In the first place, almost all Hollywood movies were made on sound stages and very rarely on location (with the exception of some westerns and adventure films). This gives the movies a studio look— all historical, geographical, and social milieus are transformed into a completely controlled and contrived environment. Wealthy studios such as MGM and Paramount generally preferred opulent sets, glossy photography, high-key lighting, and lush scores, believing that "production values" sold a film. Therefore the majority of their films were stories which accommodated such qualities—historical romances, adventure tales, screwball comedies, and extravagant musicals. Poorer studios such as Warners operated with functional bare sets, everyday costuming, and low-key lighting. The studio developed a fast-paced, hard-hitting style of editing and dialogue that deemphasized the lack of expensive production values. Setting and style together helped determine the type of stories Warners concentrated on: gangster and shyster films, working-class comedies, exposés of poverty and corruption. Warners became known as the socially conscious studio, while MGM became the home of sentimental Americana and Paramount that of sophisticated comedies.

Taken at surface level, there is nothing extraordinary about these dramatic conventions. Many of them have been basic to the art of drama since the Greeks. What is extraordinary is the sheer output of films adhering to the Formula, so that the conventions themselves became a part of the public's consciousness. Because practically all Hollywood movies adhered to the Formula, there was little opportunity for audiences to experience alternative approaches to film. For most Americans, the Formula was in essence The Movies.

The Formula became Hollywood law in 1934 with the introduction of the Production Code. The Code stated the ideological basis of the Formula, setting dictates on what subject matter could be dramatized and how it could be treated. The Code's edicts spell out in pontifical tones the moral value system behind the Hollywood Formula, decrying criminal violence and intimate sexuality while insisting upon the inviol-criminal violence and intimate sexuality while insisting upon the inviolability of law, the sanctity of marriage and the home, and the sovereignty

While Hollywood traditionally argued that it was disinterested in delivering "messages" and that movies were "pure entertainment," obviously the Code and Formula precepts do express a particular viewpoint and do seek to impose a message on the public. The Code testifies to this, blatantly stating that entertainment is "either HELPFUL or HARMFUL to the human race." Because of this, "the motion picture . . . has special MORAL OBLIGATIONS" to create only "correct entertainment" which "raises the whole standard of a nation" and "tends to improve the race, or at least to re-create or rebuild human beings exhausted with the realities of life."

In a very broad sense, a coherent ideological vision of the world is acted out in every Formula movie. The conventions place the emphasis on the individual and argue that anyone can aspire to success. Wealth, status, and power are possible in America, the land of opportunity where the individual is rewarded for virtue. Stereotypic values celebrate Americana in terms of home, motherhood, and community, puritan love and work ethic. All issues are reduced to a good and evil, black and white conflict, a them-and-us identification process where good equals us, the American values and social system. Them, the villains, are defined as those who reject and seek to destroy the proper set of values. Conflict is always resolved through the use of righteous force, with our American values winning out. The Formula helps shape not only the nature of movies, but also the values and attitudes of their public.

The Formula equated entertainment with Americanism. In *Picture*, Lillian Ross quotes one of Hollywood's more verbose and melodramatic spokesmen, Louis B. Mayer. He claimed that his mission in life was "to give the public entertainment, and thank God, it pays off. Clean, American entertainment."[7] To entertain meant to glorify clichés of Americana. Art on the other hand was quite different from entertainment and quite alien to Americanism and motherhood:

> Don't show the good, wholesome, American mother in the home. Kind. Sweet. Sacrifices. Love. . . . No! Knock the mother on the jaw! . . . Throw the little old lady down the stairs! . . . Throw the mother's good, homemade chicken soup in the mother's face! . . . Step on the mother! Kick her! That is art, they say. *Art!*[8]

MGM movies, so innocent and sentimental, not only made you laugh and cry but also made you feel that innocence and sentimentality were the right way to approach life. And they told you, in no uncertain terms, that such a way of life was peculiarly American.

Even though Hollywood would cater to anything that was popular with the public, it would always funnel that sentiment through the neutralizing influence of the Formula. Any point of view could be incorporated into a framework which so dramatized it that it inevitably conformed to Hollywood's preconceptions. Thus Hollywood presented its own vision of society by centering on a specific set of values, while minimizing and discrediting other values likewise prevalent. The movies mirrored the basic faith of the majority of the American public; they did not however, always give full expression to any variant opinions also held by that public.

All that said, it is now important to qualify such generalizations. First of all, there are a surprising number of films which manage to somehow subvert Formula values even while paying lip service to them. There is in these films an ambivalent tension between what is being played out on the surface and what is being inferred just beneath it. The Formula conventions were broad enough that a filmmaker with his own perceptions and the talent to juggle them with the needs of the Formula could express alternative, even subversive viewpoints. In the social problem film, as we shall discover throughout this book, there are frequent examples of this tension between a conventional form and a radical vision. But because its function was to call attention to specific social issues and to deal with controversial matters very much on the surface, the problem film had to speak with discretion. It is with other film genres that Hollywood could be at its most subversive. There is for example a strain of American comedy running from the Keystone Kops through Chaplin to the Marx Brothers, W. C. Fields, and the screwball eccentrics that is predicated on a hilarious anarchism and antisocial irreverence. Very rarely do these films call out for any social change or address specific issues. Instead they ridicule some of the basic tenets upon which American social interaction is founded and therefore attack the very roots of their society. All of this is done within a framework whereby the comedy keeps such criticism at a comfortable distance, putting the clowns and zanies, with all their wonderful appeal, in their own crazy universe, safely removed from the readily identifiable standard "reality." A similar case can be made for the *Film Noir* pictures of the forties with their dark insinuations about middle-class values of family and success.

But it is not simply a matter of subversive messages slipping by the studios and likewise over the heads of the audience. The public often shared the tension operating within the films, basically holding to a belief in status quo values even while questioning and challenging them. They would delight in the risqué sexual entendres of the opening café scene in *They Drive by Night* and then wallow in the sentiment of Ann Sheridan and George Raft's eventual marriage. Nor did such an undertone necessarily represent an entirely subversive viewpoint, since it was present in many "escapist" films. Escapism was intended to reassure audiences, to provide fantasies for a public exhausted with the realities of life. But even reassuring films had to allude in some way to the insecurities of the time in order to reassure. For example, Shirley Temple, often cited as Hollywood's supreme insult to Depression reality, usually played an orphan searching for a set of parents who will rescue her from hardship and provide a home and security. Errol Flynn, continually beset by official corruption and inefficiency, always had to lead his gang of pirates or brigade of lancers or band of merry men in righteous rebellion before he could set matters right. With both Temple and Flynn, their escapist fantasies work only by providing points of reference to the situations from which the audience seeks to escape.

Thus there is an intrinsic undercurrent of social irreverence functioning within the Formula, often even within the personalities of stars like Cagney and Bogart. It was this element of irreverence which audiences often found most appealing, as long as it was played out within the safe confines of the Formula where the hero eventually would go straight and the ending inevitably turn out happy. The simple fact that Hollywood films were so well attended is a clear indication that this Formula met the needs of its mass audience.

While fundamentally true, the premise that Formula values mirror public values also requires some qualifications. If a film appeals to a wide public then it must reflect something that public identifies with. However, one must remember that moviegoing was, up until the advent of television, more a compulsive social habit than a discriminating ex-pression of preference, that, as Gilbert Seldes said, "the fundamental passion is a desire to go to the movies which means to go to any movies, rather than not go at all."[9] Box-office revenue did not measure audience response to a film, did not record whether the spectator enjoyed or agreed with what he saw. It is also important to keep in mind that the popularity of Hollywood movies was dependent on Hollywood's monopoly of ex-hibition. Audiences could only popularize the films that played in the theaters and those theaters played only Hollywood films. There was little opportunity to choose movies with alternative approaches to film, so that the popularity of the Hollywood movie was never properly tested.

Hollywood represented a perfectly enclosed cultural network. The studios' complete control over production, distribution, and exhibition meant that the movies spoke with a singular voice to a mass public. That public became a partner in a dynamic relationship with the movies, re-sponding to certain films and thereby creating the need for more of the same product. Audience tastes were shaped by the movies just as the audience fed its own preferences back to help shape the next pictures. The movies spoke directly to the public, which turned around and spoke back, and in the process social values and traditions were held up for admiration, disdain, and debate.

Progenitor of the Problem Film

A brief survey of the earliest socially oriented movies—those of the decade preceding World War I—will serve as an illustration of how the problem picture reflects the predominant attitudes of the times and the commercial preconceptions of the movie industry. These early two-reelers are progenitors of the thirties and forties message movies, first because, like the later films, they appeared only when the right combination of elements was present, when the times and audience needs created an atmosphere in which such pictures were accepted; and then because they display the same tension between a concerned, progressive topicality in subject matter and an essentially conservative, moralistic narrative framework.

The early movie audience was primarily working class, living in the cities, poorly educated, and often of immigrant status. Since the film-maker had to provide these people with an easily recognizable milieu, the films centered on the common man in everyday situations. This was, furthermore, the era of muckraking reformism and Wilsonian progres-sivism. It was the time when social wrongdoing was identified with the super-rich capitalists and robber barons; the time of Upton Sinclair's and Lincoln Steffens' exposés, of Teddy Roosevelt's trust-busting. The mixture of these two factors—the sympathy for the common man and the prevailing criticism of the corrupt and wealthy—gave birth to a number of films that took the side of the poor against the rich.

In *The Rise of the American Film*,[10] Lewis Jacobs gives an excellent summary of these films. According to Jacobs, such pictures as *Burglar Bill*, *The Jail Bird*, and *Bandit King* showed criminals in a sympathetic light while others such as *The Need of Gold*, *The Miser's Hoard*, and *A Desperate Encounter* deplored poverty. Rich bankers and politicians came under attack in *Crooked Banker*, *Bank Defaulter*, *Miser's Fate*, and *The Politician*. Other social subjects included prostitution and white slavery, alcoholism, penal reform, the suffragette movement, and labor–capital strife.

These themes are presented in the form of late nineteenth-century melodrama and their point of view is fashioned by the Victorian morality intrinsic to the form. While the topics are contemporary and complex, the framework is one of old-fashioned virtues and simple homilies. Thus, in a film such as *The Ex-Convict* (1905), the problem of the reformed criminal confronted with a discriminatory society is reduced to a pat fable. An ex-convict is forced back into crime to support his wife and child, but the wealthy household which he attempts to rob miraculously turns out to be that of a little girl whose life he had earlier saved. Her grateful parents decide to help him and his family, consequently redeeming the criminal and society. The plot is resolved according to the conventions of melodrama and the central issues of the problem itself are never confronted. A surface liberal tolerance for the criminal is a pretext for a reaffirmation of traditional platitudes about virtue rewarded and a just society.

With America's entry into the war, the era of progressivism ended and the output of social problem films waned. The postwar era saw a greatly changed nation and audience. The reformist spirit was replaced by Harding and Coolidge conservatism. Meanwhile, the great wave of immigration receded and earlier immigrants became Americanized. The prosperity of the 1920s undermined older social barriers, allowing the lower classes to rise into and greatly expand the middle class. At the same time, the once aloof upper and upper-middle classes finally accepted movies as a social habit and started to attend regularly.

The films expressed the twenties' sense of optimism and prosperity. They focused on themes of sexual and material hedonism, gratifying the aspirations of the new leisure class. Among the popular cycles were De Mille's sex epics, Clara Bow's "It girl" flapper films, and Ernst Lubitsch's sophisticated boudoir comedies. The mood of positivism inhibited social criticism. An audience which now hungered after the symbols of wealth would no longer respond to films depicting a corrupt and exploitative ruling class. The upwardly mobile had no interest in films focusing on the entrapment of poverty.

Socially conscious films were rare during this era. Only a few film-makers managed to criticize the American Dream at its height. Outside the mainstream of production not only in subject matter but also in form, their films were highly sophisticated and individualized works. Most notable were Von Stroheim's *Greed* (1923) and Chaplin's *The Gold Rush* (1925), both critical of the lust for wealth; Von Sternberg's *Salvation Hunters* (1925), a portrait of waterfront dereliction; James Cruze's *Beggar on Horseback* (1923), a satire on big business and advertising; and King Vidor's *The Crowd* (1928), a remarkable study of big city alienation.

It was not until the Depression ended prosperity and leveled the middle class that a new cycle of social problem films began. A hungry and insecure audience needed the psychic relief and rejuvenation of entertainment films but also demanded that filmmakers give at least token recognition to the ever-pressing social realities of the time. The result was a move toward greater realism in style and subject matter which allowed for a substantial body of socially oriented films.

Victorian melodrama developed into the Hollywood Formula and contemporary events continued to be interpreted within the bounds of a reactionary value system. The explicitly social story material of the Depression was presented in terms of virtue rewarded, so that any potential criticism was diffused. As with *The Ex-Convict*, problems were acknowledged without really being examined. On one level, the movies' topical subject matter was responsive to audience tastes and changing times, but on another, the rigid and outmoded interpretation of that subject matter was responsive only to the economics and values of the studio system.

—PART I—

The System
Breaks Down:
The Individual
as Victim,
1930-1933

—1—

PROTOTYPES: GANGSTERS, FALLEN WOMEN, AND CONVICTS

The Gangster Cycle

Between the beginning of the Depression in 1930 and the early days of the Roosevelt administration in 1933, when confusion and desperation gripped much of the country, Hollywood momentarily floundered. Not only did the studios have to make the difficult transition to sound, they had to adjust to the rapidly changing tastes of a nation in upheaval. These two variables—sound and the Depression—created a whole new set of aesthetic demands requiring that the old Formula be placed within a new context. The studios at first experimented with extravagant musicals and photographed plays, but dwindling audience interest quickly prompted them to revert to action and melodrama. It didn't take too long to realize that the talkies required a greater surface realism. The romantic, ethereal fantasies of the twenties' films sounded ridiculous when put into words: John Gilbert's passion may have been eloquently mirrored in his face and eyes, but when he attempted to express it verbally the emotions seemed silly and banal. Correspondingly, the hard facts of the Depression demanded a shift in subject matter. Latin lovers and college flappers now seemed rather remote, completely unrelated to the changed mood and the overriding preoccupation with social breakdown. The romantic ideals of the thirties had to be more firmly grounded in a topical context.

The films of the early Depression years reflect much of the desperation of the time, both in their initial groping for new character types and settings and in their eventual preoccupation with an amoral society and the inefficacy of once-sacred values. By late 1933, with the New Deal inspiring confidence, Hollywood had found its bearings. The studios were now secure with the new sound medium and had established the dramatic conventions expressive of new attitudes. New Deal confidence and Hays Office moralism removed much of the hard edge from the early thirties cycles, but the basic groundwork for the remainder of the decade had been laid and Hollywood could now proceed with greater self-assurance.

It was during this period that the social problem film emerged as an important genre. It did not immediately spring into existence with the arrival of a major social crisis but was rather the end product of a gradual evolution. Important stylistic and narrative motifs had to be developed before the talkies could begin self-consciously to analyze the issues of the day. First among these were character prototypes—the gangster, the fallen woman, the convict, and the shyster—and a contemporary setting—the alleyways, slums, and speakeasies of the big city. Shot in a racy but essentially realistic style, these early films are the archetypal Depression movies. Though they do not really constitute problem films in themselves, the gangster, fallen woman, and prison cycles metaphorically comment on the relationship between the individual and society, taking a highly cynical attitude toward social institutions. The hero must be tough and amoral in order to endure in a society crumbling under the weight of its own corruption and ineffectuality. Dramas lingering on images of a hostile urban environment and glorifying criminal heroes seethed with antisocial undertones. Then by 1932–33, with these dramatic conventions firmly entrenched as part of popular culture, they could be readily extended into an overt discussion of modern society. The implied social criticism of these cycles quickly gave way to the exposés, commentaries, and inquiries of the problem film.

The most popular of the prototype cycles was the gangster movie. It reestablished the action movie as Hollywood's staple by grafting a realistic, fast-paced narrative style onto stories out of the headlines. For the first time, films went beyond mere talk and exploited the full possibilities of sound, utilizing the sound track to create a physical impact which increased dramatic tension. The screen exploded with "the terrifying splutter of the machine gun, the screaming of brakes and squealing of automobile tyres."[1] Furthermore, the gangsters were character types more familiar to audiences than the teacup sophisticates of the photographed plays. They spoke like truckdrivers (Bugs Raymond in *Quick Millions*, 1931), slum kids (Tommy Powers in *Public Enemy*, 1931), Italian immigrants (Rico in *Little Caesar*, 1930, and Tony Camonte in *Scarface*, 1932), and stockyard workers ("Slaughterhouse" in *The Secret Six*, 1931). And most important of all, the films adapted the Formula to make the gangster a contemporary hero. Stress was still placed on the individual but his circumstances were made more appropriate to the times. Like the traditional Formula hero, the gangster hungers after personal success, but he is different in that he can no longer fulfill this goal within the bounds of society and must pursue it through crime. The old avenues of fulfillment had been circumvented by the Depression.

Rico (Edward G. Robinson) in *Little Caesar* demonstrates an absolute faith in the American Dream by carefully following Andrew Carnegie's step-by-step formula for success:[2] he starts at the bottom and with a single-minded dedication works his way to the top, the whole time abstaining from such distractions as sex and alcohol and studying hard to learn the operation of his organization. Rico typifies the hardworking Puritan businessman, except that the corporation has been replaced by the gang and murder is Rico's main business tactic. Similarly, Tommy Powers of *Public Enemy* is a more cynical version of the early Douglas Fairbanks comic hero. Lewis Jacobs' description of the Fairbanks persona perfectly fits Jimmy Cagney's portrayal of Powers: "In all these films Fairbanks was the 'self-made man,' unbeatable and undismayed. Quick intelligence and indefatigable energy always won him success in terms of money and the girl."[3] But the only area that can accommodate Powers' drive and energy is that of the corrupt underworld. So Tommy, the true thirties go-getter, turns to bootlegging to fulfill his potential.

Thus the traditional good guy whose success affirms society had been transformed into the good bad guy whose success questions society. The films demonstrate that in thirties America only crime pays. Tommy's virtuous older brother (Donald Cook) is ambitious but stays within the law and languishes as a frustrated trolley conductor, while Tommy graduates to stylish suits, fast cars, and luxury penthouses. This of course contradicts a basic moral tenet and the films must therefore kill off their heroes to invalidate lawlessness as a route to success. But in trying to uphold society, the endings only reinforce the films' basic pessimism. The success drive either leads to frustration within the system or violent death outside it. The viewer is left with the choice between the bland existence of Tommy's brother and the exciting, doomed career of Tommy.

The Happy Ending has been temporarily turned topsy-turvy. The audience identifies with the evil gangster's aims and frustrations and is invited to laugh at the representatives of good. Tommy sneers that his brother is just a "ding-dong on the streetcar." The legal establishment is likewise hopelessly inept, something to beat. If the police manage to arrest a gangster, a mouthpiece lawyer is immediately able to secure his release. Newton (Lewis Stone), the lawyer-gangleader in *The Secret Six*, is able to clear Slaughterhouse (Wallace Beery) of murder by manipulating the jury with courtroom tricks and bribery. In *Scarface*, the manipulation becomes a running gag. Every time Tony Camonte (Paul Muni) is arrested, he uses the phrase "habeas corpus" as an open sesame for his automatic release. The gangster's downfall is usually the result of gangland rivalry or a tragic personal flaw, not police efficiency. Rico has already been toppled by his rivals and has turned to alcohol when the police kill him, while Tony Camonte is destroyed by his incestuous love for his sister.

Thus, Good is hardly triumphant, and the audience, which vicariously identifies with the gangster's flaunting of every accepted code of social behavior (e.g., Cagney mashing the grapefruit in Mae Clarke's face), has very mixed feelings about Evil being vanquished. Robert Warshow suggests that the films are emblematic of our deepest fears, that the gangster expresses "that part of the American psyche which rejects the qualities and the demands of modern life, which rejects 'Americanism' itself."

> At bottom, the gangster is doomed because he is under the obligation to succeed, not because the means he employs are unlawful. In the deeper layers of the modern consciousness, *all* means are unlawful, every attempt to succeed is an act of aggression, leaving one alone and guilty and defenseless among enemies: one is *punished* for success. This is our intolerable dilemma: that failure is a kind of death and success is evil and dangerous, is—ultimately—impossible. The effect of the gangster film is to embody this dilemma in the person of the gangster and resolve it by his death. The dilemma is resolved because it is *his* death, not ours. We are safe; for the moment, we can acquiesce in our failure, we can choose to fail.[4]

Warshow's thesis that the success ethic and Evil are one finds its most explicit expression in the films of writer-director Rowland Brown. His *Quick Millions* and *Blood Money* (1933) are the only gangster films to self-consciously connect the corruption of the gangster with that of society, to directly state that organized crime is just another form of business. In *Quick Millions*, Bugs Raymond (Spencer Tracy) succeeds by applying efficient business techniques to the rackets. He is the perfect corporate man, thinking up the plans for a protective organization and having others do the work while he collects the profits. His is less the world of machine guns and booze than of managerial manipulation. Likewise, Bill Bailey (George Bancroft) of *Blood Money* succeeds through his business acumen, making an excellent living by supplying bail money for members of the underworld. Bill's partner, nightclub owner Ruby Darling (Judith Anderson), combines legitimate business with more dubious enterprises, bluntly declaring that crime is a business like any other.

Brown continually emphasizes the many ties between the underworld and straight society, showing that the two are practically indistinguishable. Both Bugs and Bill have considerable contact with officials of law and government who seem no less corrupt than the gangsters. Bugs avoids police harassment through either bribery or blackmail, keeping files on the illicit activities of various officials. Bill backs a conservative mayoralty candidate for the same reason that businessmen support particular politicians—because the candidate's election will be good for business: "The only difference between a liberal and a conservative is that a liberal recognizes the existence of vice and controls it while a conservative turns his back and pretends it doesn't exist." In Brown's chain gang exposé, *Hell's Highway* (1932), the equation is reversed to prove that business is just another form of crime. Legitimate businessmen and government officials prove to be more criminal than the convicts, overworking and underfeeding them in order to build a highway at the smallest cost for the greatest profit.

But except for the intimations of Brown films, which were never as popular as the others of the series, social commentary in the gangster movies rarely moves beyond metaphor. They may tell us much about the attitudes of the times, but they can hardly be labeled social problem films. Economic breakdown is not an explicit issue within the films but rather an assumed backdrop for the action. Nor do the films make more than token attempts to analyze the social roots of criminality. Despite *Public Enemy*'s claim that its purpose is "to depict an environment rather than glorify the criminal," there is little dramatic or sociological connection between the film's early depiction of Tommy Powers' slum childhood and his later career as a racketeer. Similarly, the prefatory statement that *Scarface* "is an indictment against gang rule in America and the careless indifference of the government. . . . What are you going to do about it?" has nothing to do with the actual drama. Rather than indict the criminal, the film glorifies his ingenuity. We laugh with Tony when his lawyer gets him out of jail and he proves himself invulnerable to the law. The only "analysis" of a social problem occurs when a newspaper editor makes a plea for martial law. The scene is completely gratuitous to the rest of the plot—we never see or hear from the editor again—and its reactionary law-and-order viewpoint is out of keeping with the film's mockery of authority. While the police do kill Tony, no connection is made between his death and the editorial. It turns out that the scene was indeed added to the film long after its completion in order to placate censorship pressure. Director Howard Hawks disclaims it, stating that it was not part of the original script and was shot against his wishes by another director.[5]

As the addition to *Scarface* indicates, these elements of overt social analysis are flimsy attempts to mask the films' antisocial implications.

The producers' failure to effectively counter the glorification of violence and crime aroused a flurry of censorship activity which eventually killed the cycle. The censors understood that such glorification was central to the audience's experience of the films and the main reason for the gangster film's popularity in the early thirties.

Though the gangster of 1930–1932 disappeared from Hollywood films, his influence remained. The sound film was transformed by the biting dialogue, naturalistic characterizations, and fast-paced continuity of the cycle. Essential to the style and technique of the gangster films is the cynicism and topicality which verges on social criticism. Although the blatant glorification of criminal violence faded from the screen after 1932, the corrosiveness lingered on in other films. The individual's relation to society continued to be viewed with disaffection, but the reasons for such disaffection gradually emerged as central to the drama. Social criticism became a major motivating force behind the films and society was now directly indicted for the plight of the hero.

The Fallen Woman Cycle

Another group of films popular during the pre-FDR Depression years was the "fallen woman" cycle. As with the gangster film, this cycle rarely deals with the Depression in terms of social problems, but nevertheless clearly reflects the situation. The films have three basic subjects, each one demonstrating a moral breakdown within society—the unwed mother, the mistress of a married man, and the prostitute. All the films attempt to shore up morals and reaffirm America's Puritan heritage, but the drastic plot twists necessary for this reaffirmation reveal the strains of the times.

Though the films allow for the fact that crime and sin are justifiable in times of social duress, they display a heavy-handed moralism foreign to the gangster cycle. Apparently a more sensitive issue than gangland racketeering, female sexuality requires a more complicated set of rationalizations and more severe forms of punishment. It is naturally accepted that crime is a positive expression of the energetic male's rugged individualism and there is no real need to explain why a gangster is a gangster. The fallen woman's fall, however, must be thoroughly explicated and is only acceptable as an extreme necessity, a last recourse which is never a positive experience so much as a tragic degradation.

First of all, the heroine loses her chastity only for the purest of motives, usually that of true love. In the early films of the cycle centering on the unwed mother, she and her lover are prevented from marriage through extenuating circumstances. He is either a well-meaning, sincere fellow inadvertently separated from the heroine or a wealthy irresponsible playboy who abandons her in her time of need. *Born to Love* (1931), featuring Constance Bennett, "queen of the confession films," and her most frequent partner, Joel McCrea, is typical of this series. McCrea plays Barry Craig, a World War I aviator on leave, and Bennett, Doris Kendall, an off-duty nurse. With no time or opportunity to get married but still madly in love, they spend the night together. Afterwards, he returns to the front where he is soon reported missing and presumed dead while she finds herself pregnant, husbandless, and living in shame. *Common Clay* (1930), representative of the playboy seducer plot, has the pregnant serving girl (Constance Bennett) deserted by a wealthy heir (Lew Ayres) who bows to his family's class prejudice.

In these and similar films, the heroine struggles to legitimize her child. Either her lover relents and marries her or some adoring boob takes his place. *Born to Love*'s nurse weds British stuffed shirt Sir Wilfred Drake (Paul Cavanagh) for the sake of the baby; the abandoned heroine of *Common Clay* goes to court to sue for support. In both cases, the heroine suffers harsh treatment but valiantly fights on to selflessly provide her baby with a father, financial security, and social approval. And even in those films where she manages to win both true love and the baby's well-being, this happens only after the heroine has languished in a trap which seems throughout to be inescapable.

The circumstances which force her to detour around the altar and head straight for bed are rarely economic. At a time when lack of money led to countless wedding postponements and made premarital sex a necessary alternative, when families were torn apart as members scattered over the country searching for work, the early confession films avoided explicitly linking the breakdown of socioeconomic structures with the strains on morality and personal relationships. Still, with their portraits of frustrated love, their stress on sacrifice for children and the struggle for security within a tragic set of circumstances, they reflect the instabilities of the times. The continual emphasis on the need to maintain the family seems a conscious effort to reaffirm traditional mores, to reassure a shaky audience that the family unit is still the basis of American life.

This reaffirmation is strongly evident in the mistress films. The mistress character continually sacrifices her own happiness rather than have her lover break up his marriage and leave his children fatherless. In *Rockabye* (1932) the ubiquitous Ms. Bennett sends playwright Jake Pell (Joel McCrea) home to his estranged wife because Mrs. Pell is pregnant. When *Christopher Strong*'s (1933) mistress, aviatrix Cynthia Darlington (Katharine Hepburn), discovers her pregnancy, she crash dives to her death so that honorable Christopher (Colin Clive) will not have to abandon his family for her. In *Back Street* (1932), the most famous of the fallen woman weepies, Ray Schmidt (Irene Dunne) foregoes her desire to have children rather than disrupt her lover's family. She acquiescently lives out her years in their back street hideaway, fantasizing about the children she never had. The mistress is a martyr, valiantly surrendering personal satisfaction to uphold the sanctity of the family.

As the cycle developed and the Depression worsened, the fall of the heroine became ever more severe. By 1932, she was taking to the streets as a prostitute. The prostitute films best illustrate the relationship between moral and economic breakdown and hence provide the cycle's most direct, if still metaphoric, allusions to the Depression. The prostitute, like the gangster, must move outside a system that cannot accommodate her. Just as the gangster turns to crime to fulfill his success drive, so the prostitute takes to the streets to provide food for herself and her family.

Though the standard plot of these films finds the heroine beset by an economic crisis, only rarely is this crisis labeled as the Depression. It is because a husband or boyfriend suddenly becomes ill or abandons her that the heroine must quickly find some alternative means of support. Through various plot circumstances, she is unable to find work and has no choice but to use her one saleable commodity. Stranded and jobless in Panama, awaiting the return of her boyfriend, the heroine (Helen Twelvetrees) of *Panama Flo* (1932) reluctantly becomes involved in a world of crime and sin.

The title character (Greta Garbo) in *Susan Lennox: Her Fall and Rise* (1931) is also led into sin while searching for her missing lover. When she does find him, her ruined reputation prompts his rejection and, still alone, she is forced to take a number of progressively sleazy jobs which trade on her sex. Helen Faraday (Marlene Dietrich) in *Blonde Venus* (1932) becomes the mistress of a corrupt politician to pay for an expensive operation which will save her husband's life. When the cured but outraged husband casts her out, she kidnaps their son and flees across the country. The only way she can feed the boy while evading police is to become a prostitute.

The sole films to indicate any concrete relation between the heroine's prostitution and social circumstances are *The Easiest Way* (1931) and *Faithless* (1932). In the former, department store clerk Laura Murdock (Constance Bennett, again) is the daughter of an unemployed longshoreman. The film depicts a poverty-stricken environment, but the father's joblessness, it is made clear, is the result of his own laziness, not of any unemployment crisis. It is not society but her father's irresponsibility that has created Laura's revulsion for poverty and lust for the security and comfort of wealth. This leads her first to pose as a model for an ad agency (always the sign of a loose woman) and from there to become the mistress of agency president Willard Brockton (Adolphe Menjou). He keeps her in a luxurious apartment complete with lavish wardrobe and chauffeured limousine, all of which she accepts not necessarily because it is the only way (she has been employed in the department store) so much as the easiest way to get by.

In *Faithless*, Carol Morgan (Tallulah Bankhead) is a rich heiress wiped out by the Crash who becomes the mistress of a wealthy boor in order to maintain her life style. Unable to tolerate his sadistic treatment, she decides to fend for herself but cannot find a job and slips into poverty. Eventually she marries the penniless William Wade (Robert Montgomery) and when he is brutally beaten while looking for a job, she must return to a life of sin in order to pay for his food and medicine. Carol rushes into the night, declaring "There isn't anything I won't do." For the first time in the series, the sacrifice the woman makes for her man is clearly the result of the Depression.

But even in those films where the Depression backdrop remains amorphous, the implications are clear. Prostitution can be presented only as a last recourse and it can only be a last recourse within a broken-down world where all normal means of survival are cut off. The weakened or missing male figure is clearly representative of a society no longer able to support those it is responsible for.

Like the gangster films, the prostitute pictures must undercut the antisocial implications of the thesis that crime or sin is the only option available for the heroine. The conventional morality must be upheld and the women punished. But whereas the gangster is allowed to wreak havoc and enjoy the good life until the very last shootout, the prostitute continually pays the price for her violation of the Puritan code. Her career is a series of ever more degrading acts and escalating anguish. Susan Lennox has to sleep with a circus owner for the right to work in his sleazy sideshow. Later, stranded in the tropics, she is reduced to entertaining sailors in a cheap café-cum-brothel. Helen Faraday is forced to dress in rags and hide with her son in a New Orleans bordello. When the police finally catch up with her and take custody of the boy, she is left alone to languish with other tramps in an overcrowded flophouse. Noting the fact that all these women gradually proceed southward as their fortunes deteriorate, Andrew Bergman remarks "how accurately it demonstrates the really iron-clad moralism of the 'fallen woman' pictures. The heavy symbolism of deflowered women sweating off their sins in fetid tropics gave away Hollywood's assumptions about sin and its price."[6]

Even when the prostitutes find their trade profitable, they remain unhappy and unfulfilled. Susan Lennox, Carol Morgan, and Helen Faraday suffer through periods of affluence as kept women and in the end shamefully submit themselves to their one true love. Though Carol and Helen have saved their husbands' lives, they must still plead for the male's forgiveness and depend on his generosity before they can be happy again. Susan Lennox must repeatedly try to convince her lover that she is not what she really seems despite the fact that his rejection has contributed to her compromised situation.

The films make paradoxical statements: the only way to survive is through sin, thus implying a condemnation of society; but as long as a woman is sinning she must be miserably unhappy, thus upholding the established social morality. Society cannot supply the economic means to support true love and family; prostitution provides the means yet excludes the possibilities of love and family. The paradox is resolved by having the heroine overcome her economic plight through sin and then reject the sin. Both Carol Morgan and Helen Faraday can repentantly return to their healthy and stable husbands only because they have sinned to save them.

This reaffirmation of moral values is obviously rather shaky. The films final and illogical declaration that love is more important than wealth and can, after all, be achieved within society is about as believable as the gangster films' assertion that crime doesn't pay. Carol Morgan's final submission to docile Robert Montgomery completely contradicts the vitality and independence of the Tallulah Bankhead persona.

This paradox is played out on a more sophisticated level in *Blonde Venus*, the one film in the cycle with any lasting artistic merit. Director von Sternberg despised the film, his original story significantly rewritten by Paramount to follow the fallen women conventions. But although the movie in plot outline sounds very much like other anonymous potboilers of the cycle, there is a subversive subtext that points up the dilemma of Helen's and woman's position in society. Helen's descent from family normality to cabaret singer/prostitute represents a quest for identity, so that her final return to the husband she now clearly resents indicates the impossibility of finding any satisfying sense of self. As wife-mother in the opening scenes, Dietrich is desexualized, reduced to knitting in an apron with her hair pinned back and her singing career frustrated. When she does return to the stage, it is her legs that get her the job and her sexual favors the attention and money of politician Nick Townsend (Cary Grant). Her attempts to combine career with motherhood are then thwarted by her husband and officialdom. She finally gives up trying to be a self-fulfilled woman, using sex only to manipulate her way to the top of Parisian night life. In her Montmartre night club, she mocks the notion of manhood and even takes on the male role as aggressor by wearing a tuxedo. But her life is empty—"Nothing means much to me now"—and her return to Faraday, on one level a positive assertion of motherly love as self-definition, also implies a return to the tepid domesticity of the beginning, an admission of failure and despair.

According to Robin Wood:

> The film . . . can be taken as a classic statement of one of the radical tenets of Feminism: that true femininity cannot yet exist, since all available roles for women in society are determined by male dominance. Every myth of Woman is *exposed* in the film, not celebrated. It also constitutes an astonishingly comprehensive analysis of the manifold forms of prostitution—from the home to the doss-house—available to women within our culture.[7]

Though *Blonde Venus* is the only one of these films that could be described as radical, there is nevertheless an inherent tension within the entire cycle indicative of a strained affirmation. The unhappy hookers and unwed mothers find eventual normality through contorted, last-minute plot twists, with the heroine's final marriage to her love occurring only after she has endured countless indignities and years of suffering. In the mistress films, the family unit is upheld through tragedy: Cynthia Darlington's suicide and Ray Schmidt's lonely, childless aging. Despite the reassurances of the cycle, the most resonant images are those of suffering and degradation. Woman is a martyr and must endure pain no matter which course of action she takes. The films supplement the image of the individual and society established by the gangster film: the individual is an innocent victim entrapped by a broken-down society with few options open to him or her.

This strained affirmation was soon comically turned on its ear by Mae West. Through sarcastic slander, she reveled in what the fallen woman films had to disguise and circumvent, completely reversing their moral deadliness by making sin a sheer delight and woman a strong, assertive individual who didn't need any man. She quite frankly boasted, "Goodness had nothin' to do with it." And like the gangster, she became a central target for the Hays Office.

The Prison Cycle

The prison cycle combines the tough milieu, characters, and language of the gangster film with the sense of victimization and despair found in the fallen woman cycle. The gangster's final tragedy is undercut by his bold defiance which remains uncompromised even in death, but the convicts, more like the fallen women, are losers whose violation of society's codes has brought only grief and whose defiance has proven futile. The prisoner helplessly wallows in frustrating confinement, undergoing harsh punishment for what are often only apparent transgressions. The landscape of these films is usually bleak, weighted down with the deadly monotony of prison life and punctuated by spasmodic eruptions of violence. There is little hope of relief, only the ever-present dread of more brutality. In over a dozen films between 1930 and 1933, these motifs were repeated and embellished into a frightening portrait of the individual's relationship with a merciless, dead-end society.

The prison is the ultimate metaphor of social entrapment, where the individual disappears among the masses in an impersonal institution. *The Big House* (1930), the archetypal prison film, is dominated by images of mechanical regimentation. Its opening shows one man's induction into prison. Mugged, fingerprinted, measured, numbered, and outfitted in a drab, anonymous uniform, he is gradually robbed of his identity. As he is initiated into the daily routine of prison life, the prisoner is dwarfed by the size of the institution and lost in the marching multitude of convicts. Rows of cell doors open simultaneously and hundreds of prisoners tramp in unison to the yard. In the cavernous mess hall, they sit down to eat the mass-produced fodder their keepers call food. The camera tracks along a row of prisoners to reveal faces mainly individuated by the manner in which they express their revulsion for the meal.

This mechanical subjugation is even more brutal in *I Am a Fugitive from a Chain Gang* (1932). The cells in *The Big House* at least provide limited freedom within a small group but there is no relief on the chain gang. The men are chained to their beds and to one another in a large bunkhouse, a situation allowing for no mobility or privacy. A long chain that feeds through each man's leg irons is removed each morning only to be fed back through when the men are crammed onto the truck which transports them to the roadside. The men have been reduced to beasts of burden, chained together in the same way as the camp's mules. The camera lingers on the details of daily routine. At 4:20 A.M. the men are awakened, fed, and herded to the worksite; in the late evening they arrive back, have their chains inspected, are fed and shackled into bed. The soundtrack effectively reinforces this deadening regularity. Only the clattering chains, shuffling feet, pounding picks and shovels break the oppressive silence. Human communication is reduced to the guards' terse orders—"All right, pick 'em up," "OK, pull 'em through." As one convict bitterly remarks, not only do you need the guards' permission to wipe the sweat off your brow, "but first you have to have their permission to sweat." The implied lack of options that led the gangster and the prostitute into crime are here depicted at their most concrete and extreme. The human being has been deprived of his will and endlessly performs the same mechanical duties. Any hesitancy, rebellion, or even sickness only wins the prisoner a brutal whipping.

Like the fallen woman, the convict is thrust into his hell through circumstances beyond his control. He is an innocent victim with little or no recourse to justice. James Allen (Paul Muni) in *I Am a Fugitive* is wrongly condemned through circumstantial evidence. Forced at gunpoint to participate in a robbery, he is caught by police with his hand in the till. In *Ladies of the Big House* (1932), Sylvia Sidney and Gene Raymond are framed for murder on their wedding night. They are snatched up at the moment of their greatest happiness and thrust into the misery of prison while the real killer goes free. In *Numbered Men* (1930), *Criminal Code* (1931), and *The Last Mile* (1932), leading characters are likewise innocent victims.

Even those in prison for crimes actually committed suffer miscarriages of justice. In *The Big House* a knife is planted in Morgan's (Chester Morris) bunk the day before he is to be paroled, thereby getting him confined to solitary. Gangster Tom Connors (Spencer Tracy) of *20,000 Years in Sing Sing* (1933) pays the most severe price of all, being executed for a murder he didn't commit on the basis of his past record.

Often freedom can only be secured in a situation of lawlessness. In *The Big House*, it is because of Butch's (Wallace Beery) armed uprising that Morgan, by preventing Butch from slaughtering the guards, proves himself worthy of parole. In *Hell's Highway* the riot and jailbreak are actually seen as a positive force, the means to root out corruption in the prison camp. We identify with the prisoners when they kill the corrupt warden and sadistic guards. During the escape, the traditional sympathies are reversed. The posse is a bloodthirsty, mercenary mob, hunting down prisoners at fifty dollars a head. The fleeing prisoners are the targets rather than the perpetrators of violence. A deaf mute convict is murdered when he does not respond to an order of surrender he cannot hear. Martyrlike, he falls to his knees, gesticulating a prayer in sign language. The posse's cold-blooded hunt eventually arouses statewide indignation and brings the governor to the camp to inspect conditions.

The situation is viewed less optimistically in *I Am a Fugitive*. In the case of James Allen, appeals, committees, and public protest fail to move state officials to either release him or reform the chain gang. The only possible recourse left Allen is escape. As with the previous two cycles, the clearest indication of social breakdown is the necessity to move outside the law. Proper channels fail the prisoner and he must depend on the jailbreak or riot to secure justice.

This is not to suggest that the filmmakers are advocating revolt as the answer to social injustice: riots and jailbreaks are a standard part of prison films because they satisfy the needs of drama, action, and violence. The resolution of problems through legitimate means does not provide the same dramatic impact as a good shoot-em-up. Still, the frequent occurrence of rebellion against social authority adds up to a cumulative portrait of social unrest which seems to have been quite responsive to audience needs at the time. In the same way, the films' evocation of innocence living in subjugation and terror clearly reflects the despair of a nation faced with incomprehensible social and economic upheaval. Both prisoner and audience can be seen as victims trapped in a situation beyond their control. The cells and bars and chains eloquently recreate the sense of frustration and restriction in a land of lost opportunity.

This becomes apparent when comparing *20,000 Years* with its remake, *Castle on the Hudson* (1940). Even though the latter film follows the original script fairly closely, in some cases lifting scenes shot for shot, there is a pronounced change. Tom Connor's death is essentially the product of a vengeful society which automatically prejudges him as guilty. Eight years later, Tommy Gordon (John Garfield) goes to the same gallows, but the forces that lead him there are less social than universal. The motif of Saturday as the hero's bad luck day is introduced. That is the day he pulls his stickup and gets caught and the day of the fateful murder which leads to his execution. The social tension of 1933 has been replaced by the dire fatalism of 1940.

Again, metaphoric and perhaps unintentional comment falls short of social criticism. If these films are to be labeled as problem pictures, then they are very weak examples. Their attempts at overt analysis of a social issue—the deficiencies of the prison system—are brief and inadequate and their preachments for reform are backed up by the most cursory documentation of conditions. Social themes are always secondary to the melodrama built around the hero and his particular situation. Indignation against prison conditions is transformed into indignation against the unjust treatment of the innocent hero. In *The Big House*, resentment against the intrinsic evil of solitary confinement is deflected by audience awareness that Morgan is there unjustly. Our concern is focused on the wronged man rather than the social wrong.

As with the gangster cycle, the commentary often seems an attempt to justify antisocial violence. The illicit thrill of seeing the prisoners revolt is explained away by brief scenes of sadistic guards and brutal, overcrowded living conditions, by token comments on the injustice of capital punishment and solitary confinement. But once more the antisocial implications are never really undercut by the meager justifications and illogical plot resolutions. That Morgan or the prison camp convicts in *Hell's Highway* finally receive justice from society does not erase the desperate measures needed to secure that justice.

Similarly, the film's chief redeemers are rarely able to act upon their good intentions and as such one's doubts about society's ability to reform are increased rather than placated. For example, Warden Long

(Arthur Byron) in *20,000 Years* can only institute reforms that are isolated and uncertain. Long is a progressive humanist seeking not so much to punish as to rehabilitate. He does everything in his power to prohibit brutality among his staff and tries to rid the prison of corruption, refusing to show favoritism to those with political influence. But when Long grants Tom Connors leave on an honor system and Tom is then accused of murder, Long's reform system comes under heavy attack from an intolerant society. Tom gives himself up, sacrificing his life to save the warden's career, and the reforms are granted a temporary reprieve. But the cost is an unjust death and one wonders how long it will be before the unsympathetic society will attack again.

Nevertheless, the prison cycle should be differentiated from the gangster and fallen woman ones as a crucial step in the evolution of the problem film. Though its examination of the prison issue is underdeveloped, the subject matter clearly lends itself to expanded analysis. Officialdom plays only a peripheral role in the gangster films and it is hardly present at all in the purely personal landscape of the fallen woman films, except for occasional police harassment of the prostitutes. But the prison cycle places its protagonists in direct contact with social institutions and hence must take a more definite attitude toward the relationship of the individual and society.

The two chain gang films extend the rudimentary social analysis into a detailed critique and as such can be considered among the first true problem films. They go beyond the brief putdowns of brutality and capital punishment to fully reveal what is wrong in the prison camps and who is responsible. Not only do they comprehensively delineate the various physical abuses—the whippings, sweat-box tortures, poor food, and forced labor—they also attempt to explain why these occur. The problem is not simply nasty prison guards but forces operating throughout the various strata of society. The contractors and camp administrators in *Hell's Highway* exploit the prisoners to make a greater profit on highway construction. In *I Am a Fugitive*, vengeful state officials all the way up to the governor renege on their promise to free Allen because he has tried to nationally expose the brutality of their chain gangs.

Furthermore, neither film separates the social problem from the individual hero's problem. Duke Ellis (Richard Dix) in *Hell's Highway* is an habitual criminal whose problem is the camp conditions themselves. The point of the drama in *Fugitive* is to condemn the brutality the hero is subjected to rather than to prove his innocence. Both films show how the treatment affects all prisoners, regardless of their innocence or guilt. One of the most poignant shots in *Fugitive* is that of Barney Sykes' (Allen Jenkins) release from the camp. For the first time in the film he is seen in his civilian clothes, but as he crosses the yard Barney continues to shuffle as if his legs were still shackled. Although he has left the chain gang, it has not left him. Thus the dramatic tension arises out of the film's shock at the chain gang system itself, not just at the individual's plight.[8]

The prison cycle began to make the important transition from mere topicality—the use of headlines and contemporary life as a backdrop for melodrama—to social criticism in which contemporary life is confronted and commented upon. *I Am a Fugitive* is the key film of the cycle, because it explicitly parallels the prison system to Depression society. As we shall see, James Allen's victimization is not merely a matter of being caught with his hand in the till, but more a matter of being caught in American society during the Depression. In its attempt to see the issues in larger terms, *I Am a Fugitive* represents a link between those films which merely reflect social ennui and those which attempt to analyze it.

—2—

THE SHYSTERS

Never has cynicism been so attractively embodied as it is in the shyster. He quickly replaced the gangster as the hero typifying the early thirties, a lovable good bad guy who revels in an atmosphere of corruption. The shyster became an important character type in the problem film, an unethical sharpie who appeared continually throughout the thirties and forties in three basic guises: as a mouthpiece lawyer, as a crooked politico, and as an amoral newshawk. In his first appearance in the early thirties, the shyster is the character who best capitalizes on Depression breakdown. He is the only one with any real brains. In complete control of almost every situation, the shyster adroitly manipulates characters and events, always emerging from the most dangerous situations unscathed. Rather than machine-gun his rivals, he sits in his office totally dependent on his native wit, thwarting even murderous thugs with his fast-talking rhetoric.

The audience is no less prey to the shyster's charm. He is the perfect wish-fulfillment figure for the Depression, able to survive—indeed, flourish—amid the chaos. Sophisticated and witty, the shyster takes everything in his stride. He is the epitome of casual style and so are the actors who play him: Warren William (*The Mouthpiece* and *The Dark Horse*, both 1932), John Barrymore (*State's Attorney*, 1932), William Powell (*Lawyer Man*, 1932), Adolphe Menjou (*The Front Page*, 1931), Lee Tracy (*Blessed Event*, 1932). Warren William, unfortunately now overlooked, is the ultimate shyster. With arched eyebrow and a flower in his lapel, he breezes through life justifiably contemptuous of his inferiors. He is so charismatic in his rogue's role that we feel an incredible sense of frustration when the filmmakers see fit to punish him. Barrymore

31

plays upon his public image, parodying his actor's hamminess with flowery courtroom oratory. In scenes of the lawyer's private life, he mocks the drunkenness that he was so well known for in real life. William Powell, as always, displays the urbane wit of the Nick Charles character he was to become identified with. Anton Adam is a sort of Thin Lawyer Man, whose dry, casual delivery underscores the shyster's unflappability.

The Mouthpiece Lawyer

For the shyster lawyer, the courtroom is a stage. Here he is not merely actor, but also author and director. Judge, jury, witness, and the law itself are props shuffled around as the shyster sees fit. Vincent Day (Warren William) irreverently describes the judicial process: "The jury wants a three-ring circus. Barnum and Bailey with a bit of Houdini thrown in. It's worth all the lawbooks in the world." No judge or jury can resist the clever tactics of a Tom Cardigan (Barrymore) or a Vincent Day. In *State's Attorney*, Cardigan defends one of the prostitutes in the mob's ring. Before a woman judge he dramatically argues on behalf of women and motherhood. Having surreptitiously slipped a wedding band on defendant June Perry's (Helen Twelvetrees) finger, he heartrendingly describes how his own mother suffered and toiled so he could study law. An observer wryly comments: "Last week he said he was an orphan. He doesn't know who his parents are." Typically, Cardigan not only wins the case but also his charming client.

If the courtroom is a three-ring circus, then Vince Day is its P. T. Barnum. His theatrical flair is unparalleled. When the key witness against his client testifies that he could not have been knocked out by a single punch, Day suddenly whirls and punches him in the jaw, knocking the witness out. With the courtroom in an uproar Day calmly turns to the judge and asks for dismissal of the case. Johnny Rocco is accused of murder. During the trial, Day swallows the vial of poison on exhibit as the murder weapon in order to prove that it is not lethal. Self-assured, he waits for the jury's verdict and, when they find his client not guilty, sarcastically congratulates them as a group representative of American justice. Having casually bid adieu to his client and colleagues, he rushes across the street to a waiting stomach pump.

The triumph of the shyster reveals a malfunctioning, impotent legal system where miscarriages of justice are the norm rather than the exception. To substantiate this thesis, the films trace the corruption beyond the shyster into the highest political and legal offices, revealing how the shyster's gangland employers manipulate police departments and legislatures. In *Lawyer Man*, Anton Adam works for a crooked political boss, Gilmurry (David Landau), who makes him an Assistant DA and even offers him a judgeship. Similarly in *State's Attorney*, gangster Vanny Powers appoints Cardigan Assistant DA in order to get an associate off a murder charge. During a raid on a speakeasy, the police do not merely arrange for Cardigan's escape, they also see that he departs with his coat and flask.

There is little room in this world of corruption for the honest person and those who remain uncompromised are inevitably victims. To Celia (Sidney Fox), the innocent stenographer whom Day hires so that the "decent people who come in here will have somebody to talk to," integrity means joblessness. Although she has not worked for months, she quits when she discovers the true nature of Day's practice. Similarly, her fiancé's virtue only makes him an easy mark for a frameup. (Day has trouble believing the fiancé's alibi: "It's only that you honest guys tell your stories so badly.") It is because Day intercedes, using his gangland connections to find the real thief, that the boy is saved. Innocence is helpless without the cynical, corrupt shyster to serve as its protector.

The greatest example of innocence destroyed is the shyster himself, who is really an honorable man gone sour, a crusader who has become tired of poverty and defeat. At the beginning of *The Mouthpiece*, Day is an Assistant DA who becomes disillusioned because he sends an innocent man to the electric chair. He quits his office, feeling that he can never prosecute anyone again, and opens a small practice to defend the innocent. But Day gets nowhere and, frustrated, broke, and drinking, finally pays heed to a bartender friend (Guy Kibbee), "The money is with the big people who are guilty. They need lawyers too." Day is soon a very busy and very affluent shyster.

Anton Adam's career follows a similar course. He starts out as a lawyer in a poor neighborhood on the East Side, a friend and protector of the people he grew up among. He has a small office (referred to as a "charity ward"), an ill-fitting suit, and a loyal secretary (Joan Blondell) who loves him. When a wealthy lawyer offers him a lucrative job, Adam deserts the East Side for Park Avenue. He tries to remain honest but is framed by a dishonest adversary and his career is ruined. Bitter and disillusioned, he resolves to fight back, playing the game as "tough and dirty" as they do. He embraces the corruption he has always resisted: "They made a shyster out of me. I'll show them!" The shyster's failure when honest proves that the only viable response to a corrupt world is corruption. A criminal society demands that you be criminal, that you must victimize or be victimized. More than any previously discussed films except the chain gang pictures, the shyster cycle presents an overwhelming indictment of society.

Of course such blatantly corrosive criticism must be undercut. The shyster's honest roots foreshadow his eventual reformation and victory over the very forces which had previously been unconquerable and irresistible. Just as the prostitutes are distraught over the course their careers have taken, so the shyster is ever conscious of his moral complicity. When a respectable businessman fulminates at a criminal as unfit to talk to honest men, Vince Day assures the crook, "It's all right, you can talk to us." The conscience-stricken Tom Cardigan turns to drink, castigating himself as a cowardly puppet for Vanny Powers, while Anton Adam insists that his secretary leave the window closed, overruling her complaint that it "stinks in here" with a self-conscious "I like it."

Ultimately this cynical self-awareness is brought to a decisive climax through the shyster's love of a good woman. Celia's rejection of his sexual advances and "blood money" leads Vince to question his corruption. Paying her with money he earned honestly, Day admits that Celia has reminded him he has a conscience. Soon he betrays the mob, announcing that he's through with them and that if anything happens to him, a file on their activities will be turned over to the police: "I'm tired of feeling your sticky hands on me." Similarly when June Perry leaves him in disgust over his use of the courts for political advancement, Tom Cardigan is spurred on to idealistic action. Within reach of the governor's chair, he discards his political career to reveal the sordid means that got him where he is. Having found "some corner of decency still left in me," he vows to go back where he belongs and defend the poor people who start in the gutter like himself. Anton Adam is finally convinced by his secretary to buck the mob. He declares that a lawyer is not a trickster for the powerful but rather a doctor and counsellor for the poor and helpless victims of the machine. Arm in arm with the secretary, he goes "back to my people" on the East Side.

As in the other cycles, this ending contradicts the celebration of cynicism exhibited throughout the stories. The audience revels in the shyster's amoral triumphs; then, true to Formula, the shyster is reformed and the values he has attacked so vigorously are reaffirmed. Once again the conventional morality is flouted only to be upheld.

But the shyster films take this reversal to greater lengths than the previous cycles. Besides supplying the necessary moral lesson, the final reformation provides a neat cure-all for a bankrupt society. The shyster, so superior in his corruption, is similarly powerful when reformed, so that with rediscovered social conscience he is able to destroy the mobsters and politicos he has previously served. Whereas in the opening reel the honest lawyer is powerless before omnipotent social forces and has no choice but to become a part of the crookedness, by the final reel he can not only choose to go straight, but in so doing defeats those forces which had earlier suppressed him. Anton Adam ruins crooked Judge Gersham; Tom Cardigan prosecutes political mobster Vanny Powers;

Vince Day, through his death, eradicates the whole web of evil infesting the city. Thus the sense of overall corruption which permeates the films is reduced to individual cases, to easily identifiable and manageable villains. It is the shysters and their bosses who are to blame because they have abused their power for personal gain. They, not any inherent flaws in the system, have caused the breakdown. In the dramatic climax, the shyster ends his complicity, destroys the real villains, and cures society. There is no need for social change, only the need to root out the malefactors.

The shyster films localize and remove the causes of the Depression. By defining the breakdown in terms of corruption, they rarely have to refer to its true nature. The shyster's initial poverty, Celia's long-term unemployment, and a few background remarks in *State's Attorney* are the only hints that the breakdown is economic rather than moral. As Andrew Bergman writes: "It seems self-evident to note that the country's chief dilemma in 1932 was not the hand in the till, but rather the emptiness of the till."[1] But the till's emptiness did not conform to the requisites of the Formula: it could not be easily dramatized in terms of a good–evil conflict and seemed to have no happy ending. Economic bankruptcy was not as readily resolved as moral bankruptcy and it called into question the entire socioeconomic system. Instead the system is upheld through a mere reformation in ethics. Audience attitudes of social criticism are indulged and then deftly transformed into attitudes of social affirmation. The roguish shyster becomes a knight in shining armor.

The films' most accurate reflection of the deepening Depression is again not in their social analysis but in the desperate, illogical twists necessary for Formula reaffirmation. The heroes have to make great sacrifices in order to go straight: Adam surrenders his wealth, Cardigan the governorship, and Day his life. Furthermore, the long-term effectiveness of their victories is questionable. After defeating their adversaries, Adam and Cardigan take a step backwards, to positions which the films have already demonstrated as futile, to fight corruption on a neighborhood level. The fact that the frustrations of this fight led them to become shysters in the first place is conveniently forgotten, as is the fact that new shysters will arise to replace the old. It is questionable whether the films' endings ever effectively dispell the indictment that comes before.

The Politicos

The roots of the shyster cycle were in the public's bitter reaction to the dramatic reversal of the Depression. As the American Dream and the attendant myths were shattered, as scandal after scandal brought to light the wicked ways of the political and financial elite, the public felt

more and more as if they'd been suckered and adopted an increasingly
cynical stance toward the country's leaders and institutions. Pearson and
Allen's *Washington Merry-Go-Round* (1931) became a bestseller because it deflated the reputations of the dignified Washington statesmen
while a new magazine, *Ballyhoo*, rocketed to a million circulation by
lampooning the almighty. *Of Thee I Sing*, the smash hit of the 1932
Broadway season and winner of the Pulitzer Prize, satirized the whole
electoral system and displayed little faith in the government's ability to
deal with the crisis. Its chorus of politicians sing: "If you think you've
got depression / Wait until we get in session / And you'll find out what
depression really means." When the presidential candidate is advised
that you can't fool all the people all the time, he retorts, "It's different
nowadays. People are bigger suckers."

The most convenient scapegoat for the public, the ultimate Depression
villain, was Herbert Hoover. It was he who had promised a chicken in
every pot, diagnosed the Depression as just a state of mind, and insisted
that "prosperity is just around the corner." His persistent belief that official optimism would create the confidence necessary for recovery failed
to take into account either the severity of the economic collapse or the
depth of public disillusionment. As Hoover, straitjacketed by his stubborn commitment to laissez-faire, failed to meet the crisis with the de-
cisiveness required, he became the object of derision, his name synonymous with failure. Hoover jokes ("Business is turning up!" "What, is
Hoover dead?") became a staple of vaudeville routines and books soon
appeared which viciously attacked his past achievements. Arthur Schlesinger notes:

> The very word "Hoover" became a prefix charged with hate: not only
> "Hoovervilles," but "Hoover blankets" (newspapers wrapped around
> for warmth), "Hoover wagons" (broken-down automobiles hauled by
> mules), "Hoover flags" (empty pockets turned inside out), "Hoover
> hogs" (jackrabbits).[2]

The 1932 election gave the people the opportunity to directly express
their resentment against Hoover (handing him one of the worst defeats
ever suffered by a Presidential candidate) and Hollywood the setting for
some new shyster films. The glib pessimism of *Ballyhoo* and the Hoover
jokes perfectly suited the shyster hero and within a month after Hoover's
renomination, *The Dark Horse* (1932), the most cynical of the shyster
films, was released. Like *Of Thee I Sing*, it presented the electoral process as little more than a slick sales pitch bought hook, line, and sinker
by a gullible populace.

Appropriately, the film begins with a satire on the political convention. An unknown "dark horse" candidate, selected arbitrarily from a

delegate's list, is nominated for governor in an attempt to break a night-long deadlock. The party's two opposing factions, each trying to outwit the other, support the dark horse and inadvertently give him enough votes to defeat their own respective favorites. Having chosen him as their gubernatorial candidate, the party men must find out exactly who the dark horse is. What they discover is the incredibly dumb and childish Zachary Hicks (Guy Kibbee), a former county coroner (he quit because he kept getting awakened during the night and he's a man who needs his sleep) whose main concern in life is his continually aching feet. The desperate party functionaries, on the advice of their secretary (Bette Davis), hire a slick campaign manager currently serving time for failure to pay alimony. When they come to the jail to get him, Blake (Warren William again) is already at work making a speech to his fellow inmates about Zachary Hicks, the candidate for prison reform.

Blake's theory of election is to take both sides, offend nobody, and please everybody. The cynical Blake knows full well that a public which bought Hoover's promise of a chicken in every pot will buy anything as long as it is packaged properly. Even Hicks, whom Blake describes as "so dumb, every time he speaks he subtracts from the sum of human knowledge" is salable: "Hicks from the Sticks—He's Dumb but Honest." Hicks seems to be a cross between Alexander Throttlebottom, the hopelessly inept Vice-President in *Of Thee I Sing*, and former President "Silent Cal" Coolidge, who, on the rare occasions when he spoke, came out with such pearls of wisdom as "When more and more people are thrown out of work, unemployment results." As Blake tells the party men: "We're going to convince the voters that they're getting one of them. That's what voters want in these days of depression and corruption."

The major section of the film focuses on the campaign where Blake puts his theory into action. He teaches Hicks to answer all questions inoffensively, by stroking his chin and saying, "Yes . . . and then again, no." Proving that you *can* fool all the people all the time, he successfully manages to please all opposing sides. Hicks' appointments on a typical day are the vivisectionists one hour, the antivivisectionists the next; then the drys, then the wets; then the Republicans, then the Democrats. As well, Blake plans to sue Hicks' opponent, but when asked what the suit is for he replies, "I haven't thought of that yet."

The film exposes the sham of campaign pomp and ceremony. That revered forum for free speech, the debate between opposing candidates, is bitterly mocked. Blake patiently rehearses Hicks in a speech plagiarized from Lincoln, but when their opponent makes the same speech first, Blake takes the stage and reveals the fraud, assailing the speaker for doing exactly what his man was about to do. The traditional functions showing the candidate as a "man of the people," e.g., awarding prize ribbons at country fairs, being made honorary Indian Chief (shades of Coolidge), and trout-fishing in a picturesque mountain stream, are revealed as carefully staged hoaxes. Hicks poses for the newsreel camera with fishing rod in hand. Blake passes the uncomfortable candidate a fish already caught for him and directs him to hold it up and smile.

Needless to say, the corruption extends to both sides. The other party attempts to frame Hicks in a love nest, but the best campaign manager wins with Blake rescuing the halfnaked Hicks (he's been losing at strip poker) from his mountain lodge rendezvous. The film ends unrepentently: Hicks wins the election and Blake goes on to another campaign. The final shot is of Hicks riding in the victory parade, giggling like a child with a new toy. The public has gotten what it deserves.

The cynicism of *The Dark Horse*, while unremitting, is not as corrosive as it first appears to be. Like the lawyer films, *The Dark Horse* suggests that personal corruption is a viable response to a corrupt social environment. Though it significantly does not show the immediate reformation of that environment, it still sees the problems with limited scope. Wider political questions are narrowed down to a matter of corrupt politicians and a gullible public. Any real questioning of political institutions is deflected by heaping the blame on the voters. If elections are crooked, it is what the people deserve for continually buying Hal Blake's sales pitch. The public is a sucker undeserving of an even break.

The Phantom President, released a month before election day, also satirizes political campaigning, hypothesizing that the democratic process is nothing but a personality contest. The film is structured around two look-alike characters, both played by George M. Cohan. The first, Theodore K. Blair, is the most qualified man for the presidency except that he lacks the showmanship and sex appeal to win an election. The Party, vocalizing some clever Rodgers and Hart, must regretfully turn down his candidacy because you cannot elect a man who has no

> . . . flair for savoir faire,
> Who's never had a love affair.

The ability to sell oneself to the public is of greater importance than the ability to govern wisely: "It's a shame. We all know you would've made a good President."

The second central character is Doc Varney, a medicine show pitchman who has all the personality Blair lacks:

> What a smooth talker!
> What rascality!
> What personality!

The Party decides to substitute Varney for Blair in all public appearances. When Blair tries to defend the gravity of a presidential election,
protesting that the campaign is not a musical comedy, Varney corrects
him: "That's where you're wrong. That's what the voters want, a musical comedy campaign."

The election process is once again the butt of a whole series of jokes.
At the nominating convention, politician after politician makes the same
declamatory speech. The speeches are nothing more than fragments of
meaningless clichés: "And so my friends, I say to you . . ."; "Government by, for, and of the people." As in *The Dark Horse*, the public falls
easily for such campaign trickery. Varney puts the clichés into song and
sells his political platform as he sells his phony medicine show cure-alls:

> What have I got here?
> A spot remover.
> We need it to remove every blot
> That the opposing party has wrought.

Naturally, Varney wins the party's nomination for Blair.

But unlike *The Dark Horse*, the chicanery leads to social good. Varney the amoral shyster repents, and Blair the upstanding statesman
turns out to be crooked. After Blair falls prey to a kidnapping trap he
has laid for his double, Varney, prompted by true love, confesses his sins
to the public and runs for the presidency on his own merit. The public,
either miraculously cured of their gullibility or still entranced by Varney's showmanship, elects him. Varney tells the party men, "You fellows keep your hands out of the Treasury. I'm going to run this country
for the people for once."

Having reduced the Depression to corruption, *The Phantom President*
reduces the solution to the individual hero who vanquishes that corruption. Varney changes from manipulator of the good but dumb populace
to protector of the good but still dumb populace. He keeps dishonest
hands out of the treasury and looks after the interests of the people he
has been duping. The people thus elect a man who will cure all of society's ills without any change in the political system. The cynical hero's
reformation transforms the electoral process from a joke into the means
of producing an honest man for the White House.

Ironically, this upbeat ending perfectly captured the ambivalent mood
of the 1932 electorate, for lingering just beneath the general cynicism
about democratic institutions was the desperate hope that a strong leader
would still emerge to save the country. Despite their distrust of politicians, the people tentatively looked to the Democratic candidate to provide them with the leadership Hoover lacked. Roosevelt failed to make
any immediate dramatic impact, but the public gradually warmed to his

vague campaign promises of a "new deal." Will Rogers's comment reflects the guarded optimism with which the public at first viewed FDR: "If he burned down the Capitol, we would cheer and say 'Well, we at least got a fire started anyhow.' "[3]

Furthermore, it is worth noting that personality was indeed a central factor in the campaign. Hoover in many ways resembled Blair. His failure to project an image of leadership was as much an element in his downfall as his failure to act effectively. Robert Bendiner's description of Hoover echoes the film's evaluation of Blair: "With his high stiff collar and his higher and stiffer manner, he had no more flair than an assistant funeral usher."[4] Roosevelt, like Varney, was a born showman and won the people over by exuding a charm that inspired confidence. In fact, there is a slight physical similarity between Cohan in the film and Roosevelt, especially when Cohan dons his spectacles. This was probably coincidental in the film, but was later to be used more self-consciously in Broadway's *I'd Rather Be Right*, where Cohan actually portrayed the President. Roosevelt's self-assurance, his gallant courage in the face of crippling disease, marked him as a potentially great leader. And like his film counterpart, Roosevelt became the man his country needed. If he did not quite lead America out of the Depression, he did preserve its political system.

The Newshawks

The two major journalistic trends of the early thirties were a proliferation of serious political commentary and a greater predilection for sensationalist copy. The syndicated columns of Walter Lippmann, Heywood Broun, Mark Sullivan, and Arthur Brisbane satisfied a new social awareness on the part of newspaper readers, a desire to make sense of the confusing events of the day. Heightened preoccupation with lurid crime and scandal (the Lindbergh kidnapping, numerous gangland murders, etc.) gave rise to another, less wholesome, tendency: a voracious appetite for stories about corruption and murder. The writers of such stories, the muckrakers and the gossip columnists, became popular in their own right. Personalities such as Drew Pearson and Walter Winchell seemed to have a ringside seat on the events of the day and be part of the sin they reported.

Hollywood was of course far more interested in the sensationalist trend than in serious political commentary. In raiding the headlines for story material and importing many journalists as screenwriters, it was inevitable that the movies discover the affinities between the columnists' public image and that of the shyster. Soon the reporter was incorporated into the shyster's crooked city world. Like the lawyers and politicos, he at first appeared only as a minor figure on the fringe of the underworld, as one of the hangers-on who follow the gangster and report his antics to an eager public. Before long he emerged as the hero of his own popular series (at least ten films between 1931 and 1933).

The reporter perfectly embodies the shyster qualities. A tough, fast-talking cynic who prowls about unchecked in a corrupt world, continually on the lookout for trouble and a good story, he moves with speed and assurance—immediately on the scene of a news event to scoop the other papers, furiously typing out his story amidst the hustle and bustle of the newsroom. The urgency and dynamism of the world is best illustrated by the movies' dialogue (often written by ex-journalists like Hecht and MacArthur). No one talks faster than the reporters[5] and the rapid-fire wisecracks and overlapping cut-ups create a hyped-up comic velocity, a kind of verbal slapstick. The reporters are lovable roustabouts, as smooth and charming as the lawyers while at the same time somewhat rowdy and vulgar. As Hecht and MacArthur describe him, the reporter of these films is "the lusty, hoodlumesque half-drunken caballero who was the newspaperman of our youth."[6]

As usual, the shyster figure's main attraction is his cynicism. The newsman's assumptions are based on shyster society: he just takes for granted that there is corruption, that someone is on the take, and of course, he's always proven correct. The basis of his appeal is that he judges society accurately and acts accordingly. His inside knowledge of its dirty workings makes the reporter a master of the corrupt city world, but also makes him a part of it, for amorality is a necessary requisite for survival. Hecht and MacArthur comment on Walter Burns: "Mr. Burns is that product of thoughtless, pointless, nerve-drumming immorality that is the Boss Journalist—the licensed eavesdropper, trouble maker, bombinator and Town Snitch, misnamed The Press."[7] Being a part of the evil and at the same time above it, the reporter, like all shysters, combines the illicit appeal of sin with the moral righteousness of superiority.

Amorality is both an alluring and an effective modus operandi. Lacking any scruples or sentiment, the reporter is able to manipulate all situations and feel at home everywhere. He simultaneously outwits gangsters, evades police, and competes against rival papers trying to butt in on his scoop. No matter whom he confronts or what the circumstances, the journalist never fails to have a glib comeback and another devious trick up his sleeve. *The Front Page* (1931) provides the classic example of the reporter matching wits on all sides. Editor Walter Burns (Adolphe Menjou) and star newshawk Hildy Johnston (Pat O'Brien) conceal an escaped criminal from everyone—rival journalists, the police and the mayor, even Hildy's future mother-in-law—all while they try to get a story ready for the press and Hildy tries to patch up his disintegrating wedding plans. *Blessed Event* (1932) sees its columnist hero Alvin Roberts (Lee Tracy, who most frequently appeared in this cycle, having first gained attention in the stage version of *The Front Page*) continue to print scandalous stories despite various attempts on his life. When a fearsome gangster confronts him over remarks in his column, it is the nervy reporter who ends up intimidating the armed thug. In *Is My Face Red?* (1932) William Poster (Ricardo Cortez) is so much in the know that he can announce a murder in his column before the police have even discovered the body. The audience could easily identify with a hero whose success depended on his being tougher and less scrupulous than anyone else.

The reporter is willing to go to any lengths to get a story and boost his paper. Randall (Edward G. Robinson), the editor in *Five Star Final* (1931), has his staff use whatever deceit and subterfuge are necessary to dig up the facts of a long-forgotten sex murder. The paper's ace sleuth, Isabod (Boris Karloff), obtains an interview with the now repentant murderess and her husband by posing as the minister who's to officiate at their daughter's wedding. In *The Front Page*, Burns does everything to spoil Hildy's wedding because he doesn't want to lose his star reporter. In the famous ending, after he finally gives Hildy his blessings and his own watch as a wedding gift, Walter phones the police to have him arrested: "The son of a (blurred) stole my watch!"

The truth too is malleable. If it means more dramatic headlines, the journalist will not hesitate to twist the facts. In *The Front Page*, the press distort the case of Earl Williams (George E. Stone), portraying the timid and gentle man as a vicious killer because it sells better. Having just witnessed Williams meekly surrender to the police, the newsmen hastily rush to phone in stories to their papers. On seven phones there are seven different versions of the same event: "Williams put up a desperate struggle but the police overpowered him," "Williams was unconscious . . . ," "A well-dressed society woman tipped off the cops," "An old sweetheart of Williams double-crossed him."

Quite often the reporter is closely tied to the gangster. He either uses him when violence proves necessary (Walter has "Louie" kidnap Hildy's mother-in-law) or feeds off his lawlessness, exploiting the popularity of the gangster's adventures. In effect, the reporter is doing what Hollywood movies do, glorifying crime and sensationalizing violence for an eager audience. In *The Secret Six* glib newspaperman Carl (Clark Gable) is complicit in Scorpio's rise to power. Accepting gifts from the gangster, he lionizes him in the press and thereby helps his stooge win the mayoralty race. The police chief denounces him for the same reason many Hollywood movies were attacked: "And you newspaper guys. Making heroes out of these bums."

As the conventions dictate, the reporter reforms and always ends up on the side of the law. But the reporter's reformation is seldom as self-righteous as that of the lawyers and Doc Varney; indeed, it hardly diminishes his cynicism or illicit appeal. He never really undergoes a change of heart and even when he wants to quit, he finds it impossible to leave his work. Despite Hildy's denunciation of the journalistic profession and his avowed intention to get married and go into another business, he drops everything, including his girl, at the first scent of a story. Journalism is in the reporter's blood and no moral reformation can either quench his thirst for amorality or (with some exceptions) impel him to leave the sin behind. Instead he continues to satisfy his own personal needs and by the dramatic climax those needs inevitably coincide with those of the law. Carl helps bring Scorpio down and goes on to lead a campaign to "clean up" the country. Yet throughout it all he retains his cool independence and fast-talking rascality. There is little hint of social idealism behind Walter and Hildy's exposé of the city's corrupt mayor and police chief. Their real concern is in getting the story exclusively, to say nothing of beating the rap for harboring a criminal. Editor Mark Flint (George Bancroft) in *Scandal Sheet* (1931) prints a story confessing his own crime, the murder of his wife's lover. But he is prompted less by guilt feelings than by his obsession with printing all the news. This same obsession has earlier led him to file a story on his wife's adulterous affair and later, when caught and sentenced, to carry on as editor of the prison paper. Questions of morality rarely influence these heroes.

Even when the reformation is sincere, the films remain cynical. Editor Jerry Strong (Charles Bickford) in *Scandal for Sale* (1932) discovers he has scruples and abandons the big city for the idyllic innocence of the small town. But he can afford to do so only after he has resorted to some of the most underhanded tactics of the entire cycle in order to win a $25,000 bonus. The best Strong can do is get rich through any means and then leave all the evil behind. The possibility of wider social reform never comes up. Because everyone and everything is corrupt, the reporters' dubious journalism is accepted as quite normal. The films both indulge in the vice through the unrepentant misdeeds of the reporter and condemn it through the reporter's vanquishing of racketeers and debunking of Broadway slickers. Since the targets of the press are all reprehensible, the films avoid confronting the whole issue of moral responsibility.

Only *Five Star Final*, the best of the cycle along with *The Front Page*, incisively analyzes the implications of the "anything goes" ethic and openly questions a society which requires such compromised principles. It places a subtler perspective on "yellow journalism" by portraying an editor with a conscience and by making the scandalmongers' victims decent people. Randall begins as an idealistic managing editor who tries to run his newspaper in a responsible fashion, printing stories on important social and political issues. But circulation drops and Randall finally admits that "ideals don't put a patch on your pants," bowing to his publisher's demands for more sensational treatments of love nests and murders. He resurrects an old sex murder case which sells more papers but also leads the now happily married, reformed murderess and her husband to commit suicide.

Throughout it all, Randall has been cynically resigned to his scandalmongering, lightly berating himself and obsessively washing his hands. But when he is ordered to play up the couple's death with another lurid story, he rebels. In a powerfully delivered speech, Randall quits, castigating the publisher for his hypocrisy, for his inhuman, irresponsible manipulation of people's lives for the sake of profit. In *Five Star Final*, the reporter's amorality is no longer merely a whimsical means of exposing the fraudulent but also a dangerous evil in itself capable of destroying the innocent.

Yet righteousness still does not triumph. As Randall walks away from the press building for the last time, the camera focuses on a paper in the gutter. As shouts of "Five Star Final! Read all about it!" blare over the sound track, we are able to distinguish the headline: "Murderess and Husband Commit Suicide." Randall's resignation is an ineffectual gesture which may free him from the corruption but does nothing to arrest the greater evil that grips the city. The only way to survive is to join the rat race and become part of the corruption. Those with scruples are given no alternative but complete withdrawal.

Still, the cycle's portrait of society is not as damning as it could be. Much of the criticism which should be directed against the social system is instead heaped upon a gullible, sensation-hungry public. William Poster (*Is My Face Red?*) justifies his lurid gossip column, "Keyhole to the City," by claiming he is only giving the public what it wants: "I am a mirror reflecting the spirit of the times." By choosing sensationalism over responsible journalism, the readers are as guilty as the writers who provide the stories. *The Secret Six* suggests that Scorpio could never exist if there was a public that was vigilant rather than adulatory. *Five Star Final*, by showing the financial failure of Randall's socially conscious journalism, indicts the readers for the Townsends' tragedy. Randall's comments on the public sum up the press films' attitude: "I could sit on a cigar butt and look down on our readers."

To attack the public for its apathy may be accurate, but the press films never indicate the deeper reasons behind this apathy. It's simply "the spirit of the times" and no connection is made between the failure of society's institutions and the cynicism of its citizens. Throughout the thirties and forties, social unrest was to be seen as the result of an inflammatory and manipulative press acting on a public eager for violence. In this way the films continued to narrow and thereby evade social issues.

Despite its faults, the shyster cycle as a whole communicates an even more severe sense of social breakdown than the fallen woman or convict films. In the frenetic universe of the shyster, everything is a racket. Modern America is an anarchistic circus where free enterprise goes berserk. Richard Griffith accurately captures the overall feel of the shyster cycle:

> The topical films succeeded in voicing a blanket indictment of depression America because their effect was cumulative. *It's Tough to be Famous, Love Is a Racket, Beauty for Sale*—what wasn't a racket, what couldn't be bought in the third year of the depression? Nothing, answered the topical films, which found a sordid story behind every newspaper headline. Their strength as a movie cycle lay in the fact that the story was really there, and that audiences knew it. "Work and Save," the ancient maxim of individualism, had been succeeded by "Anything Goes." Success in business and love was still the goal of the American wish, but nowadays you get it any way you can.[8]

—3—

THE POPULISTS—OR, WHO'S AFRAID OF THE BIG BAD WOLF?

In their Depression study, *Middletown in Transition*, the Lynds found that in typical American Middletown there remained an essential belief that

> the system is fundamentally right and only the persons wrong; the cures must be changes in personal attitudes, not in the institutions themselves. Among these personal cures for its social woes are the following six basic qualities needed for a better world outlined in a local address: faith, service, cooperation, the Golden Rule, optimism, and character. "The typical citizen," says an editorial approvingly, "discounts the benefits of the political and economic New Deal and says that common sense is the answer to the depression. . . . He thinks hard work is the depression cure."[1]

These verities are a continual theme running through much of *Middletown in Transition* and other studies of middle-class attitudes during the Depression and can be traced to the populist movements of the nineteenth century. The populist ideology always had a particular resurgence during periods of economic depression (1837, 1873, 1895, 1907) and its precepts were resurrected in 1929. ·

Essentially a middle-class rural reaction to the industrial revolution, populism was an attempt to preserve the Jeffersonian ideals of individualism within an increasingly plutocratic society. The populists proffered traditional small mercantile capitalism in response to rising corporate monopoly capitalism, small localized government to strong

46

centralized federalism, an agrarian or small-town life style to that of the large, immigrant-laden cities, and the guarantee of equal opportunity for the individual to the growing anonymity and reduced vistas of mass society. The movement peaked under William Jennings Bryan in the final years of the nineteenth century and although it remained a strong force on the American political scene (e.g., La Follette in the mid-twenties), its basic anti-big business, antifederalist policies proved increasingly untenable.

To the populists and their Hollywood counterparts in the thirties, corruption is defined ideologically. It is not a simple matter of greedy evil-doing, but a perversion of the Puritan ethic. The Depression has been precipitated by the abandonment of the original pioneer values upon which the country was built. It is because we have strayed too far from our roots in the pursuit of progress that our political and economic institutions are no longer functioning properly. The populist critique is a highly reactionary one: reformation represents not just a change in moral standards, but a return to the past and the nation's Jeffersonian origins.

The populist films are, then, by nature sentimental, yearning for an idealized past. Their function was to explain away the Depression without any of the antisocial irreverence found in the shyster cycle and the resultant films tend to be more maudlin and less engaging. The farcical cynicism so basic to the shyster's appeal is replaced by the sentimental righteousness of the populists, the shyster's breezy dynamism by clichéd sermons. To the populists there can be no ambivalence—the shyster is forever the villain, not a charming rogue whose criminal revelry betrays our own sense of defiance. The note of reform sounded at the end of the shyster films is the one single note sustained throughout the entire length of the populist pictures: it is not society that has betrayed its citizens, but rather the individual who has betrayed society. The antidote is all those verities cited by the Lynds as the cornerstone of middle-class thought, verities that proved to be no more convincing as film than as social philosophy.

Big Businessmen and Happy Hoboes

The populists' chief target was the big businessman. Already a discredited breed, Wall Street tycoons were an easy scapegoat for the Depression. A variety of irresponsible financiers strutted pompously across the screen only to be exposed as frauds and reviled by audiences. There are two basic villains in the populist films: the greedy monopoly capitalists who acquire everything they can at the expense of everyone else, and the degenerate children of the wealthy class, spoiled and lazy wastrels who carelessly permit business affairs to deteriorate. The country's salvation is the small capitalist, the "rugged individualist" who is never a success at the expense of others and who is always concerned for the welfare of the economy and the entire community.

Populist economic theories were remarkably similar to those of Herbert Hoover. The Republican President continually lamented that his economic reforms had been undermined by irresponsible industrial and financial leaders who failed to cooperate with his policies. He also kept calling for socially responsible capitalists to turn the economic tide. His repeated stress on the "spirit of charity and mutual self-help,"[2] his "faith in the American people," and his reliance on the natural processes of laissez-faire matched the platitudinous optimism of the populist films. These parallels between Hoover and Hollywood often made the populist movies appear like commercials for a moderate Republicanism and indeed, several times during the pre-Roosevelt years, Hollywood came close to outright propaganda for Hoover.

The film of the early thirties which most thoroughly articulates this economic point of view is the Frank Capra melodrama *An American Madness* (1932), one of the few movies of the populist cycle to match the shyster films for energy and charm. Capra of course would emerge by the end of the decade as Hollywood's leading populist filmmaker, the one director whose celebration of the eternal verities made for genuinely exhilarating cinema. *An American Madness* was his first social problem film (also his first collaboration with screenwriter Robert Riskin); in story structure, character, and point of view it anticipates the *Deeds–Smith–Doe* trilogy of the late thirties.

A bank failure is the central crisis around which conflicting economic and social viewpoints are debated. The villains, the Board of Directors of the Union National Bank, are not corrupt per se, but greedy capitalists who place their own personal ambitions above the needs of the mass of Capra's "little people" and the requirements of an economy which must function for the well-being of all. They do not directly swindle their depositors but instead cling to a tightfisted no-lending policy which is dramatized as the cause of the Depression. *An American Madness*'s chief spokesman, bank president Tom Dickson (Walter Huston) opposes the board's policies on the basis that a bank should serve all the people, not just a selfish few. He recites the principles of the conventional wisdom: instead of cutting off the flow of money and strangling industry ("Unemployed money leads to unemployed men") the bank should keep it circulating so that failing enterprises can be revived and the Depression overcome.

But you say banks should lend money only to those who can put up material assets as collateral. Well, gentlemen, it isn't news that the Depression has pretty well wiped out people's material assets. But it still hasn't destroyed what Alexander Hamilton called America's *greatest* asset—CHARACTER! We must have faith in character, make *loans* on character.

Just as he would turn Senate procedure into high drama in *Mr. Smith Goes to Washington* (1939), here Capra makes economic debate gripping. Dickson's call for trust, faith, and a free market with few controls on spending has a dramatic urgency Hoover could never muster.

The drama culminates in the excitement of the run on the bank. A metaphor for the 1929 Crash, it is caused by a combination of bad luck and bad faith. An untimely robbery and some exaggerated stories about it result in the rumor that the bank is about to fail. Faced with a panicking public, Tom turns to his Board for support. Although they have the power to save the bank, the Board members exploit the run to destroy Tom and regain full control of bank policy. It was these same variables—public hysteria and socially irresponsible financiers—which Hoover continually cited as the cause of the Depression.

But Hoover's optimistic pronouncements failed to encourage business to invest in industry. Due to deflation and the debt structure, investors like Capra's Board of Directors got richer by holding onto their money.[3] Not so in Hollywood. *An American Madness* ends with a typical Capra climax, a sudden reversal of what appears to be a hopeless situation through the action of the "little people." All the small businessmen, the "bad risks" Tom had helped, now repay him in kind by depositing all their money in the bank. Such a demonstration of faith leads other panicky depositors to return their money and prompts the Board of Directors to rally to Tom's aid. The small businessman, the true agent of American free enterprise, fulfills his social responsibility and helps a friend in need. "The bank is saved—lending on character pays off!"[4]

Although the film greatly simplifies the matter, at least it views the Depression in terms of economic practice, as the result of what was a genuine speculative madness through the late twenties. Banks and stocks were indeed greatly mismanaged and, despite warnings from Hoover and other conservative economists, the bull market continued its disastrous pattern of speculative borrowing, its reliance on dubious bonds and mortgages, its dispersion and recycling of funds through networks of holding companies and investment firms, until the economy was top-heavy with credit. This pattern combined with other variables (higher production but constant wages meant decreased consumption and overextended expenditures, etc.) to create a complex of factors leading to the Crash. But within their limited scope, both Hoover and Capra were accurate in their diagnoses. Economic management with a stress on short-term gain and no sense of long-term repercussions did have a great deal to do with the Crash. The real failure of both Hoover's policies and Capra's film analysis lay in their means of treating the problem. Hoover stubbornly clung to his belief in laissez-faire, that the government itself should not interfere with the market either by imposing undue regulations or by imbalancing it with heavy government spending. Laissez-faire, of course, created the atmosphere in which such widespread speculation could occur in the first place; the downward spiral would only be countered when Roosevelt did begin to spend money and impose stiffer banking regulations. As for Capra's little people, they caught the speculative fever worst and they were the ones who were wiped out first. Their "character" too had been tainted by a hunger for fast profits, by a move beyond their status as small capitalists to corporate prominence. It was simply too late for an application of faith and character to resuscitate the ailing economic structure of modern America.

Still, populism became Hollywood's favorite ideology, the standard movie device for rationalizing the Depression. The modern financier has created a monstrous monopoly capitalism which has gobbled up the free enterprise system and thus denied the individual his equal opportunity. Corrupt bankers and greedy brokers suddenly saw their empires crumble and in a panic leapt out of their office windows or put bullets through their heads. Typical is the Winston family in *Heroes for Sale* (1933). Both father and son are venal frauds and when in 1929 they are found out, the older man commits suicide while his son is escorted off to prison. *Heroes* also includes a contrast between the old-fashioned merchant and the modern tycoon. As long as small-time, good-neighborly Mr. Gibson (Grant Mitchell) owns it, the laundry business prospers on a small scale and the workers are affluent. But after Gibson's death, the operation is taken over by a large monopoly, Consolidated Laundries, which automatically lays off three-quarters of the workers. Capitalism works fine as long as it is not abused by corporate shysters. In this way Hollywood could apparently attack capitalist economics while simultaneously upholding them because blame was deflected away from the nature of the system itself and onto the excesses of a few monopolists.

Another populist fall guy is the spoiled wastrel who has inherited all the wealth without ever having had to do any of the work. The snobbish children have lost contact with the kind of diligence which had characterized their parents and made America a strong nation. According to the Puritan ethic, their laxity is not only an abdication of responsibility but an act of gross immorality. What these youthful indolents need is a good lesson in the work ethic, and George Arliss in *The Working Man* (1933) provides just that. As shoe manufacturer John Reeves, Arliss is a rugged individualist who refuses to blame the Depression for a drop in sales: "Now don't go blaming it on the Depression. People are still wearing shoes." When an old competitor dies, his offspring take over with predictable results: "Tom's life work is being squandered by a pair of worthless brats." Reeves actually joins the competition incognito and reforms the brats, teaching them to have pride in their firm and to work hard for success. By so doing Reeves keeps faith with free enterprise, refusing the opportunity to monopolize the shoe industry and opting instead to help out his competition.

The Conquerers (1932) and *The World Changes* (1933) teach the same lesson by charting the course of wealthy families from their beginnings as pioneers to their downfall in 1929. The forefathers dare the Wild West to create a strong country but their children lose the frontier spirit and squander away the nation's well-being. Just as a commonly held attitude of the time claimed that the Depression was a form of punishment for the excesses of the twenties and the forsaking of frontier principles, so the movies depict the Crash as a purgation of the children's evil. Orin Nordholme (Paul Muni), the patriarch in *The World Changes*, refuses to bail out his stockbroker son during the Crash because the younger man is guilty of fraudulent dealings, has no pride in his work, and is motivated solely by greed. Instead, Orin remains true to the spirit of fair play and gives his money to the people cheated by his son's firm. He saves his blessings for his namesake grandson who vows to return to the land and to the values by which Orin has lived. It is also the namesake grandson in *The Conquerors* who rolls up his sleeves with the same determination as his hardy grandfather and starts to sort out the economic mess. As Walt Disney's highly popular *The Three Little Pigs* (1932) moralizes, there is no need to fear the Big Bad Wolf as long as you construct "the most solid, traditional house possible."[5]

However, as the Depression worsened, Hollywood's image of the tycoon shifted from that of shyster to that of tragic victim of his own triumphs. Rather than admit that success in the early thirties was rare, that America was not the land of opportunity, the movies portrayed success as tragic and thus sought to rationalize failure. Several films dramatized the contrast between the hero's public accomplishment and private misery. For instance, Orin Nordholme's ambition and drive are positive in that they lead to progress—the invention of the refrigerated storage car—but negative in that the resultant wealth and city life alienate him from his country roots. By betraying his heritage Orin is condemned to personal ruin. Forever estranged from his wastrel family, he dies a lonely, embittered old man. *The World Changes* suggests that ultimately he would have been better off staying in his place as a farmer, married to his childhood sweetheart.

Other heroes start out as little men who work diligently to get to the top but in the process abandon the ideals of the Puritan ethic and, as that ethic forewarns, suffer severely for it. The most sophisticated treatment of this theme is in *The Power and the Glory* (1933), directed by William K. Howard from a screenplay by Preston Sturges. The ambivalent attitude toward success is cleverly built into the film's dramatic structure. Tom Garner's (Spencer Tracy) career as a railway magnate is recalled by both his loyal assistant and the assistant's bitter wife. Each takes a different viewpoint, the one defending Tom as misunderstood, the other condemning him as cruel and inhuman. He starts out as a simple, contented rail walker but, driven by his wife's ambition and inspired by his son's birth, Tom vows to make his fortune. Along that hard road to the top, Tom loses much of his humanity and all of his happiness. He is consumed by a voracious egotism that leads him to callously abuse other people. Unlike John Reeves, Tom shows no mercy for rivals and hungrily gobbles up competitive railway lines. Whereas Orin Nordholme improves the pay and working conditions of his employees, Tom sends an army of goons against dissatisfied rail strikers. The ensuing battle causes a fire that kills hundreds.

Because he is too busy to pay attention to either his son or wife, his family life disintegrates. The boy grows into a spoiled layabout and his frustrated wife commits suicide. Tom even tries to start over, remarrying and having a second son who he hopes will be a true heir. But such hopes are destroyed when Tom discovers that his own wastrel son is the child's real father. Despite all the power and wealth, his life now appears meaningless and Tom kills himself. Not even the lowliest of prostitutes suffers as much as the millionaire businessman and, like his loyal assistant, the audience sympathizes with a simple man destroyed by success.

The Modern Hero (1934) is, according to the *New York Times*, "the story of a man who failed because he succeeded."[6] Pierre Radier (Richard Barthelmess), the illegitimate son of a drunken circus performer, lusts after success and wealth. He resorts to any effective tactic, using rich women as stepping stones to the top and coldheartedly discarding them when they have fulfilled their purpose. Naturally, Pierre must pay the price for his "modern" approach to success. His beloved son is killed in an accident and his fraudulent stock manipulations bring about his downfall. In the end, he is penniless and back with his dissolute mother. He now confesses that he has been a failure, not so much in business as in life. Among the common folk, the older but wiser Pierre has a chance to find a truer success and happiness.

The basic question of all these films is not whether success is possible, but whether or not it is desirable. Since to be rich is to be robbed of your humanity, to be left alone and unhappy, then success is of dubious benefit. Correspondingly, economic adversity may be preferable since the poor are allowed to retain a sense of compassion and identity with their fellow man. Attacking the success ethic in this way is really an argument for staying where you are when there are no other alternatives within society. Immobility and stasis are thereby pictured as positive values.

Bumper (Al Jolson) in *Hallelujah, I'm a Bum* (1933) and Bill (Spencer Tracy) in *A Man's Castle* (1933) are exuberant tramps enjoying the free and easy life of irresponsibility. At a time when millions were leaving their homes to roam across the country in search of work, Hollywood's hoboes are unemployed out of choice. William Leuchtenberg notes that the vastly increased number of hoboes during the early thirties "unlike the traditional hobo, sought not to evade work but to find it."[7] Yet in *Hallelujah* and *Castle*, both hobo heroes easily find jobs when, prompted by love, they decide to go to work. It's just that work or any other commitment is a form of imprisonment to these carefree and independent spirits. After Bumper does get a job, his fellow tramps even put him on trial for desertion and find him insane—why else would anyone want to work? Throughout the entire length of *A Man's Castle*, Bill insists on his freedom and avoids committing himself to a job or to Trina (Loretta Young). He sleeps under an open skylight so that he can see his "hunk of blue" and the migrating birds that he identifies with. The sound of a train whistle is to him an irresistible summons to move on.

Both films represent a tacit endorsement of laissez-faire. The Depression and society at large have little bearing on Bumper and Bill's situation. They are individuals responsible only to themselves, their unemployment by choice perfectly conforming to Hoover's rationalization of apple sellers: "Many persons left their jobs for the more profitable one of selling apples."[8] The only references to the social situation in *Hallelujah, I'm a Bum* are in the Rodgers and Hart songs. Though the lyrics and rhyming dialogue seem to make social statements (such as referring to the police as "Hoover's cossacks"), such statements remain in a vacuum outside the central narrative of the film. More typical of the film's spirit is the title song, a celebration of hobo life:

> Why work away for wealth,
> When you can travel for your health?
> It's spring, you hobo, sing,
> Hallelujah, I'm a bum again.

Hallelujah, I'm a Bum's down-and-out hoboes are nothing more than baggy-pants clowns (including Harry Langdon and Chester Conklin) who function quite well in their own comic universe. But when that universe is represented as a realistic social environment, as the film hints and the director claims it is, then the film is being asked to carry more than it can bear. As musical comedy it is often charming and inventive; as social commentary it is silly.

A Man's Castle, however, does open with an explicit comment on the Depression and unemployment. We first see Trina, jobless and hungry, on a park bench, eyeing the bread crumbs being tossed at pigeons by an elegantly tuxedoed Bill: "It'd be great to be a pigeon. There's always someone throwing you crumbs." Upon learning that she hasn't eaten for two days, Bill (who at this point in the film appears to both Trina and the audience to be a well-fed plutocrat) expresses shock that anybody should have to go hungry in the world. Accordingly, he treats her to a full-course dinner at a posh restaurant. Once she has eaten, he reveals that he too is broke and can't pay the bill. Instead he embarrasses the maitre d' into donating the dinner by creating a loud scene in the restaurant: "You throw out enough junk to feed all sorts of people. . . . There's twelve million unemployed but the granaries are full." The irony of apparently rich playboys throwing crumbs to pigeons, of well-to-do restaurants discarding an abundance of leftovers, of granaries standing full while the poor go hungry, represents the film's critique of the economic contradictions of modern society.

Having made this opening remark, the film shifts to romantic melodrama more typical of director Frank Borzage. Bill turns out to be a happy hobo, his tuxedo an advertising gimmick for Gilsey House Coffee (his shirtfront flashes on and off as he walks down the street). He escorts the homeless Trina to his little domicile, a Hooverville shack by the Hudson River, where they make a home together. The film's main concern henceforth is Bill's relationship with Trina, his gradual realization that an emotional commitment to her does exist. At no point do either of them ever go hungry again; indeed, they live a rather comfortable life in what looks more like a middle-class suburb than a Hooverville. Their shack is spacious, with enough room to stand and move around in. It has all the consumer conveniences, including a bed with a sliding skylight over it, a brand new stove, and a kitchen table complete with tablecloth, napkins, cutlery, and dishes. It is always warm and they somehow always have enough to eat, making Bill's complaint that Trina is too skinny comically endearing rather than tragic.

Like all the optimists in Washington and throughout the country ("Life Is Just a Bowl of Cherries" goes Rudy Vallee's famous 1931 song) who tried to wish the Depression away, Hollywood makes poverty a delight which many prefer to the rat race. The happy hoboes will never have to undergo the anguish of the tragic tycoons. Instead they rediscover the deeper, more human values of life and represent a comic variation on the populist lament against progress and desire for a past when the world was more humane.

The Political Machine and the Country Crusaders

For Wall Street to have so effectively overrun the economy, it had to have its friends in Washington. So Hollywood also unearthed a nest of lobbyists, civil servants, and politicians all working for the shyster businessman's political machine. The greedy self-seekers have infiltrated government institutions and corrupted the democratic process. Once again, in two political melodramas of 1932, *Washington Masquerade* and *Washington Merry-Go-Round*, populism decries the loss of America's virtue and argues for the rejuvenation of frontier idealism.

"The running of the U.S. has fallen into bad hands," declares *Washington Masquerade*, which then proceeds to clearly identify whose hands they are. Hinsdale (C. Henry Gordon) is an oily, Latinlike (and hence un-American) lobbyist whose influence extends through all levels of government. In *Washington Merry-Go-Round*, it is Norton (Alan Dinehart), a power-mad racketeer, who commands a chain of Senators, Congressmen, and political bosses. Through bribery, extortion, and murder, these kingpins destroy any politician who would place the country's welfare above their own. As for the current administration, it is well-intentioned but powerless to defeat such widespread and insidious corruption.

The redeemer in both films is the newly elected country innocent. Jefferson Keane (Lionel Barrymore) in *Washington Masquerade* and Button Gwinnett Brown (Lee Tracy) in *Washington Merry-Go-Round* are men of the people, idealists who arrive in Washington to honestly serve their constituents. The characters' names are a perfect barometer of the films' heavyhandedness. They are all-American. Jefferson Keane's first name is of course derived from that of the famous President and figurehead of American populism, while his second name is a homophone for keen—sharp or astute. Button Gwinnett Brown is named after one of the signers of the Declaration of Independence, of whom Brown is a descendant. The last name clearly makes him one of the common folk.

Jeff is the "people's candidate" who bucked the state machine. Labeled by the press as "a plain man speaking plainly," he defines the country's chief problem in his first big speech to the Senate:

It doesn't seem that big business has covered itself with glory in the last few years. God didn't grant his natural resources to a few people who would take a strangle-hold on it. This is the very essence of Americanism—this land belongs to the people. It is not Communistic. If we here in Washington, buried by old traditions, haven't learned it, millions have been taught by these last three tragic years. They are making up their minds that the things that belong to them are being taken away and given back at heart-breaking prices.

Jeff is not indicting free enterprise but rather, as in the business films, the concentration of wealth and power among a few unprincipled individuals. Once again, the people are not angry at the collapse of the economic system but at the "heart-breaking" prices they are being charged by greedy crooks.

Button Gwinnett Brown is described as "a one-man vigilante committee who is in Washington to destroy the Scribes and Pharisees." He bemoans the loss of the frontier spirit in the big city, complaining that to his girlfriend Washington is nothing but "a merry-go-round of embassies, parties, and tea dances, a Vassar daisy chain. If you ever got into a covered wagon, you would ask for a chauffeur." Like Keane, he opposes the corrupt machine and from his Congressional seat speaks out against Norton's graft.

Before the final triumph of their heroes, the films present us with an evil that is apparently invincible. The networks controlled by Hinsdale and Norton reach everywhere and at first easily destroy the country crusaders. After Jeff's inflammatory speech, Hinsdale hires a sexy Washington socialite, Consuelo (Karen Morley)—another Latin—to seduce Jeff into giving up the fight. The homely and aging Jeff is blinded by her attentions and quits his Senate post to please her. When Brown tries to block his appropriation bill, Norton neatly arranges for his removal from Congress by staging a trumped-up recount of his election returns.

The hero naturally makes a comeback but his victories are not easily won. Brown moves outside the Constitution to cleanse the system while Jeff virtually sacrifices his life to defeat Hinsdale. With a vigilante band of old army buddies (war veterans in Washington for the Bonus March), Button uses armed threats to get the evidence necessary to expose Norton's activities. Faced with ruin, the arch-villain commits suicide. Since he is the source of all evil, the political machine crumbles without his leadership.

In *Washington Masquerade*, Jeff is awakened from his slumber by the discovery of Consuelo's infidelity and he painfully exposes Hinsdale and himself to a Senate committee investigating the dubious circumstances of his resignation: "In the White House there's a man whose heart is heavy because of traitors like me." The strain of these revela-

tions is too much for Jeff and he succumbs to a heart attack. An on-
looker declares him a martyr: "He loved his country well enough to
die for it. That's all any man can do." The thinly disguised Republican
propaganda of Jeff's confession reveals the standard populist thesis:
Herbert Hoover, the apostle of laissez-faire, is really an okay guy who's
been betrayed by a few rotten apples. Once they have been removed,
the economy will return to its prosperous norm.

These two dramas established a pattern which many later problem
films would follow. Capra's *Mr. Smith Goes to Washington*, probably
the most famous Hollywood movie about politics, conforms almost exactly to the formula of the 1932 films. Political malfunctions are attributed to a super-shyster who controls a machine extending from
business to the press to Congress. The shyster is opposed by Jimmy
Stewart, playing the role of country innocent and popular hero Jefferson
(that name again!) Smith who is at first unseated by the machine but
finally, illogically, able to topple it. However, by 1939 the country's
situation had changed significantly and the concern with the Depression
had to a great extent been supplanted by a preoccupation with European
fascism. In 1932 the shyster's machine was the cause of the Depression;
in 1939, it was labeled as the enemy of the democratic process, the
forerunner of a fascist dictatorship.

Back to the Soil

In all the shyster films, evil and corruption are peculiar to the city,
a product of the polluted, overcrowded jungle of Manhattan. The
shyster is the classic city slicker, hustling in a world of nightclubs, penthouses and Park Avenue offices. In surveying the scene from his office
window, Anton Adam describes the city as a breeder of corruption:

> Look at the people out there. Millions of them. Scrambling over one
> another. Pushing, clawing, trying to get ahead. Every guy for himself.
> The town is full of them. Boost the guy that's riding high.

The only characters to resist the corruption are the rural innocents,
such as Celia, the country girl in *The Mouthpiece*, who comes to the
city looking for work. But as we have seen, the shyster films are more
fascinated than repulsed by the city and Vince Day is a much more
exciting figure than sweet little Celia. The populist films replace this
combination of delight and revulsion with simple moral outrage. To the
populists, the city is an entirely negative environment, the epitome of
modern progress. It is the home of the big city monopolists, the rich
society snobs, and the political machine, all of whom have contributed
to the Depression. The country, or more specifically, the soil, is the direct

antithesis to the city—a symbol of the past, of self-help, rugged individualism, and good neighborliness. Unlike the shyster city with its cynics and sharpies, the country is populated with contented farmers tilling the land and friendly small-town businessmen running the corner store.

The city–country equation is basic to most populist films. All those who would desert the land to seek their fortunes in the big city are eventually corrupted. When Tom Garner and Orin Nordholme leave their small-town homes, both they and their families lose touch with their roots and meet with tragedy. Only by the younger Orin's return to the original family homestead are the Nordholme misfortunes arrested. Conversely, when country crusaders such as Jefferson Keane and Button Gwinnett Brown arrive in Washington, things are soon set straight and the political machine is quickly finished. This glorification of the country culminated in a very popular series of agrarian romances (*State Fair*, *The Life of Jimmy Dolan*, *The Stranger's Return*, all 1933; *As the Earth Turns* and *Beloved*, both 1932) which celebrate the simple life on the land. As Lewis Jacobs describes them, these pictures, "nostalgic and idyllic in feeling, show the farmer happy in rural community life, far more fortunate in his opportunities than the city dweller."[9]

This theme receives its boldest and most sophisticated treatment in the work of director King Vidor. Vidor stands outside the mainstream of populist filmmaking, both in his daring approach to film style and in his radical reinterpretation of populism. His classic social films of the late twenties and early thirties—*The Crowd* (1928), *Hallelujah!* (1929), *Street Scene* (1931), *Our Daily Bread* (1934)—are very personal essays on the individual's relation to society that eschew most of the Formula trappings. Often cast with unknowns rather than stars, shot either on location or on sets designed to highlight mundane reality and dealing with ordinary characters in everyday situations, Vidor's pictures of this period negate the precepts of glamour and sensation basic to the Formula.

Although Vidor adheres to the classic populist belief that individual fulfillment is impossible in the urban metropolis, his city is not just a Babylon of flashing lights, nightclubs, and smooth-talking sharpies. In *Street Scene*, the city is a tension-ridden immigrant slum that is anything but a melting pot. Nor is Vidor's country landscape an idealized Eden. Life for *Hallelujah*'s black cotton pickers is characterized as much by back-breaking work and poverty as by their exuberant music and spiritualism. Still, the city and country represent moral as well as geographic universes. In *Street Scene*, escape from the slum is the main driving force behind the protagonists' actions and in *Hallelujah*, Zeke

(Daniel Haynes) falls prey to all manner of temptation and sin when he ventures to the city.

Vidor's chronicle of his ordinary couple, John and Mary Sims, thoroughly explores the differing worlds of the city and country. Their story spans two films—*The Crowd*, dealing with their lives in the city during the twenties boom, and *Our Daily Bread*, charting their search for an alternative on a cooperative farm in the Depression. Both films are remarkable for taking a stance far beyond the social conventions of their times, and *The Crowd* is one of the masterworks of American silent cinema.

The Crowd dramatizes how the individual is worn down and overwhelmed by the size and anonymity of the big city. The film is shot in two distinct styles. The first, highly influenced by the German expressionists of the time, captures the overwhelming nature of the city. Forced perspective and gargantuan sets create maternity wards and offices that are like giant factories full of faceless mobs. An ever-moving, often subjective camera and superimposed montage sequences provide a dizzying sense of the city's swarming hordes. Skyscrapers tower over the people and in one smooth, extraordinary movement the camera cranes up at a building, in through a window, and past rows and rows of desks to the dwarfed hero sitting at desk number 137. The most powerful sequence delineates John's (James Murray) vain attempts to quell the noise of the busy city as his daughter lies dying in bed. The crowd on the street moves as a mass against the solitary figure of John, arms outstretched, completely submerged by the deluge of people, by the unfeeling power of the city itself.

Set against these highly stylized sequences are the intimate interior scenes between John and Mary (Eleanor Boardman), their personal drama quietly played off against the kaleidoscopic imagery of the city. By focusing on the mundane instead of the melodramatic, Vidor creates a realistic but nevertheless engaging portrait of an ordinary young couple trying to get by. The sensitive, naturalistic acting, the everyday details of domestic life, the "slice-of-life" drama predate Italian neorealism. John and Mary's early morning squabbles at breakfast, prompted by such trivialities as a broken toilet and a cupboard door that won't close, and their frustrations on a Sunday picnic when the fire won't ignite and the food is peppered with sand, are all delicately underplayed, shifting from charming good humor to a fragile foreboding that all is not well. It is film drama rarely seen in Hollywood, treating characters that are realistically commonplace and yet are imbued with an honesty and attractiveness that is quite engrossing.

The other remarkable aspect of *The Crowd* is its inversion of the

American Dream at a time when every American was supposedly on his way to becoming a millionaire. The Horatio Alger figure turns out to be just one of thousands of eager but frustrated little guys whose ambitions have found no outlet and whose dreams have turned to bitter disappointment. John spends the whole film trying to live up to the all-American ideal, "to be somebody." Instead, he finds only token opportunities to develop any sense of identity and ends up dwarfed by mass society, his self-esteem almost completely destroyed. In the urban rat race, the success ethic has given way to the jungle ethic.

The film is Vidor's most pessimistic vision of America. John maintains his faith without realizing its falsity. He laughs, "Look at that crowd—the poor boobs. Caught in the same rut" without recognizing himself as one of them. His whole life is utterly normal. "He was born, and then [came] the responsibility of when his father died, and then looking for a job, and approaching a city, meeting a girl, falling in love, kissing the girl and sleeping together, marriage (in reverse order in that day). And children and growing up and so forth."[10] John first kisses Mary in a crowded Tunnel of Love and proposes to her on a crowded subway. They honeymoon on a cramped train to Niagara Falls and set up house in a tiny apartment with Murphy bed, portable kitchen, and the noisy El that rumbles by their window. There is nothing ennobling about their lives together. The Simses become irritable and argumentative, ultimately kept together only by their children.

When John's ship finally does come in, it is a minor triumph—a $500 prize for an advertising slogan—and that only leads to tragedy. In all the excitement over the prize, his daughter is accidentally run over by a truck. Her death, and by inference the indifference of society which ignores his pleas for quiet, lead to his breakdown, to the recognition that he is a failure, the decision to commit suicide. This is the end result of the false hopes of the Alger myth—a life out of step with its own expectations. But when his little boy tells him, "When I grow up I want to be just like you," John comes to another realization, a realization of his own limitations and of the immaturity of his dreams of grand success. His return to Mary, their little dance to the Victrola, and the family outing to the vaudeville theater all suggest a new John, no longer burdened by the need to succeed, "to be somebody." He is now quite content to accept the job of street clown he had earlier found humiliating and remain the average fellow he is. At the vaudeville theater, the Simses recognize John's ad slogan on the program and good humoredly show it to others around them. In a bold closing shot the camera pulls further and further back to reveal a vast audience all laughing. He has accepted his place in the crowd and can now enjoy life and reestablish contact with his wife and son.

The celebration of the common man's ability "to find joy in the face of adversity" is at the same time undercut by a series of ironies—his son probably will grow up to be like him; his job harks back to his mockery of his predecessor ("His father probably thought he would become President"); and in the final ambivalent shot, even in his one moment of triumph over his ad slogan, John is dwarfed by the mass audience (a double irony since the image mirrors the audience sitting in the theater viewing the film). Though John may have found some accommodation with himself, the success myths that nearly destroyed him are in no way vindicated. They are at the root of John's frustrations. The best one can expect is to simply survive the numbing brutality of the modern city. A more positive alternative for John and Mary was not to be proffered until six years later when Vidor rejoined the couple in *Our Daily Bread*.

The alternative is not just a move to the country but the development of a life style that runs counter to the one John is crushed by in *The Crowd*. *Our Daily Bread* sees the Simses, broke and unemployed, flee the city for a dispossessed farm in the hope of living off the land. But a simple return to the soil is not enough, since neither of them have any conception of how to reap the soil's bounty. A social structure must be devised which will utilize the skills of unemployed city dwellers as well as dispossessed farmers. And it must do away with the massive institutions that alienate and frustrate the individual. The new John no longer hungers for personal success in a competitive system but for fulfillment within a cooperative framework where the priority is the mutual good of all.

Our Daily Bread is a frustrating blend of daring social experimentation and naive, fuzzy wish fulfillment, of striking narrative technique and the most maudlin melodrama. Vidor attempts to adapt populist idealism to the actuality of the Depression by extending good neighborliness into a cooperative community remarkably similar to a socialist commune. In one sense, the cooperative is pure populism: the little people join together as a community to work hard and help one another. It is much like Capra's small town where a group of individuals apply their own initiative to solve their problems without any interference from government agencies. John underscores the populist nature of their project by paralleling it with the efforts of the first Pilgrims:

> When they arrived on this continent, what did they do? Stand around and beef about the unemployment situation or the value of the dollar? No. They set to work to make their own employment, build their own houses, and grow their own food. On the Mayflower, there was a planter, a printer, a doctor, a soldier, a bookkeeper and so on. And

that's what we've got here. If they got along without landlords and grocery bills, so can we. What we've got to do is help ourselves by helping others. We've got the land and we've got the strength.

But the Pilgrims had to opt out of European society entirely and Vidor sees a similar necessity in Depression America. The structure of the cooperative represents a rejection of the system and its traditional goals. To truly recapture the sense of human worth inherent in populist values, those values must be projected into a new social order. Rugged individualism, monetary gain, the whole capitalist framework are rejected in favor of cooperative exchange of goods and labor. Because they all contribute equally to the growth of the farm, the cooperative members will share the produce. They even throw together their belongings into a "common pool," apparently repudiating the idea of private ownership, so basic to American society and to populism. In Vidor's Arcadia, capitalist competition has been eliminated and the individual pursuit of happiness has merged with the collective spirit.

But collectivism and populism are ultimately irreconcilable philosophies, in Raymond Durgnat's words "converse political attitudes" which "cancel each other out ideologically while producing a double surprise dramatically."[11] The film is structured around two dramatic poles: the dynamics of group action and the emergence of John (Tom Keene) as individual leader. On the whole, group scenes provide the best and most unique moments in the film—the co-op members swarming onto the field to plough and plant it, the erection of living facilities (a stone mason builds a carpenter's fireplace and chimney while the carpenter constructs the wooden frame for the stone mason's house), and the tour-de-force ditch-digging finale. This finale is the best example in the film of communal spirit and is captured in a rhythmic montage more related to Eisenstein than the Formula. Teams of surveyors, land-clearers, and diggers all move across the countryside inexorably racing against time to irrigate the dying crop. The sequence rhythmically builds over fifteen minutes to a triumphant crescendo as the water gushes through the ditch to the cornfield. The group sing and dance, splash and slide in the mud, a climactic celebration of the cooperative spirit and the soil.

In contrast, the scenes revolving around John and his development as leader are often mawkish melodrama (particularly his affair with a stereotypic blonde floozy, and his eulogizing, complete with background violins, on the miracle of the life in the soil) or contrived set pieces where ideology is discussed and resolved with little or no dramatic subtext. These set pieces reveal a tendency toward right-wing authoritarianism completely at odds with the communal spirit. In discussing the co-op's mode of operation, the men reject proposals of "an immortal democracy" and a "socialistic form of government" and instead listen to the down-to-earth commonsense of Chris, the Swedish farmer (John Qualen): "I don't know wat dose vords mean, dem fellas been talkin'. All I know is ve got a big job, eh. And we need a Big Boss. And Yohn Zims is the man for Boss." Later the men insist John retain ownership of the farm, even though everyone has pooled their resources in common ownership. John proves to be the uncommon common man, a strong leader who personally owns and runs the farm, a rugged individualist who has at last achieved personal success.

The schizophrenia between the film's overall left-wing communal spirit and its specific right-wing pronouncements undermines the viability of the co-op proposal as a sensible, clearly defined alternative. Because the basic principles of populism—individual capitalism and private ownership—and those of collectivism are mutually exclusive, the co-op becomes a self-contradiction. Yet despite this confusion, the best sequences of the film show an artist earnestly groping toward a communal ideal that took him well beyond the established populist conventions.[12]

The other major drawback to *Our Daily Bread* is the problem inherent in the whole back-to-the-soil movement of the thirties. Unlike the Pilgrims, Vidor's co-op members and all the would-be farmers seeking their rural idylls cannot opt out of society entirely. The co-op still functions within the capitalist framework of the society at large—its survival is dependent upon getting the crop to market. In 1934, however, that market was completely depressed due to an agricultural surplus. The government was subsidizing the destruction of crops to boost their market value and, as many have pointed out, agriculture was as depressed as industry, the farm as inhospitable as the city.[13] Back-to-the-soil was no alternative, for, populist assertions to the contrary, agriculture could not be isolated from the larger economic picture.

This further indicates the limitations of populism itself. It had been established as an alternative to institutions which by the thirties were firmly established as the basis of modern social life. Mass society was a fact that could not be countered by a doctrine of self-help, by the individual's freedom to succeed through his own hard work. Rugged individualism had not only become irrelevant but had actually helped create the monopoly capitalism the populists resented. Free individual enterprise which had begun as a progressive force against mass industrialism had turned into just that, an industrial capitalism fed by mass production. Laissez-faire had been more a cause of the Depression than its solution.

The most meaningful steps taken to overcome the Depression were initiated by the New Deal and it was the antithesis of populism. A strong central bureaucracy, the New Deal accepted the fact of industrial

capitalism and moved toward controlling it by means of a planned
economy. Pragmatic rather than nostalgic, FDR voiced the obituary for
populism: "Equality of opportunity as we have known it no longer exists.
Our industrial plant is built. . . . Our last frontier has long since been
reached."[14] Paradoxically, at no other time were the underlying principles of populism accepted more enthusiastically than under the New
Deal.[15] The government's crusade for the Forgotten Man, its support on
behalf of the farmer, its curbs on finance and industry all represented
the spirit of populist idealism.

Despite its apparent obsolescence, populism contained an ideological
duality, a combination of progressive idealism and sentimental conservatism, which perfectly conformed to the Formula requirement of
pleasing all sides. The preoccupations of the populist films often seem
to coincide with those of the left. Monopoly capitalism, political machines, the modern industrial city are all familiar Marxist targets, while
both the movies and the left glorify the "common man" and defend
him against the pressures and exploitation of mass industrialism. But
the films' solutions—free enterprise, the work ethic, a return to the
land—all reflect a nostalgia for the past and clearly place their politics
in the spectrum of the right. Furthermore, the populists' "common man"
was not a member of the working class looking forward to a new egali-
tarian order but rather of the middle class looking backward to an older
set of standards where his status was more secure. To Hollywood, populism represented a something-for-everyone alternative, a safe, patriotic
cure-all which demanded change in the form of past achievement.
Capitalism is attacked by arguing on behalf of laissez-faire; social discontent is vocalized by reasserting traditional values. Populism allowed
the movies to combine innovativeness with wish fulfillment, Depression
cynicism with the American Dream.

—4—

DESPERATION—HOLLYWOOD
TURNS TO THE RIGHT

As the wait for recovery became more and more prolonged, as prosperity seemed ever more elusive, restless elements of the populace began a vague search for alternatives. Throughout 1931–32, desperation found people flirting with all manner of Depression cure-alls, from "work-sharing" to "hot money" to the Douglas Credit Plan and, most sensationally, Technocracy. Many intelligent observers predicted that there would be a revolution; Hoover's Secretary of War, Patrick J. Hurley, concentrated armed units around big cities in anticipation of Communist attacks. There was even the occasional call for dictatorship. *Vanity Fair* proclaimed, "Appoint a dictator!" while Senator David A. Reed of Pennsylvania offered: "I do not often envy other countries their governments, but I say that if this country ever needed a Mussolini, it needs one now."[1]

Nevertheless, there wasn't really much chance of either a left or right wing revolt succeeding in the early Depression years. The Communists attracted many prominent intellectuals to their side (e.g., Edmund Wilson, Sherwood Anderson, Malcolm Cowley, John Dos Passos, Granville Hicks) and campaigned vigorously among the unemployed but could garner only 103,000 votes in the 1932 election. The right wasn't on much firmer ground. Its conservative establishment was too intimately associated with the discredited policies of laissez-faire and limited government to inspire public confidence, while the more colorful figures of the extreme right—Huey Long, Father Coughlin, William Randolph Hearst—remained ominously in the background, temporarily looking to Roosevelt to meet their needs. In 1932 America simply wasn't ready to abandon its current form of government. The nation was not so much angered as stunned by the breakdown of capitalism and no amount of demagoguery from either the left or the right could arouse its citizenry. William E. Leuchtenberg has observed: "There was less an active demand for change than a disillusionment with parliamentary politics. . . . The country was less rebellious than drifting, although there were clearly limits to how long it would be willing to drift."[2] As one Depression victim told Studs Terkel: "We weren't talking revolution, we were talking jobs."[3] Hollywood's reaction to the Depression pretty much reflected that of its public. The populist films wistfully looked backward while the gangster and shyster films provided a safe outlet for audience cynicism.

Occasionally, however, like Senator Reed and *Vanity Fair*, Hollywood looked at the Hoover administration's utter inability to cope with the crisis and wondered despairingly if more drastic measures weren't necessary. In a handful of early thirties films, Hollywood flirted with right-wing solutions to the Depression. Beginning with *The Secret Six* in 1931, Hollywood moved from upholding law and order to glorifying vigilantism to advocating dictatorship. Although not even the most extreme of these films suggested fascism as a permanent solution, the cycle as a whole revealed a frightening willingness to place ends above means—even when those means meant political murder—in order to find an immediate cure for the Depression.

Because the terms of all these films are confined to the world of shyster corruption, they are able to present us with a loaded equation: since social catastrophe is defined as the product of powerful villains, then society has the right to use whatever methods are necessary to destroy those villains. Their evil is so obvious that no court of law is required to determine their guilt and therefore no regard for civil rights should interfere with their destruction. We have already seen that legal and political authority, by adhering to the rules, is impotent before the mobsters. Only the shyster who is just as corrupt as the mobs can destroy them. Even Button Gwinnett Brown, apostle of pioneer righteousness, is defeated within the system and victorious when he circumvents it, leading a vigilante group of army buddies against arch-fiend Norton. As the Depression worsened, so the movie villains' grip strengthened and the means to destroy them became correspondingly ominous. The right-wing films carefully set up the argument that to restore the system you must move beyond it.

The first films to propose extralegal methods are fairly timid and vague, elaborating only briefly on the nature of vigilantism and emphasizing that it is purely a temporary measure to be used until the corruption is rooted out. MGM's *The Secret Six* and *Beast of the City* (1932) each establish that society is handcuffed by the gangster's ability to control the police force and the courts. In the former film, Scorpio and his mouthpiece Newton hold sway over an entire city. The honest police chief is frustrated at every turn in combatting the gang, until he is finally discharged by Scorpio's stooge mayor. Police inspector Jim Fitzpatrick (Walter Huston) in *Beast of the City* finds it impossible to fight corruption from within the system. He arrests gang kingpin Belmonte on a murder charge only to see the racketeer go free a few minutes later. For his zeal, Fitzpatrick is rebuked by his superiors and demoted.

Both men have no option but to move beyond legal niceties. The police chief relies on an extralegal vigilante group of concerned and anonymous citizens, the "Secret Six." The film hints that the Six have vast power—to debar Newton from law practice, to deport many of the thugs and arrest others for income tax evasion. (This of course was the only charge that could topple gangland czar Al Capone and send him to prison, even though everyone *knew* the true nature of his activities. In the early thirties, Hollywood made use of this fact to support its thesis on the ineffectuality of the law.) But the mysterious power of the Secret Six is not put to the final test and we never see them actually bending the law. Instead, when the police arrive at the gang's headquarters, Newton opens fire, permitting the police to vanquish the gangsters in a standard shootout. *Beast of the City* also ends in a gun battle but here the police action is not so strictly legal. Once promoted to police chief, Jim Fitzpatrick does not waste any time or tolerate any restrictive formalities. Declaring that the Belmonte issue has "gone beyond . . . legal red tape," Jim leads a squad of loyal policemen willing to die for law and order into Belmonte's speakeasy and provokes a gun battle. Having given up on the courts, he simply guns the gangsters down. Fitzpatrick and his comrades-in-arms die in a blaze of glory, martyrs for their country. With the corruption removed and law and order upheld, the system can safely return to its original principles of civil rights.

Cecil B. DeMille's *This Day and Age* (1933) conforms to the same pattern, but extends the implications of vigilantism into a paean to mob action. Again the film establishes the fact that society is malfunctioning in order to justify the unconstitutional measures taken by its heroes. A group of idealistic high school students attempt to bring gangland murderer Louis Garrett (Charles Bickford) to justice through the judicial system but discover that the gangster controls the courts. Rather than just accept the defeatist attitudes of officials ("You see what we're up against"), the youths continue their campaign against Garrett, resorting to what is supposedly the only means left to them, mob action.

DeMille's glorification of the youths' vigilantism is much more frightening than the previous films' guarded endorsements. The boys are considerably more vicious, kidnapping Garrett and slowly lowering him into a pit full of rats to force his confession. In their quest for direct, effective action, any tactic is acceptable. At the mock trial, their leader declares, "There is no time for rules of evidence. Besides, we want a conviction." To reinforce the validity of the boys' actions DeMille has legitimate officials praise them. The police claim that the terrorist trial is "something too good to interrupt" and rather than stop it, they advise the "court" that any confession will be invalid unless signed before a judge. That very night the jubilant judge holds court while still in his pajamas—direct action proves contagious. The DA gloats, "Well, Your Honor, it looks like the prosecution finally has a case."

Unlike the earlier films, *This Day and Age* hints that the extralegal action should be something more than a temporary cure. The stress on the youths' sense of civic responsibility and on the school motto, "What you are to be you are now becoming," make it clear that the boys' direct action is to be taken as an omen of a better future. When the judge's wife shrieks at the sight of the approaching army of torch-brandishing students, "What is this, the revolution?" the unspoken answer seems to be a hopeful yes.

Perhaps the most disturbing aspect of the film is the obvious though unconscious parallels between DeMille's students and the Hitler youth. The imagery and symbolism of *Triumph of the Will* (1934), Leni Riefenstahl's colossal propaganda film of the Nuremburg rally, are bizarrely similar to DeMille's. Both films are infused with a chauvinistic superpatriotism. Just as Riefenstahl plays upon the invincibility of the Führer, the Party, and the Fatherland, so DeMille glorifies God, motherhood, and the American way. Each director emphasizes mass action, the aura of ritual and celebration, fire and patriotic song.

The heaviest accent is on youth and how it represents the future. Both the German and American students are specimens of Aryan superiority—blonde, athletic, and brimming over with patriotic songs. They have each banded together for a common purpose: to serve the Führer and the Fatherland; to bring Garrett to justice and see righteousness triumph. Although DeMille never actually advocates a police state or calls for a planned policy of political repression, it is not difficult to recognize the seeds of fascism in his reactionary fantasy. The contempt for due process and glorification of vigilante law are only one step removed from Hitler's storm troopers.

The next film in the cycle, *Gabriel over the White House* (1933), extends the advocacy of lynch law to its logical conclusion, openly calling for an American dictatorship. While it conforms in many ways to shyster melodrama, *Gabriel* has a much deeper sense of how desperate the situation actually was and seeks to arouse audience indignation over it.

An impassioned reporter (Mischa Auer) protests to an ineffectual President the nature of the problems:

> There is starvation and want everywhere, from coast to coast, from Canada to Mexico. Millions of dollars are poured into new battleships, farmers burn corn and wheat, food is thrown away into the sea while men and women are begging for bread. Millions are freezing without coats while cotton is rotting in fields. Thousands are homeless and there are millions of vacant homes. There were over 5,000 gangland murders last year, yet there are only five gangsters in prison, and that for income tax violation. What does the new administration say to this? What answer, what depthless plan does the government have for this indictment, to this vale of misery and horror, of lost hope, of broken faith, of the collapse of American democracy?

With the exception of the overstated stress on gangsterism, the speech is for Hollywood a remarkable cry of distress.

Having aroused audience anger over these issues, the film settles back to focus that anger onto the standard causes. President Jud Hammond (Walter Huston) is initially a conventional movie politician, responsible more to the corrupt party machine than to the voters. As ineffectual as Hoover, he dismisses the crisis with absurdly optimistic statements: "I intend to carry the country from the depths of despondency to the unsullied and sunny heights of prosperity" and disclaims all responsibility by defining issues such as unemployment as "local problems." Whereas the reporter's speech hints at a broader social breakdown, a later speech by Bronson (David Landau), a spokesman for the unemployed, narrows the causes to individuals. "The men responsible for providing work have failed in their obligations." He similarly defines the solution in terms of a strong leader: "This country is sound. The right man in the White House can bring us out of despair and into prosperity again." To effect this solution, Hammond is reformed. Upon the visitation of the angel Gabriel, the ultimate deus-ex-machina, Jud the shyster becomes Jud the savior.

The film's increased sense of desperation requires correspondingly extreme measures. To solve the country's most pressing problems, Jud must discard the legislative process which, controlled by the shysters, only serves to retard action. When Jud's cabinet place party loyalty above their country, he fires them; when Congress refuses to immediately pass his reforms, Jud suspends it and declares martial law.

Like the DeMille film, *Gabriel* frames these acts in patriotic terms. Already backed by God, Jud further justifies his dictatorship in terms of American history and institutions:

> I believe in democracy as Washington and Jefferson believed in democracy. And if what I intend to do in the name of the people makes me a dictator, then it is a dictatorship based on Jefferson's definition of democracy: a government for the greatest good for the greatest number.

He further compares himself to Lincoln, America's mythic martyr-savior, using the same quill with which Lincoln signed the Emancipation Proclamation and keeping a bust of his hero in his office. The stress on dictatorship in the name of American democracy recalls Hitler's claims that he was the instrument of the German people. And *Triumph of the Will* makes Hitler as much a gift from the gods as Jud, with the Führer descending in a chariotlike plane from the cloudy heavens to earth where his devout followers await his words.

Once he has gotten rid of Congress and the cabinet, Jud is able to apply simple, straightforward solutions to the various issues raised in the reporter's speech. He goes to the camp of Bronson's unemployed veterans and with one speech, a sort of Sermon on the Mount, restores their confidence in America and resolves the unemployment problem. He forms an Army of Construction, enlisting the unemployed as "soldiers" to work under government pay. The increased flow of money from this program will stimulate private industry which will then reabsorb the workers.

Having resolved the country's economic difficulties Jud moves to end crime. The film reasons (and not unjustly) that gangsters flourish because Prohibition has allowed them to corner the liquor market. The answer: repeal Prohibition and form federal outlets to control distribution of alcohol. When bootlegger Nick Diamond (C. Henry Gordon) resists the government plan, Jud creates a gestapolike federal police unit to wage war on this "enemy of the people." Armored tanks blow up Diamond's headquarters and he is brought before a military tribunal. When Diamond asks for a lawyer, he is told that

> this isn't going to be a court trial but a court martial. . . . By bribery, by technicalities of the law, you've escaped all punishment. You're the last of the racketeers, Diamond. And I'll tell you why: Because we have a man in the White House who's able to cut through the red tape of legal procedures and get back to first principles—an eye for an eye, Nick Diamond, a tooth for a tooth, a life for a life.

Diamond is summarily executed by a firing squad. Thus, the legal system, like the government, is discarded in the name of democracy.

After curing all other domestic ills, Jud returns to the final and greatest issue, everlasting peace and prosperity for all mankind. He gathers together representatives of all the major powers for a conference on his yacht and insists that these powers pay back their debts from the last war. When the representatives protest that they don't have the money, Jud reminds them of how much they spend yearly on armaments. By threatening them with his superior military firepower, he forces them to stop rearming. The abolition of weaponry will not only prevent future wars but will also give these countries sufficient funds to pay their debts, balance their budgets, and bring back prosperity.

Still, Jud's dictatorship is intended as a temporary solution. As Bronson has stated, the country is basically sound. Having found a "final solution," Jud's earthly work is complete and there is no longer any need for a dictator. To reassure the audience that things will revert to the pre-Depression age, the film has Jud conveniently die. He signs an international peace pact, the Washington Covenant, with Lincoln's quill and lapses into a coma. Like Jeff Keane, Jim Fitzpatrick, and Lincoln (the last two also recently portrayed by Huston), he dies a martyr for his country.

One thing *Gabriel* makes clear is the reactionary implications of the Hollywood Formula. By adhering closely to its conventions, particularly the deification of the individual hero, and adapting them to political issues, the film creates an authoritarian vision. Hammond, strong-willed and decisive, is like the lone western hero, singlehandedly protecting his homestead and community—in this case the entire country—by whatever means necessary. Using martial law and an entire army and navy instead of a six-shooter, he faces down every possible evil in the world. But what appears as an often entertaining morality play in the Old West amounts to a fantasy of American dictatorship when it occurs in contemporary Washington and is applied to social problems.

Gabriel is a fascinating curiosity of the American screen and its background is just as fascinating. It contains many references to the 1932 campaign and represents one of Hollywood's infrequent attempts through its commercial releases at direct political propaganda. Produced by Walter Wanger for William Randolph Hearst's Cosmopolitan Pictures (which also produced *Beast of the City*), the film was actually intended as a tribute to the new President. Hearst, temporarily an avid supporter of FDR, had been instrumental in getting the candidate nominated at the Democratic convention and then worked hard on his campaign. It is rumored that Hearst actually wrote many of Roosevelt's speeches[4] and *Gabriel* seems a further attempt to shape FDR's policies. Scriptwriter Carey Wilson reports that Hearst rewrote many of Jud's speeches himself and, according to Bosley Crowther, the publisher wanted to release the film on Inauguration Day.[5]

Roosevelt never adapted Hammond's radical means or "eye for an eye" directness, but there are still many similarities between FDR and his film model. Walter Wanger proudly boasts that the policies of the reformed Jud "prophesied a lot of things that later happened during Roosevelt's first administration."[6] Just as Jud took steps to involve the government directly in the running of the nation's economy, so did Roosevelt. Both men recognized the necessity of immediate action. In his inauguration speech, FDR called for "direct, vigorous action . . . discipline and direction under leadership." While he never went as far as declaring martial law, FDR did ask for "broad executive power to wage a war against the emergency, as great as the power that would be given to me if we were in fact invaded by a foreign foe."[7] Both the fictitious President and the real-life one displayed a fondness for military metaphor: Hammond enlisting the unemployed as "soldiers" in his Army of Construction and Roosevelt imploring the nation to move as "a trained and loyal army willing to sacrifice for the good of a common discipline." In "The New Deal and the Analogue of War," Leuchtenberg claims that the CCC "aimed to instill martial virtues in the nation's youth."[8] Among the many parallel policies of Jud's "New Order" and Roosevelt's "New Deal" are the repeal of prohibition, the creation of a federal police force (though the FBI did not rule under martial law), and government sponsorship of building projects staffed by the unemployed.

Furthermore, the increased power which Roosevelt claimed for the Presidency prompted many to label him a fascist. One newspaper headline boldly summarized the inauguration speech: "Roosevelt asks Dictator's Role." Earl Browder, general secretary of the Communist Party, soon declared: "For the working class the Industrial Recovery Act is truly an Industrial Slavery Act. It is one of the steps towards the militarization of labor. It is a forerunner of American Fascism." At the other end of the political spectrum, Herbert Hoover told the president of the United States Chamber of Commerce that "this stuff was sheer Fascism, that it was merely a remaking of Mussolini's 'corporate state.' "[9] The Supreme Court resisted Roosevelt's acquisition of power and ruled that his National Recovery Act was an unconstitutional overextension of federal authority.

Though Roosevelt never did become the dictator Hearst had depicted, he was the strong leader the country needed. He could neither solve all the problems in his "Hundred Days" nor could he satisfy his supporters on the far right, but he was able to create a renewed sense of hope. There is no denying that by 1934–35 such extremists as Huey Long and Father Coughlin had deserted FDR and built up substantial followings, but the majority of Hollywood's audience still believed in the President and the system. For most people, FDR had made the move beyond the law suggested by the right-wing cycle unnecessary.

Gabriel over the White House was the climax of the series. The cycle's next (and last) chief executive, President Stanley (Arthur Byron) of *The President Vanishes* (1934) resorted to much less drastic measures. Indeed, President Stanley takes his extraconstitutional actions in order to combat a threat from the right. The country is in the grip of a powerful cabal of big businessmen and politicians who have allied with a fascistic people's movement, the Grey Shirts, led by would-be dictator Lincoln Lee (Edward Ellis). Tellingly, their nefarious plot is no longer connected to the Depression but to getting America profitably involved in a European war. Through a massive publicity campaign to "Save America's Honor" and the Grey Shirts' violent repression of any opposition, the shysters arouse the populace into a prowar hysteria. With Congress and the country lined up against him, Stanley makes a reluctant move outside the system in order to avoid war. It's the same old problem: "What chance has the President got against these high-priced racketeers?"

Unlike Jud Hammond, Stanley never exercises dictatorial powers nor gets back to first principles. Rather he devises a dramatic and effective publicity stunt meant to "bring the people back to their senses." To arouse public sympathy for himself and his cause, he stages his own kidnapping on the day that Congress is to declare war. The public, apparently able to concentrate on only one thing at a time, becomes too busy worrying about the President's safety to think about war. Their mood swayed with incredible ease, they now pray for the return of the leader they were about to reject: "He preached the precious gospel of peace. In our frenzied greed we struck him down. Oh God, restore him to us so that he may lead us in the paths of righteousness." Just as the "War Gods" are about to install their own puppet in the President's office, President Stanley makes a dramatic reappearance. He arranges to have himself discovered at the Grey Shirts' headquarters, thereby discrediting the Grey Shirts, their bosses and the prowar movement. The best showman is once more triumphant.

Through its condemnation of the Grey Shirts and their antidemocratic leaders, the film assumes the guise of an antifascist film. But its method of combatting fascism and its contemptuous portrait of a submissive public have reactionary overtones. Because the masses are completely dependent on authority figures, first following the malevolent powers toward war and then listening to the benevolent President's plea for peace, the democratic process appears irrelevant. The President manipulates the people as much as his enemies do through a deceitful, illegal ruse. The film excuses his refusal to use the constitutional forums of debate by showing these forums to be bankrupt. When the democratic process fails, he takes matters into his own hands. As William Troy of *The Nation* commented:

> Lincoln Lee and his Gray Shirts are represented as criminal fanatics for no other reason than their excessive patriotism. But why is not the President subject to the same charge? Or, to put the question in a more disconcerting form, when is fascism criminal, and when is it American?[10]

But Stanley's actions are a far cry from Jud Hammond's Gestapo. That *The President Vanishes* sidesteps the Depression issues so central to *Gabriel* suggests that FDR had placated the insecurities of the earlier audience. The issues of American involvement in a European war and of fascist insurgence at home represent more an outside threat to a basically sound system than a questioning of problems within the system. Also, whereas *Gabriel* had presented a figure for FDR to emulate, *The President Vanishes* is already emulating FDR. (Like *Gabriel*, the film was produced by the staunchly Democratic Walter Wanger.) President Stanley begins a crucial radio speech to the nation with a Rooseveltian "My friends." When he tells the people "Tomorrow I go to Congress on your behalf" one is immediately reminded of the inaugural speech and the succeeding Hundred Days. To make sure that we draw the parallel, the screenwriters, Cedric Worth and Carey Wilson (of *Gabriel*), have one of the villains sarcastically refer to President Stanley's combative actions: "Well boys, how do you like the new deal?"

Though native fascism was on the rise throughout the mid-thirties, *The President Vanishes* was the last major Hollywood film to suggest a move beyond the constitution. The next films to deal with the right wing elaborated on *President Vanishes'* poorly developed antifascism. Instead of seeking alternatives to the system, the later films showed the system defending itself against those alternatives.

Epilogue: Hollywood Rejects the Left

None of the right-wing films really suggest a shakeup of society's basic power structure. Rather, they advocate temporary albeit extreme measures to restore American capitalism to its former glory. The studios were closely linked to the financial establishment and they therefore resisted any change that would threaten their status. It is perfectly natural then that the filmmakers who glorified the right should try to discredit the left and discourage any revolutionary alternative.

The films of the early thirties consistently implied that communism is an un-American evil that would destroy rather than save the nation, an addition to and not a cure for Depression woes. But the films never really discuss what communism actually is, instead basing their attack on caricatures of the evil Communists. These revolutionaries were never central characters but rather peripheral and unimportant "Reds" who popped up from time to time to stir up trouble. These villains often speak with Russian accents, disparagingly compare America to "their country," and generally embody characteristics in direct opposition to the American way—cowardice, intellectualism, insincerity. By dismissing social unrest as the product of these foreigners rather than a reasonable outgrowth of social breakdown, Hollywood hoped to immunize all the potential dupes in the audience.

One common stereotype depicted Communists as hypocrites who turned to the cause only to conceal their sense of personal failure. Typical is Max (Robert Barrat) in *Heroes for Sale*, an eccentric European intellectual whose rabid denunciations of the wealthy class are judged as little more than an outlet for his frustrations as an unsuccessful inventor. When one of his inventions does make him a wealthy man, Max stops denouncing the capitalist swine and turns against those he once termed the downtrodden slaves. Decked out in tuxedo, top hat, and cane, he rails against his former ideals and comrades: "Oh charity. It's like a snowball running down the hill—it gets bigger and bigger! The poor! The needy! A cancer on civilization! If I was running the world, I would kill everybody that needed, well, anything." It appears that "like everyone else, communists were simply waiting for the American Dream to blossom again."[11]

Another movie Red was the agitator, an uncouth, unshaven rabble-rouser who foments strikes and riots either for his own gain or out of sheer personal malevolence. The railway strikers in *The Power and the Glory* are led by a slob who claims in a heavy Russian accent that if given the chance he would punch Tom Garner in the face. But when Tom arrives on the scene and grants the troublemaker his chance, the man shrinks into the background, exposed as a cowardly fraud who is no match for the American individualist. In *Little Man, What Now?* (1934), a proletarian figure (Fred Kohler) shows up from time to time to exhort the unemployed hero to take to the streets in protest. This leftist, however, only increases the hero's revulsion of radicalism. The man is nothing more than a bully who is rude and ungrateful when fed by the sympathetic heroine (Margaret Sullavan) and who helps cause his own wife's death by refusing to take her to a "boorgwas" doctor.

Whenever the crowd is swayed by these reprehensible types, disaster follows. The central message of the agitator films is that revolution never helps the people but only causes greater tragedy. The strike in *The Power and the Glory* leads to violence and a disastrous fire which kills hundreds of strikers. In *Heroes for Sale*, rioting workers (fired because of Max's time-saving invention) ignore hero Tom Holmes' (Richard Barthelmess) pleas for moderation. As Tom predicts, defiance is futile and disastrous. The police intervene to prevent the workers from destroying the machinery and a number of people, including Tom's wife, are killed.

On the other hand, Hans (Douglass Montgomery), the protagonist of *Little Man, What Now?* rejects the rebels as "street rabble," claiming that he is satisfied and knows his place. Even after he is deprived of that place, he resists the activist alternative, feeling more a sense of personal failure than of social indignation. In the end, beaten by the police in a demonstration and thrown into the gutter, Hans spontaneously grabs at a rock to retaliate. Suddenly "coming to his senses," he is shocked and sickened by his actions, utterly disgraced at becoming one of "them." But his forebearance pays off. For not throwing the rock, the film immediately rewards him with a son and a good job. Because he rejects revolution, he averts personal tragedy.

Although this central theme of anticommunism would continue almost unbroken (except briefly during World War II) for forty years, there were at least two exceptions in the early thirties. In filming Elmer Rice's popular and prestigious plays *Street Scene* (1931) and *Counsellor-at-Law* (1933), Hollywood faithfully translated the playwright's less biased views on communism. In *Street Scene* Rice criticizes the narrow-minded dogmatism of the Party through the character of Abe Kaplan (Max Montor). But at the same time, Abe is a human being rather than a caricature: his communism a logical outgrowth of poverty and his narrow-mindedness parallel to the stifling environment of the slums. More surprising, though, is the Communist in *Counsellor-at-Law*. In this later work, the Communist is a young idealist and, although he appears only briefly, is one of the few uncompromised characters in the film. The youth has been beaten up by the police in a street rally and then charged with sedition. His old immigrant mother brings him to the office of their one-time ghetto neighbor, George Simon (John Barrymore, in another superb performance), now a big shyster lawyer. The lawyer chastises the young radical, attacking his foolish notions of changing the world. Simon offers his own career as proof that success and fulfillment are open to all men. But the youth will not be placated. Standing over Simon, the Communist angrily castigates him and everything he represents. Suddenly submissive, Simon cannot answer and there is no doubt that the Communist is meant as an heroic figure. Except for this powerful moment, he does not appear in the film. Later we hear that he has been killed and again Simon hesitates, momentarily touched by the ideals and truth the boy stood for.

But in both cases, Rice had already proven his box-office worth on Broadway and Hollywood was always reluctant to tamper with established success, even if the work strayed from the political norm. Of course Abe and the youth are only minor characters and hardly constitute an antidote to Hollywood's more typical anti-Red bigotry.

No discussion of Hollywood anticommunism would be complete without mention of the role the studios played in the 1934 California gubernatorial contest. In their attempt to quash the candidacy of Democrat Upton Sinclair, the producers utilized the anti-Red stereotypes of their feature films with great success. At the time the studios began their smear tactics, Sinclair was apparently winning over many Californians with his quasisocialistic EPIC (End Poverty in California) plan, a radical program whereby the government would take over idle factories and land for use by the unemployed. Visions of cooperative communities and a production-for-use economy excited Sinclair followers while visions of lazy tramps arriving en masse to live in the golden sun of Southern California incensed the propertied class. A huge public relations campaign was mounted to defeat Sinclair. Louis B. Mayer, a chieftain of California's Republicans, organized the film industry. The producers pooled their resources, raised one and a half million dollars (partially by assessing salaries of stars and directors) and made a series of fake newsreels. Hollywood bit players appeared as gentle old ladies rocking on their front porches and declaring themselves for Republican candidate Frank Merriam: "Because I want to save my little home. It's all I have left in this world." Others played the bearded rabble who intend to vote for "Seenclair": "Well, his system worked vell in Russia, vy can't it work here?" The *Hollywood Reporter* boasted in September: "The campaign against Upton Sinclair has been DYNAMITE. It is the most effective piece of humdingery that has ever been effected."[12] Sinclair's campaign fell apart and he lost by an overwhelming 250,000 votes. The election provided Hollywood with the opportunity to directly influence actual politics, not only to fabricate fantasies on the screen but to extend them into the real world. Their success is a barometer both of the public's fears and of the impact of repeated stereotyping by the mass media.

—5—

FROM DESPAIR TO RECOVERY:
WARNER BROTHERS AND FDR

Despair—The Forgotten Man

In 1932, the Depression was approaching its nadir. As the economy gradually degenerated, unemployment figures rose to unimaginable heights. Approximately fifteen million were out of work, while the lives of many million more were dramatically shattered. Men who had helplessly seen their jobs and savings vanish just as helplessly watched as their belongings were repossessed, their mortgages foreclosed, and their families went hungry. Once self-respecting people now shamefully moved into city-dump villages, stood patiently in breadlines, sold apples on street corners, and begged for any kind of work.

Probably the most nakedly desperate display of Depression want arrived in Washington in the summer of 1932 with the Bonus Marchers. Described by Drew Pearson as "ragged, weary and apathetic," with "no hope on their faces,"[1] between 22,000 (government estimate) and 80,000 (marchers' estimate) war veterans came by freight train from all over the country to demand relief. Specifically, the Marchers wanted Congress to pass the Patman Bill which called for the immediate payment of their World War I bonus, a certificate of compensation for their meager wartime salaries. Payment on the $500 certificates was not due until 1945, but the Bonus Marchers felt that if the government could afford to give millions to large industrialists through the Reconstruction Finance Corporation, it could also pay then and there those who had once been willing to give up their lives for their country.

But the Bonus March was, as Thomas R. Henry of the *Washington Star* put it, "a flight from reality."[2] Only the rich could successfully

78

lobby for the passage of bills. The Senate ignored the Marchers and rejected the Patman Bill. The Army brutally marched down upon the veterans with bayonets, tanks, and tear gas, driving them from the city and burning their makeshift quarters. Of all the victims of the Depression, these veterans were probably the most blatantly abused. Once glorified for making "the world safe for democracy," they were now forcibly put out into the cold by means of the same army in which they had served.

But if their government forgot them, its citizens did not. The "forgotten man" became a cultural symbol of Depression injustice. He was immortalized by E. Y. Harburg's "Brother, Can You Spare a Dime?" and one of the biggest movie hits of 1932, Warner Brothers' *I Am a Fugitive from a Chain Gang*, charted the course of the forgotten man from war hero to hobo to criminal fugitive. Like Harburg's song, *I Am a Fugitive* spoke directly to the times, times so desperate that play-it-safe Hollywood created one of its most bitter and uncompromising films.

The film's condemnation of the chain gang is placed within the larger context of society as a whole. The chain gang simply represents in extreme the stifling regimentation that James Allen has been trying to escape since the war. In tracing how Allen ends up in the prison camp, and then by paralleling the camp to the outside world, *I Am a Fugitive* offers an angry condemnation of a malfunctioning society.

The film is structured as a mini-history of America from 1918 to the Depression, the country's descent mirrored through the downfall of war veteran Allen. In the "land of opportunity" he defended so vigorously, the veteran's every effort to fulfill his potential is thwarted. Upon his return from the war, he is offered a medal and a parade but little else. While his ambitions have been transformed by his wartime experiences, his country only offers him more of the same routine he found in the army, "a factory whistle instead of a bugle call." Though he wants a "job where you can accomplish things—build, construct, create," Jim bows to family pressure and is soon cooped up in a shipping room, gazing enviously through the window at a nearby construction site.

He leaves the clerk's job to realize his aspirations but is laid off from the only construction job he can find and then wanders across the country fruitlessly searching for another opportunity. Jim's swift decline from war hero to hobo is poignantly dramatized when he tries to pawn his Medal of Honor. The pawnbroker silently refuses, pulling out a box to reveal a heap of similar medals.

Flat broke and hungry, it would seem that Jim has been reduced to rock bottom. However, when a fellow hobo sticks up a roadside diner, Jim is implicated in the robbery. Neither the police nor the courts will listen to his pleas of innocence; to them the veteran is just another bum. His attempt to avoid routine and fulfill his right to a better life is rewarded by the brutality and regimentation of the chain gang. The system has totally failed him.

By the time Jim escapes the chain gang, the country is at the height of twenties' prosperity. Using an assumed name, he is able to find a decent job in the construction industry and rise to a position of prominence. But even though he finally fulfills his life's dream, Jim still finds himself frustrated and oppressed. Entrapped by a landlady (Glenda Farrell) who, upon discovering his past, blackmails him into marriage, Jim is denied his right to happiness. He explains to Helen (Helen Vinson), the girl he loves but cannot marry, that his life is a prison from which there is "no escape . . . no freedom." His material prosperity is as ephemeral as the stock market boom and in 1929, his wife reveals his identity to the police.

Though he is safe in another state, Jim voluntarily returns to the chain gang state upon its promise to clear up his record if he will only serve a token ninety-day sentence. His faith in society is now shattered once and for all as the promise is broken and he is consigned indefinitely to the hell of the chain gang. The film through Paul Muni's performance bristles with outrage: "Why their crimes are worse than mine. Worse than anybody's here. They're the ones that should be in chains, not we!" Although a campaign to free Jim Allen is organized, the rest of society is powerless to help him and sometime later a newspaper article dismisses him as "just another forgotten man."

By the film's conclusion, the only recourse left the victimized citizen is to abandon society, to defy its laws and survive by any means necessary. Jim's second escape finds him in Depression America, a fugitive from the law living as a petty criminal, all hopes of a decent life abandoned. The final, powerful scene summarizes the paranoia, anger and despair of 1932. Appearing out of the dark, a crazed and haunted Jim greets Helen for the first time in a year. In a quickly whispered exchange, he describes his life on the road, always hunted, always moving: "I hide in rooms all day and travel by night. No friends, no rest, no peace." A slight sound triggers an instinctive cringe from Jim and despite Helen's pleas he begins to slink away, animallike, into the dark. When she calls after him, "How do you live?" his voice hisses from the black, "I steal" and footsteps are heard running away. This pessimistic fade into darkness is Hollywood's angriest statement on the Depression.

Russell Campbell summarizes the impact of the film:

> In the total structure of the film a man only wanting to go straight, to build, create, do his patriotic duty, serve society, is frustrated, thwarted, and punished by a cruel and corrupt system: specifically a

Southern chain gang, mythically America 1932. This system has no redress for its injustices; they are too fundamental. The only solution, if one is to survive, let alone counter-attack, is anti-social behavior—revolt. *I Am a Fugitive from a Chain Gang* is, I repeat, a radical film.[3]

The unhappy ending also represents a radical break from the Formula. By violating a sacred canon, it allows the film to go against the social institutions Hollywood usually upheld. Such an ending reversed audience expectations, did not give the "average fan" the satisfaction the movies were supposed to provide. According to a *Variety* reviewer,

This scene comes as such an unexpected finale that it leaves the women limp. Here they have been witnessing the rehabilitation of a fugitive and, with the apparent double-cross of a state (somewhere below the Mason-Dixon line), plus the newspaper agitation in favor of the escaped convict upon his first re-arrest, the expectation is for a favorable denouement, including the turning of the tables upon the vicious prison system which makes the chain gang possible. When the sad fade-out eventuates, as the broken fugitive shuffles off into the night, it's a shocker for the average fan.[4]

Fugitive refuses to reduce the Depression to simple villains and solve it through their defeat. Because it does not show romantic love as the ultimate cure-all for the hero's frustrations, because, in short, it does not define the universe in terms of neat dramatic conventions, *I Am a Fugitive* is free to explore its themes with an openness and honesty unusual in Hollywood movies. By breaking the ritualistic pattern of the Formula, the film provoked rather than reassured the moviegoer, and in so doing created a rare example of genuine social criticism.

I Am a Fugitive's radicalism could only be the product of the shakiest of times—when the producers were as uncertain about the viability of the Formula as their audience was uncertain about society's formulae. It is because the public was receptive to such uncompromised social analysis, that is, because it was good box office, that *Fugitive*'s ending was ever allowed. Initially, Warners' temporary production chief, Hal Wallis, cut the final scene, fearing that it was too strong. But upon his return from Europe, regular production chief Darryl F. Zanuck overruled Wallis,[5] reasoning that the ending was in keeping with the film's overall tone and that audiences would buy such pessimism. When Zanuck was proven correct and *Fugitive* became a smash hit, Warners started injecting despair into a number of their pictures. Building up an image as the "socially conscious" studio, they formulized *Fugitive*'s box-office commodities.

Blondie Johnson (1933) is typical of the studio's efforts. Otherwise a mediocre attempt to combine the gangster film with the woman's weepie, the film begins with a concrete demonstration of the premise that the social system forces you into a life of crime. Blondie (Joan Blondell) applies for relief in an understaffed and underfinanced welfare office crowded with dispirited and hungry people. Her application is rejected by a catch-22 bureaucracy designed to reduce the bulging relief rolls. Having found temporary lodgings for her family in the back of a friend's store and having quit a job to protect herself from a licentious employer, Blondie is not an emergency case: she has a place to stay and had a job, whereas others are worse off. It does not matter that her mother is critically ill, that her brothers and sister are starving, and that they can't stay in the store much longer.

Like James Allen, Blondie suffers abuse upon abuse. Her mother dies of pneumonia when their ruthless landlord evicts the family into the cold and rain. Indignant, Blondie sees a lawyer about suing the landlord. There she learns the corollary of social indifference to the poor: the protection of the wealthy. She is advised that she needs money to take legal action. Frustrated, she bitterly resolves: "Money. That's all I've ever heard. Money. I'm going to get money and I'm going to get plenty of it." When warned that there are two ways of getting money, she retorts, "Yeah, I know. The hard way and the easy way." But she has already discovered that there is no sense looking for legitimate work: "Where? With hundreds unemployed?" Burning with an anger which the half-crazed Allen cannot quite articulate, Blondie proudly declares a personal war against poverty.

Here, however, contemporary despair is little more than a plot device to introduce a tired rehash of the gangster's rise and fall. Having begun with *Fugitive*'s provocative conclusion, the Formula film ends with a reaffirmation of true love's curative powers. Blondie and her henchman-lover give themselves up to the fair and decent police and vow to reunite after they have paid their debts to society. The film, forgetting that it was social inequality that led Blondie into crime, now claims that being either wealthy or poor is irrelevant when you're in love. *Fugitive*'s shattering fade into darkness is replaced by the typical clinch.

While Warners did release a number of major films which centered on social problems (*Cabin in the Cotton, Wild Boys of the Road, Massacre, Black Legion, They Won't Forget*, etc.) *Blondie Johnson* is perhaps most characteristic of their output during the thirties. The studio gave film after film a contemporary relevance by injecting occasional scenes or comments about the Depression in a story that was otherwise asocial. *Goldiggers of 1933* safely encapsulates *Fugitive*'s despair in a couple of musical numbers and witty cut-ups. It begins with a clever satire on official optimism. A line of chorus girls dressed in over-sized coins rehearse "We're in the Money," a wish-fulfillment banish-ment of the Depression. As the girls celebrate the end of the Depres-sion, the sheriff walks in to close down the show, seizing the scenery in order to collect for unpaid bills. A wonderfully ironic touch has a zealous deputy ripping a coin off an otherwise semi-nude chorine. The girls' resigned comments establish the true situation: "It's the Depression, dearie."

This scene is followed by a montage of closed theaters and breadlines and a sprinkling of caustic wisecracks. When it's suggested they put on a show about hard times, one girl sardonically comments, "We won't have to rehearse that." Sarcasm also greets the news that some Texas cattle barons may back the show: "How can they sell cattle? Who eats anymore?" Otherwise, the film is a backstage musical which relates to the Depression only metaphorically: show people struggle to raise the money to produce a show and chorus girls romance rich playboys for their money.

The film ends with a musical number which returns to the opening scene's topicality. "Remember My Forgotten Man" summarizes the lost hope of the early thirties:

> Remember my forgotten man,
> You put a rifle in his hand.
> You sent him far away,
> You shouted hip hooray,
> But look at him today.

As the torch singer (Joan Blondell) wails her blues lament, a Busby Berkeley dance drama unfolds around her. Down-and-out veterans are seen sleeping in doorways and smoking discarded cigarette butts. When a cop starts to harass one for loitering, the torch singer intercedes, turning over the man's lapel to reveal a Medal of Honor.

A series of flashbacks within the dance condenses *Fugitive*'s history of the postwar period into three pointedly different marches. In the first the men vigorously parade to war amidst the cheers of the crowd. Next they limp home through the rain and mud, wounded and tired. Finally they are seen shuffling along to get handouts from a soup kitchen. The number ends with the abandoned singer and the forgotten men of 1933 singing before a silhouetted background of the proud marchers of 1917.

This number, Warners' answer to "Brother, Can You Spare a Dime?" places *Fugitive* protest within the safe confines of a single musical num-ber separate from the main plot. The despair central to the other film stands in sharp contrast to the happy resolution of the backstage drama. The next step for Warners was to show the forgotten man remembered.

Recovery—The Forgotten Man Remembered

In early 1932 Jack Warner was summoned by his brother to their New York office to meet with various leaders of the Democratic Party. Long-time Republicans, the Warners were being asked to join in a campaign to promote then–New York Governor Roosevelt as the man to lead the country out of the Depression. In his autobiography, Jack Warner explains why he and his brother deserted the Republicans for Roosevelt:

> I looked at my brother for some clue to this political switch and he said bluntly: "The country is in chaos. There is revolution in the air. We need a change." It was not a very original battle cry, but I had to admit the economy was a mess and almost anything would be an improvement.[6]

Once they decided on FDR, the Warners entered the campaign in full force. Jack, assigned to "help out on the West Coast campaign," organized a massive pageant at the Los Angeles Coliseum. Exploiting his radio station and the appeal of movie star associates to publicize the event, Warner attracted 175,000 to listen to FDR. It was on the train trip to the Los Angeles rally that Warner met Roosevelt: "I found him a vital and enormously magnetic man, and during that two-hour train trip we began a friendship that endured to the day of his death."[7]

After the election, Warner continued to act as a major propagandist for the New Deal. Throughout the thirties, Warner Brothers' topical films would present the administration—usually in the guise of federal judges, G-men, or benevolent civil servants—as the solution to all social problems. The adaptation of FDR into the Warners' Formula had its beginnings in *Heroes for Sale*. Originally scripted during the final panicky days of Hoover's administration but released well into Roosevelt's first term (in July),[8] *Heroes* reveals the transition from the despair of 1932 to the hope of 1933. The film tries to convince a restless populace to endure the hardships a little longer, that help is on the way in the form of FDR.

The plot is almost a carbon copy of *I Am a Fugitive*, tracing the life of a forgotten man through a series of crises from the war to the Depression. Tom Holmes (Richard Barthelmess) suffers as many indignities as Jim Allen, but unlike Allen retains his faith in the system. At his bleakest moment, Tom rejects despair and rebellion to proclaim his hope for a better life under the new administration.

The major part of the film establishes why Tom Holmes should be discontent. He returns from the war in a much worse state than Allen: a drug addict dependent on the morphine used as a pain killer for war injuries. Tom has even been deprived of his Medal of Honor because a cowardly friend has taken credit for his heroism. Like Allen, Tom is imprisoned unjustly and sent to a state narcotics farm. Again the film grants its hero a brief respite of prosperity during the twenties. Upon his release, Tom marries Ruth (Loretta Young) and works his way up in a small laundry business, earning a position of importance by installing new labor-saving machinery. But when new management uses the machinery as a pretext to throw most of the employees out of work, the disgruntled workers attack the laundry. Tom's efforts to stop them fail and he ends up imprisoned for inciting a riot. The veteran's position, his true love (his wife is killed in the riot), and his future are once more denied him.

Like Jim, Tom's second reentry into society, again during the Depression, is unsuccessful. Though he has acquired a small fortune through his investment in the laundry machines, Tom donates most of it to establish a soup kitchen to help the destitute. This charitable enterprise when added to his conviction as an agitator convinces local "Red squads" that Tom is a dangerous radical. Ordered to move on, he joins the army of unemployed transients, riding the freights across the country in search of work. He too has become a fugitive, hunted and persecuted, chased out of towns and herded into boxcars. Voicing the indignation of the forgotten man, he tells a policeman, "We're not tramps. We're ex-servicemen."

It is at this point, where the frightened Allen pronounced his despair, that Holmes reaffirms his faith. He encounters an old friend who fears that "it's the end of America," while Tom, remarkably enough, reassures him that things will get better. If the forgotten man can endure just a little longer, he will soon be remembered by Franklin Roosevelt:

TOM: No. It's maybe the end of us, but it's not the end of America. In a few years, it'll go on bigger and stronger than ever.

ROGER: You know, you're the last guy in the world that I'd ever expect to find was an optimist!

TOM: That's not optimism—just common horse-sense. Did you read President Roosevelt's inaugural address?

ROGER: He's right. You know, it takes more than one sock in the jaw to lick a hundred and twenty million people.

Fugitive's eloquent finale is replaced with the soppiest Hollywood religiosity. The film ends with a brief scene in Tom's soup kitchen where he is prematurely memorialized in a plaque: "Tom Holmes—Give Us This Day Our Daily Bread." His old landlady (Aline MacMahon) comments to Tom's little boy: "He's given up everything"—and the young boy reverently replies, "When I grow up I want to be just like my daddy." Whereas Allen found no alternative but to move outside the system, Tom demonstrates a Christian patience and tolerance of persecution because he sees the coming of a new messiah. His selfless sacrifice of all his worldly possessions provides a model for all Americans. Again, Russell Campbell has characterized the overall temper of the film:

> *Heroes For Sale* is a preachy film and the gospel it preaches is that of faith and endurance: if you just hang on, it says to the dispossessed, and trust to your president, you will live to see capitalism flourish again and the old American virtues restored triumphantly to their rightful place.[9]

The forgotten-man-remembered theme received its clearest expression in Warners' next musical, *Footlight Parade* (1933). The film's mood is markedly different from that of *Golddiggers of 1933*. The Depression specter so prevalent in the earlier musical is quickly done away with in *Footlight*'s opening scene. Stage-director Chester Kent (James Cagney) finds himself unemployed when the excitement over talking pictures cuts into stage show attendance. But the indefatigable Cagney hero can never be kept down for long and Kent soon comes up with the idea of producing stage prologues before each movie. The threat of unemployment thereafter becomes subordinated to a competition between Kent and a rival producer.

The wisecracks likewise shift from the gallows humor of *Golddiggers* to New Deal optimism. When Kent's dance director (Frank McHugh) keeps moaning that a number can't be properly rehearsed in the short time allowed, Kent confidently urges him to get moving—"Well, what are you waiting for . . . an okay from Roosevelt?" In a later scene he confronts his partners who have been embezzling his share of the profits. One of the partners tries to soothe him: "We're giving you a new deal," to which Kent responds, "And I'm the dealer." As Mark Roth suggests, Chester Kent can be seen as a surrogate Roosevelt, a strong director leading the "little people" in the chorus into the order and success of the completed show.[10] Kent is the first in a long line of Warners' Rooseveltlike characters who defeat the shysters and thus overcome every variety of social problem.

The newfound confidence is most directly conveyed in the film's climactic dance number, "Shanghai Lil." The pathetic soldiers who shuffled through the "Remember My Forgotten Man" number are transformed into stout and proud sailors marching in perfect military formations. The blues lament becomes a patriotic celebration of the country's strength. The sailors hold up flash cards so that when seen from above they form, in sequence, an American flag, a portrait of Roosevelt, and finally the NRA eagle.

Soon Warners' attempt to promote confidence in FDR became absorbed in the general excitement over the new President. In trying to mold the times, these films ended up very much a reflection of the times, for it turned out that Roosevelt did not need Warners to advertise for him. Indeed, as Russell Campbell notes, by the time of *Heroes'* release in July 1933, its optimism was already too guarded for the audience. From the moment of his famous inauguration speech, FDR executed a dramatic change in the country's mood. Arthur Schlesinger comments:

> The downward grind had been stopped; the panic of 1933 had vanished. Businessmen were recovering confidence in themselves and their system. Working people were filled with new vigor and hope. Mobs of farmers no longer gathered along country roads to stop produce from going to market or to demonstrate against the foreclosure of mortgages. The American republic and the democratic system were showing unexpected resources of vitality and purpose. Two years earlier, no one could have anticipated such a sweeping revision either of the political mood or of the economic structure. From the perspective of the winter of 1932–33, it was a record of prodigious achievement.[11]

The FDR personality was so charismatic, it began to permeate non-Warners' productions. Cosmopolitan Studios, in adapting the play *Service* to the screen, changed its title to that of Roosevelt's current book, *Looking Forward* (1933). The film dramatizes its prefatory quote from the President: "We need enthusiasm, imagination and the ability to face facts—we read the courage of the young." Universal's *Moonlight and Pretzels* (1933), using songs by E. Y. Harburg, is another backstage musical about the difficulties of putting on a show. Its final number, as described in a contemporary review, is a Depression tableau eulogizing the NRA.[12] Fox's *The Man Who Dared* (1933) is a loving tribute to Anton Cermak, the Chicago reform mayor and New Dealer who was killed by an assassin during an attempt on Roosevelt's life.

Optimism and confidence reached its asinine limit in another Fox production, *Stand Up and Cheer* (1934). Lawrence Cromwell (Warner Baxter) is a dynamic stage producer summoned to Washington to take up a new cabinet post as Secretary of Amusement. It is his task to cheer the nation out of its "depression." He organizes all the country's entertainers into traveling shows that will spread happiness throughout the land. The film shows riveters, washerwomen, poor blacks, factory workers, etc., singing away their social and racial troubles: "I'm laughin'— If I can smile, why can't you?" Cromwell defeats the shysters who would undermine his project and a "Kiddies' Brigade" led by Shirley Temple inspires so much joy that the Depression vanishes for good. The film ends with the entire country parading in columns of four and singing "We're Out of the Red" (lyrics by the ubiquitous Mr. Harburg). A deadpan review in *Variety* manages to top the film's silliness by claiming that the Depression had already been vanquished:

> (The film is) a hodge-podge principally handicapped by a national depression premise. Americans now like to think of themselves in the light of being on the upturn and having rounded that long-awaited corner. So *Cheer*'s plot motivation is basically questionable.[13]

In the space of little more than a year, Hollywood had moved from *I Am a Fugitive*'s nihilistic pessimism to *Heroes*' passive endurance to *Stand Up and Cheer*'s singing away of the Depression. After this remarkable shift, the studios would never again experiment with such radical political alternatives or question so profoundly the basis of American society. The worst had passed and, like the rest of the country, the film industry was aroused from its temporary despair. Hollywood continued to look at social problems—some of the best problem films were yet to come—but it was to do so from a position of assumed strength. By the mid-thirties a Formula had been fully developed for safely handling any issue. No matter what viewpoint the films took, that of conservative populism or liberal New Dealism, the trouble was always the same—shysterism. And in both cases, a hero-redeemer, whether the populist country crusader bearing the strength of the pioneers or the liberal New Dealer representing a strong federal government, was ready to protect the "little people," the masses of innocent victims, from all manner of social parasites and selfish profiteers.

—PART II—

The System Upheld: The Individual Redeemed, 1933-1941

—6—

UNEMPLOYMENT—
DOING YOUR PART

Although the New Deal gave the people "Action, Action, Action," it never really found a solution to the central Depression problems. Unprecedented rates of unemployment continued throughout the decade and, in 1939, nine and one-half million remained jobless.[1] The New Deal had merely placated some of the earlier anxiety until, over a period of time, joblessness came to be seen as a normal part of American life. FDR's economic "pump priming" in the form of aid to business (the NRA) and various public works projects (the WPA, the CCC, etc.) failed to effectively stimulate private industry. In Geoffrey Perrett's estimation, the New Deal was an often inventive grab bag without a definite plan for creating jobs in a deflated economy. Its major tactic was to create confidence, the sense that energetic, positive action was being taken and the matter would soon be under control. FDR's most effective palliative for the Depression was psychological rather than actual and the New Deal "a triumph of appearances over reality."[2]

Since the New Deal was more a matter of mood than policies, Hollywood, by simply promoting confidence, could appear New Dealish without endorsing any of its programs. For the rest of the decade the movies offered the familiar reassurances of the pre-FDR films—stay calm and the system will right itself—but these platitudes now sounded viable because they seemed to echo the government. In terms of concrete, realistic approaches to unemployment, Hollywood fell back on plot devices far removed from Washington's social experimentation. Not even Warner Brothers at their most politically sophisticated proposed any practical measures to meet the crisis; their New Dealism merely consisted of invoking the magical powers of the federal government. Most filmmakers adopted the populist position that unemployment is the responsibility of the individual. Either the love of a good woman or the beneficence of a socially conscious philanthropist/good neighbor would help get the unemployed victim back on his feet again without government aid. Although these self-help fantasies were diametrically opposed to the New Deal's attempts to manage the economy, they were often mistaken as examples of FDR-like energy and liberalism. Thus the aura around the New Deal helped make the movies appear socially progressive even as they clung to their basic conservatism.

Forgotten Children—Warners' *Wild Boys of the Road*

Warners' forgotten man films were the first Hollywood movies to look at unemployment as a widespread problem. In *I Am a Fugitive* and, to a lesser extent, *Heroes for Sale*, it is the collapse of an entire society which forces the heroes into the loneliness and hunger of the night. These two films established memorable images of hobo-heroes tramping across the country looking for work, standing despondently in breadlines, desperately pawning war medals. The tragedy alluded to in these early films was to be averted in Warners' subsequent productions. Tom Holmes' hopes for a better world under Roosevelt were very indefinite and, in terms of his experience, just as unlikely. In their next foray into the Depression landscape, *Wild Boys of the Road* (1933), released just a few months after *Heroes* and also directed by William Wellman, the Warners demonstrated the first concrete results of New Deal promises. The hardships and persecutions of the film's young high school drop-outs are amended in the final reel through the benevolent wisdom of a federal judge.

Following *Heroes'* pattern, *Wild Boys* first graphically depicts the injustices of Depression America before demonstrating FDR's ability to alleviate them. Somewhat modelled after the Russian film, *The Road to Life* (1931), the film is based on contemporary reports about the hordes of young people, the so-called wild boys of the road who were forced out of their homes onto the roads and rails because their parents could no longer support them. Wellman movingly portrays the effects of unemployment on a typical middle-class family, charting its decline from an affluence previously taken for granted to unexpected and unfamiliar poverty. The protagonist, Eddie (Frankie Darro), begins as a carefree student going to a high school dance in his beat-up flivver and arriving home to gorge himself on a huge piece of apple pie. Then, suddenly, Eddie's safe world is encroached upon: his best friend reveals that his family is being supported by the Community Chest and his own father is laid off indefinitely. Eddie at first brushes off the crisis with vague promises to economize but, as things worsen, comes to realize his own responsibilities. He sells his precious car to a junk dealer and offers his father the money, trying to hold back his own tears in an effort to cheer the dispirited man.

Finally Eddie resolves to leave home so that he won't be a burden to his parents: "I can't go on having fun in school while my Dad's in a breadline." Riding the rails in search of work, Eddie discovers that there are many others like him, that there is, as the title of one contemporary account put it, "An Army of Boys on the Loose."[3] The rest of the film documents the harassment and frustration these boys endure in their daily struggle to subsist. Each community they go to repulses them, treating the youths as vagrants who have come to take away jobs from their own unemployed. In Chicago, railway cops herd the boys into cattle pens for shipment back out of the city; near Columbus, Ohio, the local police chase a whole gang of kids off a train into the freezing winter. Later, Eddie's close friend, Tommy (Edwin Phillips), falls in the path of an oncoming train while fleeing the yard dicks and his leg is crushed.

Eddie is, however, no callow Tom Holmes who patiently endures, but a little firebrand who sticks up for his rights (Darro's energetic performance is reminiscent of Cagney). Upon being kicked off a train, Eddie listens attentively to an older hobo: "Why let seven train dicks chase you off the train? Why not fight back? There's a hundred of you. You're an army, ain't you?" Eddie leads his army back to the train, beating back the cops with eggs and fruit from the freight cars. Later, in another city, the youths are given permission to live in a storage yard for sewer pipes, from which they fan out to panhandle and look for work. But local merchants object to these "delinquents" and soon the police arrive at the yard with an eviction notice. They are met by organized resistance from Eddie and friends, this time armed with rocks and clubs. At least one critic, William Troy, reacted with surprise:

> Never before does one recall having witnessed an American picture whose climax is made to consist in a pitched battle between a band of ragged outlaws and the police, in which sympathy is manifestly with the former.[4]

Eddie's rebellion reaches its final stage after he is unjustly arrested for robbery and brought before the federal judge. His speech to the court is an impassioned rejection of American society:

> You're sending us to jail because you don't want to see us, not because we're menaces to society; you'll get rid of us three, but there's thousands more like us. We won't tell you who our parents are because

> they're poor and can't afford to help us. We can't go home now. Go
> ahead and lock us up. At least we'll get fed there.

But this judge listens and understands and, above all, is interested in
seeing justice done. Bearing a reasonable resemblance to FDR, the
judge steps down from his bench (providing us with a glimpse of the
NRA eagle on the wall behind him) to talk to the kids man-to-man. He
dismisses the case and promises to see that Eddie and his two friends
find jobs:

> I'm going to do my part if you do your part. Things are going to get
> better, not merely here, but all over the country. All I want you to
> do is to promise to go home when you can afford it. I know your
> father will be going to work soon.

Eddie is so happy he literally turns somersaults. The film has moved
from rebellious indignation to the celebration of a New Deal panacea
and Warners have moved from *Heroes*' tentative hope toward an actual
solution. However, William Wellman told a Toronto audience in July,
1974, that this was not the ending he originally wanted. When pressed
to reveal how the film was meant to finish, he vaguely implied that the
kids were taken off to reformatory.

As it stands, the film offers a solution but never specifies the political
and economic particulars of that solution. The social issue is brought
down to an individual level wherein the benevolent judge solves the
personal dilemma facing Eddie and his friends. This resolves the film's
drama satisfactorily without raising questions about the thousands of
other youths on the road or specifying how the NRA and other New
Deal projects will resolve their problems. Like the projects themselves,
the film is designed mainly to boost morale. Throughout the decade
Warners continued to glorify the spirit of the New Deal more than its
actual performance.

Love Conquers All

Gentlemen Are Born (1934), a melodramatic tale of four college
graduates' disillusioning experiences outside the ivory tower, adheres to
the same structure as *Heroes* and *Wild Boys*, building up a strong case
for rebellion against social injustice until the final reel when, at the
height of his despair, the hero rediscovers his faith in America. This
time though, with the "New Deal honeymoon" beginning to fade, Warners offered a more traditional solution to Depression woes. True love,
not the promises of a New Deal representative, convinces Bob Bailey
(Franchot Tone) that the catastrophe can be overcome.

The film is a compendium of problem film clichés. Bob and his fellow graduates idealistically go out into the world to make good, but, like so many Warners social victims, soon learn that the American Dream can no longer be achieved. Fred Harper (Robert Light) moves right into his father's prestigious stock brokerage and seems set until the firm's fraudulence is revealed. Mr. Harper commits suicide while Fred retreats to the country to rediscover his roots. Smudge (Dick Foran) is the film's forgotten man figure. A physical education major unable to find a coaching job, the best Smudge can do is to get himself pummeled in a boxing ring for ten dollars a fight. This prompts Bob to eulogize: "Ex-hero equals zero." When he and his wife are at the point of starvation, Smudge ends up in the usual pawn shop (with a valuable fountain pen rather than a medal), is mistaken for a robber, and is killed by police. Tom Martin (Ross Alexander), the third graduate, is a little better off. Though barely surviving as an architect's apprentice, he has the love of his wife and newborn child to keep him going: "That's enough to make any man happy."

It is Bob who articulates the college graduates' disillusionment. Observing the experiences of his friends and frustrated himself because his measly income prevents his marriage to the upper-class Joan (Margaret Lindsay), he delivers the climactic outrage speech:

> Fred was ruined before he even got started. You [Tom] have a wife and baby to support and doctor bills to pay. You work and sweat for seventeen years and then, maybe if you're lucky, you'll have enough money to send your kid to college. And what for? . . . They shot Smudge down in the streets like a dog because he was hungry. How can you live? If it doesn't make sense in dollars and cents, it's no good.

But when a chastened Joan decides that she can live on his meager salary, love disarms his cynicism. He now realizes how well off he really is: "Nothing can stop me now. We were naive and idealistic when we graduated. We thought the world was an oyster and all we had to do was open it. I forgot I had a post-graduate course."

The happy ending ignores the earlier "dollars and cents" premise of the film. If true love failed to help Smudge and his wife, how can it sustain the other couples? At a time when financial strain was tearing families apart and robbing the male of his identity as breadwinner, *Gentlemen Are Born* argues that Depression hardships brought families closer together and made better men of contemporary youth. In place of their customary liberal New Dealism, the Warners here echo the reactionary platitude that the Depression is not such a bad thing because it toughens the moral fiber of the nation.

Other films presented the same message even when depicting life among the dispossessed in Hoovervilles. Following the example of the happy hobo films, *One More Spring* (1935) idealizes its protagonists' down-and-out existence in Central Park as summer camp romance. The film at least concedes that an economic crisis forced its characters out of their homes and into Central Park, but once there it whimsically celebrates their resourcefulness at making such a congenial, almost pastoral life for themselves. As with Bill and Trina in *A Man's Castle*, once Oktar (Warner Baxter) and Elizabeth (Janet Gaynor) fall in love their problems seem trivial. Oktar constantly manages to dig up food from somewhere while Elizabeth keeps house and is dejected only when Oktar wears a shirt she hasn't had time to iron. The third member of the household, out-of-work violinist Rosenberg (Walter King) provides them all with a comfortable domicile—the park toolshed—by teaching the friendly street cleaner to play "Macushla" on the fiddle. Naturally, all ends happily. After saving the life of a banker, Oktar is rewarded with money to finance a new business. Elizabeth accepts his marriage proposal, Rosenberg finds a job, and the street cleaner can play "Macushla."

Derived from the novel of the same name by Robert Nathan, the film, as a *Time* reviewer put it, "lacks the satirical implications of its original but somehow achieves a simple and disarming charm which is likely to prove valuable at the box office."[5] The whimsicality is part of the novel but there it is undercut by an awareness of suffering and loss. The harsh social background which had made Elizabeth a whore in the book is replaced by the characterization of sweet, virginal Janet Gaynor as an aspiring actress. The bitter despair that leads Oktar to completely abandon society at the novel's end is cancelled out by his successful reentry into the business world. The fairytale tone adopted by Nathan ironically belies the realities, while for Hollywood it is the reality.

Whereas the Warners' forgotten man pictures seek to rub our faces in the dirt of unemployment and make us feel the desperation of the heroes (at least until the final reel), the romance films show us that the dirt really isn't that dirty and that it is not so much desperation as *joie de vivre* that the dispossessed experience. Nothing distinguishes these two approaches to social reality more than their photographic styles. The studio Hooverville in *A Man's Castle* is diffused with romantic soft focus and subdued back lighting. When Bill introduces Trina to the Hooverville, we see it through her love-struck eyes: shimmering in the moonlight by the Hudson River. This unreal, fairytale quality, typical of director Frank Borzage, stands in marked contrast to the gritty realism of *Wild Boys of the Road*. Wellman's documentarylike shooting, his reliance on outdoor location—the freight yards and sewer pipe city—and a straightforward camera technique, intensify the sense of realism. The hard-edged, naturalistic lighting allows no romanticization and forces the audience to take note of the squalor in which the characters live. The Warners' documentary style seeks to effectively dramatize the reality of social problems, while Borzage's romanticism yearns to transcend that reality.

Borzage's *Little Man, What Now?* again centers on the plight of a couple trying to sustain their love in a hostile environment, this time Depression-bound Berlin in the chaotic days before the Nazi takeover. Any social comment is once more shaped by Borzage's almost mystical belief in the curative power of love. As the opening credits declare, the "love of a good woman" will see the little man through "no matter how bad things are."

The film is nevertheless a more detailed portrait of social breakdown than *A Man's Castle*. Hans (Douglass Montgomery) is far more concerned with basic survival than the carefree Spencer Tracy character and must endure long periods of unemployment and hunger. Everywhere he turns he is met with abuse. The lower classes are rabble gathering ominously on street corners, always on the verge of violence, while the upper classes are decadent and exploitative. Hans' employers are cruelly insensitive to the little man's plight. His first boss, Herr Kleinholz (DeWitt Jennings), fires Hans because he gets married and is therefore no longer eligible to marry Kleinholz's homely daughter. The department store manager is a mean-spirited man who constantly harasses his workers, threatening to fire them if they don't improve their sales.

In a scene reminiscent of the ironic opening of *A Man's Castle*, Hans waits on one of Germany's most popular movie stars (Alan Mowbray). While he assists the actor in trying on every suit in the store, the excited Hans tells him how much he admired his performance in his last film, that of a desperate man driven through poverty into crime. The actor gloats over the praise and describes his next role as "a man from the wrong side of the tracks." After seeing all the suits, the star thanks Hans, revealing that he was only researching for his new film: "I only want to see how a man from the wrong side of the tracks dresses." With his job on the line, Hans pleads with the man to buy at least one suit. But the actor haughtily rebuffs him, complains to the manager, and gets Hans fired. The great humanitarian of the screen is intolerant of the needy in real life. It is an ironic comment on Hollywood's own concern for the downtrodden.

Through all of his troubles, Hans has only his love for Lammchen

(Margaret Sullavan) and his friendship with Schultz (George Meeker) to sustain him. Now Schultz has moved away from the city and Hans is too ashamed to ever face his wife again. But with the news of the birth of his son he overcomes his sense of failure and returns to Lammchen. Inspired by the love of his family, he declares, "Now everything will be different. Now I have to make good and will!" The birth of a son brings about a rebirth of love in Hans which in turn reverses his fate. Having withstood the tests to his love and rejected rebellion in the streets, Hans is delivered from further travail. At that very moment, Schultz arrives, not with a mere job offer, but with the opportunity for Hans to really "make good."

The Populist Benefactor

Schultz is one of many populist benefactors who place the interest of the people above that of their personal wealth. Like Tom Dickson (*An American Madness*) and Mr. Gibson (*Heroes for Sale*), Schultz is the ideal small-time capitalist, meeting the economic crisis with a compassion which renders the governmental action advocated by the New Deal unnecessary. Paradoxically, as in *Our Daily Bread* and *Heroes*, the scheme suggested to save free enterprise is quasisocialistic. Schultz, a truly enlightened capitalist, believes that the best way to increase sales is to allow the workers to share in the profits of the business. This incentive will both increase sales and eliminate the deadly competition of salesman versus salesman encouraged by greedy capitalists such as the department store manager. Again populism is both reformist and reactionary. The socially conscious rich man's scheme is socialistic but allows for a continuation of laissez-faire policies. The benefactors are essentially self-help individuals willing to be good neighbors and help others help themselves.

The two classic benefactor films of the thirties, Frank Capra's *Mr. Deeds Goes to Town* (1936) and Gregory La Cava's *My Man Godfrey* (1936), look at the Depression from the point of view of the rich rather than the downtrodden. Since more socially conscious millionaires are the answer to unemployment, the films advocate reform not of society but of high society. The self-seeking rich must be made to see their responsibility to the lower classes; mindless partying and snobbish intellectualism must give way to good neighborliness.

This renewal of populist values is to be achieved, according to both films, through the efforts of heroes whom one could characterize as the perfect rich man. Longfellow Deeds (Gary Cooper) is a middle-class, small-town little man who inherits twenty million dollars while Godfrey

Parkes (William Powell) is a Boston blueblood who, disappointed in love, allows himself to slip into a life of poverty. Deeds is a rich commoner, Godfrey a poor rich man. Both combine the best of two worlds: the power of wealth and the human simplicity of the poor.

The films are structured around their heroes' comic conflict with the irresponsible upper class. Deeds moves to the city to administer his estate and is immediately beset by shyster lawyers and reporters who want to exploit him. While we laugh at the country hick's naive antics— riding fire engines, feeding doughnuts to horses, etc.—we laugh even harder when his plain common sense shows up the sophisticated city slickers—the pompous opera patrons, the cynical poet-intellectuals. In the same way, when down-and-out Godfrey is taken in by the rich Bullock family as butler, we are able to observe from his rational viewpoint the family's empty-headed, irrational capers. Mrs. Bullock (Alice Brady) supports her protégé, a pianist named Carlo (Mischa Auer) who is as parasitic and pretentious as Deeds' opera patrons; cold, monstrous older daughter Cornelia (Gail Patrick) pitches stones through Fifth Avenue windows; scatterbrained younger daughter Irene (Carole Lombard) steals a horse from a hansom cab and houses it in the family library. Mr. Bullock (Eugene Pallette) is too ineffectual to stop his family's excesses but is quite aware of their irresponsible insanity: "All you need to start an asylum is an empty room and the right kind of people."

The city shysters in *Deeds* and the snobbish rich (not the rich, the snobbish rich) in *Godfrey* are the implied causes of the Depression. To the shysters, Deeds' desire to use his money to help the unemployed is the most extreme example of his abnormality. By trying to stop him so that they can have the money themselves and claiming that his philanthropy is proof of his insanity, the shysters are putting their own greedy interests above those of society and thereby helping perpetrate the Depression. The opening sequence of *Godfrey* reveals the callous indifference of the upper class. Bejewelled and elegantly gowned, the Bullock sisters visit the city dump on a high society scavenger hunt. The object of their search: "something nobody wants—a forgotten man." The frivolity of their game and their condescending treatment of the poor as curiosities contrasts sharply with the situation in the dump. The poor must also scavenge, only their hunt among the rubbish is for the basic means of survival.

Both heroes are driven to suicidal despair through their experiences with the snobs. Their psychological state is a metaphor of the country's condition. Both overcome their depression through their contact with the common people. Godfrey describes his own experience:

> I went down to the East River one night thinking I'd just slide in and
> get it over with. I met some fellows living there on the city dump.
> There were people who were fighting it and not complaining. I never
> got as far as the river.

Deeds is so disillusioned with the city that he packs up to return to
Mandrake Falls but on the way out is confronted by a destitute
farmer (John Wray) wielding a gun. The pathetic, desperate state of
the man and his attack on Deeds' lifestyle—"You never gave a thought
to all those starving people standing in the breadlines"—awakens Deeds'
social conscience. And later, when Deeds is interned as a mental case
and is so depressed he refuses to defend himself, it is again the little
people in the courtroom who rally to his defense and prod the hero
into action.

The heroes' personal depression surmounted, the comic climax comes
when they belittle the snobs and shysters and thus deal a blow to the
larger Depression. Deeds disproves all the intellectual, legal, and psychological arguments amassed against him by means of the simplest
common sense. The deep-rooted psychosis supposedly expressed in his
eccentric behavior is no different than the judge's "O-filling," the Vien-
nese psychologist's "doodling," and the claimant's "nose twitching."
Godfrey simply quits his job, rejecting Irene's immature wedding proposals and thoroughly humbling the arrogant Cornelia as "a Park Avenue brat . . . hardly deserving the comment of a butler on his off-
Thursday."

By overcoming personal despair and social snobbism, the economic
crisis is likewise vanquished. The rejuvenated hero meets the problem
head on, using his wealth to get the poor back on their feet. The common people having shown them the way, Deeds and Godfrey now
provide the people with the means for self-help. Both their plans are
similar, though Deeds' preference for farmers is more classically populist. Deeds intends to "give each family ten acres, a horse, cow and some
seed and if they work the farm for three years, it's theirs." Godfrey
(along with a syndicate of businessmen such as the now humanized
Mr. Bullock) finances a project whereby the forgotten men build and
operate a nightclub on the city dump so that they can make a profit
whenever the rich go slumming. The proceeds go not only to the forgotten men but to a housing project for their families.

Both films concretely state their preference for laissez-faire over
government interference. Godfrey rejects welfare programs in its opening scene. One bum complains to Godfrey that his business was ruined
by meddlesome police: "If only them cops would stick to their own
racket and leave honest guys alone, we'd get somewhere without all

this relief and stuff." *Deeds* provides a more thorough debate on the subject, with shyster lawyer Cedar (Douglas Dumbrille) defending the government against Deeds' plan:

> The government is fully aware of this difficulty. It can pull itself out of this economic rut without the assistance of Mr. Deeds or any other crackpot. . . . If this man is permitted to carry out his plan, repercussions would be felt that would shake the foundations of our entire governmental system.

Deeds' rebuttal is a summary of small-town populism. To him, there will "always be leaders and always be followers." Using the example of cars trying to make it up the steep hill in front of his house, he cites how "some make it and some don't" even though they all have the "same cars, same gasoline." He concludes, "That's all I'm trying to do with this money—help the fellows who can't make the hill on high." In short, Deeds proffers self-help tempered by good neighborliness. By identifying the villainous Cedar with the government, the film subtly attacks the New Deal and its proposals for social reform; conversely, by upholding Deeds and having the judge declare him "the sanest man that ever walked into this courtroom," the film defends laissez-faire as the best means of confronting the Depression. In both films, the initiative and hard work of the American people, once given a boost by the well-to-do, are all that is necessary to get the economy going again.

As before, the populist solution satisfies both left and right. The films demonstrate a sincere concern for the dispossessed but attack welfare; they rebuke the wealthy classes without criticizing their wealth, only their snobbish, irresponsible attitudes. Raymond Durgnat has pointed out that these films have often been mistaken as New Dealish: "The mere fact that a film could accept the possibility of a radical shake up, could look on such a shake up optimistically, was enough for many to associate it with a progressive, New Deal attitude." The films are, however, "sufficiently ambiguous for a New Dealer hardly to notice, or care, that, on balance, [they are] propaganda for a moderate, concerned Republican point of view."[6]

Other films picked up on the populist benefactor theme. In *100 Men and a Girl* (1937), the orchestra of unemployed musicians appears to be a WPA cultural project, but the fact that it is freely led by a generous Leopold Stokowski and subsidized by rich tycoon Eugene Pallette proves that traditional capitalism works. A Republic B-movie, *The President's Mystery* (1936), is both direct propaganda for the New Deal (its title and premise are adapted from a series of articles in *Liberty* magazine, all inspired by a mystery suggested by FDR: was it possible for a millionaire to take all his money and disappear in order to start life anew in some worthwhile activity?) and an example of pure populist self-help. The hero, James Blake (Henry Wilcoxen) begins as a lobbyist working for an evil tycoon. To protect the tycoon's interests, Blake wheels and deals in Washington to quash the government's Trades Reconstruction Corporation Bill through which many small industries would be opened as cooperatives. His dirty work done, Blake goes fishing in a small New England town where he comes face to face with the repercussions of his lobbying. Without aid, the town's cannery will be bankrupted, bringing ruin upon the whole community. Like many shysters before him, Blake is suddenly reformed and now goes to battle for the little people. He arranges to disappear, making it look like suicide, and then anonymously uses his wealth to form a cooperative in the town. The New Deal's policies are vindicated, but it is nevertheless the individual benefactor, not the government, who reforms and revitalizes the town's economy.

As in the Capra and La Cava films, a central element is the confrontation of the classes, showing how the rich are humanized by the poor—Blake through his contact with the townspeople, Stokowski and Pallette through a brash but sweet violinist's daughter (Deanna Durbin). Other screwball comedies of the late thirties also played up the motif of class synthesis: harried, overburdened millionaires and their frivolous, irresponsible children live frenetic but empty lives until they meet some carefree soul of the lower class who is not obsessed with success and thus really knows how to live.

The rich have lost their humanity in the single-minded pursuit of the success ethic and social standing. Anthony P. Kirby (Edward Arnold), the big Wall Street tycoon in Capra's *You Can't Take It with You* (1938), ends up alone, without friends and rejected by his son. The father and daughter of the Seton family in *Holiday* (1938) are cold and officious; their highbrow strictures have driven a son to drink and another daughter to neurosis. In each film the hero is a spontaneous, natural being who opts for simpler human values after making it big in the business world. Papa Vanderhoff (Lionel Barrymore) in *You Can't Take It with You* was once a big tycoon like Kirby until he realized he "wasn't having any fun" and left his office, never to return. Johnny Case (Cary Grant), the "rail-splitter" and "man of the people" in *Holiday*, makes a killing on the stock market but turns down a job in a prestigious stock brokerage and calls off his engagement to Julia Seton (Doris Nolan) in order to go on an adventurous and indefinite holiday.

A number of paradoxes are played off against one another. To be wealthy is not impossible, since the American Dream is still feasible;

it is only undesirable because it makes you a snob. To be unemployed is not to be forced into want and suffering, but is a liberating choice made by all endearingly spontaneous eccentrics. While these films appear to be socially critical, dramatizing an apparent rejection of upper-class materialism, they are essentially offering the familiar rationalizations of the Depression status quo—that unemployment makes you a richer human being.

—7—

HOLLYWOOD
AND THE WORKER

Though there was little revolutionary activity in Depression America, the decade nevertheless saw a rapid rise in militant unionism, especially after the New Deal's Wagner Act (1935) enforced labor's right to organize and negotiate. Prominent in every history of the times are accounts of the often violent clashes between angry workers and stubborn management: of Harry Bridges and the San Francisco General Strike (1934), of the GM sitdown in 1936, the "Battle of Detroit" (1940), and the Memorial Day Massacre of striking steelworkers in Chicago (1937). Even the placid calm of Hollywood was disrupted by the new militants. The production chiefs were confronted by a multitude of crafts and guilds, all insisting on the studio workers' right to collective bargaining.

Like the other vested interests, the studios fought tooth and nail against what they felt was a threat to the power structure and a harbinger of the revolution. When the three-year-old Screen Writers Guild was beginning to make headway in 1936, the studios helped form their own company union, the Screen Playwrights, and through various kinds of pressure, including blacklisting and Red-baiting, all but crushed the SWG. Even though the guild won a 1937 National Labor Relations Board election over the Screen Playwrights, it wasn't until 1940 that the studios begrudgingly signed with the union.[1]

To a reactionary management which preferred to think of labor relations in terms of a nineteenth-century patriarchy, there could be only one explanation for the rebellion of their faithful workers: they had come under the spell of "outsiders." To the *Los Angeles Times*, the San Francisco General Strike was not a labor dispute at all, but "an insurrection, a Communist-inspired and led revolt."[2] Likewise, the producers fulminated against troublemakers who led their employees against them. Jack Warner bitterly laments in his autobiography that "his" stars turned against him when they came under the influence of agents. Warner also relates how he hired an unemployed cantor out of sympathy, only to be betrayed several years later when the cantor helped organize a "violent and bloody strike" at the studio.[3] Walt Disney viewed the Screen Cartoonist Guild as the product of "outsiders" and was personally insulted by their demands: "He reacted . . . like a stern father faced by the rebellion of youth."[4]

Hollywood films naturally reflected this patriarchal viewpoint. In a series portraying the lot of the worker in America, the studios continually emphasized the rewards of moderation as opposed to the tragedy of rebellion. *The Power and the Glory* revealed that the workers were being duped and hypnotized by agitators, while *Little Man, What Now?* paid tribute to Hans' faith in the system. *I Believed in You* (1934) opens with the standard Hollywood version of a strike. When a labor agitator berates the men for abandoning a strike which appears to be lost, the workers attack him as the traitor who got them into trouble in the first place. The workers are basically good fellows who have been temporarily deceived by a villain. Having learned the error of their ways, they happily return to the conditions of the pre-strike days.

Dupes and Agitators

Two 1935 films, Warners' *Black Fury* and MGM's *Riffraff*, provide Hollywood's most thorough and direct treatment of labor unrest. While they allude to sensitive contemporary events—*Black Fury* to coal strikes in Pennsylvania and Kentucky and *Riffraff* to the San Francisco longshoremen—the films strip the labor issue of its socioeconomic rationale and completely personalize it. The strike is in each case the joint result of the individual hero's psychological turmoil and the manipulations of a scheming agitator. There is no class conflict; the central struggle is not one of union vs. management but of union man vs. union man, between loyal, contented workers and the dupes like the hero who fall prey to the agitator's inflammatory rhetoric.

To demonstrate that strikes are unnecessary, the films open with portraits of the workers' high standard of living. Whereas contemporary reports[5] describe chronic unemployment and rundown company towns, *Black Fury*'s Joe Radek (Paul Muni) is a happy-go-lucky, hardworking Polish miner with a comfortable home and well-stocked larder. Dutch

Muller (Spencer Tracy), the protagonist of *Riffraff*, is a popular, brawny, and "not too intelligent"[6] worker. He is too satisfied with his life as a West Coast fisherman and too preoccupied with his lady friends to be concerned with improving his lot through union activism. His close friend, "Brains" McCall (J. Farrell MacDonald) lives in a pleasant two-story house, demonstrating that in his case high wages and job security have already been achieved. Even when the film depicts the squalor of the overcrowded living conditions of Hattie's (Jean Harlow) family, it is done in a tone of good fun. The family is made up of lovable comic degenerates who, like the happy hoboes, are not only responsible for their own poverty but actually revel in it.

Except perhaps for their extreme popularity with their peers, Joe and Dutch are typical Hollywood workers—nice, dedicated guys who just don't have the brains to do any better. They are Deeds' "followers," members of the gullible masses who follow the evil shysters until Presidents Hammond and Stanley set them straight. Working on these shyster assumptions, *Black Fury* and *Riffraff* structure their dramas around the followers' wavering between the good and bad leaders, between the moderate union stewards opposed to the strike and the reprehensible agitators.[7]

Although the complaints of *Black Fury*'s agitator, Cronin (J. Carroll Naish), at first seem reasonable, they are mere trifles when compared to the real grievances of contemporary miners. Cronin protests that miners are not paid for "dead work," such as laying tracks or removing shale, but only for the amount of coal they bring out; he says nothing about the lack of steady work for miners or the companies' exorbitant monthly deductions for rent, medical attention, equipment, and insurance. Cronin argues that safety conditions are not adequate to prevent rockfalls; he fails to mention the frequency of more severe accidents or of such occupational diseases as silicosis. Albert Maltz, in his review of the film, drew on his own experience as a reporter in the coal fields to point out the great disparity between the film's mine and actual coal pits:

> They [the film's miners] work genially in well-lighted "rooms" ten feet high instead of lying on their bellies or crouching down, their feet in water, the roof but two inches over their heads. The fury of the speed-up that makes the miner loading coal seem like the fastest thing on earth, is never shown.[8]

But even if Cronin's quibbles do have some credence, they are quickly invalidated by the revelation that he works for a shyster agency that foments strikes in order to hire out scabs and guards to management. In trying to arouse trouble, Cronin soon shifts his attack from management to the union establishment and the present contract, the Shalerville

Agreement: "We sweat blood to pay the union officials their fat salaries. We were sold out at Shalerville." Mike (John Qualen), the moderate union steward, minimizes Cronin's arguments, claiming that rockfalls are an accepted occupational hazard and that things are much better under the present agreement than before. A strike would break the contract and thus threaten the gains already made, for the union promised no labor strife in return for higher wages and better conditions: "Don't you fellers listen to any of that radical talk. It's just gonna stir up trouble and you'll be worse off than before. . . . Always remember that half a loaf is better than none."

Riffraff's Belcher (Paul Hurst) is a "belligerent, troublemaking radical type"[9] who stirs up the men with inane pseudo-Communist clichés: "Take your necks from under the iron heel. . . . Strike the fetters from your starved bodies." He is opposed by Brains, who feels that a strike will play right into the cannery owner's hands. As in *Black Fury*, the strike will only serve to break an already satisfactory agreement with management and allow the bosses to bring in cheaper labor. Brains, lacking the charisma to appeal to the men, calls on Dutch to speak for him. Tough but dumb Dutch shoves Belcher into the water and echoes what Brains has told him—that strikes are un-American, a foreign plague brought by outsiders: "If an outside gang came sneakin' down here we stuck together and run 'em out. Well, there's an outside gang sneaked in here right now—and they're makin' you see things wrong. Brains says so."

The strike results in both films when the agitator uses the hero's popularity to sway the men to his side. In neither case does the hero's conversion from moderation to activism have anything to do with working conditions or economics. The miners' strike occurs because Joe's fiancée, Anna (Karen Morley), deserts him for another man and he gets raging drunk the night of an important union meeting. When he stumbles into the meeting and hears the men talking about whether or not to "fight," Joe immediately thinks of Anna and screams out, "Fight, sure fight. Betch m'life fight!" The men, respecting Joe's opinion, immediately rally behind him and call a strike. Albert Maltz was understandably angry: "A highly educational spectacle! Driven by the shouts of a drunken man, the miners decide to strike. There could not be a more perverted picture of the reasons and the manner any group of workers really decide to go on strike."

Dutch's shift away from moderation is attributed to his vain arrogance. Belcher begins to insinuate himself into Dutch's good graces with flattering talk of Dutch's natural leadership qualities: "You have powers to . . . help the people. You could be the biggest man on the waterfront." When Belcher talks of property commodity and labor commodity, Dutch, not wanting to appear ignorant, nods in agreement and soon begins to organize the men.

The strikes are in no way attributed to management (except perhaps for Dutch's rivalry with Nick, the cannery owner, for the love of Hattie). Even after management reinstitutes the former conditions, the unions bear the brunt of the blame. They, not management, have broken the terms of the contract. *Black Fury*'s sympathetic mine owner claims, "We try to play fair with our men, but when they doublecross us we're through with them." The film makes it almost seem as if the owner has no choice but to bring in scabs and security police. The owner even warns the shyster agency not to use mounted police or violence against the strikers unless absolutely necessary: "I want none of that sort of thing. I need the mine to operate but I want to be just." In *Riffraff*, Nick (Joseph Calleia) is at first pleased with the opportunity to bring in cheaper labor, but is more than ready to settle when the scabs prove to be less efficient workers than the union men. It is Dutch, blinded by an arrogant pride which prohibits anyone else from gaining favor with "his" men, who angrily rejects Nick's generous settlement. In each case, the conflict between labor and management is erased and the strikes are made into unnatural expressions of the workers' interests.

Both films completely ignore the way a strike actually functions, implying that the workers simply follow their leader and refuse to report to work. Albert Maltz criticizes *Black Fury*'s version of the strike action: "The strike drags on. Just how it is conducted, how it spreads to the whole coal field, we never know. The miners have no apparent organization, no committees, no relief mechanism, no pickets." In neither film do the workers offer resistance to scabs imported by management. *Riffraff*'s strikers are "stunned, helpless. They talk among themselves: 'The rotten scabs,' 'He's licked us,' 'Brains was right!' "[10] Similarly, in *Black Fury*, the men do not picket but mill around in confusion, freely allowing scabs to enter the mine. Once the scabs are inside, the strikers illogically attack the hired security police, initiating the violence themselves and thereby justifying management's action in bringing the guards onto the scene. At the same time, the frequent police and goon brutality against strikers typical of the thirties is reduced in *Black Fury* to a single vicious guard (Warners' number one heavy, Barton MacLane) who beats Mike up for his own sadistic pleasure.

What the films do stress is how the strikes threaten the comfortable life styles shown at the beginning of the films. The miners, hungry and facing eviction, are in such a desperate state that they finally agree to return to work under their pre-Shalerville contract. Joe is abandoned by all his comrades and sees his best friend Mike killed. Dutch undergoes an even greater decline. Before the strike he had moved into a cheery bungalow complete with all the latest electrical appliances, but without any salary to make payments, everything is repossessed. His arrogance and stubbornness soon alienate the men and he is voted out of the union. Hattie ends up in prison for stealing some money for Dutch and Dutch is reduced to a penniless bum living in a dingy hobo camp. The other fishermen meanwhile return to even greater prosperity when they give up the strike and go back to work with a two-percent raise.

The hero's final struggle is to undo the harm done by the strikes, to return to previous conditions. For Joe that involves regaining the pre-strike contract (rather than winning a new contract) while for Dutch it means getting back his union membership and his old job. Just as the hero's wrongheadedness created the problems, so his individual heroism saves the day. Joe, seeing that he has been a dupe (and also having a chastened Anna back at his side), resolves to hold a one-man strike for the reinstatement of the Shalerville Agreement. He single-handedly takes over the mine, charging all the entrances with dynamite to prevent anyone's entry. His action gains the attention of the federal government, which immediately perceives that there is no real cause for the strike other than the shyster agency. In typical Warners' style, the New Deal intervenes to end the strike, grant Joe his demands, and march the shysters off to prison. Through these plot twists, Warners succeeds in satisfying both workers and management while discrediting strikes: the workers appear to win but only gain what they had to begin with; management doesn't really lose since it has given nothing new to the men. The strike has been completely gratuitous. Dutch learns the same lesson as Joe and redeems himself by singlehandedly foiling Belcher's attempt to blow up the waterfront. As a result, he is allowed back into the union and returns to his original prosperity. Like Joe, Dutch now knows the dangers of radicalism and will stay in his place. He is content to merely be "the best tuna fisherman on the West Coast."

Worker discontent did not always have to take the form of a strike. Warners' *Black Legion* (1936), a condemnation of right-wing terrorist groups, speaks to the worker in almost exactly the same terms as the films attacking "left-wing" unionism. Membership in the KKK-like Legion is parallel to participation in a strike, the attempt of naive, confused workers egged on by agitators to move beyond their proper station in life. Like his counterparts in *Black Fury* and *Riffraff*, Frank Taylor (Humphrey Bogart) quickly learns that any activism against the system can only have tragic results.

Again, *Black Legion*'s case is based on the fact that the worker is well off to begin with. Before he joins the Legion, Frank seems perfectly content, working in a clean, happy factory and living in a model suburban home with his beautiful wife and cute little son. But once he gets involved in the terrorism, his life is shattered. He becomes so preoccupied with Legion activities that he neglects his family and job, and as a result loses both. Before Frank awakens to the Legion's evil and exposes it in the courts, he participates in a murder and is sentenced to life imprisonment.

Frank's downfall, like Dutch Muller's, is attributed to a dimwitted vanity which is exploited by agitators. When he loses a promotion to the much more capable Joe Dombrowski (Henry Brandon), Frank bitterly refuses to acknowledge that Dombrowski is the best man for the job. Instead of facing up to the fact that Dombrowski studied hard at night rather than listening to radio serials, Frank accepts the more soothing explanations of the Legion: he is the victim of a conspiracy of foreigners to steal jobs from "one hundred percent Americans." When Dombrowski, as Frank's foreman, chews him out for ruining an expensive drill, Frank's resentment makes him an easy mark for Legion recruiters. "How d'ya like bein' pushed around by a greaseball? Would you like to do somethin' about it or just be pushed around?" Soon, as a member of the hooded gang, Frank has his revenge, burning the Polish "conspirator's" house and running him out of town.

The Legion naturally turns out to be run by thieves who manipulate the worker dupes for a profit. Their talk about one hundred percent Americanism masks their true motive: collecting lucrative membership dues and selling "Legion" guns and uniforms. Although the film does allude to the frustrations, jealousies, and scapegoating that are the basis of native fascist movements, it ultimately narrows its analysis to a few villains and the gullible workers who fall for their pitch.

As before, the underlying assumption is that there are leaders and followers, that contented subservience is the ideal state for the worker. Those who have brains and talent like Dombrowski will rise to their level of achievement. Only someone too dumb to know better would join the Legion or participate in a strike. The film's model worker, Ed Jackson (Dick Foran) is no genius but knows his place and rejects the rabble rousers: "You never say anything that makes any sense." Like Brains or Mike, he is content with half a loaf and willingly embraces the happy domesticity that Frank so foolishly throws away.

An earlier Warner Brothers film, *Oil for the Lamps of China* (1935), presents a subtle variation on the malcontent theme. It apparently reverses the standard viewpoint in order to sympathize with worker dissatisfaction, only to prove that faith in the corporation is the best policy in the long run. The film at first questions and then vindicates its hero's blind loyalty to management. Stephen Chase (Pat O'Brien), a representative of an American oil firm stationed in China, believes that "the company always takes care of its men." But Stephen's excessive zeal in attending the company's interests only serves to destroy his personal life. His absence on business during the birth of his child results in the baby's death and his wife's estrangement. After he risks his life to save company funds from pillaging Communists and ends up in the hospital for several months, he is rewarded with a demotion. Management is cruelly indifferent to the suffering Stephen has undergone on their behalf. It would seem that the company does not look after their men but exploits their dedication.

But the film's ending proves that it is only the branch office that is corrupt and unappreciative. A long-distance phone call from the managing director in New York puts everything right. Wanting to see that justice is done to the loyal worker, the director duly rewards Steve's action with an important promotion. What has appeared to be foolish faith in the face of gross mistreatment is turned into a demonstration that true merit is always rewarded. The zealousness that is so personally destructive is ultimately seen as a positive force that brings light to China and success to Stephen.

Not all the films of the decade completely rejected the concept of unionism (or revolt against management). Samuel Goldwyn's *Dead End* (1937) represents a surprisingly strong endorsement of the striker, while *How Green Was My Valley* (1941) and *The Devil and Miss Jones* (1941), both made just before the war, give a fairly balanced version of management-labor conflict. *Dead End*'s unionist, Drina (Sylvia Sidney), is the film's heroine and is totally sympathetic in her demands for better wages and a better life. The strike occurs off camera and is only a secondary plot element to symbolize Drina's struggle to escape the slums. Still, labor is a positive force, and in a bitter confrontation between Drina and a cop, it is the representative of law and order who comes off as the villain. Drina pulls back her bangs to reveal a huge welt on her forehead where "one of you dirty cops hit me." As he had done in his handling of Communists in *Street Scene*, Goldwyn again defied convention. Drina is not a dupe, and the strike is not a plot but an heroic attempt to achieve social equality.

John Ford's *How Green Was My Valley* is not so brave. The film's ambivalence toward a turn-of-the-century Welsh coal mining strike is expressed through the father–son conflict in the Morgan family. The patriarch (Donald Crisp), the bearer of family tradition and past values, adamantly opposes the strike, claiming that "the union is the work of the devil." The sons are more modern and completely justified in their revolt against poor working conditions and decreased wages. Yet, by their militance, the youths inadvertently contribute to the breakup of the family unit, the most revered element in John Ford's populist universe. Reverend Griffith (Walter Pidgeon) attempts to reconcile the two factions, realizing that he can only temporarily delay the inevitable encroachment of progress upon the valley community. The sons and the father are both right: a union is necessary to protect workers in a world of modern industrialism, but at the same time this admission is a sad commentary on the quality of contemporary life: "Something's gone out of this valley that will never be replaced."

Ford's chief interest in the strike is in its effect on the family unit and we only learn of its outcome through the Morgans' personal tragedy. The implication is once again that militance is futile. Though we are only told "Then the strike was settled, with the help of Mr. Griffith," we must assume that the settlement was a humiliating one, for the two most militant sons angrily leave the valley for America and two other sons reluctantly follow when unjustly fired by the company. Later, the father and another son are killed in mine accidents which might have been prevented by the safeguards the union had sought. Ford remains uncommitted. He clearly prefers Mr. Griffith's moderation and yearns for the old days when unions weren't necessary, but still recognizes the justice of the union's cause and implicitly condemns management's abdication of responsibility toward its workers.

The Devil and Miss Jones matches Ford's caution by presenting its labor treatise in the form of a screwball comedy. Miss Jones (Jean Arthur) is a working-class sales clerk helping to organize union activities against the exploitation of a big department store; the Devil is Mr. Merrick (Charles Coburn), the rich, miserable tycoon who owns the store. In order to discover who is behind the unrest, the tycoon becomes a clerk in his own store. Thereafter it is the old story of the grumpy capitalist humanized by the down-to-earth workers. Merrick's utter befuddlement as a shoe clerk earns him the wrath of supervisors following his own edicts, but his fellow clerks provide sympathy and assistance. Charmed by the spunky, irresistible Miss Jones, he is won over to the workers' side and is soon picketing the store. In the end, Merrick shows up on the grievance committee to negotiate with himself. Along the way there are, as Otis Ferguson acknowledged, "little highlights of sympathetic treatment . . . the firings, the Macy plan of layoff, the fear of company spies, the young organizer with his losing minority."[11] But this apparent liberalism is again restricted to the benefactor theme: snobbish executives must become kindlier patriarchs who treat their employees with fairness, and workers need not organize once they are under the aegis of benevolent bosses. Just as Deeds and Godfrey are common-man millionaires, so Merrick is the working-class executive.

Caretakers of the Nation

As the threat of European fascism grew, the virtues of American democracy had to be extolled in order to show a united front. Thus films commenting on labor strife became increasingly scarce and after *Black Fury* and *Riffraff* the movies drastically softened their approach. *Black Legion* couches its portrait of worker malcontents in terms of a fascist threat to the nation, while in *Dead End* the labor issue is only a subplot. The last prewar labor pictures, *How Green Was My Valley* and *The Devil and Miss Jones*, treat strikes in a much less controversial fashion than earlier films and seek to placate both sides. During the late thirties, a new group of worker films emerged. Almost all produced by Warner Brothers, these pictures ignored any dissatisfaction, instead concentrating on the worker's vital role in building America and maintaining democracy.

The prototype for this cycle is *Slim* (1937), a portrait of electric linemen which, far from criticizing dangerous working conditions, makes them appear the most attractive aspect of the job. The danger of working high above the ground installing and repairing high-voltage lines is what draws Slim (Henry Fonda) from the routine of farm life. The continual movement across the country from job to job appeals to the sense of freedom and mobility often linked to the pioneer spirit. Slim's mentor, Red (Pat O'Brien), even refuses an offer to be a boss because it would permanently tie him to one place. He's his own man as a lineman, whereas a boss has too many responsibilities.

The romance of danger is reinforced by the sense of importance attached to the linemen's work. They risk their lives to bring power and light to the nation. When Slim first asks to join the line crew, he is rejected because of his youth. The job is too important, he is told, and they need experienced men. But his persistence pays off and, with Red's help, he is taken on. For the remainder of the film, the audience perceives the life and work of the lineman through the eyes of the awestruck Slim. As he learns how to "cut it" and is introduced to the various duties of his job, his admiration for Red and the lineman's ethic of hard work and loyalty grows. He even gives up his love for Callay (Margaret Lindsay) because he considers his work too vital. His education is completed when he returns to the tower to repair a broken line in a raging blizzard that has just killed Red and another worker. He and, presumably, the audience are both now fully aware of the importance and responsibility of the lineman.

Slim's portrait of the worker is completely positive: his job is stimulating and his social role vital. Any possible criticisms of his lot are ignored. There are no arguments for safety regulations and equipment such as helmets—the danger of falling tools is passed over as a comic bit with the bumbling Stuart Erwin. Nor is there the need for unions since there is no threat of unemployment and the men are paid well enough to afford expensive vacations in the big city. Any complaints about their employers (such as when Pop, the foreman, is unjustly fired) are easily rectified by moving to another job site.

Slim was in the tradition that earned Warners the nickname of "the working class studio." In their early portraits of fishermen (*Tiger Shark*, 1932), cabbies (*Taxi*, 1932) and truckers (*The St. Louis Kid*, 1934) Warners had used the workers' occupations as a pretext for the rough and tumble antics of stars Edward G. Robinson and Jimmy Cagney. Except for the addition of *Slim*'s reverential tone, glorifying the worker's importance to the country, the post-1937 cycle continued in the same vein. The films are, as Bosley Crowther points out, highly formulized and highly successful adventure yarns:

> The Warner Brothers, like Vulcan, know the pat way to forge a thunderbolt. They simply pick a profession in which the men are notoriously tough and the mortality rate is high, write a story about it in which both features are persistently stressed, choose a couple of aces from their pack of hardboiled actors and with these assorted ingredients whip together a cinematic depth charge.[12]

Films about wildcat oil-drillers (*Flowing Gold*, 1940, with John Garfield and Pat O'Brien, as well as MGM's *Boom Town*, 1940, with Clark Gable and Spencer Tracy), construction workers (*Steel Against the Sky*, 1941), firemen (*She Loved a Fireman*, 1938), truck drivers (*They Drive by Night*, 1940, with George Raft and Humphrey Bogart, and *Truck Busters*, 1943) and electric linemen (*Manpower*, 1941, a remake of *Slim* starring Edward G. Robinson and George Raft) all romanticized the dangers of their topic professions, glorifying the hero's toughness, playing up the love interest, and playing down working conditions. After the outbreak of war, it was an easy matter to extend such tributes into propaganda films that compared the unity and dedication of assembly-line workers to that of the fighters at the front. The chief element of suspense in many wartime labor films (e.g., *Wings for the Eagle*, 1942) was the question of whether some group of factory workers would be able to meet their production quota by the deadline.

Epilogue: Chaplin's *Modern Times*

Modern Times stands outside the Formula in form and viewpoint. It is a unique Depression film, grafting silent film technique and the old comic motifs of Chaplin's Tramp character onto the thirties social landscape. Unlike other filmmakers whose works we have discussed in this chapter, Chaplin was aware of the fundamental problems inherent in the system itself. Though Chaplin's allegiances clearly lie with the worker, his basic concerns extend beyond the question of management versus labor to that of the survival of the individual in an increasingly inhuman world. As such, *Modern Times* represents a full-scale critique of modern industrial society—in Chaplin's words, a study of "the way life is being standardized and channelized, and men turned into machines."[13]

The film is picaresque in structure, built around a series of episodes each resembling an early two-reeler and all tied together by a common theme. *Modern Times* was the most thematically self-conscious of Chaplin's works to date, and yet was still firmly grounded in the motifs and Tramp character of the earlier films.

Even in Chaplin's two-reelers, the central issue had been survival of the individual; not survival in extraordinary circumstances, as with other silent clowns, but in the most mundane situations. Charlie the Tramp had always been caught up in an existential conflict with the ordinary, with life itself, doing battle with social institutions, objects, physical environments, personal rivals, even his own feelings and aspirations, in short, with everything in a hostile universe. The only meaning in life is achieved through his selfless love of a pure woman for whom Charlie sacrifices everything. Victory is attained, the girl won, and society reformed only in dreams. By the end of each film, the Tramp awakens to a reality of defeat, poverty, and loneliness. His real victory is his ability to shrug it off and forever trudge down the road to new adventure.

One of the most important strands running through all of Chaplin's films culminating in *Modern Times* is the Tramp's relation to society. Much of the comedy and significance of these works arises from the contradiction between the Tramp's free spirit and the narrow social definitions imposed on him. The majority of the films are comic variations on a central paradox—Charlie cannot survive within society and yet cannot survive without it. He is continually placed in comic situations which highlight this paradox—as a lowly worker unable to adapt to the rigid job structure or the boss's oppressive demands; as a hobo masquerading as nobility and finding his natural spontaneity at odds with strict social mores; as a criminal fleeing police and avoiding religious reformers all of whom seem more immoral than the hapless Charlie. In the first shorts, these situations are merely comic bits in routinely structured plots. The irreverence toward all convention represents a general approach to life and any social comment is abstract—the disruption of order and lampooning of authority. But as Charlie developed into a more mature character and as Chaplin became more aware of theme and plot structure, a social outlook gradually emerged from the implicit comments of the early period until it was a fully articulated theme running through Chaplin's work.

One can almost measure Chaplin's degree of social awareness by the reality of the setting. Early films gave Charlie a lot of space—open parks, rural neighborhoods—where society was not intrusive and he could operate quite handily on its edges. The odd run-in with a cop presented only a minor distress. But later the social landscape became increasingly prominent, oppressive, and realistic. Beginning with *Easy Street* (1917) through *A Dog's Life* and the *Life* footage from *Triple Trouble* (both 1918) and culminating in *The Kid* (1921), the slum setting is the harrowing backdrop for Charlie's struggles to eat and survive. The milieu is Dickensian: a world of abject poverty, hostile authorities, dangerous pickpockets, and money-grubbing merchants. Yet the social horror is counterpointed by the comedy arising out of the Tramp's unorthodox and ingenious survival techniques (such as having the Kid break windows so Charlie can then offer his services as glazier). Even when the setting is changed to the affluent domiciles of the higher classes, Charlie is usually there under false pretenses, and the comedy arises from his mistaken interpretations of social conventions. Not only is Charlie out of place but he is soon out on his ear. In many of his 1916–1923 films, Chaplin highlighted the conflict between the individual and society and generally came to a guarded truce between them. The final shot of *The Pilgrim* (1923) is the quintessential visualization of the Tramp's ambivalence about society. Charlie runs along the U.S.-Mexican border, one foot on either side, unable to choose between the United States, representing law and order (and jail for escaped convict Charlie) and Mexico, representing lawlessness and anarchism with bandits shooting wildly at one another. At the very moment Charlie can finally escape society, he suddenly finds it indispensable.

Modern Times is Chaplin's most sophisticated exploration of the Tramp's relation to society. Now set in a Depression context, Chaplin's comedy takes on a more specific social outlook and finds the old truce between individual and society all but impossible to sustain. Although made in 1936, *Modern Times* has music and sound effects but no dialogue. Its silent film technique—the use of titles, pantomime acting—preserves the form of Chaplin's earlier comedies and places the Depression within the Tramp's artificial comic world, giving the film's social commentary universal implications.

Aside from the mythology of the Tramp, *Modern Times*' viewpoint was also influenced by a popular strand of artistic expression stretching from the outbreak of World War I through to the thirties which prophesies technological doom. Cubist paintings, collages and cartoons, expressionist dramas such as Kaiser's *Gas*, novels like Huxley's *Brave New World*, and movies like Fritz Lang's *Metropolis* (1927) and Rene Clair's *A Nous la Liberté* (1932) all foresee a future society where the technology meant to serve man is enslaving him, reducing individuals to mindless automatons. The opening sequence of Chaplin's film is one of the wildest and most comically hysterical manifestations of this prophesy of technological bondage. It is the ultimate confrontation between the instinctive, natural Charlie and the restrictive, deadening demands of society. As in the other works of this type, much is made of the design of the factory. The assembly line is a gargantuan geometric network of cogs and levers that grind on with unremitting rhythm and completely dwarf human beings. Charlie must become a part of the machine, tightening an endless stream of bolts rapidly moving past him on a conveyor belt. Even after he stops for lunch, Charlie cannot control the convulsive, wrench-wielding jerks and splashes his soup all over his coworkers.

This confrontation between Tramp and machine is given a series of ironic twists with the addition of the eating motif so central to Charlie's survival instincts. First, the machine makes soup eating all but impossible; then another machine is introduced to actually supersede Charlie's need to feed himself. He is strapped into an automatic feeder and, in a frenzied parody of eating, the machine goes haywire, violating Charlie and making actual ingestion impossible. An ear of corn twirls like a buzz saw through his teeth, piece after piece of creamy cake is rammed into his face, and an explosion of sparks nearly electrocutes the defenseless Charlie.

The tension between machine and eating is given another twist when Charlie returns to the job and is literally gobbled up by the mechanical apparatus. As he passes through its cogs and wheels, his body and mind become completely at one with the mechanism. He is spit out, a demented extension of the machine, running amok through the factory, maniacally tightening anything resembling a bolt. Again, chaos reigns as the Tramp obliterates the super-rational order of the plant, randomly pulling levers and switches and squirting oil on his coworkers. Finally overcome and straitjacketed, he is led away in a paddy wagon.

Later, food and machine go through an even more complex series of comic reversals. First, Charlie's foreman (Chester Conklin) gets fed into the machine and then, during break, Charlie feeds lunch to the foreman still lodged amidst the prongs and belts of the assembly line. These comic parallels highlight the conflict between the natural function of eating and the unnatural means necessary to obtain food. Raymond Durgnat compares the treatment of the food theme in *Modern*

Times and previous Chaplin films. Always food had been scarce for the Tramp, "but here it's not in short supply. On the contrary it's there in abundance for those who accept the grotesque postures forced on them by the machines."[14] The final irony is Charlie's desperate scramble to return to the factory since work is necessary to eat. Survival on one level is precluded by a form of extinction on another.

The theme of survival is the connecting thread running through *Modern Times*. Its impact is cumulative rather than climactic as Charlie tries all manner of ways to find some little corner of society in which to simply live. These attempts are divided into two sections in the film: in the first half, it is Charlie alone against society; in the second, it is Charlie and the Gamin (Paulette Goddard) struggling together to realize their love.

A dominant motif, especially in the first half, is the hostility and violence of social authority. Charlie's old foil, the cop on the beat, always suspiciously stalking the Tramp for some misdemeanor, has been replaced by an ever-present force of men who fiercely apprehend Charlie for actions now seen as threats to social organization. The police represent order and quell any rebellion against rigid conformity. Like the Big Brother factory manager who oversees his workers through a closed-circuit TV system, the police are everywhere and will never let you alone. Indeed, each sequence begins with Charlie's release from prison and ends with his being flung into the ever-ready paddy wagon. Charlie's natural humanity makes him an enemy of an inhumane system and each time he makes an innocent, generous gesture, the police pounce on him. He picks up a red flag which has dropped from a passing construction truck and when a group of marching demonstrators begin to follow him, he is arrested as a Communist agitator. Working as night watchman for a large department store, Charlie does not apprehend a trio of hungry burglars but responds to their plight and offers to share "his" wealth, serving them cake and drinks from the snack bar. The Tramp, who himself has often had to steal to eat, has a rather different definition of right and wrong than that of the law.

Whenever workers strike or the unemployed protest, the cops are there to brutally suppress the revolt. Innocently loitering in the background during a factory walkout, Charlie is suddenly and viciously shoved from behind by a policeman. The comic tone of the film here gives way to more earnest drama. Charlie backs away, looking testily at the cop, genuinely offended by the abuse. The tension is abruptly punctured when he accidentally steps on a plank and catapults a rock at the cop's head. With a greater fierceness than ever before, the cops heave Charlie into the paddy wagon. Again, the Tramp is innocent, and even if the rock (perhaps like the red flag) is taken as an uncanny realization of his subconscious urges, those urges are completely natural in light of the persecution he's suffered.

Strangely enough, the only relief the Tramp receives from the harassment and turmoil of society is in jail. There he eats three meals a day, lounges casually in his cell, reading the paper, insulated from its headlines of unemployment and strikes. When pardoned, Charlie immediately sets about to get himself returned to prison, but typically, this is the only point in the film where he has trouble getting arrested.

Once Charlie teams up with the Gamin the film changes mood. Their love is the film's strong positive force and it inspires Charlie to make his greatest effort to become part of society. The second half of the film with the Gamin constitutes a sardonic satire on the bourgeois American Dream. Sitting on the curb in middle-class suburbia, Charlie and the Gamin witness a mawkish morning farewell between husband and wife and fantasize on how their life could also abound with plenty. In a dream sequence, we see them living in a cozy, overdecorated bungalow with sunshine gloriously streaming through the windows. The aproned Gamin beams over her steak breakfast while Charlie reaches out the window to pluck grapes from bountiful vines and goes to the door to retrieve the bucket of milk left there by the cow. Characteristically, their fantasy is abruptly terminated by a suspicious cop who chases them out of the neighborhood. Later, when he is working in the department store, Charlie and the Gamin can try on fur coats, lounge on big double beds, and cavort on roller skates. The department store is society's temple of affluence, holding out the promise of material dreams come true. It is, ironically, protected by two of society's rejects who find it difficult to secure a square meal a day.

Reality for the couple turns out to be a Hooverville shack, a parody of the bourgeois bungalow reduced to the lowest level of poverty. Its walls continually capsize, its floor boards splinter and snap in two, and its only consumer conveniences are tin-can cups and orange-crate chairs. But, like Charlie and Jackie Coogan in *The Kid*, the couple are willing to tolerate its flaws as long as they are together. And, as always, the police intervene to ruin the Tramp's chance for happiness.

By the movie's conclusion, having failed in numerous attempts to exist within society, Charlie decides that fulfillment is impossible under present conditions. In previous films, there had always been enough room in the parks and hamlets and slums for the Tramp to get by, to straddle the thin line between submission to social mores and a hermetic opting out. But the spread of the machine age has swallowed up all the neutral space. The authorities are everywhere, mass institutions abound, and the possibilities for the individual to forage a meager life on his own have disappeared. In the final shot, Charlie and the Gamin again trudge down the road, but now it is a paved highway. Although they have one another and share a resilient optimism (Chaplin's "Smile" throbs sentimentally on the sound track), there is the sense that they are not off to further adventure but are making their final exit. The finale is ambivalent. It celebrates the values of love and the survival of the human spirit. The Tramp has lost none of his pluck and somehow his natural humanity will persist even if he does not. At the same time, the modern age is inescapable and serves only to stifle all the things the Tramp represents.[15]

This conclusion is revolutionary in a moral rather than political sense. The film came under fire from many intellectuals for not dealing specifically with the social issues of the Depression and for not committing itself to some form of leftist viewpoint. (Both Lang and Clair end with a vaguely left-wing harmony among capital, labor and technology.) Some contemporary critics were sorely disappointed at the Tramp's lack of commitment to anything other than his own survival. They criticized Chaplin for not glorifying the workers' strike and for not being a real agitator when he picks up the red flag. But Chaplin's critique transcends ideologies and could apply to any economic system in the industrialized world, capitalist or Communist. The film offers a positive and uncompromising commitment to human values in opposition to those of modern industrialism.

—8—

RURAL PROBLEMS

The most compelling images and documents of the thirties are those depicting the tragedy of the farmer—the works of such FSA photographers as Dorothea Lange, Walker Evans, and Russell Lee; the songs of Woody Guthrie; Steinbeck's classic *The Grapes of Wrath*; documentary studies such as *You Have Seen Their Faces* and *Let Us Now Praise Famous Men*. The socially conscious artist could not help but respond to the abject poverty of Southern sharecroppers or to the desperate exodus of the dispossessed Okies and Arkies. Urban manifestations of the Depression were often obscured by the day-to-day bustle of the city, but the farmer's victimization was too starkly dramatic to be overlooked. His plight is captured in images of droughts, dust storms, and floods, of broken and starving families sitting sullenly in rotting shacks, of disenchanted Okies migrating across the land in broken-down cars, images that crystallize the meaning of the terms "hard times" and "dirty thirties."

Richard Pells elaborates in *Radical Visions and American Dreams* that the rural disasters of the thirties came to stand for the whole tragedy of the Depression:

> Men became preoccupied with floods, dust storms and soil erosion not only because these constituted real problems but also because they were perfect metaphors for a breakdown that appeared more physical than social or economic. It gave Americans the feeling that their whole world was literally falling apart, that their traditional expectations and beliefs were absolutely meaningless, that there was no personal escape from the common disaster. It propelled every individual into a void of bewilderment and terror. Thus the crisis seemed to require a response that promised peace and safety more than further uncertainty.[1]

121

Perhaps because rural issues zeroed in on the emotional heart of Depression experience, they found little expression in Hollywood movies. In 1932 *Cabin in the Cotton* gave a reasonable portrait of the sharecropper, while 1940's *The Grapes of Wrath* was a powerful if somewhat deradicalized version of Steinbeck's saga of the Okies. Between these two films, however, lay only *Our Daily Bread* and a handful of minor B-pictures dealing with rural problems. Because the public wanted "peace and safety," Hollywood stuck to the idealized myths of populist arcadia. For the movie farmer there were no dust bowls, only state fairs, square dances, and the abundance of the soil.

Cabin in the Cotton

Even those films which dealt with rural problems showed a reluctance to break with the reassuring myths, carefully balancing their discussion of social factors to prepare for an optimistic finale. *Cabin in the Cotton*'s opening titles establish a daring interpretation of the sharecropping system in terms of class conflict—"In many parts of the South today there exists endless dispute between the rich landowners, known as planters, and the poor cotton-pickers, known as tenants or 'peckerwoods' "—and simultaneously undermine it by refusing to make a commitment to either side—"A hundred volumes could be written on the rights and wrongs of both parties, but it is not the subject of the producers of *Cabin in the Cotton* to take sides. We are only concerned with an effort to picturize conditions." This waffling is built into the structure of the drama by making the film's hero, Marvin Blake (Richard Barthelmess), a man in the middle. The son of a poor sharecropper who died of overwork, he is supported and educated by his father's landlord, Lane Norwood (Berton Churchill), who wants to exploit the young man's managerial potential. Soon Marvin is looking after the plantation store, handling all the tenants' accounts, and deciding whether or not to extend credit to "his own folks."

As the story unfolds, Marvin is caught between what are essentially two evils and is forced to become increasingly complicit in each. First he is ordered by Norwood to spy on his own people, to find out who among them is stealing cotton: "You're sort of on the planters' side now, and we're the people who keep the country going." Then his "Uncle" Joe (Russell Simpson) and the other croppers admit to their thievery and insist that Marvin be their sales agent: "I don't call it stealin', I call it takin' back what ya owe him. Lane Norwood done the stealin', been doin' it for years. Now with hard times, we gotta get our chance back."

A tortured balancing act continues through a complex series of wrongs committed by each side. Marvin is disgusted by the planters who lynch a cropper and is just as shocked when the croppers burn down Norwood's store and office. Because both sides are in the wrong, Marvin is unable to commit himself to either one. In the end, he is placed in the pivotal position between the two factions. The fire destroys Norwood's records and since Marvin has a duplicate copy he must choose between delivering it to Norwood, thus saving the man's business, or to the croppers, thus freeing them from Norwood's debt.

As the film reaches its climax, however, the balancing act shifts very subtly, indeed almost imperceptibly, in favor of the croppers.[2] The film continues to pay lip service to the equal responsibility of both classes, but also implies that the injustices of the sharecropping system itself stem more from the landlords than from the tenants. The DA to whom Marvin turns for help doesn't attack either side and on the surface retains a rational middle position. Yet the terms in which he describes sharecropping—"Thirty, forty percent interests and carrying charges. Devil of a situation. The big fish and the little fish, the weak and strong" —place sympathy with the tenants against the landlords. Most important is the emergence of Norwood as the film's major villain. When Marvin learns that Norwood cheated his impoverished father, he finally ends his impartiality. Norwood's crimes are far worse than those of the croppers: "I've argued up and down with myself a thousand times. But I know this and these books prove it—you killed my father." During the final town meeting called by Marvin and the DA to settle the situation, the film grants only token expression to the landowners' case while going into great detail over the mistreatment of the tenants. It is the discredited Norwood who states the planters' side and he is thoroughly rebuffed by the heroic Marvin:

> Work, work and for what? Nothin'. Nothin' but the long summer and the long winter, and in the end, the grave. When settlin' time comes, they got nothin' left. When their advancements are paid and the interest is taken out, nothin' for a year's sweat. A man and his whole family. You can't blame the tenant for standin' up and askin' where does he come in. And the answer is, he don't come in. He's got nothin' left.

But, having depicted open warfare between the classes, the film concludes with a fantasy of reconciliation. The meeting proves to be a democratic forum of debate where each side airs its complaints and a permanent solution amenable to both is worked out. Marvin reveals his plan for the formation of a cooperative whereby landlord and tenant will each receive his rightful share of the profits. If the upper class has seemed a little more guilty than the lower, it now readily accepts the plan, thus alleviating its share of the responsibility. Only Norwood hesitates, and he is swayed by Marvin's threats to reveal his fraudulence. Once the agreement is signed, all traces of bitterness disappear and class synthesis is reaffirmed. The final shot of Norwood amicably shaking Marvin's hand restores the equilibrium between the classes.

The film never takes the time to define exactly how the cooperative will work. While Vidor's *Our Daily Bread* may be properly faulted for not fully analyzing the problems of cooperative living, *Cabin* makes a fuzzy reference to sharing and assumes that all troubles will immediately vanish. The planters' fraudulence, exploitation, and lynching are all excused because they are now willing to cooperate. Legal investigations and government legislation are unnecessary because both sides supposedly committed equal wrongs and all things balance out. The film ultimately overlooks what it had earlier hinted at: that the planters' wrongs were committed out of malicious greed while the tenants were only defending themselves, trying to get back what had been stolen from them. It was more important to please all sides than to thoroughly analyze the thorny issues the film so tentatively raises.

Interim: *Our Daily Bread*, etc.

Although *Our Daily Bread* sees farm life more as a solution than as a problem, the film nevertheless touches upon some of the key dilemmas, both economic and natural, facing the American farmer during the mid-thirties. In their efforts to pull the farm together and turn it into a profitable, self-sustaining venture, the co-op members must confront bankruptcy, foreclosure, and drought. Each problem is vanquished through the efforts of the entire community working together—what the individual farmer could not stave off, the group can. The strongest illustration of this community spirit occurs when drought threatens the corn crop, and the whole co-op bands together to build an irrigation ditch. It is a rousing demonstration of the power of the group in confronting the forces of nature, of its greater ability to survive through mass action.

When it comes to economics, the men reject money and private property in order to build their own society based on sharing and the common good. But the co-op members still find they need money to support the farm and pay off the mortgage while the crop is growing. With a collective persistence and a bit of luck they manage to weather several crises. The first occurs when the bank sends the sheriff to foreclose and auction off the land. Imitating actual guerrilla tactics used by Iowa farmers at the time, the co-op members physically intimidate any potential bidders while themselves making absurdly low offers on the land. When the sheriff tries to close the auction, the men point out that it is illegal to do so and end up buying back the farm for $1.85. When it comes to the supply shortage, however, the film's solution is less convincing. The men scavenge and borrow whatever provisions they can but they find they still don't have enough to see them through. So Louie (Addison Richards), who turns out to be an escaped convict, selflessly gives himself up to the police so that the commune can claim the reward money. Soon the storage shed is filled with foodstuffs and one jubilant member suggests that they send a picture to poor old Louie languishing in prison.

What Vidor's plan as a whole fails to take into account is just how much the commune is still dependent upon the larger economic system. Group dynamics are not going to counterbalance the crumbling market where the co-op intends to sell its corn. In the end, the farmer, whether alone or in a group, is just as much part of the financial structure as his city cousin, and in 1933–34 that structure was unable to support their needs.

Whatever its flaws, *Our Daily Bread* does address the farmer's problems. Quite different is a trio of B-pictures that evaded the issues by simply transferring shyster conventions out into the sticks and finding a corrupt bigshot to blame. In *Golden Harvest* (1933), not economic breakdown but wheat pit speculators are the reasons behind foreclosures and farm discontent in Iowa. According to *White Bondage* (1937), the destitute living conditions of Southern sharecroppers are purely the fault of a crooked landowner who rigs the weigh scales in order to rob the cotton pickers of their due. *John Meade's Woman* (1937) traces erosion and drought to a venal lumber baron who buys up all the farms and cuts down all the trees so that rain water runs off the hills and ruins the neighboring farmland. In this way the land-hungry Meade (Edward Arnold) can kick out all the farmers and have the land for himself.

Once the farmers discover they're being exploited, they revolt and restore the country to its original purity. In *White Bondage* an investigative reporter and his girl lead the croppers against the planter and see that he winds up in jail, while in *John Meade's Woman* the displaced farmers angrily burn Meade in effigy and finally shoot him. Since the problem is defined in terms of corruption, there is no need to worry about plans to restore the land (e.g., by adhering to New Deal experiments in soil conservation) or create alternative life styles.

The Grapes of Wrath

Of all the rural problem films, only *The Grapes of Wrath* comes close to capturing the documentary feel of the photographs and writings of the period. It is perhaps Hollywood's finest contribution to the cult of social consciousness and represents the culmination of the decade's social problem cinema. The film also carries the schizoid tradition of the genre to its furthest extreme, combining Hollywood's most deeply felt outrage at social wrong and its most sentimental faith in the perseverance of "the people." This polarity can be traced to the film's marriage of two opposing strands of American culture. It welds together one of the most influential novels of social protest with the reactionary nostalgia of the Hollywood populists.

Screenwriter Nunnally Johnson and director John Ford highlight Steinbeck's optimistic belief in the indestructibility of mankind while playing down his many references to the need for mass action. The filmmakers adapt that part of Steinbeck—his respect for cultural tradition—which expresses their own concerns, while almost completely omitting the writer's angry cries for social change. These two extremes—radicalism and tradition—are personified in both the book and the film by the quick-tempered, rebellious Tom Joad and his stoic, conciliatory Ma. In the book, the two are reciprocal, neither one outbalancing the other and together creating a view of man as both a universal being with a tenacious will to survive at any cost and a social being at the mercy of a corrupt system which must be changed. The film alters this balance in Ma's favor. Hollywood's Tom Joad (Henry Fonda) retains the vestiges of Steinbeck's proletarian hero but his anger and class consciousness are outweighed, especially in the crucial final sequences, by the film's sympathy for Ma (Jane Darwell) and her struggle to keep the family together. She is Ford's populist heroine, fighting against the onslaught of progress to preserve the traditions of the family and the land. For, every time anger and frustration are filtered through Tom, Ma is always on hand to placate his rage and thus subtly undermine the social criticism. To his rebellious "They comes a time when a man gets mad . . . ," she answers with "You got to keep clear, Tom. The fambly's breakin' up. You got to keep clear."

It is through Tom's discoveries of the nature of oppression that the film presents its social themes. In a series of key encounters, Tom learns the status of the Okie in America. His first lesson occurs when he returns home from prison to find his family evicted. He meets his former neighbor, Muley Graves (John Qualen) who informs him of his people's recent history—their crops were destroyed by drought and dust storms and the banks then foreclosed on their homesteads. Muley recalls in flashback his own eviction—he and his raggedly dressed family angrily approached the big car from which the bank agent perfunctorily informed them they'd have to leave. His desperate attempts to affix blame for his plight, to find someone against whom he can defend himself, lead Muley on a frustrating chase around a bureaucratic circle. The bank agent denies any responsibility—"It ain't my fault," claiming that the land is owned by the Shawnee Land and Cattle Company. When Muley threatens retaliation against the company, the agent points out that Muley still doesn't have an individual target for his wrath—"It ain't nobody. It's a company." Even the company president isn't to blame since "the *bank* tells him what to do" and for his part, the bank manager is "half crazy hisself trying to keep up with orders from the east!" "Then who *do* we shoot?" demands the impatient Muley. The agent shrugs, "Brother, I don't know. If I did, I'd tell you. But I just don't know *who's* to blame!"[3]

Later when the Caterpillar tractor arrives like a huge monster to push Muley off his land and break down his shack, the distraught farmer again vainly tries to defend himself. He threatens to use his shotgun, but the tractor driver turns out to be an old neighbor working to support his family. He too points out that shooting him won't inhibit economic forces: "It wouldn't be two days before they'd have another guy here to take my place." The tractor rolls onward and easily crushes Muley's flimsy house. Muley and his family stand in the wake of the tractor's dust, their bodies sagging in helpless defeat.

To argue, as some critics have, that this scene is an attempt to cloud over the source of responsibility, to let everybody off the hook by saying no one is to blame,[4] is to deny the powerful sense of economic oppression that it conveys. If no single person or institution is to blame, then something larger must be at fault. The film may not specifically name the banking interests involved, but it is clear that Muley is the victim of a whole financial structure. There is also the implication that progress, a new machine age symbolized by the Caterpillar tractor, is at the root of the problem. Muley's protest to the banker and lament over his land sounds very much like the outcry of the populist farmer overtaken by progress. However, that the filmmakers are calling for a return to populist tradition only becomes clear later in the film and at this point there is as yet little inconsistency between the film's yearning for the past and the novel's cry for revolution. Whether from a populist or leftist viewpoint, the scene succinctly establishes the Okies' impotence before large, impersonal social forces and how they are forced to turn against one another in order to survive. It is one of the most eloquent expressions of social victimization ever put on film.

Tom soon learns that without their land and home his family have no status. As they travel across the country toward California, they are reduced to destitute nomads, scorned and harassed by the people they meet along the way. The migrants are an unwelcome reminder of social injustice and those better off than the Okies would rather stereotype them as subhuman than accept responsibility for them: "Them Okies got no sense or no feeling. They ain't human. A human being couldn't live like they do. A human being couldn't stand it to be so miserable." The Joads are welcome nowhere. They are chased out of one town when the villagers burn down the migrants' camp, only to be turned back by a hostile vigilante mob at the next town.

Society has deprived the Okies of their homes, their livelihood, and now their humanity. The only place the Joads are allowed to rest from their continual, fruitless search for work is in a garbage dump Hooverville. The Hooverville sequence, with its outdoor locations, naturalistic photography, and careful casting of the Okie extras, attains the sense of actuality of the FSA photographs. With the camera shooting subjectively from the front seat of their car, we see the Hooverville from the Joads' shocked point of view. They move through a labyrinth of makeshift shacks under the curious gaze of the gaunt inhabitants. When they cook a meager pot of stew, a pathetic group of hungry children enviously gather around. Ma offers to share the stew with them and they scatter to find discarded tin cans to eat from.

Legal authorities are no more sympathetic than the people they represent. The Okies, as dispossessed migrants, are clearly not privy to the rights of the average citizen. State border guards and agricultural inspectors stop their truck, ask curt questions, and insist upon inspecting their load. Although the guards allow the Joads to pass because of Grandma's critical illness, they also order them not to stop anywhere. When they do reach California, the Joads are greeted by a cop who, even though he's an Okie himself, orders them to move on out of town. Early in the film, at Grampa's roadside grave, Tom bitterly remarks that they'd better leave a note explaining the nature of Grampa's death: "Lotta times looks like the gov'ment got more interest in a dead man than a live one."

At other times officialdom goes beyond simple badgering to malevolent victimization of the Okies. One migrant describes how his children starved to death when he couldn't find work and the coroner then falsified the cause of their deaths in his official report: "Them children died a heart failure, he says. Heart failure!—an' their little bellies stuck out like a pig bladder!" In a Hooverville, a labor agent tries to hire workers without showing a license or drawing up a contract. When one Okie points out that he is breaking the law by doing so, the agent simply turns to the deputy sheriff who has accompanied him and the deputy automatically accuses the Okie of breaking into a car lot. The Okie flees and the deputy fires blindly after him, seriously wounding a woman bystander. An Okie cries out that the woman is bleeding to death, but another deputy blithely dismisses the shooting: "Boy, what a mess them .45's make."

The film details how the upper class exploits the Okies' numbers and hunger to acquire cheap labor. One migrant warns the Joads that the handbills which attract all the Okies to California with promises of work are ruses to produce a surplus of labor:

> Awright, this man wants 800 men. So he prints up 5,000 a them han'bills an' maybe 20,000 people sees 'em. An' maybe two–three thousan' start movin' wes' account a this handbill. Two–three thousan' folks that's crazy with worry headin' out for 800 jobs! Does that make sense?

Later in the Hooverville, when the agent offers to pay thirty cents an hour, another Okie expands on how surplus labor keeps wages down: "Twicet now I've fell for that line. Maybe he needs a thousan' men. So he gets five thousan' there, an' he'll pay fifteen cents a hour. An' you guys'll have to take it 'cause you'll be hungry."

The theme of class exploitation reaches its climax during the Keene Ranch strike. The Joads, desperate for a job, go to work at the peach ranch without realizing that they are breaking a strike. Then Tom comes across an old friend, Casy (John Carradine), who has become a labor organizer and is leading the strike. Casy urges Tom to encourage the new workers to join the strike, since without full support the strike will fail and present wages will drop. Tom's reply explains exactly how the Okies are forced to accept their own exploitation:

> We was outa food. Tonight we had meat. Not much, but we had it. Think Pa's gonna give up his meat on account a other fellas? An' Rosasharn needs milk. Think Ma's gonna starve that baby jus' cause a bunch a fellas is yellin' outside a gate?

Just as the Okie tractor driver destroyed Muley's home and the Okie cop chased the Joads out of town, so Tom now turns against his own people in order to survive.

But when Tom sees Casy viciously clubbed to death, the strike broken, and wages dropped to starvation level, he comes to realize the importance of what Casy said. Up until then, his rebellion had been purely instinctive—he had slugged the deputy in the Hooverville and killed Casy's murderer in spontaneous outbursts of rage. Now, with Casy's example, his revolt becomes conscious and articulate: "He seen a lot a things clear. He was like a lantern—he helped me to see things too."

With Tom having reached a conclusion which could only be radical, the film cautiously pulls back and begins to disarm the indignation it has been building. Rather than have Tom expand on his new-found consciousness, the film shifts to Ma and her efforts to preserve the family. Tom's insights are perceived as a threat to the Joads' solidarity which Ma must deflate. She convinces him not to desert the family and together they flee the Ranch for the Government Camp.

The whole mood of the film dramatically changes as the Joads move into the secure haven run by a kindly federal agent (Grant Mitchell) who bears a pronounced resemblance to FDR.[5] The camp is the antithesis of everything that the Joads have previously experienced. They are treated as decent human beings, supplied with sanitary facilities, allowed to govern the camp themselves without police interference, and put in contact with licensed agents who give them work. A small, independent populist community under the protection of an unobtrusive federal government is Ford's ideal world. It is here that Ma and the family are most secure. The Saturday night dance is almost the realization of her Oklahoma dream of a new and better life in California. She sits proudly with Rosasharn and waltzes gaily with Tom to the sentimental "Red River Valley."

When the focus does shift to Tom, it is to show his wrath being abated by the new situation. He is given a temporary job, participates in the camp's committee, and once more has a social identity. The citizens and deputies who have been persecuting them are now made into fools by the Okies. When the migrants outwit and outpunch the outside troublemakers it has a cathartic effect and gives us a sense of satisfaction that the Okies are finally coming out on top.

Here the film is at odds with Steinbeck's novel, only using those elements of the book which reinforce its own view. For Steinbeck, the camp is proof that the people, living under a collective system and within a planned economy, are capable of looking after themselves. Ford's camp also demonstrates the people's ability to self-govern, but instead of a socialist cooperative it is the populists' vision of a rural community that serves as the model. In the novel, the camp further substantiates Tom's class consciousness and is one more confirmation of solidarity as the basis for power. In the film, it is only Ma's values that are reinforced, the small-town ethos of self-help and good neighborliness.

Furthermore, instead of placing the camp sequence in the middle as it was in the book, the film puts it near the end.[6] Through this change the filmmakers give the sequence climactic weight and make it appear as the conclusion of the Joads' experience rather than as a momentary respite. It is thus less an example which impels Tom to fight for a new world order than a solution which implies a withdrawal from the modern world, a repudiation of industrialized farms and Caterpillar tractors.

Nothing indicates the film's changes from the book more than the final speeches of the main protagonists. In the novel, Tom's speech comes shortly after Casy's murder, at that point where his outrage has climaxed, where the many references to "a growing wrath" and "the murmuring of revolt" culminate in Tom's resolve to take action. But it is in the affirmative setting of the Government Camp that Tom's key statement is delivered in the film. Having carefully pruned Steinbeck's many references to the masses' unrest and the need for revolution, Tom's speech functions in a political vacuum. As George Bluestone comments, "The politico-economic tendency is merely an urge in search of a name it is never allowed to find."[7] The film emphasizes those parts of the speech which Bluestone describes as "mystical affirmation." Without the political backdrop, Tom's realization that he is part of "a big soul that belong to ever'body" makes him seem less a socialist activist than a messianic conscience at large. He represents a concept of a universalized "people" who persevere through all manner of travail:

> I'll be ever'where—wherever you look. Wherever there's a fight so hungry people can eat, I'll be there. Wherever there's a cop beatin' up a guy, I'll be there. I'll be in the way guys yell when they're mad— an' they know supper's ready. An' when our people eat the stuff they raise, an' live in the houses they build, why, I'll be there too.

Also, it is to Ma that Tom relates these feelings. The "Red River Valley" theme is gently introduced under Tom's speech, subtly shifting emphasis toward Tom's relationship with Ma, reminding us of how they had just danced together and now must part. Indignation is tempered by the pathos of the farewell, and once again the theme of Ma and the family undercuts that of Tom and politics. Tom's discontent and resolve are still present, but have been made ambiguous enough not to imply the necessity of outright political action.

With Tom having removed himself from the scene, Ma is given center stage. She sums up the film's real conclusion that no hardship can ever defeat the Okies. The populist's generalized "people," no matter what, will always be triumphant, because they are durable. Despite the breakup of the family, despite the fact that they still haven't found a permanent home or work after all their wandering and suffering, Ma remains absurdly optimistic: "Rich fellas come up an' they die, an' their kids ain't no good, an' they die out. But we keep a-comin'. We're the people that live. Can't nobody wipe us out. Can't nobody lick us. We'll go on forever, Pa. We're the people." Again this represents a major deviation from Steinbeck. In the novel, the speech is made much earlier, during the Hooverville sequence, and is presented as another of Ma's palliatives for Tom's anger, a temporary expedient to keep Tom in the family rather than a major thematic summary. Certainly Steinbeck believes that the people will go on and can't be licked, but only because, as he has Ma conclude, "A different time's comin'." In the film this last line is omitted so that the Joads' perseverance is assumed to be an inevitability, implying that no action need be taken since the victims of the situation will automatically emerge on top. Steinbeck's argument for change has been transformed by Ford into a rationalization of stasis.

The final long shot sees their car rumbling down a sunny highway framed by neat rows of California orchard trees in full bloom. It is a pacifying shot, the neat pictorial composition and bright sunshine rendering a new sense of harmony between the Joads and their environment. It also parallels the final shot of Tom, seen in silhouette disappearing over the horizon into the sunrise. Both images counter the opening sequence of Tom returning home at dusk and learning of his family's fate in the darkened, empty house of a one-time neighbor. Together, the final images of Tom and the family provide a classic Hollywood finale, the protagonists moving down the road to face new adventures with an indomitable spirit which ensures their eternal, mythic survival.

Grapes's central flaw is that of the social problem film in general. Whatever realistic discussion and social outrage are generated, must be undercut so that the audience can leave the theater secure in the knowledge that everything will be all right. Although the film retains a certain fidelity to its source and mounts a fairly angry attack against authority and economic institutions, it must prune Steinbeck's more precise indictments. Like most Hollywood problem films, *Grapes* creates a mood of indignation without supplying any specific political context through which the mood can be translated into a better understanding of the actual situation. Social criticism is expressed within a self-contained dramatic structure that first arouses and then defuses audience awareness of the need for political action.

Post–*Grapes of Wrath*

The same triumvirate responsible for *Grapes*—director Ford, studio boss Zanuck, and screenwriter-producer Johnson—tried rather dismally to repeat their success the next year by adapting another bestseller about rural life, *Tobacco Road*. But Erskine Caldwell's novel and James Kirkland's subsequent play were not nearly as strong as Steinbeck's monumental work. Caldwell's sharecroppers, the infamous Lester family, are animalistic degenerates, too lazy to do any work and completely callous toward other people. Ford transforms the Lesters into lovable comic buffoons willing to go to any lengths (except, of course, work) to get hold of some food. As a whole, the film abandons much of the book's story line and creates its own populist critique of the sharecroppers' situation.

The Lesters are being thrown off the land because Tim, their landlord (Dana Andrews), has had to give the land over to the bank due to vaguely defined "hard times." In the past, Tim and his father before him were benevolent landlords who supplied Jeeter (Charley Grapewin) with a mule and seed. But now the bank, the traditional populist enemy, intends to use the land for scientific farming. This is radically different from Caldwell's version. For all his tasteless stereotyping, he at least traces the fault to the "antiquated system" and claims it has reduced everyone to poverty. The problem lies in the failure to adapt to new times: "Co-operative and corporate farming would have saved them all."[8] The film also overlooks Caldwell's references to the bank's credit system which ensures that the farmer is continually in debt. In the novel, Jeeter's complaint echoes Marvin's: "Here I is working all the year myself, Dude plowing, and Ada and Ellie May helping to chop the cotton in summer and pick it in the fall, and what do I get out of it? Not a durn thing, except a debt of three dollars."[9]

The film looks backward rather than forward. The Lesters are rescued from their ignoble fate on the "poor farm" when landlord Tim scrapes up six months' rent to stave off the bank and stake Jeeter to ten dollars' worth of seed. The solution to the sharecroppers' economic hardship is a return to the past, to the very tenant system that Caldwell and most critics attacked as the basis of the problem. In the end, when his wife asks him when he's going to start planting, Jeeter dozes off on the front porch and mutters, "Maybe next week." He's too lazy and irresponsible to get along without Tim's help.

The underlying assumption of the Ford films, indeed of the entire cycle, is that of the agrarian romances, that to be able to work the land is to commune with the cycles of life itself. The real tragedy in *Grapes* and *Tobacco* is the farmer's separation from his beloved soil. Muley's tormented protest against dispossession is all the more poignant because eviction from the land means removal from universal processes of life and death and the loss of his heritage: "We was *all* born on it, and some of us got killed on it, and some of us died on it. And that's what makes it ourn—bein' born on it, and workin' it, and dyin' on it—and no piece of paper with writin' on it!" That life on the farm is full of hardship, uncertainty, and failure receives little play. Only *Cabin* suggests that the work is more backbreaking than ennobling (Marvin's father is literally worked to death) while *Our Daily Bread* introduces formidable difficulties only to dramatize how community spirit can overcome them. Jean Renoir's *The Southerner* (1945) therefore represents a significant breakthrough, highlighting the awesome hardships faced by tenant farmers as they struggle to make a living off the land.

The film documents Sam Tucker (Zachary Scott) and his family's first difficult year as tenant farmers. Although the film makes it clear that Sam is under intense economic pressure (the landlord will foreclose as soon as the farm fails to pay for itself), Renoir is more interested in the day-to-day, season-to-season concerns of a farm: plowing the land and planting the seeds; repairing the shack and mending threadbare clothes; scavenging for food before the crops come in. The family both enjoys and endures the forces of nature, gratified when Leadpencil, the prize catfish, is caught and worried when a flood threatens their crop. The fact that they are victimized by Devers (J. Carroll Naish), a bitter, unkind neighbor (so much for good neighborliness) is countered by the help offered by Tim (Charles Kemper), Sam's city cousin (so much for the city–country opposition). The film is a mature view of farm life, seeing nature as destructive as well as bountiful and the industry of the city as interdependent with the agriculture of the country.

Although not the best example of Renoir's lyric naturalism, *The Southerner* still goes much further than the standard Hollywood melodrama. Its location shooting is far removed from *Cabin*'s clumsy rear-projected landscapes and its realism and hardships quite different from the gingham whimsies of *State Fair*. The film does not possess either the political impact or epic sweep of *Grapes*. Its power instead rests in its simple details which by inference argue for a greater understanding of the tenant farmer's problems. Even though its ending is unfortunately trite (the young couple standing in the sunshine with their crops at harvest time), *The Southerner* presents a compelling portrait of country life.

Except in some westerns, the hardships of the farmer were rarely portrayed by postwar Hollywood. Agriculture as a social issue lost what immediacy it had with the passing of the Depression. Populist romances of agrarian bounty, however, proved to be more resilient. *State Fair* was not only remade as a musical in 1945 but again as a different musical in 1961.

——9——

THE JUVENILE DELINQUENT
AND SOCIETY

The early thirties films were more concerned with the fact of crime than with its cause, more interested in what the gangster did than why he did it. Crime simply existed as a highly attractive life style and there was no need to explain it. But with the inauguration of the Hays Code and the outcry against the gangster cycle, any further treatment of crime had to either take a pro–law and order stance—e.g., Cagney in *G-Men* (1935) and Robinson in *Bullets or Ballots* (1936)—or be "socially instructive," explaining the cause of criminality. A new cycle of films emerged that treated the criminal not as a heroic individualist but as a social problem. These films were populated by juvenile delinquents about to be initiated into big-time crime and ex-convicts struggling against an intolerant society to go straight. In both cases, sympathy is with the criminal and against the social institutions. But just as the un-repentant gangster had to die, so the reformed delinquents and cons are almost always reintegrated by a redeemer figure.

While economic breakdown was rationalized as corruption, criminality was pigeonholed as the product of bad environment. What had been only hinted at in the opening of *Public Enemy* received full-blown treatment in the late thirties. In the ex-con films, the environment is broadly defined as the prejudices of social institutions and the general citizenry which harass the hero back into crime. With the delinquent cycle, the environment is quite precise and physical: it is either the slum or the reform school. Both of these settings warp young minds. The slum traps the individual in a life of poverty and his efforts to fight against it inevitably lead him outside the law. The reform school is an even worse trap, where other toughs teach the delinquents the ways of crime and the even tougher wardens and guards completely discredit the law.

Although a couple of films had previously treated juvenile delinquency, it was Samuel Goldwyn's *Dead End* (1937) that popularized the problem and really started the cycle. It introduced the "Dead End Kids," the most believable and entertaining delinquents of the thirties—grubby, street-wise punks with an endearing coarseness. The Kids quickly capitalized on their success with a number of films, the best being Warners' *Angels with Dirty Faces* (1938), which played variations on *Dead End*'s themes and format. MGM also entered the cycle with their own style of delinquents. As epitomized in the highly popular *Boys Town* (1938), MGM's tough is a cute little mischiefmaker who is really Andy Hardy underneath. The MGM approach to the problem, though it more or less conforms to the standard established by *Dead End* and Warner Brothers, lacks the hard, guttersnipe sensibility and thereby presents a far more conciliatory brand of social criticism.

The Crime School

These films usually open with brief, vague scenes showing the young protagonists hustling among the tenements, slashing tires, and robbing candy stores, but quickly transfer the action to the reform school. Once within the barbed wire enclosure, the environmentalist issue is safely isolated and the films fall back on the prison stereotypes—the sadistic guard, the shyster warden, and the social crusader who finally wins the prisoners over by treating them with the trust and humanity they have always longed for. The prototype of the cycle is Warners' *Mayor of Hell* (1933). Its catalogue of reform school horrors includes the familiar whippings, solitary confinement, improper medical treatment, and inedible food. The blame is pinpointed to a single shyster warden, Mr. Thompson (Dudley Digges). Likewise, the problem is resolved through a tough guy hero, Patsy Gargan (Jimmy Cagney), a gangster whose ability to raise votes for the party machine has won him an appointment as Deputy Commissioner. After he witnesses the treatment Jimmy (Frankie Darro) receives, the way he is slapped around and then impaled on a barbed wire fence as he tries to escape, Patsy undergoes a transformation. Suddenly and fully dedicated to reform, he gets himself appointed warden, dismisses the nasty guards, sends Thompson away on a month's holiday, and remodels the entire operation of the school. He ends the drill camp regimentation, serves good food, removes the barbed wire, and allows the boys to govern themselves. Gargan manages to win over the most alienated of the boys, including number one rebel Jimmy, by simply trusting them and showing them kindness.

At this point, the social problem has been resolved but the entertainment film requires a more dramatic ending. This is brought about when Patsy gets in trouble with his outlaw gang and has to hide out, leaving Thompson free to take over the school and reinstitute his old ways. When the sickly Skinny dies because Thompson has put him in solitary, the boys rebel. They seize Thompson, put him on trial, and find him guilty of murder. Thompson flees to the school barn and when the boys set it on fire, falls to his death on the barbed wire he himself had erected.

The youths' revolt is quite different from DeMille's mob action in *This Day and Age*, made the same year. Rather than clean-cut, middle-class students taking righteous action on behalf of law and order, Warners' youths are lower-class delinquents rising up against a legal authority that is oppressing them. There is no chauvinist patriotism since the delinquents are rebelling against the system and those values held so dearly by DeMille's storm troopers. But the fact that Patsy had previously reformed them and now conveniently comes out of hiding to quell the boys' revolution and institute permanent reform qualifies the film's political implications. After all, it is only a single authority figure they're concerned with and once he's done away with the boys are content to abide by the benevolent judge and remain under the enlightened care of Patsy.

This early 1933 vehicle was more a spinoff of the prison films than part of the delinquent cycle. Nevertheless, all of its elements were revived in the flood of films which followed *Dead End*'s success in 1937. In fact, Warners featured the "Dead End Kids" in a 1938 remake of *Mayor of Hell, Crime School*. In the five-year period since the original version, the social climate had undergone many changes as is evidenced by the significant differences between the films. The central difference is the figure of Mark Braden (Humphrey Bogart) who replaces Patsy Gargan. Braden is an honest Deputy Commissioner without the tough guy vibrancy of Cagney/Gargan. In 1933 only a racketeer could defeat his own kind; by 1938, it is a crusading representative of the government who wins over the boys and defeats the sadistic villains. Furthermore, Braden is able to vanquish his enemies before the boys resort to an uprising. Another major alteration is the ending. Where *Mayor of Hell* looks forward to a more promising future, *Crime School* shows that future realized. The judge paroles the boys and finds trades for them. The final shot is of the boys comically perusing a book entitled *How to Break into Society*.

Within a year, Warners released another Dead End Kids' film, *Hell's Kitchen* (1939), which adhered to the same plot conventions. Besides the nasty superintendent, it harks back to *Mayor of Hell* for a hero who

is an ex-racketeer and a finale in which the boys rebel and all but lynch
the villain. But by this time the elements were becoming too predictable
to arouse any excitement. Bosley Crowther's review summarizes the
film's clichés:

> Stoically, the boys endure a lot of grievous Oliver twists, such as
> vile food, hard work and frequent torture until modified salvation
> comes in the person of an ex-racketeer who wishes to show his
> works and justify a parole by assisting with the management of the
> shelter . . . [the boys, after the racketeer is forced into hiding] make
> a pass at lynching the superintendent but end up in a burst of
> righteous glory and cake and ice cream all around.[1]

Other studios got into the act and the reform school cycle quickly
declined into B-movie status. Columbia released *Reformatory* (1938,
starring Bobby Jordan of the Dead End Kids) in which the new warden
replaces brutality with kindness and soon even the toughest guys are
going in for gym. The delinquents in RKO's *Boy Slaves* (1939) are
farmed out to a private labor camp instead of a reform school, but even
so there is still a contractor to mistreat and exploit them. The youths
finally resort to violent revolution to call attention to the injustice done
them. The State Police rescue the boys and the judge convicts the
villains. He tries to apologize to them: "We've become so enamored
with the symbols of liberty that we've forgotten its principles. You're
bitter now. I hope you'll forgive us." As with all the reformatory films,
this apparent indictment of society is really a condemnation of personal
villainy which the films' social agencies do away with in the final reel.

The Slum

A second group of delinquent films attempted to depict in fuller detail
the slum life that was reduced to a few explanatory scenes in the crime
school cycle. Though they are supposedly providing a more thorough
analysis of the relationship between slum background and delinquency,
they did not, with the exception of *Dead End*, expand on the simplistic
equations of the other films.

MGM was one of the first to dramatize slum life with *The Devil Is a
Sissy* (1936). Its typically homogenized slums are a slightly overcrowded, small town-type neighborhood where squalor means a few
overturned garbage cans and an occasional broken window. Its delinquents are like a couple of Peck's Bad Boys and running with the gang
seems a somewhat mischievous but generally enviable pastime. The
story revolves around "Limey's" (Freddie Bartholomew) attempts, as a
wealthy and sophisticated newcomer, to become one of the gang with

Gig (Mickey Rooney) and Buck (Jackie Cooper). In MGM's Pollyanna world, delinquent acts can only be inspired by a good cause, to raise money for a tombstone for Gig's father's grave. The crime for which the little rascals get arrested, breaking and entering a posh home to steal some expensive toys, turns out not to be a crime at all because it is Limey's house and his own toys.

Monogram's *Boys of the Street* (1937) also features Jackie Cooper and sentimentalizes urban delinquency. Chuck's rise from alleyway hoodlum to smalltime racketeer is explained through a simplistic reference to his family's poverty: Chuck steals to help support them. Of course, he is too nice a guy to participate in the gang's attack on the neighborhood cop and instead helps round up the crooks. As in *Devil*, delinquency is only a phase and the toughs turn out to be upstanding young men.

Quite apart from these sentimentalizations is *Dead End*, by far the most important of the slum films. Much more than a film on delinquency, it focuses on a single dead end street facing the East River and tries to dramatize how this environment shapes all the people living there. In adapting Sidney Kingsley's play, Goldwyn made only minor concessions to Hollywood proprieties: Dave the hero was changed from an intellectual cripple who defeats the villain through psychological cunning into a more virile physical hero who defeats the villain through personal combat. Except for the necessary restraint in the language, the film retains much of the play's toughness. It does not gloss over the unmitigated hardness of the kids who hang out on the street, and, though confined to a studio set, the film evokes a realistic sense of the grime and heat of an East Side summer.

The delinquents are not cute mischief-makers mollified by some reformer, but defiant, antisocial hoodlums. While their crimes are certainly the result of poverty, they do not steal to help their families. They gang up on a new kid in the neighborhood, beat up a rich brat from a luxury high rise, and plan dirty battle tactics for a gang war all as part of their everyday activities. Dave (Joel McCrea) angrily explicates the problem:

> What chance have they got against all this? They gotta fight for a place to play, fight for the likes of something to eat, fight for everything. They got used to fighting. "Enemies of Society," it says in the papers. Why not? What have they got to be so friendly about?

The youths' fates are foreshadowed by those of an earlier generation raised on the same street. Some have resorted to illegitimate means to escape poverty; others have resisted crime and never moved beyond the dead end slum. But ultimately none of them find happiness and fulfillment. Babyface Martin (Humphrey Bogart) is a killer who has returned home for a visit. He has gone the full route and represents the end product of the slum. Here the gangster is no longer the romantic individualist but a frightened and lonely creature full of false bravado. Rejected by his mother (Marjorie Main) and disillusioned by the fate of his old girl-turned-prostitute, Francie (Claire Trevor), Babyface ends up shot to death in a dark back street alley.

Similarly *Dead End*'s fallen women are not noble martyrs but victims who owe their predicament directly to society. Francie has become a cheap prostitute who rebuffs Babyface's reproaches for not getting a job with a sullen "They don't grow on trees." The same inescapable poverty drives Kay (Wendy Barrie) to her career as mistress to a millionaire. She recoils in terror at the dirt and cockroaches, at the squabbling couples and rowdy delinquents of the tenements, and flees back to the security of the luxury apartment: "I'm frightened of being poor again. I hate what it does to people. I saw what it did to my family. And to me."

Both Dave and Drina (Sylvia Sidney) remain uncorrupted and as a result are poor and frustrated. Dave, who worked nights and studied to be an architect, now goes without job or money, so that Babyface has every reason to laugh at him:

> Six years o' workin' at college and all you get out of it is handouts. That's a good one. I'm glad I ain't like you saps. Starvin' and freezin'. For what? Peanuts. I got mine. I took it. The fat o' the land I'm livin' off of.

As hero-redeemer, Dave is impotent, unable to realize his idealistic goals. His ambition to tear down the slums and "build a decent world where people could live decent and be decent" is granted no outlet.

Where Dave's education has left him penniless, Drina's legitimate job has meant low wages and poor living conditions. Her dream of escape from the slums is, like Dave's plan to rebuild them, thoroughly frustrated, the only tangible results of her strike for better pay being police brutality. Both she and Dave helplessly watch as her brother, Tommy (Billy Halop), is twisted by his environment into a violent hood and inexorably follows Babyface Martin's footsteps toward reform school. The best Dave can do is to kill Babyface, the model the boys emulate. But as he kills one criminal, Dave witnesses the birth of another—Tommy is arrested on an assault charge.

As the fortunes of the earlier generation indicate, the important factor in shaping the boys' delinquency is the gulf between their poverty in the slum and the wealth of the upper class. The inequities are summarized by the set—the back of a luxury high-rise apartment looms over the slums, looking down upon the dead end street with a cool, superior indifference. More than perhaps any other film of the thirties, *Dead End* effectively depicts a class tension which frequently verges on warfare. A uniformed doorman protects the apartment building from the neighborhood, forever sweeping the entrance clear of debris and chasing the kids away with threats of violence. The only tenant from the building to pay any attention to the kids, Mr. Griswold (Minor Watson), is likewise a threat. The father of the society brat the Kids viciously mug, he tries to apprehend Tommy only to be stabbed in the arm. Outraged, he demands and receives police action. The rich man is not the benefactor of the screwball comedies or even the kindly gentleman Drina dreams will rescue her. He is a reasonable man, a representative of his class who sends Tommy away to the dreaded reformatory in order to safeguard himself, his son, his class: "There are other boys like mine. They've got to be protected, too."

The climactic shootout brings the dramatic action to a conclusion but does not resolve the social issues. Killing Babyface does not help except that Dave can use the reward money to hire an expensive lawyer for Tommy. There is thus only a vague hope that Tommy will be let off and escape, at least temporarily, the fate of Babyface. We know that Dave and Drina will continue to fight for a better world, but there is no real sense that such a world is possible. Dave cannot even get a job let alone mount a social planning program which would replace the slums. The outcome of Drina's strike remains unknown, but even if she is granted the raise it is questionable whether it will be sufficient to take Tommy far enough away. "I can only try," is the best response she can offer. Though there are potential solutions—unionism and slum clearance—they are not so easily implemented. No neat dramatic conventions, no populist benefactor or New Deal program could whisk away the inequities of the social system which creates the slums.

Dead End raises some fairly disturbing questions and gives the audience no easy answers. Though its box office success warranted a number of spinoffs, few producers besides Goldwyn would tolerate an openended discussion of social wrong. Warners' *Angels with Dirty Faces*, the toughest of the followups, incorporates *Dead End*'s box-office ingredients, including the depiction of poverty, into a safer format. Though it relies heavily on the earlier film's plot structure, *Angels* manages by the end to twist things around so the Kids will be reconciled with society.

There is no hesitation about presenting the squalor of living conditions in the slums. Like *Dead End*, *Angels* opens with a craning camera exploring the crowded streets and dilapidated tenements. Again the Kids are tempestuous roughnecks involved in petty crime not to help destitute families but out of antisocial defiance. When they have a roll, they blow it at the pool hall: "My mother has ta work a week ta earn this much."

As in the earlier film, the Kids have two models to look up to, this time a priest, Father Jerry Connelly (Pat O'Brien) and a gangster, Rocky Sullivan (Jimmy Cagney). They, like Dave and Babyface, are products of the same neighborhood and represent the potential future for the boys. Much of the film deals with the generally unsuccessful efforts of the priest to keep the boys on the right track. He can't tear down the slums, so he settles for choir practices and a gym floor. But on the basketball court, the Dead Enders remain true to form, clawing, kicking, and tripping their unfortunate opponents. When he tries to coax the Kids out of the pool hall, Connelly is irrevocably rebuffed. "Ah, Father, there ain't no future in playin' basketball." Until the turnabout ending, the priest is an abject failure.

It is to Rocky that the boys turn for leadership and instruction. Connelly's goodness is simply no match for the charismatic and highly successful gangster. It is only when Rocky referees the basketball game and matches the Dead Enders blow for blow that Connelly's phys-ed program is effective. Much to the priest's distress, the Kids also follow Rocky in his ways of crime, earning money by helping Rocky evade the police.

Bordering on *Dead End*'s conclusion that antisocial violence is the most viable reaction to the slum environment, the film suddenly shifts emphasis. Connelly now decides that the problem is not the slums after all but the bad example that Rocky and gangsters like him set for the kids: "The hoodlum and the gangster is looked up to just like the businessman. You show them the easiest way. You unteach whatever I teach them. The kids emulate you." For the last twenty minutes of the film, Jerry abandons his attempts to get the boys into the gym for an all-out effort to get Rocky into jail and crime out of the city.

But even in captivity and facing the electric chair, Rocky remains the hero: "He'll die spittin' in their eye." To destroy Rocky's heroic image, Jerry asks him to "play yellow" at his execution. Rocky again refuses to help: "You're askin' me to give up the only thing I have left." He walks his last mile in full Cagneyesque defiance, the last shot of him a big close-up of his tough, immutable face. But once off camera, the audience hears him whimper and scream for mercy. It is a powerful moment, both for Cagney's histrionics (his cries and shadow, then the hum of voltage and a momentary dim in the light) and for the ambivalence of the action. By keeping Rocky's breakdown out of audience sight and leaving it open as to whether he's acting for Jerry or is truly afraid, the studio is able to teach us that crime does not pay and that gangsters are not so tough but still preserve the "spit in their eye" defiance of the Cagney persona. The Cagney myth remains intact and the Formula morality is upheld.

The boys are soon on their way to reform, their belief in Rocky shattered by Connelly's reports that he died yellow. By killing the bad guy, *Angels* solves the problem and comfortably avoids all those nagging questions left unanswered at the conclusion of *Dead End*. The boys are content to follow the priest to church to say a prayer for Rocky. It is assumed they are also ready to follow him onto the basketball court and into the choir stall.[2]

In *Boys Town*, MGM also resorts to the priesthood to resolve the environmental problem. According to Father Flanagan (Spencer Tracy), if the problem is the city environment, the answer is to remove the kids to the country. Armed with his faith that "there's no such thing as a bad boy," Father Flanagan sets out to create a community far away from the slums which will bring out the delinquents' natural goodness.

The major part of the film revolves around his attempt to convince his superiors in the church, his financial backers, and the delinquents themselves that Boys Town is the proper antidote to the slums. Problem after problem dissolves before the good Father's unbeatable combination of tough guy resourcefulness and prayer. Early in the film Flanagan is told that his project is "a tacit criticism of things as they are." His project is instead a paean to America's ability to right any social wrong. *Boys Town* is a microcosm of MGM's idealized America, a democratically self-governed (it even has its own court of justice) melting pot where boys of all nationalities and faiths work side by side in harmony, under the benevolent care of a purposeful leader. In contrast to the prisonlike reform schools, there is plenty of wide open space and fresh air where the boys can engage in good clean fun.

Once more MGM's delinquents lack the hard edge of the Dead End Kids. Whitey Marsh (Mickey Rooney) is the standard number one tough who resists all of Flanagan's efforts to reach him. But his toughness turns out to be nothing more than a false bravado which has been his way of coping with a tragic childhood. Whitey's defenses are broken down when his brash behavior causes cute little Peewee (Bobs Watson) to have a near-fatal accident. By the end of the film, Rooney has slipped into his true persona, the archetypal small-town kid, Andy Hardy.

Boys Town was successful enough for Warners to borrow some of its key elements and graft them onto its own delinquent conventions. In *They Made Me a Criminal* (1939), a parish priest sends the Dead End Kids from the New York slums to an Arizona date farm. Like *Boys Town*, the date farm is always under financial threat, and the drama

centers around raising money to pay the rent and continue the reformation of the boys. But the film emphasizes Warners' toughness over MGM
sweetness and the boys are reformed not by the priest (who never
actually appears in the film) but by Warners tough guy slum child John
Garfield, who is himself fleeing a murder charge.

By the time of *They Made Me a Criminal* the questions about the
slums were so familiar that they did not have to be raised. As in *Boys
Town*, a simple move to the country is the city-dweller's salvation. The
delinquents are reformed without any change in the slums or in the
economic structure that produced them. One last film, however, *One
Third of a Nation* (1939)—adapted from a highly successful "Living
Newspaper" play produced by the Federal Theater project, which in
turn had borrowed the title phrase from one of Roosevelt's speeches—
did argue that the tenements should be torn down. Instead of treating
juvenile delinquency, the film concentrates on the tenement building
itself and on the plight of its normal working-class inhabitants. It begins
by showing the unhealthy, unsafe living conditions. A fire breaks out in
a building and cripples little Joey Rogers (Sidney Lumet). His angry
sister Mary (Sylvia Sidney) fumes to a helpful passerby that the man
who owns the building should be sent to prison. The passerby, playboy millionaire Peter Cortland (Leif Erikson), turns out to be the
landlord. Having seen the error of his ways, Cortland is willing to correct the situation. The film climaxes with Peter winning Mary, thereby
synthesizing any class differences, and tearing down the old building
with the promise to replace it with a modern, clean structure. Drina's
dream of a rich benefactor who will take her and her brother away from
the slums has come true. In the process, Dave has finally been given
the chance to construct his decent buildings.

The juvenile delinquent cycle peaked in 1938 and quickly dropped
off in popularity. The Dead End Kids became involved in ever-cheaper
B-pictures, churned out in quick succession to capitalize on their popularity. With each film they became less violent and increasingly comic,
the slums more a neutral playground for their brawling hi-jinks. Universal's *Little Tough Guys* (1938) and *Little Tough Guys in Society*
(1939) and Warners' *Angels Wash Their Faces* (1939) simply borrowed the clichés of the delinquent films as a pretext for slapstick
antics. Frank Nugent summed up the course of their career: "The Little
Tough Guys seem to have acquired the head-thwacking technique of
the Three Stooges and the subtlety of the Ritz Brothers."[3] In the forties
and fifties, the remnants of the original group, led by Leo Gorcey and
Huntz Hall, were renamed The Bowery Boys and the social milieu of
their early films was completely abandoned. Among their adventures
were meetings with monsters and trips to Baghdad.

A Note on Postwar Delinquency

The year 1949 saw a brief revival of the thirties environmentalism. Two films, *Knock on Any Door* and *City Across the River*, dramatize the same thesis that juvenile crime is the direct result of slum living. *Knock on Any Door* follows the career of Nick Romano (John Derek) from slum childhood. He is more than just a raucous prankster or a Peck's Bad Boy easily reformed by the hero's kindness. Raised in poverty, the son of a criminal executed years earlier, Nick is a complex, disillusioned loser who can't quite make it in the straight world. Environmentalism is here tempered by a veneer of late-forties psychology, Derek's brooding disillusionment anticipating Brando and Dean. Another important difference with *Knock on Any Door* is the way it reverses Formula expectations. Nick appears to be an innocent victim, unjustly accused of a policeman's murder and thereby gaining our easy sympathy. It is only after he breaks down and confesses at his trial that we and his lawyer (Humphrey Bogart) discover his actual guilt. This sudden revelation calls our sympathy for Nick into question. Now when Bogart insists that the sympathy is still deserved, the film addresses with outrage the core of the problem and our responsibility in it.[4] If Nick Romano is guilty, so are we, and "if he dies in the electric chair, we killed him."

Although *City Across the River* moves out into the streets of Brooklyn and develops a documentary feel that distinguishes it from the studio-bound studies of the thirties, it still subscribes to the limited sociology of the earlier films. Thomas Pryor of The *New York Times* was one of the few critics to note this limitation when the film was released:

> Miserable tenements occasionally spaced by courtyards, and vacant lots which resemble garbage piles, remain as national eyesores and are a menace to healthy living. But just to say, as this picture mostly does, that bad housing makes for bad citizens, is to beg the question. The reasons why so many youngsters are going in the wrong direction today lie much deeper. However, in tackling this important subject through *Knock on Any Door* . . . and now *City Across the River*, to name only a few, the screen has as yet done no more than to scratch the surface, leaving the roots of the evil to flourish in the dark.[5]

Pryor is here citing the central failure of all the delinquent films, in fact of thirties sociology in general, to get beyond what were really symptoms —poor housing, overcrowding, low living standards—of much more basic processes. Only *Dead End* hints at the social structure which creates the slum and it too fails to realize that better housing does not necessarily produce better citizens.

—10—

THE EX-CON AND SOCIETY

For many Americans during the Depression, outlaws such as Bonnie and Clyde, Pretty Boy Floyd, and John Dillinger were heroes. The insecure, the frustrated, and the dispossessed vicariously identified with the criminal's triumphant defiance of the law and rigid social stratification. While the mass media generally catered to this mood by exploiting the outlaw's antisocial violence, a small group of artists sought to show why the criminal was considered heroic and thereby to create a form of social criticism. Oftentimes, the artists depicted the criminal act as a positive rebellion against society, a counterbalance to the exploitation and humiliation so many experienced. Typical is Woody Guthrie's "Pretty Boy Floyd" which compares outlaws with more respectable citizens:

> Well it's through this world I've rambled,
> I've seen lots of funny men;
> Some rob you with a six gun,
> Some with a fountain pen.

Edward Anderson's fictionalized version of the Bonnie and Clyde story, *Thieves Like Us*, similarly claims that "them capitalist fellows" are thieves just like the protagonists. He directly addresses the question of why people look to gangsters as heroes:

> The rich, Hawkins said, can't drive their big automobiles and flaunt bediamonded wives and expect every man just to simply look on admiringly. The sheep will do it and the sheep will even laud it and support it, but at the same time these sheep will feel something that they do not understand and demonstrate it, and that is known as so-called glorification of the big criminal.[1]

146

The Hollywood movie was a chief glorifier of the big criminal. The gangster, prison, and shyster cycles deified the outlaw, but, unlike Guthrie and Anderson, without explicitly linking crime to society. Sensationalism, not social criticism, was the motivation behind the gangster films. The most glaring exception is *I Am a Fugitive from a Chain Gang*. But *Fugitive*'s social criticism is quite different in mood from that of Anderson and Guthrie. Allen's criminality is a defensive stance imposed on him as a matter of survival, not a positive act of defiance against society. The only films to parallel criminality with social rebellion were entertaining westerns and swashbucklers safely set in the past. In *The Adventures of Robin Hood* (1938) the famous bandit (Errol Flynn) is fighting on behalf of the peasants against the corruption of Prince John's court, while in *Jesse James* (1939) the hero (Tyrone Power) is acting against the eastern railroad company which has violated the rights of western homesteaders.

In its contemporary outlaw films, Hollywood adapted *Fugitive*'s approach to crime whereby the criminal hero becomes an innocent victim of social persecution and the environment. But the films of the mid-to-late thirties significantly diminish *Fugitive*'s indictment. Among the earliest and most formulized of these films are *Mary Burns, Fugitive* (1935) and *The Great O'Malley* (1937). In both films, the heroes are innocent victims of police persecution who live out paranoic nightmares of desperate flight and eventual imprisonment. But legal authorities in both cases recognize their mistake and actually help rehabilitate the victims. The persecution here, not as widespread as in *Fugitive*, is an isolated phenomenon that is overcome to allow the outlaw back into society. In this way the antisocial content of the criminal-as-hero theme is transformed into a testimonial to modern America.

Garfield—Rebel Child of the Slums

The quintessential Hollywood social victim was John Garfield, Warners' rebel slum child who went through his screen life with a justifiable chip on his shoulder. Garfield is a Dead End Kid grown up and embittered, who has never found his niche in life or been lucky enough to come under the aegis of a Mark Braden or Father Connelly. Describing Mickey Borden, Garfield's first screen character in *Four Daughters* (1938), screenwriters Julius Epstein and Lenore Coffee summarize the Garfield persona:

> His dress is careless, almost shabby. But he is fortunate that his carelessness adds to his attractiveness. His humor is ironic. When he smiles (which is seldom), his demeanor is sardonic. Mickey Borden

doesn't think well of himself or the world. Poverty has done the trick.[2]

By itself, this character represents one of the studio's most effective social statements.

But as with all Warners' post-*Fugitive* rebels, Garfield must be convinced that the antisocial assumptions he's been taught through bitter experience are all wrong. In his major rebel films, *They Made Me a Criminal* and *Dust Be My Destiny* (both 1939), the Garfield hero moves from defiant outcast to good citizen, convinced during the last reel that a lifetime of injustice was not indicative of the true America. Garfield's persecution is unique, once again an isolated case. He is the victim less of social malevolence than of incredibly bad luck. Always in the wrong place at the wrong time, he is, in Archer Winston's words, "fate's whipping boy."[3] As one Garfield character puts it, "If it ain't the cops, it's a judge. If it ain't a judge, it's a couple of mugs. If it ain't mugs, it's a screwy foreman. It always happens to me."

Johnny Bradfield, the protagonist of *Criminal*, is a hardened, corrupt boxer who believes life is a "sucker game." His slum background and boxing career have taught him the jungle ethic. Johnny's rejection of friendship—"Friends nothin'. Nobody's got friends. My manager's a friend, for 50%, as long as I'm ridin' high"—is borne out when the manager frames him for murder. He descends from champ to fugitive, chased across the country by a fanatical policeman (Claude Rains) and finding refuge with the Dead Enders on their rehabilitation ranch. Away from shyster city, his hard shell is melted by social worker Peggy (Gloria Dickson) and soon Johnny is helping reform the kids and save the ranch from financial ruin. When the obsessed detective finally catches up with him, Johnny's new life and Peggy's charm so affect the cop that he lets Johnny go and closes the case. Society has now unmade a criminal.

Dust's Joe Bell undergoes the most relentless persecution of all Garfield characters. Just released after serving a bum rap, he is picked up as a vagrant and sentenced to ninety days by a judge who labels him a tramp. "We're tramps if you call guys looking for jobs tramps," Joe sneers. In a labor camp, Joe is antagonized by a bigoted warden. When the warden dies accidentally, Joe flees, certain he will be accused of murder. Although Joe yearns for "a place to hang my hat," society won't let him have it. Each time he finds some security, his identity is discovered and the ominously vigilant police renew their chase.

Throughout the whole ordeal, Joe's girl, Mabel (Priscilla Lane), retains her faith in society and, unable to convince Joe to surrender, she finally turns him in, confident that he'll receive a fair trial and be set free. To Joe, this is the worst betrayal of all, because he knows that there is no justice for him. And when the DA bases his case on Joe's "bad character," Joe's prognosis appears to be true. He's not being tried for a specific crime, but for being a member of a particular social class. But character witnesses and a sympathetic jury prove Mabel right. Joe's lawyer equates his innocence with his basic rights as an American citizen. Joe is just like a lot of others "and if they're to be judged, then America is not much of a democracy. . . . You should prove to Joe the world's not against him, that it will give him a chance." Social rebellion has been built to a climax and then purged, the rebel reintegrated and society reaffirmed.

Despite the final reversals, the Garfield films, especially *Dust*, are often quite powerful as social statements. If the persecutions are familiar and the finale all too predictable, Garfield's cynicism still rings true. The rebel we encounter throughout the film provides an indictment which withstands the happy ending.

Fritz Lang and *You Only Live Once*—We Made Him a Criminal

The most memorable film of the cycle, Fritz Lang's *You Only Live Once* (1937), makes no concessions to the Formula. In recounting the persecution of ex-con Eddie Taylor (Henry Fonda), Lang rejects both the happy ending and the possibility that society can redeem itself. Believing that man's cruelty to his fellow man is a universal characteristic, the director even goes so far as to implicate his audience in the hero's murder. All the elements of universal destiny—man's flawed nature, Eddie's own weaknesses, social prejudice, and simple chance—interact to condemn the hero. But whereas the fate motif serves to diffuse society's responsibility for the hero's lot in the Garfield films, Lang makes social institutions the specific agents of fate. The universalities enhance, not diminish, the social criticism: Lang's criticisms do not just apply to American society in the Depression but to all societies at all times.

In *You Only Live Once*, Lang sets up the odds against his protagonist and watches him struggle against them. Like Garfield, Eddie is the product of slum poverty and an unjust legal system. A "three-time loser" whose next conviction means life imprisonment, he determines with the encouragement of his wife Joan (Sylvia Sidney) to go straight. But once more society will not let him find a place to hang his hat. A narrow-minded populace fed on newspaper sensationalism and lurid crime magazines insists that once a con, always a con. On their honeymoon, Eddie and Joan are evicted from a motel by a henpecked proprietor and his shrewish wife: "Convicts and their wives aren't welcome here." Just after he has begun work as a truck driver, Eddie is fired for falling behind schedule: "No ex-con is going to mess up my schedule." Even other convicts ridicule his attempts to go straight, warning him not to put on "the high hat" because he'll always be "one of us." When he refuses to help his old cronies pull off a bank job, they make sure he never escapes his past by framing him for the crime. As with Joe Bell, his faith in society is beaten out of him by his experiences. Arrested for a crime he didn't commit, Eddie has good reason to believe that he'll be condemned on his record.

But for Lang, there are no redeemers to save Eddie from societal prejudice. Joan, whose faith echoes Mabel's, convinces Eddie to give himself up. But the moment the police arrive, her illusions are shattered as a cop taunts Eddie to draw his gun: "Go ahead Taylor. You'll save the state the cost of a trial." Joan at first refuses to sneak a gun into the jail for Eddie: "If you get the gun, you'll kill somebody"—but is convinced by his bitter, irrefutable answer: "What do you think they're going to do to me?" Once Eddie escapes, she joins in his flight from the law, no longer hesitant to resort to crime in order to survive. Society has not only made Eddie into a criminal, it has made his redeemer one as well.

The priest, the most common redeemer figure of the delinquent films, is here an ineffectual do-gooder. The prison chaplain's (William Gargan) exhortations to keep the faith are completely alien to the convict's life experience. In fact, it is Father Dolan's interference with Eddie's escape, his attempt to convince the desperate inmate that his pardon is genuine, which panics Eddie into killing him. Dolan's well-intentioned bumbling actually makes Eddie the murderer society has always said he was. A third redeemer figure, Public Defender Stephen Whitney (Barton MacLane), is unable to arouse the jury's sympathy the way Joe's lawyer does and instead loses faith himself in the legal system. Realizing that Eddie is the product of society, he refuses to blame him for Dolan's murder or to cooperate with the police in their pursuit of the fugitive couple. Stephen's last futile gesture on behalf of the fugitives takes him outside the law. Feeling that Eddie can no longer be saved, he offers to help Joan escape the country while he works to clear her name. But Joan is unwilling to abandon Eddie and accompanies him into the police ambush that kills them both.

The difference between Lang's vision of America and that of the Garfield films is further illustrated by contrasting the two fugitive couples' lives on the road. Whereas Joe and Mabel are always bumping into friendly citizens eager to help, Joan and Eddie live out a relentless nightmare that is relieved only by their deaths. When Joe decides to rob a delicatessen, his resolve is undermined by the generosity of the proprietress who gives him free sandwiches and allows him to buy food on credit. But when Joan and Eddie steal gas for their getaway car, they are exploited by the gas attendants. While one attendant is on the phone reporting the theft of all their cash, the other attendant empties the cash register. Their lie is then compounded by overdramatized news reports and the manhunt for the couple is intensified. In Lang's America, good does not counterbalance evil.

The somber mood of Lang's landscape, the grey, rain-swept roadways and dark alleys of his couple's flight, contrasts sharply with the open, sunny spaces Joe and Mabel inhabit. Images of entrapment recur throughout the film. Lang composes his shots so that space always seems to be closing in on the couple. We see them through window frames, surrounded by boxcars in a freightyard and finally through the telescopic lens of a marksman's rifle. The expressionistic camerawork presents an entire environment as a prison. Even the bars of Eddie's real cell create shadows that fan out to encompass the whole screen. Society's literal prison symbolically reaches out to embrace everything and entrap Eddie no matter where he flees.

Lang's most significant deviation from the Garfield films and Hollywood conventions is his manipulation of audience reaction so that we too are implicated in society's victimization of the couple. Where *Dust* voices our doubts in order to satisfy them, *You Only Live Once* makes us question our own role in society. Lang edits the robbery sequence so that we assume that Eddie is guilty. In sequence we see Eddie angry at the loss of his job—"And to think I wanted to go straight"; the bank holdup where the robber remains anonymous beneath a gas mask; a hat with the initials E. T. left at the scene of the robbery; the escape truck crashing in the rain; and a frightened Eddie running home to Joan. Although we know the "jailbird" assumptions have been unfair, we are skeptical when Eddie claims that he's been framed. It is only with his pardon, when it is too late to help him, that we realize our mistake. Like the prejudiced society we have taken his guilt for granted. Later, as the police move in for the kill, Lang reminds us of our own culpability. By filming the couple's death through the crosshairs of a policeman's rifle, he makes us identify with social authority. Along with the cop, we aim the rifle and pull the trigger.

As with *I Am a Fugitive*, much of the film's impact comes from the shock of the unhappy ending. The director builds up a typical case against society, fuelling our antisocial indignation, but instead of relieving it turns it against us. Rather than leave the theater with the comforting knowledge that Joe Bell has gone free, we are forced to recognize that "they" who made the hero a criminal and "we" in the audience are the same people.

Lang's next film, *You and Me* (1938) is a strange follow-up to *You*

Only Live Once, almost constituting a rebuttal of the earlier film's pessimism. It again deals with a couple (here both are ex-cons) who are trying to fulfill their love and go straight in society, but this time they succeed. The grim, unrelenting reality of *You Only Live Once* is replaced by an offbeat musical comedy with a "fairy tale"[4] atmosphere. Joe (George Raft) and Helen (Sylvia Sidney), are subjected to many of the same hostilities as Joan and Eddie, but this time they come across a redeemer who is effectual, a department store owner who makes it his policy to hire and rehabilitate ex-cons. Joe's return to crime is not the result of persecution but of his own overreaction to the fact that Helen has lied about her past. When he robs the department store, he is not even accused of a crime but greeted by the fatherly remonstrances of the still tolerant proprietor. The film ends not with the couple's inevitable death but with their reconciliation and the birth of their baby. The last shot shows Joe's gang of once-hardened criminals gathered around the baby making funny faces and goo-goo sounds.

You and Me subscribes to all the clichés that *You Only Live Once* tries to shatter and Lang himself has rejected the film's essential phoniness: "I don't think *You and Me* is a good picture. It was—I think deservedly—my first real flop. . . . I wanted to make a didactic picture teaching that crime doesn't pay which is a lie, because crime does pay very well."[5] Still the film should not be too readily dismissed, for Lang's method of expressing the conventional message is decidedly unconventional. In attempting to find the most effective way of teaching that crime doesn't pay, he experiments with Brechtian techniques. Through fantasy sequences, songs, and didactic lectures, he interrupts the flow of character identification to highlight the thematic relevance of the drama. As in *You Only Live Once,* the ultimate aim is to provoke the moviegoer, to make him think about what he sees on the screen after he has left the theater.

The didactic sequences are easily the best in the film. To teach us our lesson Lang provides us with a teacher. After the gang is caught in the store, they are led to the toy department where they lounge about like kindergarteners on rocking horses and wagons while Helen lectures them at the blackboard. She carefully works out the net expenditures and gains of robbery to prove mathematically that the gang would make more profit through legitimate means. For once, the criminals are reformed not by moral arguments but by economic ones. In the film's opening scene, Lang demonstrates that crime is wrong, not necessarily because it's unjustified but because you get caught at it. While an unseen chorus sings "You can't get something for nothing, / You have to lay it on the line," the camera moves down aisles of tempting consumer commodities. As the music fades, the film cuts to a woman shoplifting one of those luxuries promised to all but denied to most. When caught, she pleads, "I've never had something like this . . . I've never done this before." Instead of giving us a serman about crime being immoral, Lang advises us that it's just not practical.

A Note on the Postwar Outlaw

With the coming of World War II and its focus on an outside enemy, the image of the criminal as victim or rebel faded. As part of the war effort, Hollywood had to promote the idea of a united country, without class divisions and without injustice. In films such as *Air Force* (1943), the Garfield outsider comes to identify with the goals of the armed forces and in so doing achieves a sense of belonging he's never had before. Similarly, in *Passage to Marseilles* (1944), an escaped convict played by Humphrey Bogart, the forties' great cynic hero, is reintegrated into society through the need to fight a common enemy. During the postwar years, the outlaw's defiance was depicted as a neurotic impulse. James Cagney's Cody Jarrett in *White Heat* (1949) was neither a go-getter seeking an outlet for his success drive nor a victim of the environment. He was instead a homicidal maniac suffering from a mother complex and hereditary madness. Richard Widmark became a popular criminal villain playing psychopathic types in films such as *Kiss of Death* (1947) and *The Street with No Name* (1948).

One exception to these trends was Nicholas Ray's *They Live by Night* (1948), an excellent adaptation of Anderson's *Thieves Like Us*. Reminiscent of *You Only Live Once*, the film depicts a Bonnie-and-Clyde-like couple on the run who do not want to be criminals but have no real alternative. When Bowie (Farley Granger) naively escapes prison with the idea of raising enough money to hire a good lawyer and clear his name, he unwittingly triggers a chain of events which leads to his death. Forced to participate in a series of robberies by his fellow escapees T-Dub (Jay C. Flippen) and Chicamaw (Howard Da Silva), he is soon labeled a notorious public enemy by a sensationalist press and, like Eddie, is blamed for murders and robberies he had nothing to do with. When Bowie tries to go straight and disappear with Keechie (Cathy O'Donnell) until the furor dies down, his gang won't let him. The criminals again accept society's attitudes, but for Ray these attitudes do not involve prejudice so much as greed. T-Dub tells Bowie: "This is a business, son . . . So to speak you're an investment. And you're going to pay off." Inevitably, a police manhunt bears down on the young couple and their flight ends in the police ambush of Bowie.

The central difference between the Lang and Ray films is a matter of focus. While Lang places societal malevolence within a larger framework, Ray directs his anger more specifically at the American social system. The society Bowie and Keechie live in is corrupt and exploitative. There are two kinds of thieves: the supposed "enemies of society" and the more legitimate crooks. When Bowie protests over the high price of a used car, T-Dub explains the facts of life to the innocent youngster: "They're thieves. Just like us." The "vultures" on both sides of the law will not let Bowie go straight as long as they can use him to sell newspapers or rob banks. In a corrupt society, there is no room for innocence.

Like *Knock on Any Door, They Live by Night* is a throwback to the thirties. But by the mid-fifties, Ray was explaining social rebellion in terms of psychological alienation. In his classic study of juvenile delinquency, *Rebel Without a Cause* (1955), Jim Stark's (James Dean) problems lie in his relationship wtih his father. Fritz Lang in *The Big Heat* (1953) also abandoned the social premises behind crime to concentrate on the sadism of the criminal, on a thug (played by Lee Marvin) who is a vicious psychological cripple. Gangster films well into the sixties continued to see the criminal in terms of personality—*Kiss Me Deadly* (1955), *Baby Face Nelson* (1975), *Al Capone* (1959) and *The Killers* (1964). Like the gangsters of the early thirties, these heroes moved in their own isolated underworld which may mirror the institutions of modern society but is not explicitly connected to them. Crime and violence are simply accepted as part of a life style.

Not until the late sixties and seventies was the outlaw placed back within a social context. But by this time, the problem film as a self-conscious genre no longer existed and the films' social commentary is just one thematic strand of many or sometimes just a vague mood of discontent. Arthur Penn's *Bonnie and Clyde* (1967) revived the fugitive couple in order to make a new kind of statement. The protagonists are not innocents whose criminality is the product of their environment, but dumb hoodlums whose nihilistic deeds are the only possible form of individual heroism in an unheroic, stultifying society. Subsequent films, such as *Cool Hand Luke* (1967), *Butch Cassidy and the Sundance Kid* (1969), and *Easy Rider* (1969) similarly play upon the theme of the outlaw as the last individualist whose very existence represents a defiance of the Establishment.

By the mid-seventies a new cycle of films about fugitive couples— *Badlands* (1974), *Sugarland Express* (1974), and Robert Altman's remake of *Thieves Like Us* (1974)—have their protagonists act out an impulsive, inarticulate rebellion which sets all of society's repressive power against them. Although no longer stated directly, the assumption remains that criminality is a natural response to a criminal society.

——11——

DIFFERENT PROBLEMS,
SAME SOLUTIONS

Most of the social problems we have discussed so far have been intertwined with the larger breakdown of the Depression. Forgotten men, Okies, agitators, and criminal-victims are all figures moving in the landscape of despair and want that was peculiar to the thirties. However, the studios did touch upon other problems not so intrinsic to the Depression—for example, the role of the doctor in society and the treatment of racial minorities. If these problems are not exclusive to the times, the films, with their individual hero-redeemers and benevolent New Deal officials, are allegories of America's ability to overcome its own weaknesses during the Depression.

The Doctors

To Hollywood, medicine, like everything else in the thirties, was a racket. The profession's failure to fulfill its social responsibility is attributed to unethical doctors who neglect poorer patients for the substantial remuneration obtained by satisfying the hypochondriacal whims of the wealthy. When it comes to treating real maladies, the doctors are incompetent. In MGM's *Men in White* (1934), perennial villain C. Henry Gordon's ineptness nearly causes a patient's death. In *A Doctor's Diary* (1937), sloppy surgery costs a violin prodigy his arm, while in *The Citadel* (1938), a brilliant and honest doctor loses his life at the hands of a charlatan. Each time, a fraternal conspiracy among these doctors keeps them rich and safe from censure.

If it isn't a shyster, it's a stodgy, conservative medical establishment which blackens the name of the profession by inhibiting valuable scientific progress. In *Arrowsmith* (1931), a State Veterinarian opposes Dr. Arrowsmith's (Ronald Colman) development of a serum that will save the countryside's cattle from disease. In *The Story of Louis Pasteur* (1935), Paul Muni spends more time in his fight against Charbonnet (Fritz Leiber) and the French Medical Academy than he does battling a deadly rabies epidemic. The title character in *Dr. Ehrlich's Magic Bullet* (1940) (Edward G. Robinson) has his research into the cause of syphilis (demurely referred to as "the reward of sin") interrupted when the government cuts off his funds.

Rebuffed by their contemporaries, the researcher heroes persist in their work even if it means setting up laboratories in their own homes: Arrowsmith in his kitchen, Pasteur in his basement, and Dr. Manson (Robert Donat) of *The Citadel* in his greenhouse. They represent humanitarianism and progress threatened by a malevolent society and the final vindication of their research sees that malevolence tempered and reformed. The doctors not only cure physical ills but also the society's selfish preoccupation with personal reward over the welfare of mankind.

The Citadel, directed by King Vidor, is the most explicit study of the interrelationship between medicine and society, the only film of the period to connect social and physical diseases. Dr. Manson and his colleague Dr. Denny (Ralph Richardson) discover a typhoid epidemic among their working class patients and trace the cause to the leaky sewer system. But Denny's letters to the Ministry of Health produce no response. The film thus implies a class basis for disease that is later amplified when we see the rich pampered and coddled for imaginary ailments. The only way the doctors can overcome the typhoid epidemic is to blow up the sewer. Within a few days a new sewer is being constructed and the doctors' radical activism is justified. Manson also discovers the cause of miners' tuberculosis is occupational, but the film never delves into the implications of this discovery, i.e., the culpability of the mine owners and the laws which protect the status quo. It is not profit-motivated industry which prevents further research (as in Carol Reed's *The Stars Look Down*, 1940), but the mob mentality of the superstitious miners.

Another important theme of the medical films centers on the doctor's personal conflicts between the demands of his profession and his private life, between his calling as a doctor on the one hand and as a research scientist on the other. Dr. Arrowsmith finds that his long hours in the lab keep him away from his wife Leora (Helen Hayes) and seriously undermine his marriage. At the same time he is torn between a career in research where his work will benefit all men for all time and his practice as a doctor where the immediate needs of his patients must be met on a daily basis. After many months of experimentation, he finds that his discovery has also been made by a French scientist who publishes it first. Disappointed, he realizes that research goes on without him and he plunges into his work, not in an easy domestic practice, but with patients whose needs are great—West Indian natives ravaged by bubonic plague. In *Men in White*, young Dr. Ferguson (Clark Gable) must choose between an arduous training under Dr. Hockberg (Jean Hersholt) and an easy, lucrative practice. His snobbish fiancée (Myrna Loy) insists that he choose the latter and only comes to appreciate the importance of his work after witnessing his performance at the operating table. His conflict is happily settled—he ends up with both the girl and the career he wants.

Again it is *The Citadel* which most clearly roots the doctor's conflict in a social basis. Dr. Manson's work among Welsh miners and his research into tuberculosis reward him with frustration and poverty—he is reduced to piercing the ears of prostitutes (the film's amusing version of the original novel's somewhat harsher reason for the doctor's treatment of prostitutes). He then encounters the affluent fraternity of Harley Street practitioners and becomes part of their world of fee-splitting, expensive consultations, and unnecessary therapy for the very rich. Manson soon sports a shyster moustache, smokes expensive cigars, and drives a flashy new car. Society has narrowed the doctor's choices to a life of dedication and poverty or a career of racketeering and wealth.

Manson's social conscience is reawakened by Denny's death and by a subsequent grief-stricken walk through a disease-ridden neighborhood. As he passes through the slums, he witnesses children eating garbage, a blind beggar sitting unattended on the sidewalk, and an ambulance careening dangerously through the narrow, overcrowded streets. Poverty is the disease which Manson must fight to cure. Like so many reformed shysters, Manson returns to the slums and applies his abilities to those in greatest need.

But when he deserts Harley Street he is censured by the medical association, not for his new-found class-consciousness but for his use of radical new pneumothoracic surgery. In this way his radicalism shifts from a social basis to a purely technological one. Manson, like Pasteur and Ehrlich, concludes the film with a passionate plea for scientific progress, not social reform. Yet even the scientific issues which the films dramatize had been resolved. In the cases of Pasteur and Ehrlich, their discoveries had been vindicated long before the thirties; the surgical methods Manson uses had also been accepted in the United States by 1938 (which the film intimates by making the discoverer an American who has already overcome prejudice back home). Except for *The*

Citadel, the medical series makes little direct social analysis. Few of the films take place in Depression America and their pleas for liberal reform are merely generalized variations on the thirties' sense of political liberalism.

Warners and the Minorities

Racism did not gain Hollywood's consideration as a serious problem until the postwar period. Rather, throughout the thirties, racial and ethnic minorities were depicted in the most stereotypic and demeaning fashion. As we shall discuss in a later chapter on minorities, gestures toward racial-ethnic equality were rare, tentative, and then never central to a film's drama. Two noteworthy exceptions were Warners' *Massacre* (1934) and *Bordertown* (1935), which reworked the studio's social outcast dramas to fit Indian and Chicano protagonists. Richard Barthelmess moved from WASP hero Tom Holmes in *Heroes for Sale* to Joe Thunder Horse in *Massacre*, while Paul Muni graduated from James Allen to Mexican-American Johnny Ramirez in *Bordertown*. Both heroes undergo a similar odyssey during which they discover the nature of social persecution, impulsively rebel against it, and finally return to the system: Joe with faith that the New Deal will correct the situation and Johnny with an acceptance of his place in society.

Massacre is the more interesting of the two, detailing Indian conditions more fully and self-consciously than *Bordertown* does those of the Chicanos. In its opening sequences, the film attacks racial and sexual stereotypes by showing how whites react to Joe on a predetermined basis, either as a figure out of adventure folklore or as a savage stud. ("I'd be his squaw anytime," one female fan purrs provocatively.) The only way for Joe, as an Indian, to become successful in the white world is to cater to its misconceptions, to star in a wild west show as everyone's caricature of the Indian. Known to his public as Chief Joe Thunder Horse, he gallops across the rodeo arena sporting feathers and breechcloth, brandishing a tomahawk and a bow. Even when in his normal suit and tie, Joe is seen not as an individual human being but as a racial-sexual symbol. One seductress plants a feathered bonnet on his head before embracing him. In analyzing sexuality as an important basis for racism, the film is far ahead of its time. (It is worth noting, however, that this same sexual stereotyping is exploited by the film's ads: "Would you risk the kisses of the *savage* suitor? See what happens when white arms quicken his lawless blood.")

The film also demonstrates how Joe has been robbed of his heritage. Successful, Joe is truly the white man's Indian. He not only acts out their stereotypes on the stage, he imitates their manners and customs in his off-stage life. Like his affluent white friends, Joe even has a black man-servant. When he is called back to the reservation because of his father's illness, Joe rediscovers the world he has forsaken. Reentering the real world of the Indian, he learns of his true heritage and of its rape by the white culture. When he sees a movie crew filming the same Indian caricatures he had promulgated in the rodeo, he angrily smashes the camera and protests to his people: "You don't have to do things like this." Despite the fact that native burial rites are disallowed and Chris-tian funerals compulsory, Joe buries his father according to Indian custom.

Most important, Joe is repulsed by the poverty of his people and the corruption of the white Indian agency which keeps the natives in debt. It is here, however, that the film degenerates into Formula clichés. The agent and his cohorts epitomize evil. Agent Quisenberry is played by Dudley Digges as if he were still the sadistic reform school warden in *Mayor of Hell*; Dr. Turner (Arthur Hohl) is an addict who hoards all the drugs for himself and refuses to treat the Indians; and Shanks (Sid-ney Toler) is an undertaker who maliciously charges exorbitant funeral rates in order to force the Indians further into debt. The audience focus is shifted away from the cultural-economic rape of the Indian to Shanks's rape of Joe's sister Jenny.

Joe's first angry reaction leads him outside the system and he murders Shanks in revenge. But he soon realizes that violent rebellion is fruitless and that not all government officials are like Shanks and Quisenberry. He flees to Washington to seek government aid from the benevolent New Deal's Indian Affairs Commissioner. Like Joe, the New Dealer is angry about the Indians' exploitation, even hinting that the problem goes beyond shysters. The film approaches its most radical statement in the Washington sequence as the Commissioner links the Indians' plight to "the most powerful interests in the country":

> Every move I make is blocked by the same organized groups that have been bleeding the Indians for years: water power, oil rights, cattle ranges, timber—whatever the Indian happens to own, they manage to get it away from him. They control public opinion and legislation and they've got me hog-tied.

But the film carefully avoids further specification of who these interests are and the drama quickly reverts to the more easily vanquished shysters. With the New Deal behind him, Joe returns home to battle Quisenberry. The villain is sent off to prison, Joe is offered a job with the Indian

Commission, and the future looks bright. Who the interests are and how they are going to be overcome turns out to be irrelevant to the melodrama.

What is important is that Joe has learned to trust in the same way Tom Holmes does in the final moments of *Heroes for Sale*. His rebellion has been replaced with faith in the New Deal so that when the Indians revolt, Joe quells the uprising:

> Burning the courthouse won't stop it. They will only send soldiers and shoot you down, and we don't want another massacre! . . . Now go back to your reservation where you belong. You won't get a square deal by breaking the white man's law.

In her discussion of the film, Karyn Kay maintains that this speech represents the most significant political statement in the movie:

> Joe is a pragmatist now. He seems to understand the futility of a sudden, unorganized uprising. Having passed through an initial stage of irrational aimless violence, he now embraces practical politics, the policies of the New Deal government. The only possible justice is working through the system.[1]

Whether dealing with Forgotten Men, workers, or ex-cons, the Warners' message was always the same.

Massacre was adapted from Robert Gessner's angry 1931 study of the nation's Indian reservations. Hoping to arouse as large a public as possible to action, Gessner welcomed the Warners' offer to film the book and wrote the original story himself. He incorporated many of the facts and situations from his 1931 study into a fictionalized drama, but "needless to say the story I wrote is not on the screen in its entirety."[2] The corporate powers and government bureaucracies which Gessner specifically indicts become anonymous; the Indians' revolt which "was the climax of my story: an oppressed people revolting" is undermined; and the harsh realism is twisted beyond recognition by such entertainment values as

> a rape motif, brake-screeching pursuits, a scarred maiden, a torture chamber, the hero shot by the villain and a sunset ending over the Grand Canyon with the heroine in the hero's arms while war chiefs on white horses ride thundering in the background.

Gessner was left with the vague hope that the limited social realism "slipped" into Hollywood's "bourgeois form" may have some impact on public opinion since the movies reach such a large audience.

While Gessner's aims were revolutionary, Warners had a more pragmatic political goal. Karyn Kay suggests that Warners too was trying to sway public opinion: the film was released as the New Deal's Howard–Wheeler Indian Rights Bill was being prepared. However, just as Warners' *Massacre* is a watered-down version of Gessner's original, so the final bill was compromised into ineffectuality. Neither the film nor the New Deal effectively helped the Indian cause; Joe's faith in the system has not been vindicated.

There was no chance of Warners' other ethnic opus provoking change. *Bordertown*'s main concern is not the Chicanos' oppression but a turgid melodrama around the hero's trial for a murder really committed by an insane Bette Davis.[3] What social comment there is acts as a sedative against revolt. Again the individual hero moves from a discovery of oppression to initial revolt against the system to reconciliation.

Johnny Ramirez begins as an eager idealist but soon learns that the American Dream is not open to Chicanos. After working his way through night school, his law practice fails because his people are too poor to afford a lawyer. When he does get his big chance in court, Johnny is defeated by a smooth-talking upper-class shyster who insults the Chicano. Angered, Johnny assaults the lawyer and is debarred by the presiding judge: "Frankly, you don't deserve to be a lawyer. Once a ruffian always a ruffian. You don't know any better and you can never change." A bitter Johnny traces his downfall to his ethnic background and social class: the other lawyer won "because he had a million dollar education and I have a five and ten cent one." Against the advice of his padre (Robert Barrat)—"Remember the virtue of our people: patience"—and the wishes of his mother, Johnny departs on a search for wealth and success.

Just as Joe had prospered only when he was not among his own people but competing as a white man in the white man's world, so Johnny finally works his way up the "steps of success." On a bordertown strip of nightclubs and gambling joints, he moves from bouncer to owner-manager of a club. His ambition still unsatisfied, he begins courting socialite Dale Elwell (Margaret Lindsay). Their sexual roles are functions of the stereotypes they hold of one another: to him, she represents "real class," all the status he has been denied; to her, he is "savage and primeval danger" and arouses the same physical excitement the women feel for Joe in *Massacre*. Their relationship can never be legitimized and she greets his marriage proposal with a haughty laugh: "It's impossible. I could never marry anyone like you, Savage."

The film ends with Johnny, disillusioned over the corruption and meanness of success, returning to his ghetto home. He says his confession to the priest, prays with Mama, and all three walk down the church aisle. The padre asks, "Well, Johnny, what are you going to do now?" and Johnny gives a familiar reply, "Come back and live among my own people where I belong." Whereas *Massacre* advocates change within the system, *Bordertown* hypothesizes that for a Mexican-American success is fruitless and undesirable, that true virtue lies in accepting life as it is. Johnny has learned the padre's lesson of patience and no longer holds impractical ambitions. *Bordertown* celebrates complacency and denigrates the desire for change as unchristian and detrimental.

The system breaks down. Shyster Warren William is the picture of cynicism. Even hung over, he can contemptuously waltz his way through the court, destroying a witness' credibility with a few clever questions and a charming smirk. *The Mouthpiece*, 1932.

The individual as victim. Ex-hero equals zero. Richard Barthelmess, one of Warners' many Forgotten Men who followed Paul Muni down poverty road. *Heroes for Sale*, 1933.

The search for alternatives. Back to the soil. King Vidor's cooperative community says a prayer of thanks for the earth's bounty. The film combines sentimental populism with an earnest radicalism. *Our Daily Bread*, 1934.

The Hollywood worker: leaders and followers. A befuddled Paul Muni (center) is duped by shyster agitator J. Carroll Naish (left) into leading a disastrous strike. They have all forgotten: "Half a loaf is better than none." *Black Fury*, 1935.

Life in the Hooverville. Well-dressed Happy Hobo, Spencer Tracy, proudly shows Loretta Young his home by the Hudson. *A Man's Castle*, 1933. Scruffy, hungry Okies mill about, angry at exploitative job contractors. *The Grapes of Wrath*, 1940. The correlation of style and message: the romance of the studio-lit Hooverville versus the documentary realism of the exterior location.

The criminal and social environment: The slum set looms over gangster Humphrey Bogart and delinquent Dead End Kids. None of them can escape their formative environment. *Dead End*, 1937.

Images of entrapment: We made him a criminal. Sylvia Sidney and
Henry Fonda in doomed flight from the social definitions that hem them
in and determine their fate. The environment as prison. *You Only Live
Once*, 1937.

Native fascists: The lynch mob. Spencer Tracy's view of Main Street
America from his jail cell. Good neighborliness is about to explode into
mob violence. *Fury*, 1936.

Native fascists: The Legion. Humphrey Bogart is about to join all the dupes who fall for the Legion's "100% Americanism" pitch. He's tired being pushed around by all those foreign "greaseballs" who are stealing the good jobs. *Black Legion,* 1937.

Native fascists: Edward Arnold (right), Frank Capra's ultimate villain, the ruthless tycoon whose lust for power makes him the enemy of free enterprise and the democratic way. Here he shows no mercy toward vanquished rival H. B. Warner. *You Can't Take It with You,* 1938.

International fascism. The Spanish Civil War as exotic backdrop for romance between peasant rebel Henry Fonda and reluctant enemy spy Madeleine Carroll. This rare example of Hollywood's "Premature Anti-Fascism" created an extraordinary stir at the time. *Blockade*, 1938.

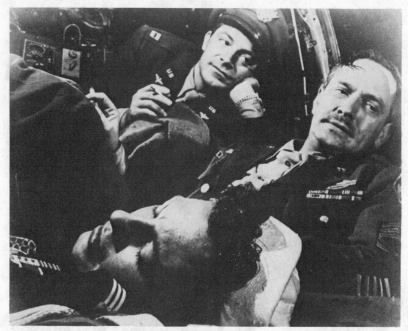

Nervous from the service. Three service branches, three economic
classes, three sets of problems. Dana Andrews, Frederic March and
Harold Russell head home to face civilian life. *The Best Years of Our
Lives,* 1946.

Passing: The White Negro. Could you ever guess that Mel Ferrer and
Beatrice Pearson are really the same race as their minister? Like Jeanne
Crain in *Pinky,* they are whites ruined by Negro blood rather than
blacks persecuted by a racist society. *Lost Boundaries,* 1949

Down, down, down. John Garfield descends to the bottom of the world to discover his brother's body. Cain and Abel meet Freud and Marx in the corruption of modern capitalist America. *Force of Evil*, 1949

Robert Walker swears on Helen Hayes' bible that he is not now, nor has he ever been, a Communist. A right-wing, comic book view of the Red menace preying on our innocent America, vulnerable because of its own liberalism. *My Son John*, 1952

Hollywood goes slumming. Rich movie director Joel McCrea is dressed by the costume department to go out and research the "real world" of poverty. Preston Sturges satirizes the paradoxes of the social problem film. With the fastidious Eric Blore as the disapproving butler. *Sullivan's Travels,* 1941

—PART III—

Fascism and War

—12—

NATIVE FASCISTS—
LYNCHING AND LEGIONS

As the decade progressed, fascism, both internal and international, superseded economic dislocation as the chief threat to the American way of life. During the middle years of the Depression, the European fascist regimes inspired many neofascist organizations throughout the United States. Lawrence Dennis, William Dudley Pelley and his Silver Shirts, and "General" Art Smith and his Khaki Shirts made a brief impact with their militaristic chauvinism. Far more prominent were the social salvationists, the "radio priest" Father Coughlin, Dr. Townsend, and especially Huey Long who until his assassination appeared to be a potential rival for FDR in the 1936 election. But without the charismatic Long and his powerful Louisiana machine, a third party coalition was convincingly trounced by FDR and the native fascists thereafter declined.

Hollywood, as always, was reluctant to take sides in a controversial issue. In the pre–New Deal days it had proffered vigilantism and dictatorship as a solution to the Depression, but by the mid-thirties the studios shied away from such a blatant stand. By 1934, the last of the protofascist cycle, *The President Vanishes*, balances an endorsement of extraconstitutional action with an attack on a Pelley-like group of militants. Although native fascism was at its height between 1934 and 1936, Hollywood remained silent. The widespread popularity of Sinclair Lewis's cautionary novel, *It Can't Happen Here* (1935), and the play based on it (1936) did not outweigh the studios' fears that its portrait of a Nazi-like American dictator was too radical.[1] Only after the American right had died down did the studios openly repudiate their earlier flirtations with fascistic solutions. In two films on lynching, *Fury* (1936) and *They Won't Forget* (1937), the mob is now condemned as an irrational, bigoted perverter of law and order; *Legion of Terror* (1936) and *Black Legion* (1936) view the members of vigilante groups as gullible dupes rather than responsible citizens cleansing society of corruption as in *This Day and Age* and *The Secret Six*; and Capra's films just before the war, *Mr. Smith Goes to Washington* (1939) and *Meet John Doe* (1941) warn against would-be dictators taking over the reins of government.

Lynching

Lynching in the thirties was of course not necessarily related to fascist movements but was a prominent issue in and of itself. The number of lynchings had reached a peak during the first half of the decade (sixty between 1930 and 1934),[2] provoking an all-out campaign to stop them. A total of 130 anti-lynching bills were presented in Congress between 1934 and 1940[3] and a nationwide public relations crusade produced pamphlets, lecture tours, mass meetings, and at least one art show ("An Art Commentary on Lynching" in early 1935).[4] National concern reached a peak with the introduction of the first important federal measure, the Wagner-Costigan Bill, in 1934 and the horrifying lynching of a young Florida Negro, Claude Neal, in 1935. Thereafter, the frequency of lynchings dramatically declined (in 1936 to eight from fifteen the year before)[5] and continued to diminish throughout the rest of the decade. So, with the appearance of *Fury* in 1936 and *They Won't Forget* in 1937, Hollywood joined the attack on mob violence at a time when it was still in the forefront of the public's consciousness.

Lynching does not always represent an overt political viewpoint, for a lynch mob is not a permanent organization in quest of political goals. Still, the numerous occurrences of lynch law throughout the thirties created a consistent pattern which was decidedly right-wing in character. The Depression lynch mob was generally made up of white, middle-class conservatives and was most prevalent in the South and California. It usually performed its deed with the tacit approval of local law agencies and acted against those deemed to be threats to the nationhood. The mobs' targets were the typical phobias of the right—blacks, Jews, Communists, and labor unionists—and their defenders in Congress were Southern conservatives.[6] On the other hand, lynching was perennially condemned by more progressive elements within society—Northern liberals, civil liberties groups, and racial organizations (especially the NAACP). There is, essentially, a distinct overlap between those sympathetic to fascism and those likely to join a lynch mob, between those opposed to fascism and those opposed to lynching.

Fury and *They Won't Forget* are not explicitly antifascist and yet, in their analysis of some of the sociocultural bases of mob mentality, they touch on many of the values at the root of fascism. In the same way as the pro-lynch film *This Day and Age* was implicitly fascist in its endorsement of mass conformism and "direct action," so the anti-lynch films are implicitly antifascist in their condemnation of such values. The malleable mobs of *Fury* and *They Won't Forget*, easily given over to righteous violence and repressive action against any kind of outsider, are a seed bed for fascism.

Fritz Lang's *Fury* concentrates on the formation of the lynch mob, precisely detailing the types who join the mob and their reasons for doing so. In evoking the transformation of simple, small-town folk into vicious, hate-filled murderers, Lang blasts open the myths of populist America and good neighborliness. Beneath the friendly veneer of the rural community, he reveals the unspoken frustrations, the boredom, ignorance, and violence waiting for a scapegoat against which to explode.

The familiar, reassuring Capra stereotypes are replaced by an ominous group of bigots, bullies, and gossips. The film rhythmically builds to a powerful tension as vignette after vignette charts the townspeople's relentless course toward lynch action. In the barbershop a small-minded local fumes against the radical ideas being taught in schools; a montage of hatchet-faced women shows the progress of a rumor which ends up condemning the kidnap suspect held in the town jail; in the hardware store, staunch advocates of law and order discuss the case amidst a display of knives, sickles, and ropes; a rock is pitched through the jail window and the sheriff catches a glimpse of figures scurrying out of sight; an out-of-towner taunts the local rowdies in the bar that "real men" would stick up for the kidnapped girl. The camera tracks down the street as a mob gradually grows and bears down on the jail. The camera movement is a dramatic visualization of how the mob's rage is focused on the prisoner in the jail.

Once the mob has gathered and faces the sheriff and his deputies, the violence escalates to a new plateau. Beginning with taunts at the sheriff ("I'm Popeye the sheriff man," a youth mimics), the mob's fury erupts into violence as they surge forward, overcome the guards, and break into the jail. Grins of almost orgiastic delight come across the people's faces while they construct a pyre of office furniture. Again Lang pinpoints telling details: a woman ecstatically hurls a torch to ignite the pyre; as the jail burns, another woman falls to her knees in evangelical frenzy; a mother holds her child up to get a better view; and a young boy chews ravenously into a hot dog. The crowd, their faces distorted by the dancing flames, watch their helpless victim as they would a parade or a movie. When the prisoner struggles frantically at his cell window, they sadistically hurl rocks to drive him back into the fire. With the belated arrival of the state militia, the mob scatters, but only after throwing dynamite into the flames to ensure the death of their victim. In this brilliantly constructed sequence, Lang has shown America in its most warped form. In the name of manhood, God, and law and order, the hypocritical townspeople have committed obscene brutalities. The populist myths stand decisively refuted.

As in *You Only Live Once*, Lang frames his social criticism in a larger context and the town's actions become symbolic of man's flawed nature. Just before the rumor ignites the community's hatreds, the barber talks about how all men are capable of committing violent crime:

> People get funny impulses. If y' resist 'em, you're sane; if y' don't, you're on the way to the nuthouse, or the pen . . . Would you b'lieve that in the twenty years I been strokin' this razor across throats here that many a time I've had a impulse to cut their Adam's apples wide open?

This theme receives its fullest play in the film's second half, after the mob scene. By having the kidnap suspect, Joe Wilson (Spencer Tracy), escape death (the dynamite blows the cell door open), Lang shows us that the lynch victim is as capable of hatred and murder as the lynch mob. Joe convinces his brothers to initiate legal proceedings against the lynchers while he remains in hiding, concealing his survival so that the citizens will be charged with murder. Supplying evidence to his brothers and listening to the trial over the radio, Joe gains a perverse satisfaction as he hears the defendants squirm in the face of the damning proof against them. Unable to continue the grim charade, one brother makes the point that the roles of victim and victimizer have been turned around. Joe castigates him for "feelin' sorry for those lynchers" and his brother protests, "You're as bad as them! You're lynching me!"

Again Lang makes the audience feel responsible through subtle manipulation of our identification with the characters. Much of the lynch scene is presented from Joe's and his fiancée Katherine's (Sylvia Sidney) points of view: his panic as he sees through the bars of his cell window the mob gathering on the street; her hysteria at the sight of Joe trapped in the inferno, surrounded by frenzied murderers. Our outrage at the townspeople naturally supports Joe's plans to prosecute and bring them to justice. Lang plays upon this, showing the community enter a conspiracy of smug silence, refusing to testify against the lynchers in order to protect their friends and the reputation of the town. Therefore we delight when Joe arranges through his brothers to screen newsreels of the lynching which unquestionably indict his would-be murderers. But as the trial proceeds and the citizens of Strand gradually break down and beg forgiveness, they become humanized and it is Joe who seems to be the hate-filled monster. Having felt the same desire for revenge as Joe, having gone along with his plan of vengeance, we too are guilty of the lynch mentality.[7] Our culpability is further emphasized by the subtle parallel between our response to the lynching and that of an audience in the film which views the newsreel. After his escape, Joe bitterly describes a theater he hid in: "The place was packed. They liked it. They got a big kick out o' seein' a man burned to death. A *big* kick."

The second half of the film, by reversing the roles of victim and victimizer, is brilliant in conception but does not quite work dramatically. The buildup to the lynching is too powerful to follow, making the trial anticlimactic. Furthermore, Joe's survival strains credulity and undermines the whole first half—the lynching turns out not to be a real lynching after all. But the worst sin is the happy ending which almost completely nullifies the universal guilt premise. Prodded by Katherine, Joe makes a last-minute appearance in the courtroom, thereby saving the lynchers from a murder rap and freeing himself of guilt. His final speech condemns lynch law, claiming it has destroyed in him "a belief in justice and an idea that men were civilized, a feeling of pride that this country of mine was different from all others" at the same time as it points toward the absolution of all parties: "Those people were wrong . . . But maybe it's done them some good. I don't know. All I know is that the only way I could go on living was to come here today." The film ends with Joe and Katherine happily embracing in front of the judge and, as Robert Giroux of *The Nation* remarked, we leave the theater satisfied:

> Nobody's hurt; Joe and his girl are ready to marry and start life over, and the lynchers have had a big scare. The whole business is, I suppose, just one of those messes which human beings are always getting in and out of.[8]

Whereas *You Only Live Once*'s ending made us question our own role in Joan and Eddie's murder, here Lang lets us off the hook. If Joe is not guilty, then neither are we.

If the Langian pessimism is compromised by an MGM-imposed happy ending (the director detests the final embrace as "coy"[9]), *Fury* remains a minor masterpiece. Warners' *They Won't Forget* is allowed to be much more cynical in its final analysis, and while it never achieves the power of *Fury*'s best sequences, it is still a compelling portrait of lynch-law mentality. Like *Fury*, its main strength lies in its depiction of the small town and the transformation of the self-righteous citizenry into a lynch mob. It again captures the sense of boredom and frustration that makes lynching a perverted form of entertainment, showing a crowd gathering in the square outside the courthouse to cheer on the prosecutor as he railroads a schoolteacher to his execution.

A major difference between the two films is their stress on the responsibility of social authority and the media for the lynchings. Lang, concentrating on larger themes of universal malevolence, is satisfied with a few pointed illustrations: a Chamber of Commerce type gloats over the publicity of Joe's arrest; the governor delays sending the militia lest it offend the townsfolk during an election year; the press view the lynching in terms of saleable sensationalism—"What a shot this is . . . We'll sweep the country with this stuff." In *They Won't Forget*, the spontaneous passion of the mob is placed in a much more political milieu. Here, the mob is a manipulated agent of community leaders and officialdom who opportunistically inflame and exploit the people for personal gain. Claude Rains' District Attorney Griffin is a cynical Machiavelli, using the rape-murder of schoolgirl Lana Turner to further his own career. He stage-manages the entire event, first, indicting the suspect—Northern schoolteacher Hale (Edward Norris)—not on concrete evidence but on the fact that it will fan North–South factionalism in the town and generate greater publicity in the case. His courtroom tactics are flamboyant, tacitly encouraging press sensationalism and ultimately the lynching itself.

The press is much more malevolent than in *Fury*. They do not merely sensationalize the case but convict the teacher before the trial, using the headlines to further arouse the lynch spirit in the town. The reporters are predators, tricking the distraught Mrs. Hale into giving personal information about her husband's dislike of the town and then misrepresenting him as an enemy of the South. When she faints during their visit, they scavenge her personal belongings to find newsworthy items.

More so than *Fury*, *They Won't Forget* gives us a sense of the parallels between lynch mob mentality and fascism. Both the lyncher and the fascist follower are prone to manipulative leadership, their irrationality controlled by powers who use them for their own ends. Nor does the film underestimate the success of these powers. Griffin achieves his stated goals, gaining both his conviction of Hale and statewide prominence. The one honest official, the liberal Governor who commutes Hale's sentence, sees his political career dishonored when the mob spurns his decision, pulls Hale off a train and hangs him.

The film's finale is much more consistent than the final embrace in *Fury*. In a rather ambivalent scene, Mrs. Hale confronts Griffin with his guilt, but Griffin remains unrepentant, legally clear of the whole affair. He offers her a token check in recompense and promises to bring the lynchers to trial himself. He has acquired power because he lacks conscience and is willing to use any means to achieve his ends. When his campaign manager ponders whether Hale really was guilty, Griffin calmly muses, "I wonder."

Both films are really generalized warnings against the blind mass conformism which overrides judicial and governmental institutions and, especially in the case of *They Won't Forget*, against the dangerous manipulators of that conformism. Where both films fall down, however, is in their failure to confront the more specific causes of lynching. The only data to indicate that lynching is not an isolated phenomenon is a brief speech made by the prosecuting DA in *Fury*: "Your Honor, in the last forty-nine years, 4,176 human beings have been lynched by hanging, burning, cutting in this proud land of ours . . . a lynching about every four days!" While both films cry out against the bigotry of the mob, neither pays more than token attention to the central motivation behind lynching, racism.[10] A liberal lawyer in *They Won't Forget* claims that "hatred, fear, and prejudice" are witnesses to the Hale case, but those hatreds are defined as North–South animosity. Although the film is loosely based on the case of Leo Frank, a Northern Jew, anti-Semitism is never mentioned in the film. The Leo Frank character is made over into the WASPish Robert Hale and the film opens with a timorous disclaimer of its origins. The references to the hatred of the Negro are mere asides. When news of the murder first filters through the town everybody just assumes that the Negro janitor (Clinton Rosemund) is the killer. Even before the police accuse him, the Negro, trained by experience, breaks down and cries that he is innocent. But when Griffin passes the Negro by as too commonplace a suspect, the film defines the most volatile of all hatreds as sectional, not racial. *Fury* does not even make oblique reference to racism. According to Fritz Lang, Louis B. Mayer censored his attempts to include scenes of blacks reacting to the trial:

> I had a scene showing a group of Negroes—an old man, a very beautiful buxom girl, and a young Negro with two children—sitting in a dilapidated Ford car in the South listening on the radio to a transcription of a lynching trial. As the state attorney spoke about the high incidence of lynching in the U.S. each year, I had the old Negro just nod his head silently without a word. Mayer had this scene, and others like it, removed because at that time I think even he was convinced that Negroes should be shown only as bootblacks, or carhops, or menials of some description.[11]

Although *They Won't Forget* hints at the role of the landed gentry in lynchings and *Fury*'s barbershop bigot fumes against radicals in the schools, neither film really discusses other common, nonracial causes for lynching. *Fury* is based on a California lynching case, but makes no reference to the political motivations of the vigilantism so rife in that state throughout the thirties. Indeed, the mobs were made up of the landowning class and their targets were the same as those the studios knock in their films: labor organizers and supposed Communists. While such writers as Carey McWilliams (*Factories in the Field*) and Steinbeck equated this activity with fascism, Lang would never have been allowed to make any such connection (coincidentally enough, he had just recently fled Nazi Germany). Only *The Grapes of Wrath*, by showing mob action against the Okie Hooverville and the murder of Casy by the landowners' thugs, would hint at the political causes of lynching.

Even when taking the films at their own level, as discussions of the ethics of lynch law, the two films fall prey to a basic flaw. Both Joe Wilson and Robert Hale are innocent (or so it is assumed in the latter's case though never actually stated). This deflects the condemnation of lynching itself, no matter what the status of the victim, to a condemnation based on the fear that the mob could be mistaken. The Formula, by demanding good guy heroes, prohibits a more subtle argument. Lang tried to subvert the conventions by transforming his innocent hero into a guilty monster and making the lynchers sympathetic, but *Fury* still does not match Lang's earlier *M* (1931) for lack of compromise. There the protagonist is guilty of a series of brutal child murders, yet Lang still denounces the lynch mob activities of the criminal underground who hunt him down as well as the capital punishment the state would administer. Lang was aware of the limitation of his American film and claims that to make a true picture of lynching "one should have a white woman raped by a colored man, and with this as a basis, still prove lynching is wrong."[12]

Despite their shortcomings, both *Fury* and *They Won't Forget* strongly denounced social repression at a time when it was becoming increasingly clear that a violent totalitarianism was overwhelming all human and social laws. The link between the anti-lynch and antifascist argument is made explicit in two wartime films, *Talk of the Town* (1942) and *The Ox-Bow Incident* (1943). Both films conform to the conventions of the earlier films: their analysis of lynching is confined to the small town and to victims who are both innocent and nonracial (although one is Mexican in *Ox-Bow*, his nationality is not at issue). But here the attacks against mob violence are more directed toward affirmation of American justice and civilization as safeguards against barbaric tyranny.

Talk of the Town is pointedly ideological: its victim of the mob's wrath, Leopold Dilg (Cary Grant), represents free speech while his chief detractor, industrialist Andrew Holmes (Charles Dingle), stands for autocracy. Dilg has criticized Holmes, denounced his factory as an unsafe firetrap, and attacked his political domination of the town. Holmes in turn has burned down his own factory for the insurance and now, utilizing his complete control over the press and the courts, has framed Dilg for arson and aroused public opinion against him. These two elements established, a third figure enters the scene, Professor Michael Lightcap (Ronald Colman), symbolizing reason and justice. Through Lightcap's transformation from a detached, ivory-tower "library philosopher" who refuses to get involved to a crusading defender of Dilg's rights, the film affirms the ability of the system to deal with the threat to free speech.

The Ox-Bow Incident, an allegory set in the American West of the 1880s, is closer to *Fury* in that it concentrates on the types who make up the lynch posse. But unlike the irrational mobs in *Fury* and *They Won't Forget*, the posse conducts itself in a much more reasoned fashion. Although their violence may be the result of moronic ignorance or self-righteousness, the posse members still act in a premeditated manner. Theirs is not a spontaneous outburst but a conscious usurpation of individuals' legal rights.

Where both wartime films vary the most from their Depression counterparts is in their final thematic statements. The films' liberal redeemers summarize the central message that law is the basic requisite of freedom and civilization. In *Talk of the Town*, Lightcap rushes into the courtroom with the real arsonist just as the mob is closing in on the defenseless Dilg and makes his appeal to the mob; in *Ox-Bow*, Gil Carter (Henry Fonda) reads a letter written by one of the dead men to the lynchers. Both Lightcap's editorial and the letter stress the value of law as the basis of freedom and the need to be ever ready to defend it against the tyranny of lynch mobs. To Lightcap, the law is what "makes you free men in a free country." The world is "crying out for this very law" and "you ought to guard it." Likewise, the cowpuncher expounds that man "can't take the law into his hands and hang people without hurting everybody in the world" because law is "the very conscience of humanity."

In each case, the redeemers and the lynch mobs learn from their experiences and it is evident that they have become immunized against further outbreaks of inquisition. At *Talk of the Town*'s conclusion, Lightcap assumes a seat in the Supreme Court from where he will keep a vigilant eye out for any further injustice. In *Ox-Bow*, all the lynchers penitently contribute to a collection for the victim's widow and there is even the intimation that Gil, upon delivering the letter and money to the woman, will stay on with her "to look out for his kids."

Again the central flaw of the films' argument lies in the victims' innocence. The lesson the citizens learn does not spring from their revulsion of lynching itself, but from the horror of having gone after the wrong man. In fact, *Talk of the Town* seems to endorse lynch-like actions when they are used against a real villain. The methods Lightcap resorts to in exposing Holmes are not qualitatively different from those of the corrupt industrialist. He beats up and kidnaps Clyde Bracken (Tom Tyler), Holmes' villainous plant foreman, and forces him under threat of physical violence to confess to the arson. He justifies his actions with a casual "Sometimes there are extenuating circumstances." In the courtroom, Lightcap wields a gun to quell the mob and then uses his smooth oratory to sway them over to his side. The only difference between Lightcap and Holmes is one of morality. Lightcap has the license to go outside the law because he's on the side of good. In short, the ends justify the means; the downfall of Holmes is more important than the principles of law.

Two postwar lynch films, *Intruder in the Dust* (1949) and *The Lawless* (1950) deemphasize antifascism in favor of a now timely antiracism. The would-be victims in both films are racial, a black in the former and a Chicano in the latter. The films adhere to many of the cycle's established motifs—the innocent victim, the small town which is no populist paradise, the community's carnival atmosphere in *Intruder* and the inflammatory press in *The Lawless*. *Intruder* ends, like *Talk of the Town* and *Ox-Bow Incident*, with a sanctimonious message. Chick (Claude Jarman, Jr.) and his Uncle John (David Brian) resolve that everything will be all right, that Lucas Beauchamp (Juano Hernandez) is still there as a reminder to all of the lynching that nearly took place. Uncle John observes Lucas walking proudly down the main street, "There goes my conscience." Chick corrects him, "There goes *our* conscience, Uncle John."

There are however significant variations that distinguish these two films. Lucas is a tall, dignified hero whose real crime is that he's uppity, that he refuses to live up to the white man's subservient image of his race. Paul Rodriguez (Lalo Rios), the Chicano in *The Lawless*, is a frightened youth whose flight from the police is distorted into a series of major crimes by racist witnesses and the most callous press since *They Won't Forget*. When Paul is finally captured, a woman reporter comforts his mother ("I'm a mother too") and then phones in an inflammatory report to her paper: "Rodriguez stood there . . . Mud-covered. Sullen. Cruel. A trapped animal. . . ."

The Lawless adds some fine twists to the genre's conventions. The town's liberal newspaper editor, Larry Wilder (Macdonald Carey), bears some resemblance to redeemer figures such as Michael Lightcap, Gil Carter, and Uncle John, moving from a stance of noninvolvement to one of commitment against the mob. But Larry is a more politicized man than his predecessors, his noninvolvement a conscious rejection of his previous activism as a crusading New York reporter. However, the events surrounding Paul soon shatter his hopes for peaceful neutrality, and he reluctantly takes a stand using his paper to organize a defense fund for Paul and then helping the sheriff sneak him out of town and the reach of the mob. But this reluctant redeemer himself becomes a victim of the mob. Since they cannot get at Paul himself, the lynchers attack his defender by destroying the newspaper office.

It is in the after-effects of the lynching where *The Lawless* differs most from the other lynch films. Larry's speech to the crowd is not a cure-all editorial but a bitter admission of defeat. Unlike *Intruder*, only a handful of people have really learned anything. After a brief period of despair, Larry realizes that there is no escaping social responsibility and resolves to keep up the fight. But having identified himself with the Chicano cause, he has himself become a member of the oppressed class. The only place where he can start his paper again is with the small press that prints a Chicano community circular. The film offers the hope of a redeemer figure, but realistically places him outside or, at best, on the edge of the system. He approaches the primitive printing press and turns for help: "Can you show me how to start?"

Legions

The prejudices and frustrations which exploded into mob action in the lynch films are channeled into cryptofascist organizations in *Legion of Terror* and *Black Legion*. The films are based on the Ku Klux Klan-like Black Legion which was formed in Michigan, Indiana, and Ohio during the mid-thirties. The Legion was a secret organization made up mostly of unskilled workers who donned hoods and robes and indulged in terrorist acts against such "un-American foreigners" as immigrants, Jews, and Catholics. Its ritualistic murder of WPA worker Charles Poole near Detroit in the spring of 1936 gained the Legion not only national prominence but also the attention of police investigators who quickly put an end to the organization.[13]

Like *The President Vanishes*, whose treatment of the Grey Shirts foreshadowed them, the two Black Legion films concentrate on the bigotry and violence of vigilante groups and almost completely ignore their sociopolitical nature. Hollywood makes them appear like lynch mobs meeting once a week under the leadership of fanatics and racketeers. Although this image is not entirely inconsistent with actuality, the films refuse to credit the right-wing groups of the thirties with any political aims or programs. Rather than admit that these movements grew out of discontent, frustration, and the desire for radical change, Hollywood makes them into isolated terrorist gangs.

The President Vanishes' treatment of the Grey Shirts serves as an important precedent, establishing many of the conventions through which fascism was to be handled. The film refers to an actual fascist movement—William Pelley and his Silver Shirts, at their height in 1933–34 —but only superficially exploits the movement as a pretext for violence. The Grey Shirts are seen in a vacuum, not arising from any kind of social need and aspiring to only one political end—power. Their leader, Lincoln Lee (Edward Ellis) is a wild-eyed maniac who sees himself as a Christlike messiah fulfilling his destiny. Although Pelley also believed himself to be "inspirationally instructed" and seems to have been every bit as crazy as Lee, he nevertheless represented and articulated a particular political viewpoint, closely modeled on Nazism (i.e., "the forcible removal of the Jew from office"). Pelley did train a militia, but his main efforts went into publishing and disseminating literature in order to spread the word and create a national movement. With Lee, the focus is exclusively military. His group beats up any opposition to their prowar campaign while really trying to generate so much chaos that they will be able to seize power.

Lee is a megalomaniac patriot ("Save America's Honor" is his battle cry) backed by big business and political shysters. This is the equation —a radical nationalist movement backed by Wall Street—which, Raymond Gram Swing predicted, a year after the film's release, would doom democracy in the United States.[14] But by 1936–37 the threat from an internal fascist coup had diminished so that the later films replaced Lee's nationwide military organization with purely local vigilante activities. Rather than center on the fanatical leader, the Legion films focus on the duped followers. Like the lynch films, they serve as admonitions to common folk against the menace to civil rights in their hometown communities instead of alarums over plots in high places.

In most other ways, the Legion films follow *The President Vanishes'* lead. Again they base their stories on an actual organization but concentrate on its violence rather than its politics. In both films one-hundred-dred-percent Americanism is nothing but a ploy which the racketeer leaders use to attract members and make themselves richer. In *Black Legion*, the Legion heads' talk of a "bigger and better Legion" sounds like ambitious salesmen seeking to increase their revenues through uniform and gun sales. The *Legion of Terror* is similarly run by a crooked editor and racketeer, so that the film's final editorial against being duped by the Legion schemes sounds like a warning for consumer protection. As before, there is some basis in fact for this portrayal. The real Legion did have some elements of racketeering and its political ambitions were vague, restricted mostly to terrorism. Yet by the mid-thirties the organization had started to move into local Michigan politics and by 1936 nearly one hundred of its members were in public office in Pontiac and surrounding Oakland County (including a city treasurer, a member of the legislature, and top police, fire, municipal, and judicial officers[15]). The murder of Charles Poole was prompted by his opposition to a Legion candidate in the upcoming election. Similar murders of other political opponents (the municipal president of Ecorse and a Highland Park newspaper publisher) were planned until police investigations broke up the Legion. In contrast, *Black Legion*'s version of the Poole murder is completely apolitical. Ed Jackson is shot by a panicky Humphrey Bogart when he runs off to inform on the Legion, not ritualistically murdered for defying the Legion's political goals.

Still, *Black Legion* does make a genuine attempt to study the psychology of the men attracted by the cryptofascist ideology. Frank Taylor is a worker whose ambitions to be promoted and fulfill the American Dream are frustrated. His dissatisfaction needs a scapegoat and the Legion provides him with one. By assigning blame to "outsiders" who he is told are depriving native-born Americans of their jobs, Frank does not have to confront the fact of his own limitations. But these limitations are exclusively personal, not social. It is Frank's lack of intelligence and his failure to apply himself which lose him his promotion. Even without it, he lives well and has a steady, decent job. His complaint over the promotion is, then, rather minor and it is entirely his own gullibility which leads him into the exploitative arms of the Legion. He is a disappointed sucker being conned by clever racketeers.

In reality, of course, social circumstances were an important factor in the rise of the Legion. According to David Chalmers in *Hooded Americanism*,[16] most of its members were migrants from the hill country of Mississippi, Kentucky, and Tennessee who were "generally ill-adjusted to the monotony and discipline of factory life" and "too uneducated and unskilled to hope for anything better than insecure, low-paid, seasonal work." Unlike Frank Taylor, most Legionnaires could hardly partake in America's abundance and what began in the early thirties as a social club whose members could exchange leads on jobs soon became a sect resorting to violence against the "un-Americans" who stole all the good jobs. Its earliest success was in regaining jobs for two members by threatening their employer with violence unless he took them back. Thus the Legion was a reaction, however bizarre, to the Depression. Like most fascist groups, its major appeal was the reduction of the almost incomprehensible variables of economic breakdown to easily identifiable targets.

Just as they have distorted the nature of the problem, so the two films easily resolve it by capturing the gangster ringleaders. *Legion of Terror*'s hero (Bruce Cabot) arrives with the State militia who shoot down the escaping chieftains and round up the members. Frank Taylor finally turns against his exploiters and gives evidence which leads to the arrest and imprisonment of his fellow legionnaires. Similar circumstances did destroy the Legion, with the Poole murder case leading to the revelation of all its activities, sending eleven members to prison and removing almost one hundred legionnaires from the Oakland County payroll. But the deep-seated disaffection lingered, only to be gradually placated by the war and subsequent prosperity.

—13—

FRANK CAPRA'S
SUPER-SHYSTERS
AND LITTLE PEOPLE

The little man . . . quietly said: "Mr. Capra, you're a coward."
"A what?"
"A coward, sir. But infinitely sadder—you are an offense to God.
You hear that man in there?" Max had turned on the radio. . . .
Hitler's raspy voice came shrieking out of it. "That evil man is des-
perately trying to poison the world with hate. How many can he talk
to? 15 million—20 million? And for how long?—20 minutes? You,
sir, can talk to *hundreds* of millions, for 2 hours—and in the dark.
The talents you have, Mr. Capra, are not your own, *not* self-acquired.
God gave you those talents. . . . And when you don't *use* the gifts
God blessed you with—you are an offense to God—and to humanity.
Good day, sir."
. . . In less than 30 seconds he had ripped me open with the truth:
exposed the fetid pus of my vanities.[1]

Thus, in a passage from his autobiography reminiscent of one of his
own movies a big, successful Hollywood director is suddenly shown
the light by a "little man." Frank Capra accepts his responsibilities with
messianic fervor: "to totally commit my talents . . . to the service of
man . . . my films had to *say* something." The message of Capra's films
was to be "the rebellious cry of the individual against being trampled
to an ort by massiveness—mass production, mass thought, mass education, mass politics, mass wealth, mass conformity." Capra was to champion the little man against the Hitlers of the modern world, against all
the forces within society which would compartmentalize, stifle, and

179

oppress the individual. Between 1936 and 1941 Capra made a remarkable series of films—*Mr. Deeds Goes to Town, You Can't Take It with
You* (1938), *Mr. Smith Goes to Washington* (1939), and *Meet John
Doe* (1941)—the most popular and most critically analyzed films of
the social problem genre.

Capra the committed filmmaker did not forget the lessons he had
learned as Capra the master of movie entertainment; he now simply
placed his characters and stories within a political context. His purpose
was to "integrate ideals and entertainment into a meaningful tale," so
that the films are not so much about politics as they are about people
whose crises reflect political viewpoints. By thoroughly engaging us in
the lives of his characters (Capra's forte as a director), he engages us
in his social and political concerns.

Even today, despite material that is naively optimistic and often downright corny, these films continue to have a strong impact on audiences.
Capra describes their universal appeal in summarizing *Mr. Deeds*: "He
was the living symbol of the deep rebellion in every human heart—a
growing resentment against being compartmentalized. And when Mr.
Deeds routed the mass predators, using only his simple weapons of
honesty, wit, and courage—audiences not only laughed, they cheered!
Longfellow had struck a blow for their *own* individual dignity and di-
vinity." The filmmaker's belief in his material transcends the limitations
of his *Saturday Evening Post* sentimentalities and gives the films a power
that critical qualifications cannot quell. More than any other major
director, Capra took the Formula to heart, but in so doing created his
own unique cinema style. Adapting the conventions of the early thirties
problem film genre, he transformed the shyster film into a full-blown
study of American fascism. We have already seen how the big businessmen with their kept politicians and all-powerful press were established
as Hollywood scapegoats for the Depression. In the series of films from
Mr. Deeds to *Meet John Doe*, Capra shifted the image of the omnipotent tycoon from root cause of the Depression to overt menace to
democracy. Corruption became less a personal quest for money and
more a conscious conspiracy for power. Capra's super-shysters moved
from exploiting the political system for their own economic ends to
seeking its overthrow.

There were precedents for this portrait of shyster-as-fascist in earlier
non-Capra films. In *Washington Masquerade* and *Washington Merry-
Go-Round*, both made in 1932, the government was under the thumb
of powerful business interests and had to be rescued by a man of the
people. Two years later, *The President Vanishes* depicted a super-capitalist plot against the government: using their control of Congress, the
judiciary, and the press, a cabal of munitions manufacturers attempt to

install their own puppet in the White House. They even back a paramilitary fascist group, the Grey Shirts, to suppress any open opposition to their plans. Although none of these corporate bigshots articulate any ideology or are concerned with changing the political system per se, they are fascistic in their subversion of the democratic process and their contempt for the people. It was Capra who gave an ideological basis to the monopoly capitalists' action. But, most important, Capra created a dramatic structure that shapes the audience experience of his films to parallel the argument he is making. The films make their case on an emotional level by thoroughly involving the viewer in the processes of decision-making taken by the characters. No matter how cynical the viewer is, by the end one wants to believe in the films' faith and hope. One is almost converted by Capra and that is his greatest achievement as a committed filmmaker.

Conversion is a central motif within the films' structure. It is the experience most of the characters undergo along with the audience. Capra's three classic comic heroes,[2] Longfellow Deeds, Jefferson Smith, and Long John Willoughby/John Doe (Gary Cooper) are all Christ figures who enter the temple of the Philistines, are crucified, and then rise again through the supplication of the little people to smite their malefactors. Deeds goes to the cynical big city, Smith to the corrupt Senate, and Doe right into the temple of moneyed power, all carrying with them the virtues of honesty and fair play Capra associates with small-town America. There is a double conversion in operation here: first, the cynics, city folk, and hangers-on (and we in the audience) must be converted to the cause of the hero; then the hero himself, passing through a deep moral crisis of doubt and near suicide (the crucifixions can never be fully consummated), must be converted back to the cause by his newly won disciples.

Built into this basic plot are the audience's own cynicism and doubts. Our relationship with each of the heroes (and with the Vanderhoff/ Sycamore family in *You Can't Take It with You*) begins ambivalently. We are laughing at as much as with Deeds, Smith, and the John Doe PR gimmick. Deeds' antics with tuba playing, fire engines, and doughnut-eating horses, the Vanderhoffs' outrageous life style, and Jeff Smith's awestruck Washington sightseeing and adolescent clumsiness are all comic idiosyncrasies which on the one hand are endearing but on the other quite laughable. And congregated around the hero are a collection of wonderfully tough-minded, wisecracking big-city types whose sarcastic jibes at him reflect our own initial response to his apparent gaucheness.

Thus the audience's own resistance to the hero's sentimental goodness is accommodated within the story and given full expression. It is then that loyalties begin to shift, that the hero's moral superiority becomes apparent. The shift is managed through each hero's romance with a goodhearted city girl who is the first to recognize his true worth. Reporter Babe Bennet in *Deeds* and secretary Clarissa Saunders in *Smith* (both played by Jean Arthur) begin as manipulators of the hero, the former for a highly popular satiric newspaper series on the bumpkin millionaire and the latter to keep the junior Senator in the dark on the matter of graft. Very quickly, both fall in love with their prey and begin to see in him the ethical qualities they have abandoned in the big city rat-race and, by refusing to compromise themselves any further, they become the first converts to the hero's cause. In *Doe*, it is reporter Ann Mitchell (Barbara Stanwyck) who first takes the Doe philosophy seriously, whose fervor inspires Long John and turns the PR ruse into a legitimate idea.

This shift in sympathy is furthered by the interaction of the cynics, some of whom convert to the hero's cause and some whose wisecracks and scheming by now are turning sour and cruel. There are scenes where the hero's naiveté is not the butt of the comedy but suddenly refreshing, even superior, when set against the cynics—Deeds with the opera board and the poets, Grandpa Vanderhoff with Henderson the Internal Revenue Man (Charles Lane), Smith with his filibuster.

An illustration of this conversion process is John Doe's first radio appearance, a hokey speech perfectly typed as "Santa Claus socialism."[3] Yet the content of the broadcast is secondary to the dynamics of the scene, which absorb the speech's sentimentalities into a key dramatic event. Capra begins by ridiculing the whole affair and then, by refocusing on Long John's moral dilemma, turns it all into a very emotional and sincere statement of the film's point of view. Before the broadcast, the Doe idea is still a gimmick to everyone but Ann: her editor Harry Connell (James Gleason) has Long John photographed with midgets, representative of the "little people"; a rival newspaper offers John an envelope of money if he goes on the air and exposes the entire thing as a fraud; and his hobo friend, "the Colonel" (Walter Brennan) continues his campaign to get Long John away from all these "heelots" for some fishing. But amidst all the hoopla, Capra provides a quiet moment between Ann and John, shot mostly in closeup on her. As she hands John the speech and gives him a pep talk, there is a new intensity in her tone. She has invested the radio speech with the uplifting, populist philosophy of her late father and has created a John Doe in his image, a John Doe she now takes very seriously. The tension then sits not in the speech itself but with what course of action Long John will take.

Throughout the speech, Gary Cooper takes us through some wonderfully modulated transitions in Long John's thinking. He begins comically, all vulnerable clumsiness and confusion, intimidated by the contrived hype of the broadcast, by an uncooperative microphone, and by his own wavering voice. There are cutaways which telegraph the two poles of moral choice for Long John: on the one hand there is the exasperated Colonel, the skeptical Connell and the man with the pay-off envelope; and on the other there is Ann, concentrating fervently on John as if willing him through the speech. The rhythm of these cutaways, as Barbara Stanwyck's eyes moisten and as even Connell, with some wonderful doubletakes from Gleason, registers pleasant surprise, as Cooper finds his voice and wins over the audience, involves us in a dramatic event in which Long John undergoes the first step in his moral development. Capra then adds one more element. He cuts away to D. B. Norton (Edward Arnold), the financier publisher behind the Doe stunt, listening with calculating malevolence in his mansion. On top of all this action rides the content of the speech itself (about the power of the little people in the world when they all pull together) which, because it is delivered within such an emotional, moral context, is given a greater impact and increased credibility.

The broadcast scene not only moves the action forward, incorporating all of the major characters and beginning the definition of their eventual relationship to one another, but also introduces the Doe philosophy as a serious theme. With this scene, the whole film shifts gears, moving the audience closer to an acceptance of Capra's populism before quickly pulling back. Capra momentarily pricks the dramatic intensity of the speech, as John, unable to reconcile the meaning of Ann's words with his role as a hired fake, bolts out of the radio studio and heads for the open road with the Colonel where he refutes the whole event with comic misanthropy. But a few scenes later, John is recognized in Millville by his fans and forced to confront the effect he has had on their lives. With this scene, John fully accepts the truth of the Doe philosophy and we are moved a little further along in our own conversion process.

In all these films, this process climaxes when the hero himself despairs and must be won back to the cause. Behind his disillusionment are the negative cynical attitudes which had in the beginning been played as comic irreverence. In the end, his apparent or actual betrayal by all those he trusted—Cedar, Senator Paine, D. B. Norton, and most important, Babe, Clarissa, and Ann—threatens to destroy the hero and with him the only positive ethic the films have proffered. What makes Capra's films so strong and rousing is the final conversion scenes when all the cynics and little people rally around their hero in a dramatic demonstration of his, and Capra's, philosophy. The sentimentality of these cries is secondary to the climactic force they bear within the dramatic structure, since they must inspire the hero's resurrection and propel the action to its final conclusion. When Deeds finally speaks for himself at the hearing, when Smith begins his filibuster, and when Doe takes Ann in his arms and turns away from the ledge, the action itself is primary and exhilarating, the forces of good rising renewed against insurmountable odds. Because the action and the populist ethos are so closely tied together, our involvement in the story necessitates (if only temporarily) our support of that ethos.

But if Capra can convince us on an emotional level, he cannot do so on an intellectual level. The weakest parts of the trilogy are those that try to interpret populism in concrete dramatic terms. The heroes themselves are of course walking embodiments of the ethos, so well conceived and performed that the screen personae of Cooper and Stewart were shaped (in Cooper's case, reshaped) by these roles. But as soon as Capra attempts to show what the heroes embody beyond their own personalities in larger political terms, he falls back on symbolism that is maudlin and unconvincing. Deeds' innocence and Smith's idealism are rooted in their small-town origins. While the concept of the farm boy in the big city is basic to the dramatic conflict, it does not follow that such small-town innocence is always morally superior and could ever be the basis of a viable political alternative. The dramatic device does not translate as a credible value system. Moral principles and populism are not necessarily synonymous; to do the right thing does not require that you come from a small town or have a blind allegiance to hackneyed symbols of America.

Deeds sentimentalizes over Grant's Tomb, Smith over the Lincoln Memorial and Capitol Dome, and Long John over baseball and the little people. This naive, simple-minded patriotism passes through major crises in the films that all but destroy it. In the end, the heroes may have evolved into a more sophisticated understanding of social and political processes, but they have not developed a more complex vision of life to reflect this understanding. Instead their faith in the innate goodness of man is simply renewed, their initial beliefs merely validated by such a severe test. This is Capra's limitation as a social filmmaker. Despite the power with which he conveys his message, he has nothing new to tell us. He can only fall back on platitudes.

Where Capra excels is in dramatizing the frustrations and anxieties of modern life. All the social and economic forces that thwart and suppress the individual are symbolized by a rich collection of shysters, tycoons, and power barons. With each film, Capra refined the image of his villains, concentrating more and more evil power within their grasp so that the real villain in the end is fascism. His fascination with the villains and the increasingly impervious mechanisms of their power tinges Capra's films with desperation. He has to come up with ever greater miracles of faith and goodness, and then not to vanquish the evil but merely to contain it. He begins in *Deeds* with a generalized shyster city, moves in *You Can't* and *Smith* through a single apolitical super-capitalist and ends in *Doe* with an overt would-be fascist dictator. With each succeeding film, corruption is increasingly identified with an individual villain (marvelously played by Edward Arnold) who gathers ever greater power to himself and becomes increasingly political in his aspirations.

In *Mr. Deeds* corruption is identified as an environment rather than an individual. The city is peopled with crooked lawyers, upper-crust snobs, cynical journalists and pretentious intellectuals who conspire to destroy the all-American hero. In *You Can't Take It with You*, Capra makes Anthony P. Kirby (Arnold) the personification of shyster city values. Kirby is a ruthless Wall Street tycoon who is in the process of finalizing a series of mergers that will gain him a monopoly of the country's munitions industry. Though he seems to be preparing to capitalize on the imminent war, Kirby is not politically motivated; he sees war strictly in terms of profits. He becomes a threat to American values when he finds it necessary to liquidate a block of houses inhabited by a cross-section of populist good neighbors led by Grandpa Vanderhoff. But the specific political issue of fascism is not yet uppermost in Capra's mind and the film concentrates on Kirby's personal drama.

The conversion motif in *You Can't* is not focused on the hero but on the villain. The hero is not so much Jimmy Stewart's Tony Kirby, Jr., who is quite secondary to the action, but rather the entire Vanderhoff/Sycamore family; because they have already established their particular brand of insane populist utopia, they experience no moral crisis. Instead it is Kirby, the villain, who must make the choices that motivate the moral action of the film. Therefore, much of the film, unlike the original play, concentrates on him and his interaction with the Vanderhoff/Sycamore clan. It is thus a drama of conversion without the complexities of the *Deeds–Smith–Doe* trilogy and instead plays up the simple-minded aspects of Capra's populism. Because, in Donald C. Willis' words, "the movie opposes unhappy wealth with fun, daffy poverty, with nothing in between," it is locked into "the fatuous reality of its conclusion, which has Anthony P. Kirby giving up his millions to play the harmonica."[4] All tycoons are lonely and frustrated, all the unemployed are eccentric artists happily doing their own thing. Kirby recognizes the emptiness of his life and with only the opposite extreme to serve as an alternative is soon playing a "Polly Wolly Doodle" duet with Grandpa Vanderhoff.

What is interesting is that two years later in *Smith* the Edward Arnold villain is long past redemption. Jim Taylor operates a machine that controls an entire midwestern state's industry, press, and government, and has even extended its tentacles into Congress. Taylor is now grooming his own state's senator, Joseph Paine (Claude Rains), "The Silver Knight," for the Presidency. As yet, however, political power is purely a means for the super-capitalist to protect and extend his business interests. Taylor's greatest concern is that the Senate pass Paine's bill for a state dam. Having anonymously appropriated land, the super-shyster will then be able to sell it at a high profit.

But Taylor's well-laid plans are undermined when the naive Jeff Smith inadvertently stumbles upon the plot. Taylor first discredits Jeff in an effort to have him voted out of the Senate. Then, when Jeff exercises the "American privilege of free speech in its most dramatic form" by filibustering against Taylor's project, Taylor uses his machine to prevent any pro-Smith sentiment from being published in the state's papers. His hoodlums even attack Jeff's scout troop and destroy their press to prevent them from printing handbills. Taylor succeeds in completely stifling Jeff's speech and turns the state against him. Twenty-three hours after the filibuster begins, baskets of telegrams and letters are wheeled into the Senate chamber, all condemning Jeff. Exhausted and apparently defeated, Jeff passes out, his faith in the democratic processes having failed him.

The conclusion is an example of a Capra miracle akin to Kirby's conversion. Taylor's stooge, Senator Paine, suddenly has an attack of scruples and, during a hysterical suicide attempt, discloses the truth of Taylor's corruption. The gaps in the film's dramatic structure (Paine has been morally uncomfortable with the proceedings, but unlike the Kirby character his conversion has not been thoroughly set up and motivated) are hurdled and simply overlooked in the frenzy of the film's closing minutes. (An additional scene was shot but cut from the final film.) A miracle, a declaration that good always conquers evil, is the final affirmation despite the implacable power Taylor mustered against the defenseless Smith. Taylor's defeat is not entirely convincing and indicates that Capra's view of modern society is not as rosy as it appears. In his contemporary review of the film, Meyer Levin noted a deep-rooted cynicism:

> For aside from the miraculous intervention of a resourceful boodler, the film suggests there is no way to break the throttling hold of the tycoons upon the throat of democracy. Mr. Taylor is completely successful in strangling the press and the radio, in strong-arming the resistance of a few kids and a few reformers.[5]

Taylor is still not overtly fascistic, but his methods and monopolistic aims are clearly antidemocratic, tending toward a strong concentration of power that is authoritarian in character.

It is finally in *Doe* that the Arnold villain's true colors emerge as he mounts an all-out campaign to establish a fascist dictatorship in America. D. B. Norton has all the money he needs and now wants political power. Armed with a private police force and motor guards, D. B. attempts to use the John Doe movement to catapult himself into the White House. Manipulating the electoral potential of the unwitting club members and buying up the votes controlled by labor and political bosses, D. B. will neither gain power through democratic means nor exercise it constitutionally. He announces his intentions in a tone that is bluntly fascistic: "These are daring times. . . . We're coming to a new order of things. There's too much talk going on in this country. Too many concessions have been made. What the American people need is an iron hand." Hollywood's typical shyster heavy has become an American would-be Hitler.

For the first time, fascism is not merely a plot but a popular (i.e., middle-class) movement trading on fervent patriotic platitudes. The film realistically details the characteristics of native fascism, dramatizing how would-be dictators represent themselves as "men of the people" acting on behalf of the common folk who are oppressed by big businessmen and politicians. Huey Long trampled the legislative and judicial processes while invoking the same patriotic symbols and myth figures as the populists. In Sinclair Lewis's *It Can't Happen Here*, Buzz Windrip, "the professional common man," rises to dictatorship by dramatically brandishing Old Glory, while *Gabriel over the White House* defends Jud Hammond's dictatorship in the names of Lincoln and Jefferson.

But Capra splits the fascist movement into two separate elements— John Doe, the movement's sincere populist orator, and Norton, the authoritarian backstage manipulator—and in so doing courts ideological trouble. The two elements are intended as opposing good–evil forces, but as we have noted, Capra's vision of good (at least at an ideological level) consists of sentimental clichés of patriotism, good neighborliness, and the spirit of Christmas. His political ethic is nothing more than a surface jingoism that is no match for the power of evil marshalled against it and in fact closely resembles the requisite orthodoxy upon which fascism is built. As Gerald Mast complains, Doe's sentimentalities are "exactly parallel to Hitler's own."[6] Just as Doe and Norton are inseparable parts of the same phenomenon, so Capra's naive brand of

populism at times seems indistinguishable from the ideology it is supposed to counter.

This ideological kinship can be seen in Capra's treatment of the
"little people." As long as they function as individuals within a community, that is, a small town full of good neighbors, then the little
people represent a healthy, positive, albeit Pollyanna-like society. The
testimony of Bert, the soda jerk from Millville (Regis Toomey), is a
long catalogue of little triumphs over life's hardships when people just
get together and start helping one another. People are given jobs (a
relief administrator complains, "If this keeps up, I'll be out of a job"),
the economy picks up, and everyone lives a much happier life without
any large-scale programs issued from on high. But the success of the
ethic revolves around its figurehead John Doe whom they do put on
high and that success catapults the ethic into the kind of mass movement
it supposedly defies. The rally in Wrigley Field with a huge collection of
John Does hidden under umbrellas has turned all of those individuals
into a mass of followers and the proceedings have the flavor of the
Nuremberg Rally. But Nuremberg quickly turns into Calvary and the
John Does into a mob who readily accept Norton's denunciations of
their hero. Despite protests that "the idea is still good," it is the leader,
not the idea, that the people follow; the movement immediately dies
when that leader is discredited. Even in the end, when it appears that
the clubs may revive as a more populistic grass roots movement rather
than a grand national drive, there is a preference for a leader: "We need
you, Mr. Doe. . . . We are going to start up our club again . . . only it
would be a lot easier with you." Capra's politics are so underdeveloped
that they blend too readily into the sphere of social activity he so vociferously opposes. The film's celebration of the principles of democracy
—a free people's ability to govern themselves—stands in direct contrast
to their relationship to John Doe.

Capra's ending reinforces the interdependence of the charismatic
populist and the fascistic power broker. As equal components of the
Doe movement, John and Norton cannot function without one another
and the conclusion is necessarily even more tentative than that of *Mr.
Smith*. Having discovered Norton's true motives, John has tried to expose him. But just as Taylor could easily discredit Smith, so Norton
destroys Doe. The movement in tatters and his credibility ruined, Long
John decides to go through with the suicide protest which had begun as
a hoax and would now restore belief in himself and the movement. But
Ann and several of his original followers arrive upon the scene as do
Norton and company, all to prevent John from committing suicide. His
decision to live or die perfectly encapsulates the dilemma. As long as
he lives he's a fake and the movement is dead; yet if he kills himself

Norton still has the power to suppress any news of the suicide and therefore squelch the movement's revival. There can be no final victory, only a stand-off.

Despite the ideological vagueness, despite Capra's own dissatisfaction with his inability to find a clearcut solution ("No answers this time, ladies and gentlemen. Back to the drawing board"[7]), the finale works surprisingly well. Even though Capra pulls out all the dramatic stops to make it play as if good were triumphant (the last shot is the Liberty Bell ringing), there is an underpinning of doubt and dread that gives the film added resonance. When Doe and his followers turn their backs on Norton and leave him standing in the snow, it is a small but nevertheless positive gesture. John cannot rebuild a national mass movement without the financing and media at Norton's disposal. Nor can Norton manipulate his way to ultimate power without the unwitting cooperation of the John Does of the world. The hope Capra leaves us with is that John Does are no longer so unwitting, that they do intend to start up their clubs again, even if not on the old mammoth scale. The little people may not be able to vanquish evil, but they will not be vanquished by it either. Connell's final challenge, "There you are, Norton, the people! Try and beat that!" is an assertion of their will to go on fighting and not to bow under to Norton's yoke. In this sense, Capra's ending is not simply a fairy tale victory but an insight into an evil so powerful and ominous that only constant vigilance can keep it at bay. Considering the state of the world in 1941, that is a very positive and yet realistic insight.

Like all lasting works, Capra's social parables touch at a central truth and do not really flinch from the ramifications. Capra did not raise the specter of fascism just to wish it away, but to face it head on. Norton and Doe live on to do further battle in an eternal struggle and Capra is on hand to sound the rallying cry for the world's John Does. It is a testament to his success that these films had such an impact when they were released and continue to touch audiences in such an elemental manner.

—14—

MORE PLUTOCRATS
AND WOULD-BE DICTATORS

When *Meet John Doe* was released in May 1941, America's chief concern was with the fascists abroad, not with those at home. Huey Long, the only American fascist figure to truly capture the public imagination, had done so by directly addressing the dislocation of Depression America, accusing Roosevelt of moving too slowly toward the economic democracy that Long had promised under his "Share Our Wealth" program.[1] But Long had been dead nearly six years and those who had sought to take up his mantle, such as Gerald L. K. Smith and Father Coughlin, had failed miserably. And once America finally entered the war, not only was fascism designated the official Evil plaguing the world, but the war itself removed many of the social concerns upon which fascism could feed. As heavy industry began retooling for war production and the armed forces began their rapid expansion, the tide of unemployment receded. The three million new workers hired to man the assembly lines were thinking about preserving democracy, not overthrowing it. The red, white, and blue banners that hung in the factories provided a stark warning: "Time is short."[2]

Films on native fascist movements now became an extension of Hollywood's propaganda efforts. To a degree these films followed Capra's lead. The power plays of Robert Forrest in *Keeper of the Flame* (1942) and Hank Durban in *Pilot Number Five* (1943) are reminiscent of D. B. Norton's schemes, cynical plots by villains obviously meant to be Hitler surrogates. Like Long John, the heroes in these films eventually discover the truth and march out to teach the entire world the importance of eternal vigilance on behalf of freedom. But for all its propagandistic fervor, *Meet John Doe* still depicts the relationship between charismatic political leaders and the mass of followers as ambivalent. The later films, however, reduce the dynamics of this relationship to that of a power-hungry fanatic whose designs are thoroughly evil and a naive populace which is easily duped, indeed almost brainwashed, into a blind, reverent allegiance. This became Hollywood's orthodox view of fascism—it all boils down to a shyster leader tricking the innocent masses.

Keeper of the Flame takes the idea of duping the people to a particularly absurd extreme. Robert Forrest dies a great American patriot, revered as a war hero and champion of the people's rights. War correspondent Steven O'Malley (Spencer Tracy) comes home from the European front to write a book about Forrest that will hold him up as an example for the rest of the world: "In Europe I watched most of the decent things change and I could always think of what Robert Forrest stood for—decency. That's why I want to write a book about Forrest." But O'Malley's research into Forrest's life and death reveals an incredible fraud. The supposed hero was in reality a power-crazed, would-be dictator on the verge of a fascist coup. Forrest's wife, Christine (Katharine Hepburn), has murdered her husband in order to stop him and now reveals to Steven that Forrest was once a genuine humanitarian who became a cynical exploiter of his own image. Christine's description of Forrest's megalomania directly parallels native fascism with the war cause: "I saw the face of fascism in my own house. Hatred, arrogance, cruelty. I saw what German women were facing. I saw the enemy. . . ."

In Forrest's private bunker, Christine shows Steven her late husband's private files and reveals the roots of popular fascism, its prejudice, bitterness, hero worship, and blind patriotism: "Of course they didn't call it fascism. They painted it red, white, and blue and called it Americanism." She pulls out articles ready for release, intended "to stir up all the little hatreds of the whole nation" (anti-Semitic, anti-Catholic, anti-Negro, anti-labor), and lists of all those frustrated losers who long for the power and prestige of a uniform, who will serve as "America's first storm troopers." *Keeper* here provides one of Hollywood's most thorough analyses of the appeal of fascism, but is still restricted by its purpose as war propaganda to highlight only the obvious negatives of fascism. Unlike a Huey Long, Forrest addresses narrow phobias, not broadly based social and economic discontent, and his program is restricted to repressive violence rather than constructive reforms. In the end, Forrest's widespread popularity is more public relations trickery than a response to his genuine ideology—an ideology of which most of his followers are totally unaware. His fascism is a plot, not a popular movement.

As in many films of the time, *Keeper*'s endorsement of democracy is at odds with its view of the public as gullible dupes. Many, including Steven and Christine, believed in Forrest as the great humanitarian, reverently elevating him to the status of greatness and in the process sometimes losing all their capacity to reason. This hero worship is perfectly acceptable when the object of adulation represents "the decent things"; it becomes a problem only when he represents something else.

Christine kills her husband but maintains his heroic image because she believes the people need a hero—"I had to destroy the image—no, the man, to preserve the image." Steven opposes her, claiming that Americans don't need false heroes, that they should know who their enemy is, both in Europe and at home. But when Christine is killed by Forrest's fanatical secretary (Richard Whorf), Steven writes his book about her, memorializing her as a martyr who died for her country. Just as the film opened with a montage of a shocked populace reacting to Robert Forrest's tragic death, so it ends with the same populace reacting in a similar fashion to the news of Christine. Christine has replaced her husband in the hearts and minds of the people. Thus, despite his professed trust in the people, Steven creates another hero for them to revere. The point the film seems to be making is that the people need real heroes—not false ones—to follow but rarely seem capable of distinguishing between the two.

In *Pilot Number Five*, ambitious lawyer George Collins (Franchot Tone) is the dupe. He goes to work for a Huey Long-type governor, Hank Durban (Howard Freeman), and, despite the warnings of his fiancée (Marsha Hunt) and his best friend (Gene Kelly), gets embroiled in Durban's corruption. Too late, Collins realizes that Durban is really exploiting the little people he pretends to serve and is interested only in his own absolute power. Collins exposes the governor, helping to bring about Durban's downfall, but also ruins his own career in the process. Then, the outbreak of war provides Collins with the opportunity to get back at all the fascist powers who would rob the people of their freedom. He volunteers for a suicide mission and crashes his plane, kamikaze-style, into an important Japanese aircraft carrier. Like Christine, he ends up a martyr-hero who has redeemed his past mistake.

Clearly the film is meant to explain fascism; according to Gene Kelly:

> The picture started out to be something bigger and stronger than it finally emerged. The original idea was a statement against fascism, to draw a parallel between the malpractice of political power in America and the kinds of fascism that had drawn America into the war. It was a warning against incipient fascism, somewhat based on Huey Long and the danger of one man's gaining control of a state.

But the studio shied away from taking that kind of a stand at that time, which isn't hard to understand—we were in the entertainment business and this was wartime. So the script was defanged.[3]

In 1943, Hollywood was not really interested in the ideology or roots of fascism. To suggest that would-be American dictators genuinely appealed to a broad-based public, that they were a response to democracy's failures, was unacceptable at this point. Fascism simply became an un-American aberration, an evil psychosis which could only be cured through the application of American values and knowhow. Throughout the war, the disease was explained not in political but in familiar moral terms. Hitler was the biggest shyster of them all and the Third Reich the most corrupt political machine ever.

Two films of the forties did view native fascists not as a parallel to Nazism but as distinctly American phenomena. Both Orson Welles's *Citizen Kane* (1941) and Robert Rossen's *All the King's Men* (1949) defy the conventions of the Formula, using unorthodox narrative techniques to highlight the ambivalence of power and the tension between the protagonists' public and private lives. The films provide sympathetic portraits of genuine American types. In *Citizen Kane*, Welles creates a portrait of the turn-of-the-century corporate baron, modelled on such figures as William Randolph Hearst and Samuel Insull. Likewise, *All the King's Men* is a thinly disguised biography of Huey Long, tracing his rise from country lawyer to the Louisiana governorship. The politics of Charles Foster Kane (Welles) and Willie Stark (Broderick Crawford) are bound up in the complexities of their personalities. Their fates are determined by their social backgrounds—Kane's wealth, Stark's poverty—and their personal dramas represent microcosms of larger, social ones. Both combine progressive political platforms with dangerous right-wing methodology, a real concern for the people with a megalomaniacal need to control them. They do not appeal to dupes, but to the dispossessed. The masses' allegiance is neither blind nor irrevocable, but a positive response to the leaders' call for change.

Fascism and politics are not Welles's major concerns in *Citizen Kane*, but in portraying how Kane is corrupted under the influence of money and power, Welles touches upon the central paradox of American authoritarianism. Kane is a true plutocrat who operates on the edge of politics, even running for office but never threatening to become a dictator. Still, his obsession with power and his assumption that he can do or buy anything, including governorships and presidencies, when combined with the peculiar evolution of his political thinking, mark Kane as a distinctly American right-wing figure.

Kane's political platform, as a newspaper publisher and then as a gubernatorial candidate, is vaguely left-wing. Just as Hearst began his career fighting political corruption and big business monopolies, so Kane crusades against business trusts and slum landlords. But Kane's progressivism is always self-centered: "If I don't look after the interests of the underprivileged, maybe somebody else will—maybe somebody without money or property. . . . And that would be too bad." He magnanimously offers the people enough token reforms to placate their discontent without surrendering any of his real power over them.

When he runs for governor (as did Hearst, on an anti-big business platform), his campaign once again displays both a genuine desire for social reform and an obsessive egotism. Kane promises "to protect the underprivileged, the underpaid and the underfed" but his main platform, an all-out attack against his opponent, Boss Jim Gettys (Ray Collins), gradually declines into an ego-gratifying attempt to prove that he is more powerful than the political machine. Caught in an extramarital affair and threatened by Gettys with exposure, Kane refuses to give up his political ambitions and quit the campaign. To the end, he insists on his own superiority: "Don't worry about me. I'm Charles Foster Kane. I'm no cheap, crooked politician trying to save himself from the consequences of his crimes."

The limitations of Kane's liberalism are best summarized by his disillusioned friend, Jedediah Leland (Joseph Cotton), who points out that Kane's beloved working man is "turning into something called organized labor, and you're not going to like that one bit when you find out that it means that he thinks he's entitled to something as his right and not your gift." Kane's progressivism is really a disguise for his need for power. He is like Doe and Norton combined into one complex figure, carefully balancing a sincere concern for the people with a condescension toward them which reinforces his own superiority.

Although Kane's formal political career comes to an end with his defeat in the election, his newspapers and wealth assure continuing influence as a political power. Like Hearst (whose career Arthur Schlesinger, Jr., characterizes as "a long trajectory from left to right"[4]), Kane moves from a liberal stance toward the extreme right. In the opening newsreel sequence, he is seen posing on a balcony with Hitler and offering his endorsement in much the same way as Hearst did in 1933. While the film includes no further references to its model's right-wing activities (in 1934, Hearst unequivocally equated fascism with Americanism: "Whenever you hear a prominent American called a 'Fascist,' you can usually make up your mind that the man is simply a LOYAL CITIZEN WHO STANDS FOR AMERICANISM"[5]), Kane's megalomania, his ruthless attempts to manipulate public opinion, and his mistrust of the working class clearly place him in the spectrum of the right.

But just as he cannot bend Jim Gettys to his own will when discovered in his "love nest," so Kane can never really buy the affection of the people. With his newspaper empire he can indeed help mold public opinion, but he cannot sell something that is basically unwanted. The readers react favorably to Kane when he echoes their views and attacks their targets, such as big business and Gettys' political machine. At other times, Kane fails to convince the people that "fraud" caused his election defeat or that Susan Alexander is a great opera star. Just as Kane cannot be foisted upon the public unless they want him, so fascism or any ideology cannot succeed as a popular movement unless it in some way expresses the people's will.

The dependence of political figures on public support is also a key theme in *All the King's Men*. If Kane fails to win the public's affection because his social concern is perceived as hollow, Willie Stark is elevated to an unimpeachable position of power because he is in direct touch with the people. Willie is one of them, a hick whose personal corruption reflects the larger corruption of the people debasing themselves before Willie's demagoguery. When he begins his political career, Willie is an idealistic champion of the underdog's rights. His early attempts to overthrow a corrupt political machine fail because it is too powerful to defeat by legitimate means. He unsuccessfully battles the machine as a lawyer in the courts, as the head of a citizens' movement, and twice as a political candidate. He learns how to win the crowd's approval by using their own language: "Nobody ever helped a hick but a hick himself." But popular support and the sincere desire for reform are not enough to win the election. The party bosses "deliver" the city vote and overwhelm Willie's strong rural backing.

In an abrupt cut the film jumps from the defeat of one election to the campaign of the next and a new Willie Stark. He has realized that the only way to defeat the party machine is to create his own machine. He wins with an expensive campaign paid for with political deals and bribes from the very groups he's opposing: "I'd make a deal with the devil if it'll help me carry out my program."

Once governor, Willie embarks upon a legislative policy that will effect meaningful change. Using any means necessary to achieve his ends, he railroads building programs through the state house. His legislation calls for higher and cheaper education, new hospitals with free treatment for the poor, and the building of new roads and bridges in underdeveloped areas. But his methods increasingly enmesh him in criminal corruption. In order to effectively institute his programs he finds he needs complete control; in order to gain and maintain that control he must resort to ever greater criminal acts. It becomes increasingly difficult for Willie to distinguish between the means and the ends until power itself becomes the only end. Programs that were begun with the intention of helping the people ultimately result in a series of concrete monuments to Willie's own achievement. Bigger and better construction projects become a substitute for actual change. Stark Highway, Stark College, Willie Stark Library have little relation to the people's needs. A newsreel narrator points out that "You don't need a four- or six-lane highway for a horse and buggy."

Parallel to the erosion of political ideals is the disintegration of Willie's family life—estrangement from the wife who taught him law, bitterness from the son whom he has left crippled. Yet when the need arises Willie trots them out to pose before the newsreel cameras as the happy Stark family. His rapport with the people also becomes perverted. He still speaks from their point of view and they still respond, but the spark of idealism has turned into cleverly manipulated public relations. In 1984 fashion he plasters the state with billboards and banners proclaiming, "The people's will is the law of this state—Willie Stark." During impeachment procedures against him, Willie buses the hicks into town and stages a rally reminiscent of *Meet John Doe.* He speaks to them messianically, believing that he is the people and that any act he performs is thereby democratic:

> Your will is my strength, and your need is my justice, and I shall live
> in your right and your will. And if any man tries to stop me from
> fulfilling that right and that will, I'll break him. I'll break him with
> my bare hands. For I have the strength of many.

For Rossen, fascism is not just a conspiracy hatched by an individual villain and the fascistic personality is not the incarnation of pure evil. Willie Stark is a complex man molded largely by social circumstance. Despite his evil, Willie has still done more for the people of the state than any of his predecessors. He starts out in an honest attempt to end corruption and in the process creates a new and greater corruption. Willie, like Kane, is Norton and Doe indistinguishably mixed together, but without the comforting option that Doe can repudiate Norton.

The redeemers are just as corruptible as Willie and are effectual against him only when they resort to his means. The liberals, represented by the patrician Stanton family and their close friend, Jack Burden (John Ireland), turn to Willie to act where they cannot. They help him rise to power and become complicit in his corruption. Jack is especially guilty. The fact that he is the film's narrator places Willie's story within Jack's particular perspective. He is the other half of Willie, beginning as an idealistic reporter turning his back on the decadent affluence of his mother in search of his own social vision. Impressed by Willie's integrity, he helps bring him to the public's attention and devotes his energies to Willie's cause. In the process, he becomes Willie's "hatchet man." He constantly expresses his guilt feelings but fails to do anything about them. Too weak to fight Willie, he initially runs away; only when his boss is dying, and unable to oppose him, does Jack decide to take positive action and reveal the truth about him to the people.

The other liberals, Judge Stanton (Raymond Greenleaf), his niece Ann (Joanne Dru), and nephew Adam (Sheppard Strudwick), are likewise corruptible, all willing to appease Willie's demands at the expense of their own principles. The Judge's revulsion at Willie's tactics is eventually proven suspect when it is revealed that the Judge himself is guilty of self-serving "indiscretion" committed in the distant past. Ann, once Jack's fiancée, becomes Willie's mistress, and Adam, although hesitant about Willie's corruption, becomes director of his new hospital. Like Jack, they all become enmeshed in Willie's immorality and are helpless to act against it. The judge's impeachment proceedings are easily quashed by Willie's less orthodox but more effective methods and Adam finally concludes that the only way to free the state from Willie's grip is through assassination. For Adam this decision is the final abasement of his liberalism, an expression of despair that he knows will result in his own death.

As to whether the cycle is complete with Willie and Adam's deaths, that is left ambiguous. Jack claims that he has learned to resist Willie's corruption and that he will attempt to educate the voters so that they will not support another Willie Stark. His claims are, however, immediately undercut. When the dying Willie calls for him, Jack comes running, still the faithful follower. Nor will knowing the truth about Willie eradicate the conditions that produced him. The people respond to Willie because he appears to answer their needs and until those needs are met, they will always be ready for other Willie Starks.

Broderick Crawford's energetic performance is crucial to the film's success, encapsulating the blunt bravado and galling charm of a Willie Stark. No matter how cruel he becomes, Crawford never loses our sympathy. Like Kane, Willie emerges as a tragic figure whose fatal hubris not only brings him down but seriously undermines the social fabric of democracy.

A year later, Crawford gave the same character a comic personification with Harry Brock, the arrogant multimillionaire junk dealer of *Born Yesterday* (1950). Harry, like Willie, is a lower-class stiff who has worked his way up to the top through any and all means. In his employ are highly paid advisers (including one former Assistant Attorney General) and his past is a history of crooked deals with municipal and state governments. Now he is promoting the biggest deal of all, the formation of an international combine which will reap a fortune from all the junk lying around Europe after the war. To prevent any interference from Congress, Harry relies on the influence of his own personal Senator. As in Capra, fascism is the most extreme perversion of monopoly capitalism.

His relationship with his "dumb blond" mistress Billie Dawn (Judy Holliday in her definitive performance) is analogous to that of the fascist leader with the people upon whose ignorance he thrives, but this political allegory never takes away from the marvelously human and engaging characters. Harry is really just a slob who's always followed the rules of the game: "I don't know what I'm doin' so wrong. This is America ain't it? Where's all this free enterprise they're always talkin' about?" And the dupes have never been so warm-blooded as Billie. With her two mink coats, lavish wardrobe, and luxury apartment, she admits that "I'm stupid and like it. . . . So long as I know how to get what I want, that's all I want to know." She is Harry's "silent" partner who on paper controls a majority of his affairs and whose signature is required on everything pertaining to Harry. Without her unwitting cooperation, Harry would be powerless.

To make Billie more acceptable in Washington social circles, Harry hires journalist Paul Verrall (William Holden) to educate her. Paul represents the crusading liberal conscience who arouses the people to the danger in their midst. He writes articles like "The Yellowing Democratic Manifesto," is continually critical of how the government has been corrupted, and is committed to enlightening the unaware: "A world full of ignorant people is too dangerous to live in." Under his tutelage, Billie gradually comes to understand what Harry represents: "Sometimes selfishness even gets to be a cause, an organization, even a government. Then it's called Fascism." Billie comes to equate Harry pushing Senator Hodges around with "pushing a few million people around" and to realize that Harry can only get away with his "kind of shenanigans if nobody cares about it." Billie rebels, giving up her role as Harry's kept woman and silent partner to become Paul's wife, but she still maintains majority control over Harry, making her a responsible watchdog over his subsequent dealings.

Billie is the ideal postwar political heroine, representing a vigilant people safeguarding the interests of all against those who would selfishly abuse them. The fact that the people can rise up and easily defeat the fascist threat, in contrast to *Meet John Doe*'s standoff, constitutes a new optimism borne out of the war experience. Crusaders like Paul and informed individuals like Billie are the hope for a new world. But the optimism is a trifle sugarcoated and naive. Loud, dumb Harry Brock is perhaps too simple a target. In real life, 1950 saw Joseph McCarthy riding high, dispensing his "justice" against the Paul Verralls without any opposition from the Billie Dawns.

—15—

INTERNATIONAL FACISM—
FROM PACIFISM TO WAR

It soon became evident that the real fascist menace came from abroad, from the expansionist policies of the German, Italian, and Japanese dictators. Fascist aggression in Ethiopia, the Rhineland, Spain, and Manchuria proved that cries of "Tomorrow the World" were not to be dismissed as idle threats. European war became an inevitability and American participation an unwelcome but distinct possibility. But until the Axis powers became openly hostile, the pros and cons of fascism were debated furiously by the American public. While the right contended that it was the best means of dealing with economic depression and social unrest, the left protested against it as a violation of basic human rights and the tenets of democracy.

The chief political thrust of the American right was isolationism, a stubborn insistence on remaining uninvolved in European affairs. The American reaction to World War I had been one of profound disillusionment. Feeling that it had been unnecessarily dragged into a futile war, the country rejected any other invitations for international involvement. In speaking out against American participation in the League of Nations, Henry Cabot Lodge summed up the isolationist viewpoint that was to prevail until the advent of World War II:

> We would not have our politics distracted and embittered by the dissensions of other lands. We would not have our country's moral force abated, by everlasting meddling and muddling in every quarrel, great and small, which afflicts the world.[1]

With the advent of the Depression, Americans became increasingly preoccupied with their own problems. The New Deal initiated a policy of "economic nationalism" and, according to William Leuchtenberg, "isolationism became a kind of national secular religion in the 1930s."[2] Throughout these years, the prevailing view of war was that it was only another plot by shysters to lure the common people into tragedy while making businessmen and bankers wealthy. This attitude found expression in a number of popular books and articles of the early thirties such as *The Road to War* that depicted America's entry into the war as a terrible mistake. Also important is a cycle of pacifist films beginning with Lewis Milestone's peerless *All Quiet on the Western Front* (1930), continuing through *Journey's End, The Case of Sergeant Grischa,* and Howard Hawks' *The Dawn Patrol* (all 1930) to William Dieterle's *The Last Flight* (1931) and Ernst Lubitsch's *Broken Lullaby* (also known as *The Man I Killed,* 1932). Though somewhat dated in their stilted dialogue and mawkish acting, the best scenes of these films, particularly *All Quiet,* reverberate with outrage at the waste and destruction of war. The films deal not so much with World War I as with the universal premise of war. Except for generalized accusations against kings, cabinets, and manufacturers, there is little political insight as to why the Great War was fought. The nationalities of the characters—German in *All Quiet,* French in *Broken Lullaby*—are therefore secondary to the principle that all wars fought by all peoples are evil. In fact, nationalism is cited as the basic root of war and international brotherhood as its antidote.

These films are hardly isolationist in intention, yet their pacifism is the emotional base for popular support of isolationist policies. The useless horror of war was the common ground of both pacifists and isolationists and this 1930–32 movie cycle directly fed the sentiments of neutrality. The major difference was the pacifists' mistrust of nationalism as opposed to the superpatriotism of the America Firsters. The pacifist avoids war for humanitarian reasons, the isolationists out of a sense of national priority.

Two subsequent films illustrate this difference, *Gabriel over the White House* and *The President Vanishes. Gabriel's* chief executive is not so much against war as he is against the United States being exploited by devious foreign nations. To President Hammond, European powers have continually "plucked" the American Eagle: first they dragged the United States into the 1914–18 war; now they have worsened the Depression by failing to pay their debts and by forcing America to spend billions on the arms race. *The President Vanishes* also provides the standard isolationist interpretation. America is about to be drawn into another European war through the machinations of profiteering industrialists who declaim: "What did the last war cost us? A few million casualties. But it also brought us the greatest era of prosperity that this

nation has ever seen." President Stanley defeats the warmongers' plot
and at the film's end assures America that "so long as I remain President, not one American will be sent to a foreign land. . . ." Both *Gabriel*
and *The President Vanishes* claim that the problems of European countries are of no interest to America, that her sole concern should be with
solving the problems of her own Depression.

Isolationism continued to be a major force in American politics
throughout the Depression decade. As late as 1937 a Gallup Poll on
the question "Do you think it was a mistake for the United States to
enter the World War?" drew a yes from 71 percent of those polled.[3]
Congress's response to the acts of aggression abroad was the Neutrality
Act of 1935, prohibiting the sale of munitions to any nation at war. But
with each new German, Italian, or Japanese atrocity, a segment of the
American public was converted away from isolationism toward interventionism. The radical left were the first converts, rallying many liberals to the cause in Spain in 1936–37. Although his administration
took no positive action against Franco, FDR's "quarantine speech" indicated his recognition of the fascist threat. As the thirties drew to a
close, American public opinion was polarized between those who recognized that deliberate nonparticipation in foreign quarrels would be both
difficult and immoral and those who believed in "America First"; between the New Deal liberal left and the anti–New Deal right. Then,
with America's entry into the war, one of the major tasks facing the
country was the transformation of a divided nation into a united front.

The movies during these years reflected public opinion and the nation's foreign policy. They shifted from pacifism in the early thirties to
a period of silence on the subject of war in the mid-thirties to vague,
infrequent warnings about European fascism in the late thirties and
finally to militancy at the turn of the decade. Pacifist films became no
longer tenable as the world braced itself for the new conflict, but neither
were antifascist films possible in an atmosphere rife with isolationism.
The studios were under continual pressure from isolationists—Senators
Wheeler and Nye, the Catholic Church, and hundreds of patriot groups
and German-American organizations—who inhibited all but a handful
of films from taking a stand on Germany. Another important reason
behind Hollywood's hesitation was its dependence on foreign markets.
To openly criticize a foreign power would not only jeopardize the box
office of that country, but potentially that of any other nation friendly
or neutral toward the offended state.

Thus those few films which did treat fascist oppression had to tread
carefully, usually setting their stories in a hazy political landscape where
no specific terms were ever used. The Nazis and Jews in Germany, the
Republicans and Loyalists in Spain, all went unnamed. Even these

tentative gestures came under heavy censure from foreign embassies and local isolationists. Only as the public mood shifted and war approached could the movies become more openly critical of international fascist powers. Hollywood's gradual move toward militant opposition to the Axis charted the country's own slow, inexorable progress from isolationism to commitment. Upon his declaration of war, FDR mobilized the industry to rationalize the struggle to a country fed on isolationism for twenty years. Apparent contradictions had to be reconciled. The very filmmakers who at the beginning of the thirties had found the Great War purposeless were now explaining why the American people must fight the Germans all over again.

China

The fact that Japan invaded Manchuria in 1931 and spent the rest of the decade trying to overrun China goes all but unmentioned in the American cinema. China was presented as a world of mystery and intrigue, a never-never land populated by wise old men, hard-working peasants, and pillaging warlords (*Shanghai Madness*, 1933, *Shanghai*, 1935, *The Good Earth*, 1937). In *The Good Earth*, the military chaos of the city sequence is caused by uniformed "republicans" and any political rationale for their actions is entirely absent. The only explicit political commentary is reserved for the Chinese Communists. In *Shanghai Express* (1932), a devious Red ringleader serves as the heavy in Von Sternberg's highly atmospheric (and tongue-in-cheek) China. An Eton-educated Chinese Communist and his rebel troops in *Oil for the Lamps of China* (1935) try to requisition the profits of the Atlantic Oil Company and thereby deny energy and light to the countryside. In each case, the Communists are merely used as handy cardboard villains, but the fact that they were chosen over any other political group indicates Hollywood's bias. In the later thirties several films (*Exiled to Shanghai*, 1937, *Daughter of Shanghai*, 1937, *West of Shanghai*, 1937, and *International Settlement*, 1938) made the vaguest references to the Japanese aggression, but it was more as a timely background for familiar melodrama of newsreel men and smuggling rings than as political comment. Although the latter two films mention the bombing of Shanghai, there is little else in them that relates to the actuality of the situation.

The General Died at Dawn (1936) also uses China as a mystical backdrop for spy melodrama, but expresses quite a different political viewpoint. Writer Clifford Odets and director Lewis Milestone convert the conventional format into a political allegory about tyranny and freedom. The Chinese warlord, General Yang (Akim Tamiroff), symbolizes fascism, terrorizing the countryside, looting villages, and exacting taxes from impoverished peasants. The hero, O'Hara (Gary Cooper), is made into a defender of the proletariat. He explains his commitment to the oppressed as the result of his own background in the slums of an American city and makes a plea to the conscience of America:

> Yang is a head-breaker, strike-breaker, heart-breaker. He's having his moment, but the people will arise to walk proud and tall on this earth . . . What better thing is there for an American to do than fight for democracy?

The film opens with a little lesson in economics reminiscent of the thirties' agitprop theater which spawned Odets. Starving Chinese refugees flee through the crowded streets from the advancing Yang. A snobbish Englishman looks on and remarks to his wife, "These people can take suffering and death. They're used to it. The only thing they can't take is paying taxes." At this point, O'Hara approaches him from the crowd and asks for a light. When the gentleman apologizes that he doesn't have a match, O'Hara socks him in the jaw.

ENGLISHMAN: I told you, I don't have a match.
O'HARA: And these people don't have the pennies to pay General Yang. Think about it.

When it comes to the political situation in China itself, the film is vague. Its antifascism seems to have been aimed not at the Japanese but at the Chinese themselves. Since it is an allegorical conflict between an autocratic militarist and a people's movement, one could relate Yang to Chiang Kai-Shek and O'Hara to the Communist Party. This interpretation is substantiated by the fact that the Chinese Nationalist Government opposed the film and during World War II pressured the United States not to release it.[4] But unless you were well versed in Chinese internal politics and looking for a hidden political statement, this subtlety would escape you. The general audience saw it, at best, as a vague attack against fascism and more likely as a playfully exciting thriller.

Ultimately the film is more a battle of wits than of ideologies. O'Hara falls in love with and is then betrayed by Judy Perrie (Madeleine Carroll) who feels an allegiance to her father (Porter Hall), a spy for Yang. Once her father is dead, she can switch sides back to O'Hara. He then outwits Yang by convincing the pompous general to prove his army's loyalty by ordering them to shoot one another. One reviewer failed to notice any political connotations, commenting on how the film owed less to Odets' then-renowned left-wing politics than to his ability as a writer of good melodrama: "Sophisticated cinemaddicts were less surprised at the speed with which Hollywood had apparently caused Play-wright Odets to modify his creed, than at that with which Odets had obviously acquired Hollywood's technique."[5]

General established the means by which fascism could be dealt with acceptably: as a subtle undercurrent in an otherwise amusing spy melodrama. As the war drew closer, the undercurrent became ever stronger, but the spies and melodrama were retained and the political discussion restricted to the terms of a morality play.

Spain

The Spanish Civil War crystallized for many the fallacies of isolationism. The democracies' failure to support the popularly elected Spanish government on the grounds of nonintervention seemed absurd beside the German and Italian support of the Spanish military. The German-Italian involvement proved that Ethiopia and the Rhineland were not isolated incidents but part of a larger imperialistic policy. The liberal left saw Spain as "a testing ground for fascism" and the war became an important symbol in thirties' politics, the last great cause. Thousands of Americans, Canadians, Englishmen, and Europeans joined together in the International Brigades to fight for the Loyalists, while many at home raised money for food, medicine, and weaponry. Emotions ran just as high on the right. Most reactionaries saw the Spanish issue as a Communist conspiracy, since Russia was the only country to help the Loyalists and the American Communist Party was at the vanguard of the antifascist movement. The Catholic Church exerted its vast influence on behalf of Franco, who had aligned himself with the Church hierarchy in Spain.

As always, Hollywood tried to capitalize on items "hot off the press" while avoiding any of the controversy. *The Last Train from Madrid* (1937) used the Civil War as the setting for a Grand Hotel-type soap opera, with an assorted group of fugitives gathered in a hotel waiting to escape from the besieged city. Why Madrid is under attack and the people must flee is irrelevant. As Frank Nugent complained, its "sympathies, neither Loyalist nor Rebel, are clearly on the side of the Ruritanians."[6]

Adding to the studios' natural reticence was the pressure exerted by both the left and right against any film which attempted to take sides. The left successfully thwarted a pro-Franco film from being produced at Fox[7] while the right managed to stifle all pro-Loyalist films with the exception of *Blockade* (1938). Though *Blockade* was released, producer Walter Wanger was sufficiently intimidated to greatly emasculate the film.

The final product bears many similarities to *The General Died at Dawn*. Though its antifascist message is more forthright than that of the earlier film, *Blockade* still hides its message in an inoffensive spy story. Its plotline, originally devised by Odets and Milestone,[8] is basically the same as *General*'s. Madeleine Carroll repeats her role as the reluctant spy torn between her love for the people's hero, this time Henry Fonda, and her loyalty to her father who works for the enemies of democracy. At the film's end, with the converted heroine's help, Fonda manages to outwit the villain, here a Nazi-type spy instead of a warlord.

Blockade contains many of the evasions of its predecessor. Although the opening title reveals that the setting is Spain in 1936, the two opposing sides are never labeled and the real issues of the war never discussed. Peasant farmers Marco (Fonda) and Luis (Leo Carillo) defend their valley against an unnamed invader who suddenly shows up one night to drive them off their land. There are some vague declarations that the people are fighting for their freedom, but any political bases for this fight are ignored. Instead the melodrama quickly shifts to the real dangers, the "enemies among our own people"—spies. The central conflict of the story is with enemy agents, including the ambivalent Norma (Carroll), who have blockaded the seaport in order to starve the people into submission.

Despite these shortcomings, the film is a more effective political statement than *The General Died at Dawn*. Spain was a much more recognizable situation than China and if the viewer had any knowledge of international affairs he would have found it fairly easy to identify which side was which and what they stood for. Additionally, the scenes set aside for political comment are more powerful and direct than in the Odets–Milestone film. Whereas the suffering of the people is merely alluded to in *General*, here we actually see the anguish caused by the fascist aggressors, even if they are not named. The Madeleine Carroll character is something more than a romanticized spy figure and is not just converted to the people's cause by her love for the hero alone. Screenwriter John Howard Lawson makes her the object of audience identification through whose eyes we see the suffering of the townspeople starved by the blockade. In the film's most effective sequence, Norma walks through the town and is confronted by scenes of deprivation. As she observes the desperate women in church with their dying children praying for a supply ship, as she sees a mother catatonic with grief, sitting amidst the rubble of the school where her children were killed in an air raid, Norma recognizes the evil of her own complicity and resolves to make up for the harm she has done.

An English reporter (Reginald Denny) who has accompanied her through the town editorializes on what he sees. He points out that what is occurring in Spain is a war against civilian noncombatants and that unless such aggression is stopped here, it will soon be unleashed on London and New York. Declaring that "the world must know about this," he sends home a series of articles fired with indignation, calling for action to help the Spanish people. He makes it clear that it is something larger than Spain that is at issue and although the film never quite defines that *something*, the reporter's comments only make sense if taken in the context of German-Italian aggression in Spain.

Marco's final speech is an outright call to action. After Marco has foiled the blockade, his superior officer rewards him with leave from the front so he "can find a little peace." Angrily turning away from the officer, Marco looks directly into the camera which moves toward him in a dramatic closeup and delivers his reply to the audience:

> Peace? Where can you find peace? The whole country's a battle ground. There is no peace. There is no safety for women and children. Schools and hospitals are targets. And this isn't war, not war between soldiers. It's not war, it's murder. It makes no sense. The world *can* stop it. Where is the conscience of the world? Where is the conscience of the world?

In this speech, at least, the film is blatantly anti-isolationist. The many contemporary critics who attacked it for its timidity[9] overlooked the fervor of its better scenes. When one considers the pressure on the film-makers during and after the making of the film, one can better understand the compromises they made. According to Winchell Taylor in a *Nation* article, "Secret Movie Censors,"[10] there was a private campaign waged in Hollywood to intimidate Walter Wanger. Many theater chains refused to exhibit the film and those that did play it were confronted with union sabotage and organized demonstrations. When Wanger, Lawson, and director William Dieterle attempted to make a less compromised portrait of European fascism, *Personal History*, they suddenly found that they could get no financial backing despite *Blockade*'s substantial box office. Apparently Wanger's Catholic financiers had been pressured by the Church into withdrawing their support. John Howard Lawson adds that Wanger was told that he would never get another loan to finance a picture if he made *Personal History*.[11]

It was not until 1943 that Spain was again the topic of a Hollywood film. Even then, with America actually at war with the fascists (though not with Spain), the studio's approach was so timid that *For Whom the Bell Tolls* makes *Blockade* seem like a *Daily Worker* tract. Paramount's intrepid studio heads carefully edited out almost all usage of the word "fascist" from Dudley Nichols's script and substituted "nationalist" for it.[12] Any other political references were similarly excised, except for Robert Jordan's (Gary Cooper) single discussion of the whole affair: "The Nazis and Fascists are just as much against democracy as they are against the Communists. They're making your country a proving ground for their new war machinery . . . so they can get the jump on the democracies." James Agee soundly condemned the film's evasions, particularly Jordan's comment: "The context makes it clear that they [the fascists] are just Italians who, in company with German Nazis and those dirty Russian Communists, are bullyragging each other and poor little Spain, which wants only peace and quiet."[13] On the film's release, Adolph Zukor declared, "It is a great picture without any political significance. We are not for or against anybody."[14]

Other films on Spain, *The Fallen Sparrow* (1943) and *Confidential Agent* (1945), adhere to the spy format but show a little more courage than *For Whom the Bell Tolls*, using many of the previously forbidden words in reference to Spain. *The Fallen Sparrow*'s hero, Kit (John Garfield), a veteran of the International Brigade, clearly links Franco with his German benefactors, recalling how he was tortured by Nazi guards in a rebel prison. Denard (Charles Boyer) in *Confidential Agent* openly declares that he is both a Republican and a foe of the fascists. The films, of course, were no longer relevant to the Spanish situation in that Franco had been firmly entrenched since 1939 and instead were just part of the general wartime propaganda against the enemy.

Germany

Hitler and the Third Reich represented the most dramatic manifestation of totalitarianism and attracted most of the attention during the thirties. Controversy over political repression was abetted by fascination with the histrionic Führer, the columns of goose-stepping troops, and the frenzied mammoth rallies. Further stories of book burnings, persecution, and an arms buildup at first reinforced isolationist aloofness, but quickly prompted others to mobilize public opinion against the potential threat of Nazism.

Despite public interest, Hollywood kept quite silent until almost the eve of the war. The first movie to supposedly deal with Nazi Germany, *Are We Civilized?* (1934), was a low-budget, non-studio feature released the year after Hitler's rise to the Chancellory. It presents a European country under the heel of a totalitarian government whose methods include the suppression of free speech, book burning, and the stirring up of racial and religious intolerance. But *Are We Civilized?* never dares to name either the country or the political party and its politics are a mélange of pacifist clichés. Its hero (William Farnum), a naturalized American visiting his native land, delivers a banal sermon on brotherly love, illustrated with a montage of great leaders reminiscent of the worst in D. W. Griffith—Moses, Buddha, Christ, Washington, Lincoln, etc. The mob he has been addressing turns on him and kills him, but his final words have affected the fascist leader (whose daughter happens to be engaged to the hero's son). His reformation promises that the hero's pleas will be fulfilled and undercuts whatever warning the film has made against the dangers of fascism. This piece of hokum understandably failed to gain much attention; within a year, its producer was screening it in church basements as an "educational" film.[15]

The Borzage Trilogy

Director Frank Borzage made a trio of films set in pre-Nazi Germany —*Little Man, What Now?* (1934), *Three Comrades* (1938), and *The Mortal Storm* (1940)—which are among the earliest Hollywood features to allude to the political strife in Europe. Like the Depression Hooverville in *A Man's Castle*, the turbulent Germany of the twenties is an amorphous backdrop against which Borzage's protagonists struggle to find meaning and love. The names and ideologies of political parties are not that pertinent since they are part of a milieu that is more spiritual than real. The chaos of the setting is largely an external manifestation of the characters' inner conflicts.[16] But as American attitudes gradually changed, the films' political setting became more oppressive and important in its own right.

In the first film, *Little Man, What Now?*, the director shows an anarchic, broken-down society ripe for a fascist takeover. The ever-growing legion of unemployed are restless and the film conjures up a sense of foreboding as they turn toward political extremism. One worker limps into his office after being beaten up at a street rally the night before and bitterly comments that "there are too many organizations. First the Communists, then the . . ." He is cut off before he can name the second group, clearly the Nazi Party. Throughout, the social landscape threatens to consume Hans and Lammchen, but Borzage undercuts the sense of foreboding by granting his lovers a happy ending.

In 1938's *Three Comrades*, Borzage presents a similarly ominous Berlin encroaching upon his three protagonists—Erich (Robert Taylor), Gottfried (Robert Young), and Otto (Franchot Tone) and their female companion Patricia (Margaret Sullavan, the heroine of all three films)—but with some very significant changes. Whereas Hans in the earlier film is frightened by what appear to be roving street mobs, Gottfried feels that the unrest is too pervasive to remain detached from: "Too many people are closing their windows and whistling in the dark."

The political parties are given slightly more definite qualities. Gottfried's mentor, Dr. Becker (Henry Hull) is a fairly positive figure, vaguely standing for some sort of social humanitarianism. At the same time, powerful businessman Breuer (Lionel Atwill) espouses an autocratic credo, arguing for "order and discipline" and remarking that there is "a group I'd like to join." Also significant is the mood of the ending. Instead of the happy resolution of *Little Man*, the two surviving characters of *Three Comrades* must flee from a Germany which now seems completely hostile.

But again politics is secondary to romantic melodrama. The film fails to identify either Dr. Becker's allegiances or Breuer's group, which viciously breaks up Becker's meeting and kills Gottfried. The main interest is the love relationship of Erich and Pat, dwelling particularly on her fatal disease and final, willful death. The death imagery and sentimental fatalism so characteristic of Borzage serve to further de-emphasize the politics.

To screenwriter F. Scott Fitzgerald, however, the politics were central; he intended the film as a chronicle of the rise of Nazism. According to Aaron Latham, who read the various drafts of the original script, Fitzgerald wanted to fully detail, through titles and graphs, the economic and social crises that led to the fall of German democracy.[17] But even before Borzage's direction could alter the focus of the film, Fitzgerald's screenplay was radically revised by producer Joseph L. Mankiewicz. One of the most significant changes Latham notes is in the ending. In the Fitzgerald version, Erich and Otto stand by the graves of their two dead comrades with Berlin and the sound of street fighting in the background. Otto comments, "There's fighting in the city," and the two, joined by the ghosts of Patricia and Gottfried, walk determinedly back toward the city. Fitzgerald saw this scene as the culmination of the whole film's thematic movement: "The march of four people, living and dead, heroic and inconquerable, side by side back into the fight."[18] When the film reached the screen, however, Otto's comment is answered by Erich—"South America is so far away. I wish they were coming." Otto says, "They are" and now the four walk away from Berlin. Whatever sense of the need for commitment that Gottfried has conveyed to the audience is now completely contradicted by the comrades' flight. The film's mood of anti-isolationism, its hint of impending war, is thus converted into the assertion that you can run away and remain uninvolved.

The film was further transformed by Louis B. Mayer who, in one of Hollywood's more groveling attempts to appease all sides, invited a representative of the Nazi government to attend a private screening and discuss any potential objections to the film. When the Nazi demanded various cuts and Mankiewicz refused, Mayer called in Joseph Breen of the Hays Office to effect a compromise. Breen's solution was to slightly alter the film to indicate not the rise of Nazism but of Communism. Mankiewicz naturally balked and threatened to resign, but by the time the film was released there were no references to either Communists or Nazis. According to *Time*,[19] other alterations included the removal of scenes depicting the Jewish problem and political book burnings and a change in the date, restricting the story to 1920—long before Hitler's rise to power—instead of to the more contemporary period of Fitzgerald's screenplay.

A third Borzage film set in Germany, 1940's *The Mortal Storm*, is more outspoken. The social circumstances that threaten to tear Borzage's characters apart now move to the forefront. The street gangs have become uniformed Nazis singing their anthem with arms extended in a Nazi salute. The targets of their violence are either religious or political, and the harassment the lovers experience is less a metaphoric comment on their ability to love than a condemnation of political oppression. Martin (Jimmy Stewart) and his Jewish lover Freya (Margaret Sullavan) try to escape to Switzerland but as they cross the border Freya is shot by a Nazi patrol and dies in Martin's arms. Unlike *Three Comrades*, the potential sentimentality of the death is played down and indignation emphasized. The camera moves into a closeup not of her tragic demise but of Martin's look of helpless rage.

The film ends with the resolve to fight that was cut out of *Three Comrades*. Otto (Robert Stack), one of Freya's stepbrothers, comes to realize what Nazism has done to his family and rejects the Party. He proclaims that he is glad of Martin's escape to Switzerland from where he will be able to fight Nazism. The implication is that Otto too will now battle that which he once believed in.

The Mortal Storm is also important as the first Hollywood film to deal with the Jewish problem and the concentration camps, although it only uses the word "Jew" once. The Roth family's cohesiveness and security are shattered with the broadcast announcing Hitler's rise to the Chancellory. As the Aryan stepsons and the future son-in-law, Fritz (Robert Young), become increasingly involved in Nazi activities, they are alienated from the father and daughter whom the Party condemns as non-Aryans. The stepsons move out, Fritz and Freya end their engagement. The father (Frank Morgan), a respected university professor, first has his classes boycotted, then his books burned, and finally is arrested and killed in a concentration camp. Though the film does not come out and say that Professor Roth is persecuted because he is a Jew, it locates his trouble in his refusal to retract his scientific findings that all human blood, Aryan and non-Aryan, is alike.

More than with any of his films, in *The Mortal Storm* Borzage's romanticism finds an even balance with social criticism. His concern is still with the conflicts of his characters, but here the Roths' struggle to survive and final ruination has a more explicit political meaning. The environment has become too pervasive for Borzage's characters to realize their love and comradeship. Previously Hans and Lammchen had been able to fulfill themselves despite the violence around them and the four comrades were spiritually reunited in their escape to a more peaceful world. But in *The Mortal Storm*, Martin, Freya, and the Roth family are completely thwarted by the Nazis. Martin and Otto's flight is not toward disengagement but is the beginning of a battle to restore a world where individuals can live and love freely.

Confessions of a Nazi Spy—Up from Isolationism

Louis B. Mayer's interest in the Nazi emissary's view of *Three Comrades* was of course a cautionary measure aimed toward the retention of MGM's European market. Warner Brothers did not have quite the same worries since they had already lost the German market: in 1936 Warners' German distribution agent, a Jew, was murdered by the Nazis and Jack Warner promptly closed down offices there.[20] Added to this was Jack's friendship with Roosevelt, who by 1938 was unofficially preparing for war. Charles Higham relates how the President brought the case of a Nazi spy ring in America to Warner's attention long before the story became public and then tacitly approved the preparation of a screenplay based on FBI information. Warner contract writer Milton Krims worked closely with FBI investigator Leon Turrou, infiltrating meetings of the German-American Bund and attending the trial of the various spies. Krims prepared an extremely factual screenplay with a documentary approach and a *March of Time*-like narrator.[21]

The final product, *Confessions of a Nazi Spy* (1939), released six months before the war started in Europe, was exceedingly daring for the time. It is the first Hollywood film to portray the Nazis as a threat to America. Essentially an investigative crime melodrama, the film documents the FBI's inquiry into American-based Nazi spies. Sprinkled throughout the story are brief but pointed attacks made by the authoritative narrator against Nazism. Edward G. Robinson as the Leon Turrou character even goes so far as to say "It looks as if Germany is at war with the United States."

The film is also important for establishing the stereotypes that were to be associated with the Nazis in most subsequent anti-Nazi films. Though we are informed that Germany is an imperialistic state currently involved in the suppression of political opposition and religious minorities, the greatest stress is on Nazism as a pure evil, the concoction of the psychologically abberrant. George Sanders as Franz Schlagel enacts the archetype of the clever, dispassionate sadist who will go to any lengths to achieve his evil ends. Paul Lukas' Dr. Kassel is the fanatic intellectual for whom Nazism represents a source of righteous power, while Kurt Schneider (Francis Lederer), a typical Nazi follower, is a classic dupe in the Frank Taylor–Joe Radek mold. As in later war propaganda, our emotional condemnation of the Third Reich is based completely on the repulsiveness of the individual Nazi characters.

The film came under severe attack. According to Charles Higham, members of the cast received threatening letters and telegrams, the German Consul in Los Angeles fought to cancel the film, and the German-American Bund sued Warners for $5,000,000. (The suit was subsequently dropped when leader Fritz Kuhn was jailed for misappropriating Bund funds.) The German government protested against the picture as "pernicious propaganda poisoning German-American relations" and had the film banned in Italy, Japan, Sweden, and Yugoslavia.[22] But despite all the publicity surrounding both the actual trial and the film's release, *Confessions* was a commercial failure. The poor box office, when combined with the controversy, was enough to inhibit Warners or any other studio from producing similar films for more than a year.

Then in the summer of 1940, anti-Nazi films finally began to trickle out of Hollywood. The earliest of these dramatized life inside Germany, editorializing against the political atrocities but not yet calling for American involvement. *Four Sons*, like *The Mortal Storm*, was released in June and dealt with a European family whose loyalties are split by the rise of Hitler. Set in Czechoslovakia on the eve of the Nazi invasion, it reveals the fifth column espionage work that prepares for the ruthless blitzkrieg. One son (Don Ameche) tries to subvert the efforts of his Nazi brother (Alan Curtis) but by the conclusion both are dead on opposite sides of the same battlefield. After a third son is killed in the Polish campaign, the mother flees with her daughter-in-law and grandchild from a country now gripped in totalitarian oppression. They find refuge with the only surviving son, living a life of freedom in America.

The Man I Married (July 1940) and *Escape* (October 1940) present Germany through the eyes of visiting Americans and chart their movement from indifference to anger. In the former, an American woman visits the country with her German-born husband and sees him slowly won over to the fanaticism of the Nazi ideology. In *Escape*, a young American returns to his native Germany to visit his mother, only to find her in a concentration camp awaiting execution. Both Americans undergo the very process the U.S. populace was going through: they begin as uninformed, detached onlookers and gradually become more and more outraged at the atrocities they witness. But interventionism is not yet the answer. Like *Four Sons*, each film still sees America, the land to which the surviving characters flee, as a haven far removed from danger.

Soon, however, the American heroes' transformation was taken one step further. Suddenly prevented from escaping to the United States, they resolve to fight Hitler and encourage their countrymen to do likewise. *Foreign Correspondent* (August 1940), Walter Wanger's belated adaptation of *Personal History*, directed by Alfred Hitchcock, was the first to take a bluntly prowar stance. American journalist Johnnie Jones[!] (Joel McCrea) arrives in Europe completely ignorant of any crisis, but through his unwitting entanglement in a Nazi plot to sabotage a peace movement and provoke world war, Johnnie comes to realize that he and his country must take militant action. At first he tries to escape to the United States but when his plane is shot down he remains in London to broadcast to the world what is going on. During the blitz, he makes a direct appeal for military involvement: "The lights are going out in Europe. . . . Ring yourself around with steel, America."

In *Arise My Love* (October 1940), another journalist, Augusta Nash (Claudette Colbert), is too enamored with her lover to notice the impending tragedy. When their idyll is broken by the German invasion, they too set out for America. However, their ship is torpedoed and as they are washed up on the Irish shore, they resolve, like Johnnie Jones, to remain in Europe and fight the war. In Fritz Lang's *Man Hunt* (June 1941), it is a Britisher (Walter Pidgeon) who moves toward a commitment to antifascism. A big-game hunter, he begins by stalking Hitler, not to kill him, but purely for the challenge of outmaneuvering the world's most protected quarry. When the hunter succeeds and has Hitler in his rifle sights, he does not shoot him. But by the end of the film, his contact with Nazi Germany (in the familiar person of Gestapo chief George Sanders) convinces him to hunt down Hitler for real. Each film serves as an allegory against isolationism: the protagonists' desire to remain uninvolved is put to too severe a test and they are pushed into action by the outrageous villainy of the Third Reich. By September 1941, *A Yank in the R.A.F.*, as its title clearly indicates, was suggesting quite strongly that America become involved in the fight against fascism.

Of course, for the most part the films remain apolitical entertainments. With the exception of the final declaration of commitment, the message is made between the lines. The studios remained reticent even as Hitler marched through Paris and bombed London. Mitchell Leisen, the director of *Arise My Love*, shot alternate takes of all the anti-Nazi scenes with toned-down dialogue in order to protect himself as much as possible.[23] Fritz Lang was told by Darryl F. Zanuck not to show too many swastikas in *Man Hunt* and when Lang shot it the way he wanted, Twentieth Century-Fox changed much of the film.[24] Isolationist pressure continued unabated and as late as September 1941 Senator Gerald P. Nye spoke out rather floridly against prowar propaganda in Hollywood movies:

> At least twenty pictures have been produced in the past year all designed to drug the reason of the American people, set aflame their emotions, turn their hatred into a blaze, fill them with fear that Hitler will come over here and capture them, that he will steal their trade. . . . [The movies] have become the most gigantic engines of propaganda in existence to serve war fever in America and plunge the Nation to her destruction.[25]

Perhaps because it restricted its discussion on the necessity of war to the past, Warners' *Sergeant York* (July 1941) is one of the least compromised prewar calls to arms. Without referring to fascism, the film telescopes the thirties' movement from pacifism to acceptance of war's inevitability. Alvin York (Gary Cooper) begins as a highly religious conscientious objector who refuses to kill because it "goes agin the Book." But long, hard study of the Bible and the history of the United States convinces him that the Good Lord thinks it admissible to sometimes fight to defend your own rights and those of your countrymen. When York does kill dozens of Germans and captures 132 more, he does so because it is the only way he can prevent the Germans from killing his fellow soldiers. Like the other heroes, York finds war a necessary evil: one must kill to prevent killing. *Sergeant York* is the culmination of the prewar cycle, accurately mirroring the nation's dread of war while attempting to find positive, humanitarian justification for the coming death and destruction.

The Great Dictator

By far the most courageous and inventive of the prewar antifascist films is Chaplin's satire *The Great Dictator* (October 1940). The film is important for its thorough treatment of the Jewish problem and its direct condemnation of Hitler as well as for its attempt to integrate its politics into the main body of the film. Chaplin is not adding topical allusions to an established format but rather developing a mode of expression to comically perceive the nature of Nazism. He seeks to expose Hitler's backside so that we laugh at his mystic bilge and ultimately recognize his true homicidal insanity.

As with the other films, pressure was exerted to halt production. Chaplin's distributor, United Artists, warned him that the film would be subject to heavy censorship and probably unsuitable for foreign release. Many others advised him against the project and during production he received many threatening letters and calls.[26] Chaplin, however, was in a position not only to override such pressure but to make the kind of direct political statement the other films balked at.

He builds his comedy around two characters, the little Jewish barber and Adenoid Hynkel, Dictator of Tomania (called "the Furor"), both played by Chaplin and both representing opposite sides of the old Tramp. The Barber has inherited all of Charlie's innocence and humanity while Hynkel exhibits his mischievous cruelty and streak of sadism. Thus, instead of the comic paradoxes between good and evil, nature and society being contained in the Tramp alone, they spring from the contrasts between the Barber and the Dictator. Since both represent extremes of good and evil, both are in a sense insane: Hynkel because he retains the elements of Charlie's violence without the compassion to offset it and the Barber because he is too innocent to cope with the modern world. The Dictator has grossly perverted Charlie's alleyway scrappiness, using it to gratify his monomaniacal need for complete power. The Barber, driven even crazier by the machinery of war than was the factory worker by the assembly line in *Modern Times*, is released from an army hospital a pale ghost of his former self. Almost completely lacking Charlie's pluck, this childlike innocent is hopelessly ineffectual and often downright stupid, pathetically ill-equipped to face the insanities of the new modern world—anti-Semitism, storm troopers, and concentration camps.

Hynkel is the more intriguing character. Chaplin does not just burlesque Hitler but tries to understand him. The raving hysteric of the opening scene whose mad rage of epithets literally wilts the microphone (translation: "The Furor has just referred to the Jewish people") is also a human being whose evil has cause and explanation. His vanity and power lust make him an easy pawn for such clever manipulators as Garbitsch (Henry Daniell), whose devious suggestions constitute the real policy of the Party. His vanity also pits him against the strutting Napaloni, as the two dictators try to outdo each other in everything and anything until Hynkel finally tops his rival by invading Austerlich.

The Dictator's demented fantasies are revealed in the famous dance with the globe. As he glides ethereally about the room with the balloon globe, coyly bouncing it off various parts of his anatomy, Hynkel is suddenly revealed also to be an innocent. He is a child at play in a fantasy of world domination. The discrepancy between the delicate grace of the dance and its sinister connotations points up both the brilliance and the savagery, the childishness and cruelty of Hynkel. An overeager embrace bursts the balloon, the globe is destroyed, and the Dictator is left like a disappointed, pouting infant.

Other satiric bits illustrate the rationale for political repression. Not satisfied with having just the leaders of a strike executed, Hynkel first orders all three thousand strikers shot ("I don't want any of my workers dissatisfied") and then extends his tortured logic of escalating violence to shoot all brunettes since the strike leaders were all brunettes. He overlooks the fact that he himself is a brunette. The political basis for anti-Semitism is unmasked as Garbitsch cynically advises his Furor that perhaps increased violence against the Jews will take the people's minds off their stomachs. The Jews are made scapegoats to distract the populace from the real problems of economic strife in Tomania-Germany. The only time the persecution relents is while Hynkel attempts to dupe a Jewish financier into loaning the necessary funds for the invasion of Austerlich.

The ghetto scenes depict the effects of Hynkel's policies on the Jews. Chaplin contrasts the oppressors' comic lunacy with the very frightening results of that lunacy. Storm troopers march through the streets singing a ridiculous hymn to the super-race: "The Aryans, the airy, airy, Aryans, as we go marching by." As they proceed through the ghetto, however, these Keystone Kops segregate shops by painting "Jew" on windows and viciously beat up dissidents. When the naive barber objects, the troopers almost lynch him. Chaplin thus directly links Nazism with anti-Semitic policies. The brutality of those policies is further revealed as the Barber is arrested and imprisoned in a concentration camp (although Chaplin had no idea what the actual camps were like and later commented that had he known he could never have made fun of the Nazis[27]).

The ghetto scenes are less effective than the Hynkel satire, marred by an often heavy-handed sentimentality. Chaplin's Jews sometimes appear as overly noble victims who too easily arouse our sympathy. The Barber, because he is a one-dimensional common-man type, is no match for the Dictator either in terms of the film's good–evil conflict or in terms of audience appeal.

The contrasts between victim and victimizer are given an ironic turnabout in the finale when the disguised Barber is mistaken for Hynkel. This is Chaplin's most extreme use of his masquerade/role reversal motif wherein the social outcast replaces the look-alike insider; the common man Jew is taken for the anti-Semitic Dictator. But rather than play upon the satiric richness of the situation, Chaplin drops all comic pretense, in essence stops the film and speaks directly to the audience. There is nothing the Tramp could possibly say as he has been robbed of his cunning, so Chaplin himself steps forward to plead with his audience to stop the dictators and create a world of freedom for all. Besides breaking with the dramatic structure of the film, the speech (despite Chaplin's passionate delivery) is banal and sentimental.

One cannot help but suspect that a biting, satiric finale more typical of Chaplin would have made the point more effectively. In fact, according to a *Time* article on the original script, Chaplin initially intended for the final escape speech to be nothing more than a dream Charlie has in the concentration camp:

> With . . . cheers and happy song echoing in his ears, Charlie wakes up back in the concentration camp, a storm trooper glowering down at him. Charlie smiles and the storm trooper starts to smile back. Then his lips freeze and he bellows Charlie Chaplin's curtain line: "Get up, Jew! Where the hell do you think you are."[28]

This comic irony sounds like a much more scathing and effective conclusion than the pretentious preachment for brotherly love.

With *The Great Dictator*, Chaplin's Tramp reached the end of his road. A society in its final stage of disintegration has declared war on all those values Charlie holds most sacred. Conformity has reached the absurd level of the super-race and all deviants must be incarcerated or liquidated. The neighborhood cop has become a Gestapo agent or a storm trooper. Trekking down the road is no longer possible since fascism will reach everywhere; Hannah (Paulette Goddard) and the Jaeckel family have already fled to freedom in Austerlich only to find themselves back where they started—Hynkel's troops invade and confiscate everything. Instead of giving us the final shot of Charlie shuffling hopefully toward the horizon, the Tramp simply disappears and it is Chaplin urging us not to turn our backs but to stand up and fight. *The Great Dictator* is blatantly anti-isolationist. Unlike the other antifascist films of 1940, Chaplin does not proffer an idyllic America for his Jews to escape to: "There is no promised land for the oppressed people of the world. There is no place over the horizon to which they can go for sanctuary. They must stand and we must stand." Modern society has finally forced the Tramp out of existence. The highway Charlie took back in 1936 proved to lead nowhere.

Epilogue—A Brief Survey of Wartime Propaganda

The whole isolationist stance was obliterated by Pearl Harbor. Suddenly Hollywood was officially sanctioned to produce films which attacked fascism. Whereas FDR once could only tacitly encourage anti-isolationist pictures, he now appointed a coordinator between the government and movie industry whose duties were "to consult with and advise motion picture producers of ways and means in which they can usefully serve the National Defense effort." Producers, distributors, and exhibitors responded by forming the War Activities Committee which sought to "emotionalize and glorify 'the blood, sweat and tears' of war, the sacrifices demanded, and the ends for which America and her allies were fighting."[29] Now that it was approved and was potential box-office, the European issue became a movie staple. In the four years from 1942 to 1945, twenty-eight percent of Hollywood's production dealt with the war.[30]

During this time, the social problem film all but disappeared and was absorbed into the wartime propaganda film, which in many ways seems an outgrowth of the problem cycle. Hollywood applied the same conventions it had used on internal matters to the external threat. The issues and answers were as clear-cut as always: fascism replaced corruption and the united front class synthesis. The celebration of America which inevitably popped up at the end of the problem film now took over center stage.

The enemy was presented according to the stereotypes established in *Confessions of a Nazi Spy*: as brutal sadists and obsessed fanatics devoted to the quest for power. They stood in opposition to everything that was honest and worthwhile, to the American way of life, liberty, and the pursuit of happiness. So, despite a government recommendation to clarify the issues of the war, the films rarely depict ideological matters on anything other than a "we're for freedom, they're against it" basis.

In films such as *Hitler's Children* (1943) and *Tomorrow the World* (1944), democracy versus totalitarianism is really a fight between good and bad people, not between political viewpoints. In the former film, totalitarianism is represented by American-born Nazi Karl Bruner (Tim Holt) and freedom by Anna Muller (Bonita Granville) a German-born American. The girl is noble and friendly while the boy is neurotically fanatic. Karl is reformed not through a change in ideals but because he is repulsed at the way in which Anna is whipped and beaten by his brutal superiors. *Tomorrow the World* similarly identifies the Nazis as nasties. Emil (Skip Homeier) is a twelve-year-old member of the Hitler Youth who like Karl has been thoroughly indoctrinated in Nazi ideology. So brainwashed are Hitler's followers that they are incapable of thinking and feeling for themselves and must blindly act out the implanted demands of their master. After he is orphaned, Emil is taken to America to live with his uncle (Fredric March) and proceeds to create dissension and hatred in the typical American small town. The vicious little monster reviles his uncle's Jewish fiancée (Betty Field), spies on his uncle's war department work, and bludgeons his cousin.

Although the film preaches patience and understanding in overcoming such hatred, young Emil is reformed only when he is threatened with violence by the neighborhood kids and with arrest by the police. Like the shysters, the Nazis have to be either reformed or killed.

Except for *The Great Dictator*, only one film actually took a detailed look at Hitler and his party leaders. *The Hitler Gang* (1944) traces the rise of the Nazi Party, following its progression from 1918 when Corporal Hitler is a paranoic in a German hospital to a blood purge after his ascension to power in 1934. But rather than analyze the background which fostered the Nazi movement, the film views the rise of the Third Reich as series of murders, double-crosses, and underhanded plots and Hitler (Robert Watson) as a deranged psychopath at the head of a gang of cutthroat mobsters.

Although the Japanese were dealt with less frequently, their stereotyping was far more vicious and racist. Epithets such as "yellow rats" and "yellow cowards" had to be dropped out of deference to America's Chinese allies,[31] but the movies' "sneaky Nips" and "lustful Japs" clearly foreshadow the "dirty gooks" of a later war. The Japanese are portrayed as being particularly savage to white women, capturing Amelia Earhart (Rosalind Russell) in *Flight for Freedom* (1943) and doing their worst to Allied nurses in *So Proudly We Hail* (1943) and *Cry Havoc* (1943). *The Purple Heart* (1944) and *God Is My Co-Pilot* (1945) detail Japanese abuse of prisoners of war, accusing the enemy of trying to brainwash their stalwart American foes. The major characteristic of the movie Japanese, anathema to all Americans, is their sneaky, two-faced fighting techniques. The surprise attack on Pearl Harbor had established this image and it was followed through in, among other films, *Across the Pacific* (1942) and *Blood on the Sun* (1945).

In dramatizing America's role in the war, one of the most prevalent motifs is that of conversion from passive isolationism to active commitment. Like many prewar heroes, such sleeping giants as John Garfield in *Air Force* (1943), Cary Grant in *Mr. Lucky* (1943), Alan Ladd in *China* (1943), and *Lucky Jordan* (1943), and, most prominently, Humphrey Bogart in *Casablanca* (1942–43), *To Have and Have Not* (1944), and *Passage to Marseilles* (1944) are finally awakened from their indifference when they come in contact with the totalitarian repression of the Nazis. They enter the fray amidst a fanfare of patriotic music and assurances that "This time I know our side will win" (Lazlo to Rick in *Casablanca*). A variation on the conversion theme is provided by *Watch on the Rhine* (1943). A refugee resistance leader from Europe, Kurt Muller (Paul Lukas), persuades his American in-laws of the necessity to fight by describing the dangers of Nazism. When a Nazi collaborator threatens to reveal Kurt's identity, Kurt murders him and escapes with his relatives' assistance. Before returning to Europe to rejoin the battle, he explicates the same lesson learned by Alvin York —violence is evil but is sometimes also the only way to rid the world of a greater evil.

Another large group of films celebrated America's allies, portraying them as Americans with funny accents fighting for the same principles of liberty and motherhood. Among these films are *Mrs. Miniver* (1942) about England, *This Land is Mine* (1943) about France, *Hangmen Also Die* (1943) about Czechoslovakia, *Edge of Darkness* (1943) about Norway, *Dragon Seed* (1944) about China, and *Mission to Moscow* (1943), *North Star* (1943), and *Song of Russia* (1944) about the Soviet Union. One of the most straightforward statements on the need for unity is made in Hitchcock's *Lifeboat* (1944). A group of shipwreck survivors of disparate social, national, and racial origins are stranded together in a lifeboat. The group is controlled by a willful and treacherous Nazi until they finally band together and destroy him. Hitchcock describes the film as an allegory on the need for "the democracies to put their differences aside temporarily and to gather their forces to concentrate on the common enemy, whose strength was precisely derived from a spirit of unity and of determination."[32]

Americans in combat also had to put aside their class and ethnic differences in order to survive. *Action in the North Atlantic* (1943), *Bataan* (1943), *Sahara* (1943), *A Walk in the Sun* (1945), and *The Story of G.I. Joe* (1945) portrayed combat units that looked like the old neighborhood gang from the thirties' slums—Poles, Italians, Irishmen, Jews, Negroes, etc., who successfully merge together (usually under a WASP leader) in battle.

Homefront unity received some attention in films which attack civilian complacency and, by extension, isolationist attitudes left over from the prewar years. The social problem film was restricted to those films which depicted American issues as a parallel commentary on Europe. *The Male Animal* (1942) and *The Talk of the Town* raise the question of freedom and justice in America in order to reaffirm it as a strong safeguard against totalitarianism. As we have seen, *Keeper of the Flame* and *Pilot Number Five* present would-be American dictators in order to highlight the nature of foreign dictators.

Other films glorified the efforts of the war worker whose performance on the assembly line was essential to the cause. In some cases, the factory was just another arena for espionage around secret weapons (*Joe Smith, American*, 1942) or enemy sabotage (*Saboteur*, 1942). Warners' *Wings for the Eagle* (1942) tried to create drama out of the struggle to meet factory quotas by the deadline. The relation between plant worker and flier is illustrated through riveter Jake Hanso (George Tobias) and his pilot son, Pete (Russell Arms): "Me on the assembly line, you in the air. A double play, eh kid? Hanso to Hanso."

The two most popular homefront melodramas were *Mrs. Miniver* and *Since You Went Away* (1944). Both deal with idealized middle-class families, one British, the other American, bravely seeing the war through while their men are in the battlefield. Insecurities are resolutely overcome by the stalwart wives and sweethearts who sacrifice their domestic roles to work in factories and hospitals.

Several comedies were created out of civilian shortages and hardships. In *The War Against Mrs. Hadley* (1942), a snobbish and isolationist society woman (Fay Bainter) is taught the necessity of sacrificing her own self-interests for a greater purpose, just as all those rich tycoons learned to care for the unemployed during the Depression. *The More the Merrier* (1943) and *Doughgirls* (1944) used the chronic bed shortage in wartime Washington as a pretext for romantic comedy. As the thirties screwball comedies synthesized the classes in a struggle against the Depression, so these forties comedies find everyone buckling down together to win the war.

Wilson and *The Searching Wind*: A Post-Mortem

Wilson, although made in 1944, is clearly confident of the war's outcome and extends the theme of unity beyond the war, suggesting that the allied nations join together in the postwar era to form a more effective League of Nations. The film's story returns to the prewar era and condemns the isolationism that kept the United States out of the League. With the assurance of hindsight, it postulates that isolationism is no guarantee against war and that the pacifist cause is best served by international unity. Woodrow Wilson's (Alexander Knox) defense of the League against its detractors and his warning that it is "the only hope the world has to avoid wars in the future" is clearly meant to parallel the post–World War II period.

Likewise, *The Searching Wind* (1946) is a heavyhanded chronicle of America's neutrality between the wars, of its refusal to recognize and act against the fascist threat. The film's message is conveyed through a series of confrontations between American Ambassador Alexander Hazen (Robert Young) and foreign correspondent Cassie Bowman (Sylvia Sidney). Hazen is stationed in Europe at key moments during the rise of fascism—Rome in 1922, Berlin in 1928, Spain in 1937, and Paris during the Munich Crisis. In each instance, he absolves himself and his country of any responsibility, while Cassie's warnings are ignored by him and the public. During Munich, he comes close to taking a stand against Hitler, but fears of a possible war in which his son, Sam (Douglas Dick), would have to fight lead him once again to turn away from commitment: "What right have I got to give away other people's lives? I won't have to fight. Sam will." But, as his father-in-law (Dudley Digges) points out, Alex has made sure that his son will have to fight: "All we can do is compromise. Compromise and compromise. There's nothing like a good compromise to cost a few million men their lives."

With the war's end, Cassie and Alex decide to forget their differences and get married. But when Sam, now crippled from the war, accuses his parents' generation of having helped to cause the war, Cassie sides with him against Alex. The film concludes with Sam's declaration that we must not make the same mistake again: "I don't mind losing my leg as long as it means a little something and helps to bring us out some-place." Sam expresses a constructive attitude far removed from the despair of the lost generation. The veterans of the early thirties films were incapable of envisioning any future, but this disillusionment has here given way to a new idealism.

Both films are self-conscious, preachy "message" pictures, but even though neither was a box-office success, they were indicative of the importance now placed on repudiating isolationism. *Wilson*'s producer, Darryl Zanuck, was totally committed to its political viewpoint[33] and used the film to project the spirit of wartime unity into a future world where all men are committed to one another and peace can thrive at last. With *The Searching Wind*, director William Dieterle (with script-writer-playwright Lillian Hellman) was finally allowed to express the militant antifascism that had been bowdlerized in *Blockade* and aborted in *Personal History*. The theme of the two pictures could be labeled "let's not make the same mistake again." Post-mortems on isolationism, they constitute the studios' final rejection of the principles they had been so afraid to contradict a few years earlier. Hollywood was quick to pick up on the idealistic and what proved to be too fragile hope of the postwar world.

—PART IV—

The Postwar World

—16—

READJUSTMENT—
"NERVOUS FROM THE SERVICE"

The war, in fostering both a sense of national pride and an economic boom, had created a solvent and healthy America. But, despite this, Americans could not easily forget the Depression and looked forward to the postwar world with mixed feelings. Many believed that the cessation of wartime production and the influx of returning veterans would cause another economic collapse. This prospect, combined with memories of what followed the last war—race riots, labor turmoil, left-wing violence, right-wing terrorism, government repression—and the growing possibility of a future war with the Soviet Union, provided ample cause for dread. Still, buoyed by wartime triumphs abroad and undreamed-of prosperity at home, Americans could not be totally downcast. Instinctive insecurities were counterbalanced by an optimism which saw America on the threshold of unprecedented triumphs.

Just as they had tried to calm public jitters throughout the Depression, so the Hollywood studios now attempted to ease the transition from war to peace. Working from a stance of economic confidence, the filmmaker no longer had to rationalize the collapse of the entire social structure. Since America was supposed to be solvent, the individual's conflict with it must lie in his own inability to adapt, that is, in his own personal neurosis. In her study of forties movies, Barbara Deming concluded: "Not doubts about society but—the other quantity in the equation—fears concerning one's identity find sharpest utterance."[1] In 1939's *Dust Be My Destiny*, John Garfield was a misunderstood victim of social forces beyond his control. By 1945, in *Pride of the Marines*, Garfield's failure to fit into society lay in his own psychological trauma at being blinded in combat. Society need no longer rid itself of corruption to prove to Garfield that it is indeed just; Garfield must, with society's help, cure himself of his neurosis.

Whereas the thirties problem films addressed a severe crisis of faith, the forties films were able to interpret the various problems—alcoholism, mental health, veteran readjustment, even racism and labor unrest —as pockets of distress in an otherwise sound society. In the thirties, Hollywood had confronted the problems of the forgotten men and the Okies reluctantly, trying to placate fears over issues too pervasive to be ignored. The later problem film, however, was more an assertion than a defense of American democracy. These films appear to be dramatizing the country's ability to question itself, to confront problems and work toward resolving them in an open and free society. But by safely confining the issues to individual cases, the films avoid truly testing the extent of America's openness and freedom, placing their confidence on a shallow footing.

Though the emphasis shifted from corruption to neurosis, the basic formula for treating social problems remained the same. Movie treatment of the first major postwar problem, the readjustment of war veterans to civilian life, goes through various reductive stages so that the veteran is happily reintegrated by the film's end. First of all, the films deemphasize those uncertainties that could potentially question society. Troubling fears of another war or depression, for example, are dealt with briefly and then glossed over or forgotten. The films concentrate instead on more personal physical and psychological traumas: learning to live with a handicap; getting reacquainted with one's wife, girl, or family; wanting to get something better out of life after being so close to death.

The films begin by showing these difficulties as common to all soldiers, but soon localize them to the neurotic protagonist. While the hero's compatriots quickly reintegrate themselves into the healthy society, he remains defiantly alone in his resentment and insecurity. The central drama then becomes one of his struggle, aided by the tolerant agents of various institutions, to overcome his neurosis. In order to, in Barbara Deming's phrase, "wind the hero safely home,"[2] one further reduction is required. If at first the hero suffers from the various normal insecurities, the film invariably focuses on one in particular, usually his relationship with his girl. The hero cannot overcome the other doubts as easily as his peers can because of his psychotic fear of rejection in this most important relationship. As soon as the girl proves to him that she still loves him, the other difficulties vanish.

The reaffirmation of the love relationship is tied in with that of society. The girl is always associated with officialdom. She either works for the army as a volunteer or a nurse or is aided by the service in recapturing her man. When more conventional methods of therapy fail, army doctors and psychiatrists contrive, in Hollywood's best Cupid fashion, to bring the estranged couple together again. In the few films where there is no girl, the compassionate doctors provide the love needed to cure the hero of his psychosis. Whatever the case, this army which specializes in Tender Loving Care provides unquestionable proof that any doubts about society's desire and ability to resolve the problems are unfounded.

The prototype for the series is *Pride of the Marines*. War hero Al Schmid (Garfield) is blinded at Guadalcanal and retreats into bitterness. He refuses to be helped or consoled by the hospital staff, throwing away his Braille alphabet and spurning their attempts to teach him to feed himself. Al's antisocial behavior is explained by a nightmare he has after being told he is permanently blind. In his dream, horrifying recollections of his injuries in battle are dwarfed by his fiancée's rejection of him. On awakening, Al decides never to tell her that he's blind but to simply say he's not coming back to her. He rationalizes that he doesn't want to be a burden, to have Ruthie (Eleanor Parker) waste away her life as his seeing-eye dog.

A later scene in the hospital ward shows that Al's anxieties are indicative of broader doubts. The wounded veterans in the ward discuss their various fears about peacetime life, including that of getting reacquainted with their girlfriends and wives. Only Al remains aloof and cynical during the conversation. The point is made immediately that problems such as Al's are being easily overcome by other soldiers. One of his wardmates relates how he got over his marital uncertainties by simply calling his wife and finding out how she felt about him. Fears about society are likewise unwarranted. Their country will take care of them —there is a GI Bill which will send them to college and, if all else fails, there is the American tradition of standing up for your rights and hollering until you're listened to. The most optimistic of the group declares that he's going to be a lawyer and maybe a Congressman. He's going to do everything in his power to ensure that the mistakes made in 1918 won't be made again.

Where Al differs from his fellow soldiers is in his stubborn refusal to face up to his fears. By the end of the conversation, he alone remains unconvinced about the state of the nation: "We can make things work in peace as we did in war, don't you see, Al?" "No, I don't see." The allusion to social issues gives Al's fears a more general basis, but this is just as quickly dispelled and Al's problem is clearly identified not as social but as psychological. The trouble is not with a country which is doing everything in its power to help but with Al Schmid.

The issue thus localized, the solution is fairly easy. His fiancée Ruth remains patient and loving and the army arranges a reunion between her and Al. She confronts him, labeling his fears as self-pity, and when she tells him that she doesn't pity him but loves and needs him just as he does her, Al's neurosis dissolves: "We'll have problems, but all married couples have problems." The film even intimates that physical handicaps may disappear when Al is able to faintly discern that a cab's top is red. Perhaps there is hope that his vision will return. But they agree, "Whichever it is, we'll do it together."

In 1946 a spate of similar films appeared and others continued to crop up into the fifties, many playing upon the conventions established by *Pride*. By far the best is the Samuel Goldwyn/William Wyler film, *The Best Years of Our Lives* (1946). It created the images and motifs by which the wartime generation measured its difficult but gratifying passage into peace. Three veterans, a working-class flyer, a middle-class sailor, and an upper-class army officer, hitch a ride together on a cargo flight to their old hometown, Boone City. Each experiences the pangs of anxiety as he faces his loved ones for the first time in years. In the archetypal return scene, Al Stephenson (Fredric March) surprises his family, with wife Millie (Myrna Loy) emerging from the kitchen aproned and unprepared, moving down the corridor to him in a state of wonder and disbelief. By following the lives of its three protagonists from their arrival home to their final readjustment, *Best Years* charts most of the major themes related to returning vets.

Prominent among these themes is that of the handicapped veteran and in the performance of real-life amputee Harold Russell, *Best Years* towers over other films in the cycle treating the same issue. Russell's Homer Parrish casually and good-humoredly performs all manner of everyday tasks from lighting cigarettes to drinking beer with the two hooks that have replaced his hands. When we first see Homer, he has already accepted his handicap so we don't witness any emotional trauma over the loss of his hands. As Al Stephenson comments, "They don't bother him, so they don't bother us." The fact that the hooks are real and that Russell is not an actor gives Homer an instant verisimilitude and makes him an inspiring character. Though Homer's story line through the film closely parallels Al Schmid's, it is secondary to Russell's impact as a genuine amputee and does not severely undermine the overall impact of the movie. Like Al, he rejects his fiancée Wilma (Cathy O'Donnell) out of fear that she is going to reject him: "I don't want you to be tied down just because you have a kind heart." His anguish is over her attitude toward his handicap rather than over the handicap itself. Nevertheless, when he removes the harness holding the hooks and sits there with his two arm stumps describing how helpless he is, and she gently tucks him into bed and kisses him goodnight, the boy-keeps-girl contrivance is entirely beside the point.

Similar but far less effective dramas are acted out by the other crippled veterans, paraplegic Ken Wiloceck (Marlon Brando) in *The Men* (1950) and blind Larry Nevins (Arthur Kennedy) in *Bright Victory* (1951). Ken is almost a carbon copy of Al Schmid, bitterly rejecting the hospital staff's help and deciding to end his engagement without even seeing his fiancée. He is entirely caught up in his self-pitying uncertainty about Ellen (Theresa Wright). But the helpful hospital staff (this time with the wardmates pitching in) play Cupid by ordering the recalcitrant veteran from the hospital and into the arms of his faithful girl. Larry Nevins finds himself unable to believe the reassurance of his doctors and GI friends that life "won't be quite so black tomorrow" until he falls in love with Judy (Peggy Dow), a girl he meets on leave. Judy's love is clearly the key to his recovery but Larry decides to return home to the girl he promised to marry before the war. Finding that his fiancée does not have the faith or strength to see him through, Larry returns to Judy and with her support begins to study law.

Perry (Bill Williams) in *Till the End of Time* (1946) and Moss (James Edwards) in *Home of the Brave* (1949) are crippled veterans who have no girlfriends. Nevertheless, the films narrow their problems down to a single fixation and the solution to a savior who cures them through love. Perry's belief that he can do nothing for himself because of the loss of his legs leads him into a state of sullen withdrawal. The girl whose love could inspire him is replaced by his mother and a friendly army officer who prod him to go out into the world. When Perry is called on to help a friend in trouble, his mother encourages him to put on his artificial legs and answer the call: "A man lost his legs at 39 and he became President." Perry, on artificial legs and crutches, arrives at the bar in time to help his buddies thrash the troublesome patriots group. The psychosomatic paralysis that prevents the Negro Moss from returning to civilian life is analyzed as a guilt complex over his white friend's death in battle. A dedicated psychiatrist/parent figure (Jeff Corey) forces him to confront his guilt feelings and thereby overcome his paralysis.

The same plot device of the good woman rescuing the hero with love and understanding is applied to veterans experiencing emotional trauma. Fred Derry (Dana Andrews) in *Best Years* is the most interesting of the psychologically damaged veterans. He returns home with citations and ribbons, an heroic bombardier who has been involved in a momentous global war and has lived daily with the imminence of death. Now he finds himself unqualified for decent jobs because his experience amounts to "two years soda jerk, three years dropping bombs," and must settle for working again in the drug store behind the soda fountain. His war bride, sexy, blonde Marie (Virginia Mayo), turns out to be a good-time B-girl, quickly disillusioned with her Freddy once he's out of uniform and out of money. In the end, the embittered Fred is like the rows upon rows of bombers waiting for the scrap heap. As he wanders through the airplane graveyard, he cannot resist climbing into the cockpit. There, in the film's most dazzling sequence, he relives his war experiences. Camera movement, music, and editing recreate the sensation of takeoff and flight, the awesome power and size of the aircraft, and the frightening but invigorating pressure on the bombardier. This surreal sequence more than any other captures the paradox of the war veteran, his exhilaration and pain in remembering the past and the obsolescence and frustration of his experiences in peacetime. But Fred is soon rescued, first by the junk dealer in the plane yard who offers him a decent job recycling the old bombers into prefab housing, and then by Peggy (Theresa Wright), the girl who does understand and love him. In the final scene at Homer's wedding, the now-divorced Fred is reunited with Peggy: "It may take us years to get anywhere. We'll have no money, no decent place to live." Her response is to stare up at him, eyes sparkling with the love that conquers all.

Cliff Harper (Guy Madison) in *Till the End of Time* finds that he can no longer relate to his sedate, middle-class parents, who still see him as the child he was before the war. When Cliff tries to explain his wartime experiences to them, they don't want to listen. They can't understand why he doesn't immediately go out to look for a job or finish his college degree. Cliff feels that he's completely alone in the world, has nothing to live for until he falls in love with Pat (Dorothy McGuire), a soldier's widow who gives him the inspiration he needs. With her help, he finds a job and conquers the bitterness he feels over the three and a half years he has lost and the college degree he would have completed. Complications are created only by Pat's hesitancy over their relationship and then are resolved when she rushes back into his arms for a fadeout embrace.

Specific social concerns beyond the personal trauma of the veterans are not central to most of the films. Again it is *Best Years* which develops this aspect the furthest. Behind the action there are references to larger issues—the prospect of another Depression, the possibilities of atomic war, and the bigotry of ultra-right patriots—all of which indicate an atmosphere of general uncertainty. Then, in the foreground, are Al Stephenson's struggles at his bank to ensure that deserving GIs receive loans to get them started no matter what their collateral. Al is the classic populist benefactor, like Dickson in *An American Madness*, fighting the bank for the right to loan on character—"His collateral is in his guts." But as played by Fredric March, Stephenson is far more than a one-sided idealist. A nascent alcoholic, he is straining as much as Homer and Fred to find his civilian bearings, to develop some meaningful career options and to reestablish contact with his wife and his children who have grown up in his absence. March's performance is full of comic wit and perceptive observation. When he rises at the big bank dinner to make his speech, it is not an assertion of Capra-like idealism but a drunken combination of insights and insults that alternate between making the point and embarrassing the guests.

In the other films of the cycle, the only social theme separate from the heroes' angst is a concern about bigotry. Ultra-rightism and racism are a minor but recurring motif within the cycle. The "old prejudices" still existing back home are not too far removed from the fascist attitudes the GIs have fought to destroy. Like *Best Years*, *Till the End of Time* attacks the xenophobic patriotism of those who would deny minorities their rights as Americans. In *Crossfire* (1947) veterans discover one of their own to be a psychopathic anti-Semite, while in *Home of the Brave* the black GI is virtually paralyzed by the racial taunts of his fellow soldiers. For blind southerner Larry Nevins in *Bright Victory* it is a self-revelation to discover his close friend is actually black. Thereafter, his mother's comments about "them niggers" offend him while his father's explanations that the war has taught the younger generation the evil of racism send him apologetically back to his black buddy.

From This Day Forward (1946) stands somewhat separate from the rest of the cycle as it concentrates almost entirely on the veteran's economic and social fears. Ex-sergeant Bill Cummings (Mark Stevens) waits in an overcrowded Army Employment Center and begins to recognize this situation as parallel to his many frustrations at getting work before the war. The heart of the film are his memories of the hard times during the Depression, as he is kept waiting and told to fill out endless forms, he instinctively assumes his postwar experience will be as fruitless as his prewar one. The only thing that saved him previously was the outbreak of war—first a job in a war plant, then in the service. Now, with the war plants closed down and thousands of men reentering the job market, Bill wonders if America will be able to avoid another Depression.

After voicing his doubts, the film concludes with a love-generated optimism. Bill's spirits are lifted by his resilient wife, Susie (Joan Fontaine), who has always seen him through his moments of despair. Bill gets a job interview, Susie announces her pregnancy, and his chronically unemployed brother-in-law gets the chicken farm he's always dreamt of owning. Once more the future bodes well and no matter what happens Bill and Susie still have one another.

The difference between this and the other films is that Bill's fear is not portrayed as neurotic; he is simply one of many whose fears have been shaped by society. The drama is not that of Bill overcoming his anxieties at a personal level but of his learning to live with them and hope for the best. The crisis is in his relationship with society, not with his wife. The film's cautious optimism is an accurate reflection of audience attitudes. Despite America's underlying doubts, the economy would hold its own and the GIs prosper.

—17—

THE MINORITIES

Anti-Semitism

Although many of the Hollywood moguls were themselves Jewish, Jews rarely appeared on the screen except as secondary characters and then usually as comic stereotypes. The producers insisted that any sympathetic portrayal of Jewish problems would only provoke more anti-Semitism and refused to deviate from an upper middle-class WASP image of America that was more in keeping with audience aspirations. It was not until the postwar era that two major studio films, *Crossfire* (1947) and *Gentleman's Agreement* (1947), confronted anti-Semitism as a serious social issue in the United States. And even then, despite the films' substantial box-office returns, no further films on the subject were released.

Up until this period, the Jew usually appeared as one of many ethnic types inhabiting the big-city neighborhood. Along with the boisterous Italians, hard-working Poles and brawling Irish, the friendly Jewish miser added color and humor to the urban melting pot. Representative of this "benign" stereotype is Herman (Harry Green), the heavily accented Jewish tailor in *This Day and Age*. Herman is the only member of the business community who refuses to pay protection dues to the mob. Although he is standing up to the gangster with proud declarations about life in a free country, the film makes clear that an equally important motivation is his unwillingness to part with money. When his shop is bombed by the mob, he emerges from the rubble, surveys the destruction, and summarily estimates that the "damage is worth $550." In Warners' *Mayor of Hell* (1933), one of the delinquent boys brought before the judge is a Jew. But whereas the other kids' parents are either drunks, widows, or simply unable to cope, Izzy's father is too preoccupied with his business to care for his son. Later, when Jimmy Cagney institutes self-government at the reformatory, Izzy "naturally" becomes treasurer and takes over the small school store. Sidney Miller, who plays the role, was to become Hollywood's perennial Jewish juvenile; in *Boys' Town* he again is elected treasurer of the progressive reform school.

Street Scene (1931) and *Counsellor-at-Law* (1933), both adapted from Elmer Rice plays, are the only films until after the war to refer to anti-Semitism as an American phenomenon or to present the Jew as a person rather than a type. *Street Scene* centers on the Jewish inhabitants of the New York melting pot. Sam Kaplan (William Collier, Jr.) is the hero, a frustrated youth caught between his love for Rose (Sylvia Sidney) and the demands of law school, between the life of poverty in the overcrowded tenement and his ambitions of affluence. On top of this, he must live with the anti-Semitic prejudices of his neighbors who label him the "little kike" and harass Rose over her relationship with a Jew. Although somewhat diminished by Collier's mawkish performance, Sam is still a fully developed character, a Jew who does not simply function as comic relief around the theme of money.

The other Rice play filmed by Hollywood, *Counsellor-at-Law*, dramatizes what happens to the Jew who escapes the ghetto. George Simon (John Barrymore) has worked his way up from the slums to become a prominent shyster lawyer but can never escape prejudice against his economic and ethnic background. Though he marries into high society, his snobbish wife and her two children from a previous marriage will not let him forget what he is. With his roughhewn manners and his Jewish friends, he fails to become "one of our kind" and, by the film's end, the wife leaves Simon for a young WASP sophisticate (Melvyn Douglas). Like Sam, Simon is a complex, ambivalent character. He is intelligent and charismatic and yet at the same time has betrayed his origins. As he is reminded by a radical youth from his old neighborhood, in breaking away from poverty Simon has aligned himself with the people who once exploited him.

As the war approached, the theme of foreign persecution of minorities began very tenuously to appear in the movies. Until the actual declaration of war, however, explicit references to German anti-Semitism were infrequent and veiled. *The Life of Emile Zola* (1937) makes but one fleeting reference to the anti-Semitism behind the Dreyfus affair. When the corrupt French military staff need their scapegoat, they peruse a list of suitable candidates. The camera scans the page, moving in on the name of Dreyfus and the designation "Jew" opposite it. One of the generals smugly remarks, "Yes, he'll do fine." Similarly, *The Mortal Storm* makes only subtle allusions to the Roth family's ethnic origins, preferring to call them non-Aryans rather than Jews. Chaplin's *Great Dictator* stands alone in its refusal to compromise the issue, to openly satirize Nazi anti-Semitic policies.

As the trend toward war propaganda developed, the miser image was replaced by another, more positive stereotype. The Jew became an innocent victim, ennobled to elicit greater sympathy. Dreyfus is shown to be a good family man and a dedicated officer with a clean record; Professor Roth is a lovable patriarch and respected professor; and Chaplin's Jews are sentimentalized common folk.

During the war itself, persecution of minorities was a major theme of anti-Nazi propaganda. Wartime combat films that called for a national unity against a common foe emphasized America's own tolerance toward various racial and ethnic groups. Combat units were made up of the gang from the old neighborhood, a microcosm of America's melting pot. In films such as *Air Force, A Walk in the Sun*, and *Objective Burma*, the Jew is an important member of the battalion. In *Action in the North Atlantic*, a Jewish merchant marine (Sam Levene) even becomes the heroic spokesman for American democracy: "You've got a right to say what you want. That's what we're fighting this war for. The Czechs and Poles, they didn't have a chance to say or do what they wanted."

Still, Hollywood remained guarded toward the subject. Jews were almost always minor characters and never too Jewish. Alvah Bessie, screenwriter of *Objective Burma*, recounts Jack Warner's attitude toward the film's Jewish soldier: "I like the idea of having a Jewish officer—what's his name, Jacobs?—in Burma. See that you get a good clean-cut American type for Jacobs." The actor cast in the role, William Prince, fulfilled Warner's requirements as a "good looking, American-type *goy*." Also, when the film's hero, Errol Flynn, finds Jacobs and his fellow soldiers dead, the camera shows their name tags in close-up. Jacobs' tag lacks any religious designation, whereas the others' are all stamped with "P" or "C."[1]

The early rehabilitation films continued to stereotype the Jew as a positive symbol of democracy but for the first time since 1933 referred to American anti-Semitism. In *Pride of the Marines*, Lee Diamond (Dane Clark), a Jewish GI, reminds Al that he's got no monopoly on handicaps: "Guys won't hire me because my name is Diamond and I celebrate Passover. There'll always be people like that. But we've got a stake in this country—in making it so people won't be like that." In *Till the End of Time*, it's his Jewish friend, Maxie Klein, that Bill remembers lying in a Guadalcanal foxhole when he confronts the bigoted American War Patriots.

With 1947's *Body and Soul*, a socially conscious Hollywood film again centered on a Jewish protagonist. Charlie Davis (John Garfield) and his parents are similar to the thirties neighborhood types, struggling to get by with a small candy store on the Lower East Side, but are also, like the Kaplan family in *Street Scene*, multifaceted individuals. While their Jewishness is not made central to the film, neither is it shunted aside. There is none of the previous subterfuge in identifying the characters' background. When a welfare worker asks Mrs. Davis (Anne Revere) her religion, she openly answers "Jewish." Once Charlie has risen out of the slums to become boxing champ and is preparing for a big bout, Shimmy, a Jewish delivery boy, tells him that the whole street has bet on him. Charlie is their hero, the Jew who will disprove the things being said about them in Europe. The film confronts the familiar theme of greed but Charlie's hunger for wealth and success is not stereotyped as a product of his Jewishness. (His boxing career is vigorously opposed by his mother, who answers his "I wanna be a fighter" with "So fight for *something*, not for money.") It is instead equated with the acquisitive values of American society.

That same year, anti-Semitism became a major, if short-lived, box-office attraction. Several productions on the subject were announced: Samuel Goldwyn was preparing *Earth and High Heaven*, a drama about a Jewish–Gentile marriage; MGM planned production of Sholem Asch's *East River*; Arthur Miller's *Focus* was scheduled by the independent King Brothers; and Twentieth Century-Fox was shooting *Gentleman's Agreement*.[2] According to James Agee,[3] RKO quickly made and released *Crossfire* in August to beat out the others. Its surprising commercial popularity was duplicated by Fox's *Gentleman's Agreement*, released in November. Goldwyn, ranting that Zanuck had "stolen my idea," canceled *Earth and High Heaven*, afraid that the public would soon be tired of the anti-Semitism theme. The other two films were never made but the fact that they were announced and that *Crossfire* and *Gentleman's Agreement* were so successful indicates the high level of audience receptivity to the theme of anti-Semitism in 1947.

Crossfire is essentially a taut, atmospheric thriller in which the motivation for the crime happens to be anti-Semitism. The issue is identified with the pathological hatred of Marty Montgomery (Robert Ryan), who drunkenly rages at Samuels (Sam Levene), "No Jew is going to tell me how to drink his stinking liquor." The word "Jew" is no longer taboo and Ryan uses it with sadistic relish. He shoves Samuels around, insulting him as a "Jewboy," and finally beats him to death. His inability to conceal his antipathy ultimately tips off the police:

You know, the guys who played it safe during the war. They live off the fat of the land and don't dirty themselves. They end up with nice apartments. Some of them have names like Samuels, some of them have funnier names. You know the type.

As an examination of anti-Semitism, the film has many weaknesses. Montgomery's bigotry is exceptional, a virulent neurosis, and the film fails to relate his case to more common and subtle instances of bigotry. The only reference to anti-Semitism as a wider problem is made by police Lieutenant Finley (Robert Young) in a generalized sermon about the need to stand up against prejudice: "This hating Jews comes in different ways. There's the you-can't-join-the-country-club type and the you-can't-live-here type." But the central example of prejudice Finley uses is that of Irish immigrants arriving in America over a hundred years ago, and the only anti-Semite we actually see is Montgomery. There are no attempts to show Montgomery's social background, to explain why and how he came to focus his hatred on the Jews. When Finley tracks down Montgomery and shoots him, the problem is dramatically resolved for the audience. Because Marty's psychosis lies outside one's general experience, the spectator's own values are never called into question.

Just as the villain is so nasty that he can elicit no sympathy ("He's been dead a long time"), so the victim is once again noble. Samuels is a war hero (as the Sam Levene character was in *Action in the North Atlantic*), wounded at Okinawa and honorably discharged. He gets mixed up with Montgomery only because he tries to help a troubled member of Marty's platoon who has the jitters about returning to the civilian world and his wife. Samuels is such a good Jew that even those who harbor prejudices would probably object to his murder. Revealingly, in the original novel, *The Brick Foxhole*, the victim is homosexual. The limitations of Hollywood's liberal-mindedness were never clearer. The fact that the theme could so easily be changed from homosexuality to anti-Semitism indicates the superficiality with which it is treated. And though the film exudes confidence in America's tolerance, the producers obviously feared that their audience would not have related too well to the murder of a homosexual.

Gentleman's Agreement, a rather turgid, self-conscious treatise, never generates the dramatic tension of *Crossfire*'s murder mystery. Paradoxically, it is the more effective study of anti-Semitism. Its central device —a magazine journalist decides to pose as a Jew to give his story on anti-Semitism "some angle that will humanize the problem and make people want to read it"—forces the audience to confront the subtle, almost invisible bigotry of apparently tolerant people such as themselves. As we discover along with the writer how the "nice" people change their attitudes toward a person because of his Jewishness, we cannot so easily dismiss anti-Semitism as a psychosis.

Through a series of painfully manufactured but revealing confrontations, the self-righteous writer, Phil Green (a stolid Gregory Peck) telescopes "a lifetime of hate into a couple of weeks." Each of his experiences highlights a different facet of American anti-Semitism. Phil encounters the blatant, unreasoned hatred of a bigot who uses epithets like "dirty Yid" as well as the "polite" hatred of the genteel, upper-class WASP establishment that refuses to rent him a room at a swank hotel. Equally pernicious are the discriminatory hiring policies of Phil's own magazine and the way people automatically stereotype him in terms of Jewish "character traits." At the magazine, for example, a staff member assumes that Phil had a desk job during the last war. There are even self-deprecating Jews such as Phil's secretary, Miss Wales (June Havoc). She obtained her job by changing her name and hiding her Jewish background and now objects to Jews who are too Jewish. "The kikey ones," she tells Phil, "will spoil it for the rest of us."

The film's major conflict centers on Phil's fiancée Cathy (Dorothy McGuire). She owns a vacant house that she refuses to rent to Phil's Jewish friend Dave (John Garfield), not because she herself objects but because the neighborhood would be upset with her. Likewise, Cathy asks Phil to drop his masquerade for their engagement party since her friends "wouldn't understand" and "it would cause a lot of unnecessary trouble." It is "the Cathy's everywhere," the film contends, that are most to blame: "all the nice people who hate anti-Semitism but do nothing about it," who enter a gentleman's agreement, a "conspiracy of silence" not to upset the status quo.

At its most challenging, the film hints that Cathy's reluctance to speak out may actually be indicative of a deeply ingrained, subconscious anti-Semitism. When Phil first confides to her his intention to write his article from the point of view of a Jew, she blurts out in alarm, "You aren't one, are you?" After Phil's son, Johnny, is beaten up at school, Cathy's intuitive response is to reassure the tearful child, "It's all right. You're not a Jew." Phil angrily accuses her of bestowing on Johnny "immediate superiority—being a white Christian" to which she impatiently retorts: "I'm tired of always being in the wrong. I'm just facing facts. I'm glad I'm a Christian and not a Jew. Just like I'm glad I'm rich and not poor, healthy and not sick." Cathy's true feelings are thus bared. To her, being a Jew connotes only negative qualities.

But Cathy's latent anti-Semitism is quickly retracted to afford a happy ending. With her engagement threatened, Cathy meets with Dave to discuss Phil's accusation. The film's "real" Jew assures her that Phil is wrong, that she's not anti-Semitic but merely complacent. Cathy suddenly sees the light and resolves to rent Dave her house. Phil in turn overcomes his solemn righteousness and the couple get back together. They will move with Dave's family into the restricted community and valiantly fight any abuse directed against them or others. With such zealous liberal activism, "the problem" will be overcome and the world will be a better place in which to live. As Mrs. Green (Anne Revere) proudly remarks to her son, "This isn't going to be the American century or the Russian century. Maybe it's going to be the human century."

Phil's masquerade as a Jew is a precursor of the "passing" films about blacks made in 1949. In both cases the films use this device to contend that there is no essential difference between the various races and ethnic types. Phil points out to his shocked secretary when his actual identity is revealed that he is "the same man as before, the only difference is a word—Christian." Still, this stress on the Gentile rather than a real Jew represents an evasion. The persecution Phil endures arouses audience indignation not only because it is innately wrong but also because Phil, as an Aryan, does not really deserve it. At any point, the audience can say, with Cathy, "It's all right. You're not really a Jew." The final effect on the spectator can perhaps be seen in a crew member's comment to screenwriter Moss Hart: "I'll be more careful in the future; I won't ever ill-treat a Jew in case it turns out that he's really a Christian."[4]

Furthermore, the concept of all races being the same denies the ethnic group their cultural attributes. *Gentleman's Agreement*'s only statement on the nature of being a Jew is made by a noted Jewish physicist (Sam Jaffe) whom Phil interviews,

> I'm going to start a movement saying that I'm not a Jew. Since Jews are not a race and most do not really practice their religion, why therefore do they still call themselves Jews? Because the world still makes it a disadvantage to do so and they call themselves Jews out of pride. My movement is stopped before it starts.

Although this definition allows the Jews some strength and affirmative pride, it also dismisses their entire cultural religious history in order to assure the audience that we're all the same, that Jews are really goys.

Gentleman's Agreement was the second and last film in the short-lived cycle. Few subsequent films of the postwar period included Jewish characters. Even Garfield (who had commented on his role in *Gentleman's Agreement*, "That was a part I didn't act. I felt it with all my heart"[5]) retreated from such roles, playing a Cuban revolutionary in *We Were Strangers* (1949) and Hemingway characters in *Under My*

Skin (1950) and *The Breaking Point* (1950). Hollywood's abandonment of the theme may have been partially inspired by the growing controversy around the founding of Israel, but a more important factor was probably the HUAC investigations. The old stereotype of the Jewish intellectual as Communist was again becoming popular. By 1949, when Stanley Kramer set about to film Arthur Laurents' *Home of the Brave*, he changed the central character from a Jew to a black.

The Negro Problem

The Jewish miser-merchant stereotype seems a minor transgression when one considers the frequency and intensity of debasement which the blacks have suffered at Hollywood's hands. Blacks have always been presented by Hollywood in terms that are acceptable to its white audience and that conform to current attitudes toward the Negro. One of the earliest film dramas was Edwin S. Porter's *Uncle Tom's Cabin* (1903); the American film's first artistic milestone, *The Birth of a Nation* (1915), is grotesquely racist; and Hollywood's commercial blockbuster *Gone with the Wind* (1939) likewise plays upon racial caricatures.

Several writers[6] have catalogued the American screen's black stereotypes and charted their development. There are two basic categories to which all movie blacks conform: The Good Negro (the faithful, submissive "tom" and "mammy" and the no-account, harmless "coon") and The Bad Nigger (the savage, rapacious "brute" and the rebellious, villainous "buck"). Donald Bogle traces the evolution of these two types over the years as they were placed into different contexts and "guises":

> With the Griffith spectacle, audiences saw the first guises. The brutes, the bucks and the tragic mulatto all wore the guise of villains. Afterward, during the 1920s, audiences saw their toms and coons dressed in the guise of plantation jesters. In the 1930s, all the types were dressed in servants' uniforms. In the early 1940s and the 1950s, they donned the gear of troubled problem people. In the 1970s, they appeared as angry militants. Because the guises were always changing, audiences were sometimes tricked into believing the depictions of the American Negro were altered, too. But at heart beneath the various guises, there lurked the familiar types.[7]

Until the problem cycle, blacks were almost always confined to bit roles and racism was hardly ever an issue. The earliest films specifically about Negroes, the "all-black musicals" *Hearts of Dixie* (1929) and *Hallelujah!* (1929), perpetuated a patronizing image of the black as entertainer. Both are set in an idealized South, an idyllic dream world where the childlike darkies sing and dance all day long. At no time do the films suggest that living conditions are anything less than perfect and virtually no whites intrude to create a potentially racial confrontation.

Hearts of Dixie abounds with romanticized clichés of the Old South, with Negro cotton pickers singing spirituals while the *Nellie Bly* steams down the Mississippi. Its story is structured around the two basic Good Negro types: the tom, in the person of old, kindly grandfather Napus (Clarence Muse) and the coon, as created by the incomparably shiftless Stepin Fetchit. Although *Hallelujah!* is a much more sophisticated film, director King Vidor's attempt to "depict the Southern Negro as he really is" still follows a plotline designed to incorporate the director's favorite stock images of the black: "I made a list of scenes suitable for an all-Negro sound film—river baptisms, prayer-meetings accompanied by spirituals, Negro preaching, banjo playing, dancing, the blues."[8]

Hallelujah centers on its hero's struggle to channel his passions toward goodness and away from evil. When he is the Good Negro, Zeke (Daniel Haynes) is a happy cotton picker singing and dancing with his family, or he is the evangelical preacher wailing out spirituals, performing riverside baptisms, and holding frenzied revival meetings. But Zeke's innate animalism often gets out of control. Once the devil gets into him, Zeke lusts after the sensuous city whore, Chick (Nina Mae McKinney), loses his money in crap games, fights in barroom brawls, and ultimately murders the faithless Chick and her lover in a fit of rage. In the end, Zeke serves time on the chain gang and returns home purged. He has learned his lesson and is again content to pick cotton and marry the good, down-to-earth Missy Rose (blues singer Victoria Spivey).

But such a summary does not do the film justice. The emotionalism must also be seen within the larger context and tone of the film, which is highly operatic. If the blacks are badly stereotyped, they are also everymen in a stylized musical morality play. And though Vidor's preconceptions about his characters today seem racist, Zeke and Chick still come across as full-blooded human beings. Under Vidor's direction, Nina Mae McKinney and Daniel Haynes invest their roles with such charm and vitality that they transcend the stereotypes. Many of the later, more sympathetic and realistic screen blacks never come to life as Chick and Zeke do.

Throughout the thirties, black servants and lackeys continued to provide comic and musical relief from the Depression. In a handful of films about social oppression, however, blacks were employed in minor roles to serve as a kind of background commentary. Though these appearances hardly counterbalanced the more demeaning caricatures, they constituted the movies' first self-conscious references to racial oppression and created a number of new variations on the familiar types. The most important of these new black stereotypes was the noble victim. In early films, he stands as a ready symbol of a general rather than specifically racial oppression. For instance, the presence of minor Negro characters in both chain gang films of 1932 automatically connotes social persecution and thereby helps establish sympathy for the beleaguered white inmates. In *Hell's Highway*, black prisoners sing a woeful spiritual during the funeral of a white prisoner, while in *I Am a Fugitive* it's a Negro member of the chain gang who selflessly helps James Allen escape. Later in the decade more attention was paid to the particular plight of the black himself. When a white girl is murdered in *They Won't Forget*, the immediate suspect is a Negro janitor who is so terrified that the police will pin the crime on him that he agrees to give false testimony. But once on the stand, the black confesses to his lie, declaring that he cannot send an innocent man to die. While each of these films alludes to the persecution of blacks, they again must make the victims long-suffering to ensure sympathy and must erase any trace of rebellion or bitterness to project a mood of appeasement.

This noble Negro stereotype was carried over into the early forties. In *Of Mice and Men* (1940), Crooks (Leigh Whipper) is the most oppressed of the ranch hands, the scapegoat for both the bosses and the workers. He is segregated from the rest of the hands and forced to live by himself in his own barn stall instead of the bunkhouse. Bitter over his segregation, he refuses any whites entrance to his stall and at first taunts Lennie (Lon Chaney, Jr.), venting his frustrations on the slow-witted giant. But soon the black warms to Lennie and welcomes him into his stall. The Negro is allowed some bitterness and anger but in the end is brimming over with generosity and humanity.

Three years later, Whipper played a similar role as Sparks, the Negro preacher in *The Ox-Bow Incident*. He is one of seven men who oppose the lynching, made sensitive to the white victims' plight by the experience of his race:

> Ah saw mah own brother lynched, Mistah Carter. Ah was just a little fellah—but sometimes Ah still wake up dreaming about it. . . . Oh, they made him confess, but it wouldn't have done him any good not to, and confessin' made it shorter.

But the film's sympathy is tinged with condescension. Every time Sparks appears, the soundtrack swells with a reverential spiritual. Like his predecessors, Sparks ends up as a long-suffering tom, self-consciously dignified but completely submissive.

In the wartime combat films, the noble black, like the Jew, was included as a representative of his race fighting alongside other nationalities and ethnic types against persecution. But, almost always, the black had to be elevated to hero status in order to be accepted as equal. In *Bataan* (1943), Wesley Epps (Kenneth Spencer) is a demolitions expert who valiantly rescues a white comrade. Oliver Cromwell Jones (Ben Carter) of *Crash Dive* (1943) is based on Dorie Miller, a Negro messman who gunned down four Japanese planes during the attack on Pearl Harbor. In *Sahara* (1943), Tambul (Rex Ingram), a Sudanese officer among a group of Allied soldiers, sacrifices his own life to save his white comrades.

Besides the noble Negro, the other important stereotype to emerge was the "tragic mulatto," the black whose fair skin allows him or her to pass as white. The genesis of this type is found in the character Peola (Fredi Washington) in *Imitation of Life* (1934), who grows up with a white girl and comes to expect the same kind of life that whites have. Peola's pale skin allows her to "pass" and therefore achieve the status she yearns for. But her fat, Aunt Jemima-like mother, Delilah (Louise Beavers), continually sabotages her efforts, forcing her to live as black. Peola rejects her mother's Christian stoicism and goes out into the world as a white. Peola's struggle is not for black equality but to be identified as white and her tragedy is that she cannot escape her heritage. After her mother dies of a broken heart, Peola realizes the error of her ways. At the funeral she hysterically repents, finally accepting her mother's role of submissive Negro.

The stereotypes of the noble, patient martyr and the pale-skinned pretender came into full flower in the postwar era. Just as anti-Semitism had been the theme of 1947, so the Negro became the problem of 1949. The self-effacing black who embodied white values was the perfect expression of the prevalent integrationist belief that all men are the same under the skin. A flock of "white" black heroes became fully acceptable to American society by denying any sense of their black identity.

The first of these characters is Peter Moss (James Edwards), *Home of the Brave*'s emotionally disturbed GI. By means of sessions with an Army psychiatrist, the film dramatizes Moss's memories of his past, the social background and racism that led to his paralysis. First, the film is careful to point out that Moss is a professional who has proven himself worthy to be considered equal and a part of white society. He has a high-school education and is a skilled surveyor who has heroically volunteered for a dangerous mission. Except for a brief scene in which his family is in the background, he is always in the company of whites—at high school, on the mission, and in the hospital.

Also important is his passivity. Although continually insulted by a fellow GI, TJ (Steve Brodie), Moss hardly ever defends himself. Except for a few indignant retorts, he generally remains calm and dignified even if deeply hurt inside. He stands by in self-pitying silence and allows other whites—first Finch (Lloyd Bridges) and then Mingo (Frank Lovejoy)—to defend him against racial slurs. Not only has Moss proven himself capable of being white, he endears himself by posing no threat. His quiet dignity cancels out any sense that he may be uppity.

The film deemphasizes external social conditions and plays up Moss's neurosis so that his problem seems as much his own fault as that of racist America. Moss's trauma stems from his own oversensitivity and a frustrated desire to be accepted by white society. A childhood memory describes the roots of his "feeling different": "I learned that if you're colored, you stink. You're not like other people. You're alone. You're something strange, different . . . Well, you make us different, you rats." His relationship with Finch is important to him because being accepted by a white is a means of overcoming his own sense of inferiority. So when Finch momentarily slips, calling him a "dirty yellow-bellied ni . . . nitwit," Moss is broken because such rejection reminds him that he is different and not really one of the boys. He recoils with resentment and when Finch is killed shortly thereafter is initially glad. But these feelings soon create such a guilt complex that he cannot leave Finch on the island, and this results in the psychosomatic paralysis.

Moss is cured of his trauma when he is assured that he is not different, that his blackness does not mean that he cannot be part of white society. His gladness at Finch's death does not have racial roots, the psychiatrist explains, but is a completely normal relief all GIs feel when their comrades die instead of them. The psychiatrist finally forces Moss to walk by taunting him: "Get up you dirty nigger and walk!" Moss's anger lifts him out of the bed and across the room. But by the time he reaches the object of his hate, the white doctor, he falls gratefully into his arms. His greatest moment of rebellion against the white racism that has defined and stifled him ends in an embrace of thankfulness that the white man is helping him.

The lesson he has learned from the doctor ("Sure, I'm different. You're different. We're all different. But underneath we're the same") is now validated by Mingo (Frank Lovejoy). The two form a partnership, intending to open up a restaurant-bar after the war. Mingo accepts Moss as his equal, but the message is undercut by the fact that Mingo has lost one of his arms and is thus not a whole human being. It is on this basis that he convinces Moss to join him in the restaurant venture:

MOSS: It wouldn't work. A lot of people wouldn't like a col-
           ored . . .
MINGO: A lot of people wouldn't like a one-armed bartender.

The black's equality is thus defined in terms of a crippled white.

By framing the drama in terms of black neurosis ("You're too sensitive. . . . The people who call you names are sick, maybe sicker than you. You've got to learn to face their names"), the film sidesteps institutionalized racism. As Manny Farber put it: "This gets a big laugh, particularly from Negroes in the audience who doubtless think of all the jobs they didn't get because of their oversensitivity."[9] TJ is the film's major allusion to white racism and his gross insensitivity is absurdly blatant. In one instance Moss offers the men some fried chicken and this leads TJ to ruminate: "You can't take it away from them, they sure can cook. They're great comedians too. Just lookin' at them makes me laugh. 'I's not lazy, boss, I's jes' tired.'" Later, as Moss embarks for home, TJ remarks how lucky he is to be returning as a Negro war hero, how he'll be the "king of Lennox Avenue" and will "have all those high yellows lookin' up at him." TJ's racism is an easy target for audience indignation and can be summarily dismissed as another form of sickness: "Don't worry about him. He's just a crud, a crud who hates everybody."

The overall message is clearly integrationist. Blacks should be allowed to enter white society as equals, that is, as white black men. The barriers to this integration are found in blacks, with their inferiority complexes, and in some whites, with their patronizing view of blacks. The film sees both barriers being easily hurdled: Moss is cured and whites like TJ are readily counteracted by liberals such as Mingo and the psychiatrist.

The next two films in the cycle present essentially the same kind of analysis. Both *Lost Boundaries* and *Pinky* center their discussion on the mulatto who is able to pass as white and thus fulfill what Moss can only dream about. The Carter family of *Lost Boundaries* and Pinky look physically white and, as highly educated professionals, are culturally white. Scott Carter (Mel Ferrer) is a doctor who has just married pale-skinned Marcia (Beatrice Pearson), and Pinky (Jeanne Crain) is a nurse engaged to an unsuspecting white doctor, Tom Adams (William Lundigan). In both cases the characters find professional fulfillment only when they are accepted as whites. Finding that a black doctor cannot earn a living, Scott relents and agrees to pass only for a year until he is established. Then another job opportunity, his own practice in Keenham, New Hampshire, convinces him to continue his masquerade. For twenty years the Carters live and work in the town as whites and become respected and popular members of the community. Their two children grow up as whites, the only hint of their racial origin being their predilection for music, their "natural rhythm." Pinky has received her education in the North where she has been regarded as white. Her return to the Southern shantytown of her youth is intended only as a brief visit before she marries Tom and embarks upon the life of a well-to-do Boston blueblood.

These idylls are shattered when the truth about their color is revealed. Scott obtains a navy commission during the war but, on the very day that the townspeople warmly send him off, an intrepid navy investigator arrives with the news of the Carters' mixed blood. Not only is Scott denied the commission but he is ostracized from the community. The people huddle in groups and gossip over telephones: "Have you heard about the Carters?"—"They're all Negroes"—"You can't trust anyone." Though Pinky comes to live in Negro shantytown, she is initially taken for a white. When she gets into an argument with a black couple over money stolen from her grandmother, Pinky is politely questioned by the sheriff while the black couple are searched and molested. The sheriff's attitude abruptly changes, however, after he is told that Pinky too is black. Later, when she wants to make money, the skilled nurse must resort to taking in laundry. Just as Phil Green discovers in *Gentleman's Agreement*, white society is hypocritical, treating individuals according to predetermined labels. The same people the Keenham New Englanders and the Southern sheriff respected are suddenly spurned when it is learned that they are of black origin.

An important ingredient in Hollywood's treatment of the mulatto in these films is the fact that they are all played by whites. The rejection the characters suffer seems more poignant and undeserved when portrayed by white actors meeting Hollywood's standards of glamor and beauty. The social issue then, just as with the Jewish problem in *Gentleman's Agreement*, becomes more the tragedy of whites who are ruined because of their Negro blood and less the persecution and oppression of blacks by a white racist society. This is particularly noticeable in *Lost Boundaries* when the Carters' son Howie (Richard Hylton) is told the truth. His disbelief and sense of revulsion provide a far more climactic moment in the film than the community's reaction. He flees to Harlem where he observes the life "his people" lead, hanging around street corners and living in rundown tenements. (This scene is given added punch by the use of location footage, designed to stress the low-life in the ghetto.) As he lies in his cheap room, Howie imagines the faces of his family, each appearing in closeup on the wall over his bed —smiling, healthy, warm, and white. But the faces of his family dissolve into the faces of blacks, each black face displaying prominent Negroid features and void of any vitality. Howie and the audience wallow in degradation and feel utter ruin at the idea of being black. Later Howie finally does accept his blackness with pride, but only when he is back with his white family living in white Keenham.

In the same way, Jeanne Crain's "perfect porcelain-white face"[10] makes her blackness acceptable without forcing us to confront it. And although Pinky finally asserts her blackness as a positive force, the film subtly implies that she is an incomplete person. Living as a white, Pinky would have been entirely fulfilled, marrying Tom and pursuing her career as a nurse; as a black her expectations are narrowed and she must reject Tom (interracial marriage was always objectionable), and live a celibate's life in her all-girl nursing school-cum-convent.

To a certain extent, the films place the burden of responsibility on the blacks. Both the Carters and Pinky are condemned for being dishonest to themselves and their community. The tragedy of the Carter family is not just that they are blacks mistreated by whites but that they have lied to their children and thus betrayed their heritage. The drama in *Pinky* centers strictly on the heroine and her gradual acceptance of her racial identity. In each case, the social criticism is not so much concerned with white racism as it is with blacks knowing and accepting their place. Indeed white society and its institutions come off quite well, demonstrating the willingness and power to resolve the problems in each film. *Lost Boundaries* ends with the news that the navy now accepts officers of all colors and races and with a soul-stirring sermon on brotherly love by Keenham's minister. So effective is the sermon that the entire congregation sees the error of its ways and apologetically welcomes the Carters back into the community. Pinky is forced to recognize her blackness and fulfill her social needs in the South through the efforts of Miss Em (Ethel Barrymore), her old, crotchety white patroness. Impelled to care for the dying woman, Pinky is at first resentful but gradually comes to terms with her own identity under Miss Em's wise tutelage. When Miss Em dies, leaving her estate to Pinky with "confidence in the use which she will put it to," the town almost reaches lynch fever. But an upstanding white judge defies the angry stampede and ensures that Pinky retain the property. Thus she is able to open her nursing school only through the charity and justice of the white upper class.

Other black characters conform to the standard racial stereotypes, confirming that Hollywood had not progressed too far. Except for the ghetto hoods glimpsed during Howie's odyssey through Harlem, all the blacks in *Lost Boundaries* are dignified professionals. One of Scott's fellow graduates who can't find a position in a hospital is indignant but nevertheless resigned to his fate: "I can always go back to work for Mr. Pullman. I've done it before and I can do it again." Jake Walters (Frederick O'Neal) in *Pinky* is a lazy, no-account "coon" lying around in his hammock or stealing money from Granny while his wife, Rozelia (Nina Mae McKinney), is a "razor-totin' " spitfire. Aunt Dicey (Ethel Waters), Pinky's grandmother, is a mammy, the strong black woman serving as faithful domestic for whites. Yet Ethel Waters' performance manages to imbue Dicey with a humanity which minimizes the character's stock servility. Apparently, Waters was so insistent on going beyond the stereotype that she clashed with the original director, John Ford, and helped bring about his removal from the project because, in producer Zanuck's words, Ford's "Negroes were like Aunt Jemima. Caricatures."[11]

The last black hero of this cycle represents a dramatic departure from the preceding "white" blacks. Lucas Beauchamp (Juano Hernandez) in *Intruder in the Dust* is a black who is stubbornly and proudly himself. He never once adopts white values, either by passing (he's too dark) or by overproving his worth in a bid for equality. It is his aloofness and forthright humanity that make him a threat to the whites and gain their resentment. When Lucas visits the general store, the white crackers taunt him, but Lucas remains unperturbed, half smiling to himself. His silence is not a noble dignity that quietly represses anger and suffering, but an almost smug superiority that refuses to condescend to foolish insults.

The film's adolescent protagonist, Chick Mallison (Claude Jarman, Jr.) is particularly frustrated by Lucas's refusal to be subservient, to fulfill the expected social role of nigger. Lucas has helped Chick by rescuing him from the icy creek in which he had fallen and then by taking him into his home, drying out his clothes and feeding him. Chick feels his white supremacy undermined by the tall black and attempts to pay the man for his assistance. But Lucas firmly refuses any money and when Chick sends him a gift, Lucas returns an even better one, delivered by a white boy "to add to the insult." It is only with Lucas's arrest for murder that Chick finally begins to feel superior: "They're gonna make a nigger out of him for once in his life anyway."

Lucas is not in jail so much for murder as for behaving independently of whites. Chick's Uncle John (David Brian), the liberal lawyer who takes Lucas's case, automatically assumes the black man's guilt and pinpoints the source of his trouble: "If you weren't so proud you wouldn't be here now waiting to be lynched." Even while in jail and dependent on the white lawyer and Chick to prove his innocence, Lucas remains in complete control. Seeing John is "too full of notions," Lucas turns to Chick and instructs him on how to discover the truth: dig up the body of the victim, extract the bullet and discover which gun it was fired from. Although Lucas cannot act on his own behalf, it is only through his prudence that Chick and the law can discover the real murderer.

Intruder in the Dust is by far the best of the 1949 cycle of films on blacks, but it was also the least successful commercially. This may be the result of the film's relative militance. Its insistence on treating Lucas as a human and not a "problem," and its portrait of the whites as the sole cause of racism (Uncle John: "He wasn't in trouble, *we* were in trouble") failed to conform to the attitudes of the time. Other practical factors contributing to its box-office failure were its lack of major stars and the fact that it was the fourth film on the subject within the year.

The next important film to look at blacks, *No Way Out* (1950), returned to the noble professional stereotype and introduced its most successful proponent, Sidney Poitier. He appears as Dr. Luther Brooks, a black who is distinguished among his race and thus equal to the whites. Brooks has passed his tests with "all A's" and now thanks the hospital chief surgeon, Dr. Wharton (Stephen McNally) for treating him as special, thereby giving him the breaks needed to get ahead. But the film immediately places Brooks in a crisis which threatens to destroy all that he has won for himself. Two white brothers are brought into the hospital with gunshot wounds received during an attempted robbery. When one dies, Brooks is immediately accused by the surviving hoodlum, Biddles (Richard Widmark), of murder and suspected by Wharton of incompetence. The main drama revolves around Brooks's attempts to prove his innocence and, by extension, prove himself a competent doctor and social equal. Against him are ranged the prejudices of white society. Racist Biddles denies permission to perform the autopsy on his brother that would determine the cause of death; the liberal chief coroner refuses to open an inquest, afraid that a scandal about Brooks's color would inhibit politicians from funding the hospital; and the dead man's wife (Linda Darnell) also won't cooperate, conditioned by her destitute lower-class background into assuming that a black man could not possibly be a doctor.

Despite these frustrations, Brooks nobly perseveres, continually repressing his own anger and that of his fellow blacks. When Biddles plans a raid on the black ghetto, the doctor first tries to dissuade his black friends from fighting back and then warns the police of the ensuing riot. Even after he is ambushed by the psychotic Biddles and forced to fight in self-defense, Brooks tends his assailant's wounds before caring for himself. The long-suffering Negro remains ever faithful to his Christian-integrationist code: "Don't you think I'd like to put the rest of these bullets through his head? I can't . . . because I've got to live too. . . . He's sick . . . he's crazy . . . but I can't kill a man just because he hates me." The Poitier character is a kind of loyal tom who endures and patiently waits for white society to recognize his rights rather than go out and demand those rights. To be too insistent would only threaten white society and thereby prolong racial inequality. The film naturally upholds Brooks's faith: the dead brother's widow learns from Wharton's mammy maid the warmth and motherly affection of the black race and allows the autopsy; it proves to the hospital staff that Brooks was right; and Biddles, the film's most dangerous racist threat, is arrested and thus removed.

The film is chiefly notable for its portrait of the racial tensions of the urban ghetto. The residents of "Nigger-Town" are not all as conciliatory as Brooks. His mother, tired of living in an overcrowded, decaying slum, disparages him for not making enough money. His brother, though he also studies to better himself, decides with their mother's approval to ambush Biddles's friends before they can attack the ghetto. The most prominent spokesman for black militancy is the hospital's elevator operator. He explains to Brooks that he's had enough of trying to be the white man's equal, that that's not good enough and from now on he's going to fight back. Though Brooks is the focal point for audience identification, we are not totally unsympathetic toward the militants. The whites are attacking them and their desire to defend themselves is only natural. If the race riot takes place in the middle of the film, before the optimistic resolution, and is soon dwarfed by the personal confrontation between Biddles and Brooks, *No Way Out* is still unique in its admission that such tensions exist.

Subsequent films followed the examples of Luther Brooks's integrationism, centering on the need for tolerance in both races: Negro athletes struggle to prove themselves worthy to compete with the white man in *The Jackie Robinson Story* (1950) and *The Joe Louis Story* (1953); *Bright Victory*'s blinded veteran must confront and overcome his racial bigotry when he discovers that his close friend, another blind GI, is black; in *The Well* (1951) the blacks and whites of a small town torn with racial strife join together to rescue a girl who has fallen into a well. By far the most important figure to emerge during this time was Poitier, who became Hollywood's first black superstar by playing the integrationist role. His character either nobly sacrificed himself for whites (*Edge of the City*, 1957, and *The Defiant Ones*, 1958) or overproved himself in order to be accepted in white society (the 1967 film *Guess Who's Coming to Dinner?*). Poitier gave expression to the liberal values of the period, carrying the late forties conventions through to the sixties and seventies, when a new black stereotype emerged—the aggressive, superhero, super-stud of *Shaft* (1971) and *Sweet Sweetback's Baadasssss Song* (1971).

Chicanos and Others

During the early fifties, Hollywood produced a flurry of films on ethnic minorities. Some atonement was made for past sins in the studios' reexamination of the American Indian. Beginning with *Broken Arrow*

(1950), the Indian was viewed as a human being who is either mis-understood or exploited by shyster white men. "Cowboys and Indians" took on a more complex texture in this and subsequent films throughout the fifties, including *The Savage* (1952), *Sitting Bull* (1954), *White Feather* (1955), *Walk the Proud Land* (1956), and many others. All of these, however, were set in the past and dramatized from a slightly broader perspective the frontier wars. Only *Jim Thorpe—All American* (1951) moved into the twentieth century and for the first time since *Massacre* alluded to more contemporary problems facing native Amer-icans.

The Japanese, so viciously maligned during the war, were also wel-comed back into the human race and were depicted as sympathetic people whose interaction with American culture creates racial violence. Typical is King Vidor's *Japanese War Bride* (1952) in which a Korean war veteran returns to his California hometown with a Nipponese bride and must tolerate racial abuse from the community. *Go for Broke* (1951), *Bad Day at Black Rock* (1954), and *Three Stripes in the Sun* (1955) all dramatize the Japanese as victims of American bigotry.

Of the films dealing with minorities, some of the most interesting are those that focus on the Chicanos, whose problems, ignored for the fif-teen years following the making of *Bordertown*, again assumed a certain prominence on the screen. Two Ricardo Montalban B-pictures, *Right Cross* (1950) and *My Man and I* (1952), merit little attention, blandly conforming to all the problem picture clichés. Chu Chu Ramirez (Mon-talban), the fruit picker in *My Man and I*, is exploited by a nasty white shyster who cheats him out of wages and then has him arrested. Yet throughout his ordeal, Chu Chu maintains his patriotic optimism (he even becomes a naturalized citizen), confident that everything will work out. He is the standard friendly, happy Mexican whose faith in America is upheld when the injustice is rectified. In *Right Cross*, Montalban is more bitter, but society still proves to be liberal and the problem turns out to be the hero's own neurosis. Johnny Monterez resentfully spurns society, assuming that he is accepted only because he is a boxing champ and will be rejected as soon as he loses his crown. But as usual, Johnny is cured of his neurosis by his manager's all-American daughter (played by girl-next-door June Allyson) who convinces him through her love and loyalty that the "Gringos" really like him for himself.

In terms of their social analysis, *The Lawless* and *The Salt of the Earth* (1954—based on a real-life strike and using the miners as actors) stand among the most daring of problem films. Neither was made within the confines of the studios—*The Lawless* was a low-budget independent released through Paramount, while *Salt* was made outside the studio system altogether[12] by blacklisted writer Michael Wilson, producer Paul

Jarrico, and director Herbert Biberman—and this freedom is reflected in their more radical interpretation of racial oppression. Here there are no Marty Montgomerys or TJs to blame. The lynch mob violence in *The Lawless* and vicious labor strife in *Salt* are deemed to be typically middle-American. By stereotyping the "spics" as lazy and no good, the people find a scapegoat for their hatreds and a rationale for injustice.

Each film exposes the shabby working and living conditions of the Mexican-American community. The only job opportunities open to the Chicanos in *The Lawless* are as fruit pickers making "six bits a day" for torturous labor. Though there are easier ways to make a living, they are restricted to "Anglos." Because of their meager, unstable income the only houses the Chicanos can afford are flimsy shacks lacking indoor plumbing and located "on the other side of the tracks" in the slum known as Sleepy Hollow. *Salt* goes further and provides some historical background on how the Chicanos' rights were violated by white industrialists. The community once owned the land but the zinc company moved in, took over the property, and offered the Chicanos the limited choice of moving or accepting employment at low wages. They are forced to live in management-owned houses and buy at management-owned stores. The houses are again flimsy shacks with poor sanitation and plumbing; the stores sell goods at inflated prices and thereby entrap the workers into a state of continual debt. Safety provisions for Chicano miners are lax, especially when compared to those in neighboring mines manned by whites. Whereas white miners are allowed to work in pairs, the Chicanos must perform dangerous chores individually. When the Chicano workers protest to the company, the manager warns them that he will find someone to replace them. "Who? A scab?" charges a Chicano; "An American," retorts the manager.

Racism is clearly linked to social authority. In *The Lawless*, a peaceful dance in the Chicano community is invaded by white hoodlums and a rumble erupts. When the police arrive, eleven Mexicans and only one white are arrested. White business leaders unofficially intervene and the Chicanos are forced to accept full responsibility for the violence. The newspapers then report that the incident was a battle between two gangs of "fruit tramps." In *Salt of the Earth*, the police conspire with the mine owners to defeat a strike, disrupting the picket line and arresting one of the spokesmen, Ramon (Juan Chacon). Snarling racial epithets, two deputies viciously assault him and then charge him with resisting arrest. Later, as the strike continues, the police evict the miners from their homes, carelessly damaging their possessions in the process.

The films' portrait of the Chicano personality does not conform to the conventional Hollywood stereotype of the noble victim seeking only to gain acceptance from the white man. Sunny (Gail Russell) in *The*

Lawless and the strikers in *Salt* are proud, bitter, and militant. Through her small newspaper Sunny agitates for change, and with other community leaders helps reduce gang warfare among juvenile delinquents. She is quite articulate, never hesitating to speak out, often with caustic insight. When white businessman Prentiss agrees to pay the fines for the Chicano youths if they plead guilty to the brawl, she protests: "So he gets rid of his guilty conscience by paying money and our boys are made to admit guilt." Sunny understands the issues and sees through the various guises of white liberalism, whether it is the double-edged benevolence of Prentiss or the cynical detachment of Larry. She has resolved to fight against all odds and not even Larry's romantic persuasions will discourage her. The strikers too are militant and articulate. They debate the issues at union meetings, thoroughly defining their goals and examining the nature of their foe. Every tactic management uses against them the obstinate Chicanos outmaneuver, and every cunning argument for a return to work they refute with solid reasoning.

However, in trying to offset Hollywood clichés and fulfill its "socialist realist" purpose of promoting the working class and oppressed minorities, *Salt of the Earth* relies too easily on political slogans ("This installment plan is the curse of the working man") and a romanticized image of the proletariat. Throughout his book on the film's production, for instance, Biberman continually betrays his stereotypic vision by describing his actor-miners as "stalwart people" whose "unfailing humility" is nothing but "the customary modesty of working people."[13] Just as the workers are defined as Classic Heroes, righteous and strong, so their oppressors must be Classic Villains, vicious and weak. The sheriff and his deputies, the mine foreman, and the company representative are caricatured as capitalist baddies whose ruthless hatred is motivated only by their pure evil.

In contrast, *The Lawless* presents us with characters whose attitudes and behavior are as diversified as human experience. While Sunny's dedication is somewhat larger than life, there is also Paul's confusion and fear in the face of hostile whites, Roberto's destructive bitterness which lashes out violently at his detractors, and Mr. Rodriguez's defeatist withdrawal. Nor are all the representatives of authority "vicious toadies." Some cops are blatant racists but others offer genuine sympathy even while they follow orders and arrest the Chicanos. Despite Sunny's condemnation, Prentiss is well-meaning and does genuinely want to see the unjustly arrested youths set free. Both films offer the classic leftist solution to racism—unite and fight—but *The Lawless*'s guarded optimism is a more accurate appraisal of the situation. Director Joseph Losey and scriptwriter Geoffrey Homes (pseudonym for the blacklisted Danel Mainwaring[14]) understand that such unity is rare, that the fight will be tough and that any change will be hard to come by. *Salt* idealizes the whole question of Chicano–white relations, making the poor automatically indivisible and omnipotent. It conforms to a rigid good–evil Formula and its rousing finale, like Hollywood's Happy Ending, is amplified from the specific strike to universal connotations of "the meek inheriting the earth." Ultimately, socialist realism is not substantially different from Hollywood wish fulfillment.

—18—

MORE NEUROSES— ALCOHOLISM AND INSANITY

Until the mid-forties, alcoholism was rarely dealt with in a serious fashion by Hollywood. A number of gangster films named Prohibition as a cause for crime, but few films portrayed the drunkard as anything other than a comic figure with an endearing weakness rather than a problem. Only with Prohibition a major issue in the 1932 election did the movies take up the issue of alcoholism—D. W. Griffith's low-budget independent *The Struggle* (1931) and MGM's very loose adaptation of Upton Sinclair's *The Wet Parade* (1932). The Griffith film is a combination of hoary sermonizing and a highly intimate portrait of a working-class alcoholic (Hal Skelly in a chilling performance). MGM's crude and confusing polemic thoroughly distorts Sinclair, first condemning the evils of drink (characters are killed, go insane, and are blinded by bad illegal booze) and then condemning Prohibition for creating more trouble than alcohol ever did.[1]

Aside from Fredric March as the ruined movie star in *A Star is Born* (1937), alcoholism was absent from the screen as a serious theme until the postwar years. Then it fit in well with the general trend toward problems as individual neurosis and held out a logical solution—going on the wagon—which could provide the necessary optimistic ending. The major film of this cycle is Billy Wilder's *The Lost Weekend* (1945). Like *Pride of the Marines* and countless other postwar films, it centers on the hero's identity crisis and its resolution through the efforts of the patient heroine. The film is a case study of an individual alcoholic, a frustrated writer named Don Birnam (Ray Milland) and the hell he undergoes on a weekend-long binge. It documents the anguish and humiliation of the hero as he pursues his single-minded goal of getting the next drink: hiding bottles so well from his ever-watchful brother that he himself cannot find them; stealing the money set aside for the cleaning lady; getting caught snatching a woman's purse in a nightclub and being humiliatingly ejected. During his lost weekend, Don is arrested and imprisoned in the alcoholic ward of a hospital and beset by DTs. Then, trying to hock his prized typewriter, he finds that the pawnshops are closed for a holiday. Finally, in utter shame, he steals his fiancée's coat and exchanges it for a gun with which to commit suicide.

In dealing with these surface experiences of alcoholism, *Lost Weekend* is a powerful and effective drama. It is less effective when it tries to explore the roots of alcoholism. It locates Don's problems in his particular situation. Like the veterans, his problem is insecurity, a lack of self-respect which leads to a writer's block: "I've never done anything . . . Zero, zero, zero." Rather than confront and overcome the problem, he escapes from it through drinking: "The reason is me . . . what I'm not."

The solution is again the determined heroine. Don's fiancée, Helen (Jane Wyman), determinedly nurses her future husband back to health, ignoring his abuse and rejection. But Don's despair is so much deeper than any of the veterans' (his lost weekend is a movement toward the decision to kill himself) that the reformation seems especially contrived. Even Helen is on the verge of giving up and admits that only a "miracle" can save him. Just then, Nat (Howard da Silva), the friendly neighborhood bartender, arrives with the typewriter Don had left behind in the bar. Helen convinces Don that this is an omen: "Someone, somewhere, sent this typewriter back. Why? Because you're to stay alive! Because he wants you to write!" Don, suddenly inspired, discovers the ending for his book that has always eluded him and is thus liberated from his writer's block and therefore from his alcoholism. With Helen he envisions a store window filled with "a pyramid of books! A novel by Don Birnam." His whole identity crisis has hinged on the elusive ending; now that he's found it, everything else falls neatly into place.

This abrupt reversal can probably be attributed to studio insistence. Charles Jackson's original novel concludes with the drunk hero crawling into bed after another binge without any sense that anything has or ever will change: "This one was over and nothing had happened at all." The film's hero, on the other hand, could never be such a negative figure. Studio head Buddy Da Silva told director Billy Wilder, "If the drunk wasn't an extremely attractive man, who apart from being a drunk could have been a hell of a nice guy and wanted to be saved, the audiences wouldn't go for it."[2] Paramount had been reluctant to make the film in the first place, afraid that it wasn't commercial enough and sensitive to pressure from liquor interests and prohibition groups.[3] When the film was released, though, it was a runaway box-office and critical success. It won four Academy Awards (Best Picture, Best Actor, Best Screenplay, and Best Director) and inspired a rather mediocre spinoff, *The Smash-Up* (1947).

The Smash-Up is variously referred to as a woman's version of *Lost Weekend* or "Lost Weekend with schmaltz."[4] It again deals with alcoholism through an individual case history, detailing with melodramatic flourish the various personal horrors of the experience. First, nightclub singer Angie Conway (Susan Hayward) needs a double before performing; then, once she gives up her career for marriage and motherhood, she needs several drinks to ward off the frustrations and boredom of being the complacent housewife while hubby goes on to be the big singing star. The film's feminist viewpoint is lost in the soap opera mechanics of the plot in which a near tragedy (Angie burns the house down and nearly kills the baby) finally reconciles Angie to her lot in life and the alcoholic crutch is readily discarded. Ultimately the film is about Susan Hayward wallowing in softly lit, sumptuously designed luxury far removed from Wilder's hard-edged realism.

Lost Weekend established alcoholism as an acceptable movie subject. In the next decade, films such as *The Small Black Room* (1948), *Come Fill My Cup* (1951), *I'll Cry Tomorrow* (1955)—also starring Susan Hayward—and *The Bottom of the Bottle* (1956) continued to examine dipsomania in terms of personal melodrama.

Mental illness was another problem that Hollywood shied away from for a long time. The only major thirties film to deal with the subject was *Private Worlds* (1935) which merely used a mental hospital as a colorful backdrop for a series of romantic entanglements between hospital staff and patients. In the early forties, Hollywood adapted psychoanalysis to its various genre conventions. *King's Row* (1941) placed psychology at the service of small-town soap opera, but in so doing introduced a theme which would be picked up in later films. It presented emotional disturbance as similar to physical illness and the Freudian psychoanalyst as the doctor who can cure the "disease." Parris Mitchell (Robert Cummings), motivated by the disastrous end his insane lover (Betty Field) meets because she goes untreated, travels to Vienna to study under Dr. Freud. He returns to his hometown where he successfully tackles the phobia of old friend Ronald Reagan and the neurosis of his new-found lover.

Lady in the Dark (1944) uses Liza Elliot's (Ginger Rogers) illness as a pretext for beautifully filmed musical dream sequences. Through psychoanalytical interpretation of the dreams, Liza comes to better understand herself, resolves her problems, and determines which man she should marry. *Spellbound* (1945), a Hitchcock murder mystery, makes psychoanalysis into a form of detective work. Psychiatrist Constance Peterson (Ingrid Bergman) delves into the psyche of her lover (Gregory Peck) in order to discover the truth about a murder he's implicated in. Scrutinizing her subject's dreams for clues the way Sherlock Holmes sifts through evidence, she solves the mysterious riddle. But when Constance breaks the case, she not only captures the real murderer, she also gets her man.

The Snake Pit (1948), Hollywood's first serious exposition of mental illness, simply dresses up psychology in problem film conventions. It too presents its case history in terms of detection. After immersing the viewer in the bizarre, almost hallucinatory experience of the breakdown which leads to Virginia Cunningham's (Olivia de Havilland) internment in a state mental hospital, the film follows the efforts of psychiatrist Dr. Kik (Leo Genn) to crack the case. With the help of drugs and shock treatment, the good doctor searches her past for the key to her illness. He finally locates "what went wrong" as a guilt complex over first her father's and then her fiancé's death. Like *King's Row*, the film exudes confidence in Freudian methods. Once Dr. Kik explains the problem to Virginia, she is automatically freed of the fixation and released from the hospital.

While it accepts the methods which society offers as a cure for mental illness (endorsing such controversial practices as electric shock treatment and the heavy use of memory drugs), *The Snake Pit* is critical of the conditions in mental hospitals. Much of the problem is the sadistic nurses and unfeeling doctors who hurt Virginia more than help her. One particularly sadistic nurse starts off by falsely accusing Virginia of stealing and then maliciously has her transferred to the ward for the hopelessly insane, "the snake pit." A doctor, eager to make room for new patients, ignores Dr. Kik's warnings and prematurely brings her before a Board of Examination hearing, thus causing a serious setback in her recovery. To a certain degree, the nastiness is the product of being overcrowded and understaffed. The head nurse has a breakdown due to the pressures of her work and the unfeeling doctor justifies his behavior as resulting from "no space and no money."

The solution, it's implied, is to put more money into the treatment of the mentally ill. An influx of funds would make the otherwise healthy system work more effectively. The ending demonstrates that with time, even the most deeply disturbed patients can be cured. Virginia befriends and patiently attempts to establish contact with Hester (Betsy Blair), a catatonic girl who attacks anyone who approaches her. As Virginia bids farewell, Hester utters her first sounds, a major step on the road to recovery.

Still, the film's most resonant images are those delineating Virginia's terror and miscomprehension at what is happening around her. From Virginia's perspective it catalogues the abuses patients suffer, climaxing in the famous "snake pit" nightmare. The ward ceases to be part of the hospital and becomes a deep hole filled with writhing, tormented creatures who surround a helpless, confused Virginia. It was these scenes which generated public controversy and, according to Darryl Zanuck, led to significant changes. The producer boasts that twenty-six states responded by passing legislation covering mental hospitals.[5] This assertion conforms to the film's reformist view. The validity of Zanuck's statement or, at least, the effectiveness of the legislation is called into question by the testimony of inmates such as the late Hollywood actress Francis Farmer. Her experiences from 1945 to 1953 in a Washington state asylum, described in her autobiography *Will There Really Be a Morning?*, belie *The Snake Pit*'s optimism. Her story parallels Virginia's, but she found no Dr. Kik and no easy cure:

> For eight years I was an inmate in a state asylum for the insane. During those years I passed through such unbearable terror that I deteriorated into a wild, frightened creature intent only on survival . . . I was chained in padded cells, strapped into straitjackets, and half drowned in ice-baths. . . . The Asylum itself was a steel trap, and I was not released from its jaws alive and victorious. I crawled out mutilated, whimpering and terribly alone.[6]

—19—

POSTWAR LABOR PROBLEMS

If labor had made giant strides throughout the thirties, creating powerful industrial unions and building up a massive membership, the war years saw those gains consolidated and accepted as a standard part of industry. Wartime increases in production and decreases in the labor force found corporations realizing high profits and hungering for workers. The result was a greater readiness to accommodate unions' demands. For its part in the war cause, labor tacitly adhered to a no-strike policy (with a few exceptions) that helped foster further good will between management and worker and create a new public image for itself as responsible and just. The strike, as a means of resolving issues, was replaced by labor–management committees; the era of militance and violence seemed, temporarily at least, at an end. Despite a series of national strikes in the winter of 1945–46 (General Motors, November 1945–February 1946; United Steel Workers, January–February 1946; UMW, April–May 1946; The Railway Brotherhood, May 1946) and the resurgent right's attack on unionism as a seed bed of communism, this basic harmony persisted throughout the postwar era.

King Vidor's *An American Romance* (1944) and Louis de Rochemont's *The Whistle at Eaton Falls* (1951) express this new tolerance toward organized labor without in any way championing strikes or discrediting management. Both films turn labor–management disputes into very personalized conflicts in which all sides appear moderate, reasonable, and responsive to one another. In *An American Romance*, the strike is seen through the eyes of two people, self-made auto magnate Steve Dangos (Brian Donlevy), who opposes unionization, and his son, university-educated engineer Teddy (Horace, later Stephen, McNally), who is spokesman for the workers. As such, the issue is less class warfare and more family debate between the old populist individualism and the new spirit of cooperative collectivism. In *Whistle at Eaton Falls*, the debate is funneled through one individual, Brad Adams (Lloyd Bridges), a union leader who is improbably appointed president of the business when the former head dies. Now Brad, faced with balancing the books, must reevaluate his former union stand and dismiss workers in favor of labor-saving machinery. In both films, the men strike and their demands appear completely reasonable even while management's position remains sympathetic.

The Vidor film is an epic wartime hymn to American industrial achievement and individual enterprise, and the strike is accordingly downplayed. In fact, it is practically nonexistent. Steve simply arrives at the plant to find it empty, the strikers not even bothering to form a picket line. Instead, everyone gathers in the board room to listen to young Teddy politely explain to his father and old friends the "organization's" demands. At no time is the word "union" used and Teddy's speech is conciliatory in the extreme. There are no "unreasonable demands," no attempt "to take over the Danton Plant . . . or tell you how to run it," just "the security of knowing where every man stands no matter who is in the front office and the dignity of knowing just what he's entitled to as a matter of open agreement." Steve must give way to changing times and agree to the contract, but this represents neither a glorious victory for labor nor a crushing defeat for management. It's just another step in America's industrial evolution.

Vidor's original script, entitled *America*, did include a sit-down strike, but the Bureau of Motion Pictures of the Office of War Information requested it be changed because most strikes recalled the very kind of capital–labor violence the War Labor Board was trying to prevent.[1] The screen version does show some hard feelings between Steve and Teddy but the outbreak of war has them side by side at the plant turning out a bomber every five minutes. Labor and management must set aside their quarrels for the greater cause.

The philosophical debate of *Romance* is replaced by hard economic realities in *Whistle*. All the honorable intentions of labor and management cannot alter the basic fact that either Brad must lay off the workers and install the new machinery or the business will go bankrupt. However, the strike takes a violent turn and the film goes melodramatically awry with the introduction of a thirties-type agitator who has been hired by an unscrupulous rival firm to hasten the company's demise. Ultimately the very technology which threatened the workers comes to everyone's rescue as Brad and some loyal machinists develop a new device that saves so much time and money that the nasty rivals can be outbid for new contracts. Brad can then reopen the plant on a 24-hour-a-day basis with all the workers rehired. Management and labor are reconciled but the initial economic premise of their antagonism has been overridden by clichéd shyster conventions.

Two of the best and most controversial American features on labor strife appeared in 1954—*On the Waterfront* and *Salt of the Earth*. (It is interesting that, like Hollywood's 1935 twin features on labor, *Riffraff* and *Black Fury*, these two films deal with the waterfront and mines.) Both break from Hollywood conventions, upholding unionism as the basis of collective democracy and siding exclusively with the workers as exploited victims. *Salt* portrays the Chicanos' strike against the exploitative owners as a victory for the workers in the class struggle. *On the Waterfront* focuses on intraunion corruption, with longshoremen oppressed by the gangster president of their local gaining freedom through the efforts of an individual hero.

Waterfront carefully builds up its case against union boss Johnny Friendly (Lee J. Cobb), exposing the methods through which he deprives the union members of fair working conditions. He keeps the workers continually in his debt, forcing them through his control of waterfront hiring to take loans at heavy interest. ("If you don't borrow, we don't work," comments one union member.) By means of physical terror and a spy system, he quells any potential revolt. When a parish priest (Karl Malden) attempts to organize the men against him, Friendly infiltrates the meeting with a spy and then sends his thugs to beat up the participants. The men are thus faced with the choice of either cooperating with Friendly and being rewarded with work or opposing him and being deprived of their livelihood. The penalty for opposing Friendly too vehemently is death. When first Joey Doyle and then Dugan try to expose the labor boss's corruption by testifying at a police investigation, they are executed.

Salt is equally thorough, for the first time in an American feature portraying a strike exclusively from the militant workers' point of view and providing documentarylike details on the specific whys and hows of a strike. The Chicanos have legitimate complaints concerning their working conditions, demanding the same safety regulations and pay as the white miners receive. After negotiations fail to achieve these ends and a miner is injured, the men walk out. The rest of the film shows us how they organize and implement their strike: they hold union meetings where issues are democratically discussed and voted on; they form picket lines and fight to keep scabs out; they solicit support from outside by printing and distributing leaflets; as food supplies dwindle, they pool their resources and help each other's families. They are not dupes under the sway of agitators, but rational, intelligent beings engaged in a struggle for human betterment.

In both films, the heroes must make difficult moral decisions before taking effective political action. *Waterfront*'s conflict is dramatized through Terry Malloy (Marlon Brando). He begins as an indifferent member of Friendly's operation (he unwittingly helps "set up" Joey Doyle and then acts as spy at the church meeting) but gradually undergoes a crisis of conscience, recognizing his complicity and resolving to free himself—and the others—of Friendly. Although *Salt*'s strikers are from the outset absolutely certain of their cause, the men still have an important lesson to learn. They must accept their wives' demands for equality in the same spirit as they require equality from the mine owners. At first they condescendingly dismiss the women's complaints about unsanitary conditions—"Leave it to the men." But when the Taft-Hartley injunction prohibits the men from picketing, the women form the picket line so that the strike can continue without breaking the law. As the women assume new and important roles and as the men are left with the "women's work," the husbands start to realize that their mates' demands are as valid as their own.

The films resolve their social conflicts with the characters' realization of the need for united mass action. The striking miners accept the women as partners, whites from the neighboring mines accept the Chicanos as equals, even the kids are part of the action. So when the sheriff and deputies start to evict one family they are confronted by the entire community. As fast as the law can remove furniture from the home, the workers return it through the back door. The law can do nothing when outnumbered and intimidated by mass organization, and management must concede defeat.

This same theme—that if everyone takes a stand together Friendly can be overcome—is the major line throughout *Waterfront*. Here, though, it is focused on an individual whose action in testifying before the police commission is held up as a model for the others to follow. Whereas *Salt*'s climax is clear-cut and didactic, *Waterfront*'s climax is confused and inconclusive. Although blacklisted from work by Friendly and ostracized as a fink by the men, Terry defiantly shows up at the hiring gate to demand his right to work. Friendly's thugs brutally beat Terry while the men stand by and watch. Then, suddenly no longer intimidated by Friendly or mistrustful of Terry, the men rally behind the informer: if Terry does not work they don't either. Bloody, battered, and semiconscious, Terry must now valiantly stagger into the ship's hold to once and for all assert his rights. The men follow him into the ship, leaving Friendly alone and defeated.

According to director Elia Kazan and screenwriter Budd Schulberg, this final sequence is a dramatization of "vital democracy" in action, yet upon close examination it yields to no concrete political interpretation. While it is certainly powerful dramatically, in terms of the film's thematic buildup the scene seems gratuitous. It is solely because of Terry that Friendly is defeated: *he* informs on the boss; *he* defies the process of hiring only "good" workers; and *he* leads the men into the hold. If the sequence illustrates mass action, why do the men hesitate to support Terry? Has he not already proven himself through his testimony, which represents an irrevocable rejection of Friendly and a blow for freedom for the men? If they still fear Friendly, then why do they rebel *after* Terry is beaten up as an example? And why is so much stress placed on Terry's ability to walk alone and unaided into the ship? If he had been too weak to make it, would the men have simply gone to work without him and thus somehow reinstated Friendly's power over them? These questions remain unanswered, almost as if they would intrude upon the hysterical emotionalism of the scene.

The meaning of the sequence has been debated by Lindsay Anderson and Robert Hughes in the pages of *Sight and Sound*.[2] Hughes's defense of the film fails to account for the confusion of the ending; while Anderson's analysis is more valid, his claim that the final sequence is "implicitly (if unconsciously) Fascist" seems overstated. Though the emphasis is most decidedly on Terry's individual action, he does not represent the strong leader to whom the "craven" men turn; he has no pretensions to being a leader except as an example. He is just one of many who have rebelled (Doyle, Dugan, and, the filmmakers make clear, others who have been murdered before them). The men do appear weak and docile beside Terry, but are hardly "leaderless sheep in search of a new master." They are just not as exciting as Marlon Brando and it is because it is his big scene that the men are hardly noticeable. It is more overdramatics than unconscious fascist tendencies that have taken over the scene. Kazan has admitted that "Possibly I over-exploited the end. My first wife used to say that when I felt uncertain about a scene, I would make it more forceful."[3]

But even the defeat of Friendly does not necessarily free the men. The film makes clear that Friendly is a part of a larger system. There are references to "Mr. Upstairs," to Friendly's police connections, and a shot of an anonymous man watching the hearings on television and informing his secretary that he will no longer see Mr. Friendly. Although the precise nature of Friendly's contacts is never identified, Friendly obviously does not function in isolation; even if he is defeated the system will remain. *Waterfront's* final image, the giant doors of the ship slowly closing on the men inside, is ambiguous. They are now free from Friendly but the sense of a larger entrapment still lingers in the image of the closed doors.

There is no ambiguity in *Salt*. The system is not represented as an elusively defined power structure but as traditional bad guys. Management representative George Hartwell (David Sarvis) is a stereotypic "bloated capitalist," impeccably dressed in a gabardine suit and Panama hat, coolly viewing the strike from his Cadillac. Hartwell, the sheriff, the foreman, and even the company president whose magazine picture the men jeer are cardboard villains who crumble before moral right. In direct contrast to the film's depiction of power is the description in Biberman's book of the forces marshalled against the production and distribution of the film. Unions prohibited any members from working on it and labs throughout the country refused to develop the film. The filmmakers also had to overcome opposition and violence from the community in which they were shooting; the deportation of the leading lady; infiltration by the FBI; attacks in Congress; an industrywide conspiracy to block its release; and the loss of an eight-year antitrust case. This account provides a truer glimpse of the awesome, almost intangible forces of repression. That the filmmakers continued to fight to get their picture seen even after they lost the suit, that the film is now a college campus favorite, is far more encouraging than the facile victory won over the bloated capitalists in the film itself.

Regardless of their shortcomings, both films demonstrate a mature view of militant labor far removed from the distortions of *Riffraff* and *Black Fury*. In 1935, the strike was a feared weapon and unionism could only be upheld if any indication of militancy was totally discredited and if management was always sympathetic. In the war and postwar films, labor's strike action is valid as long as its demands are moderate and management is again sympathetic. By 1954, strikes were an accepted part of American life and outright militancy was portrayed as the only course of moral action the worker could take. Not only is management corrupt but there is some vague sense that such corruption extends throughout the social system and that mass action is the only means to keep it in check. Still, *Salt of the Earth* had to be made outside the studio system and *Waterfront* concentrates on the traditional right-wing target of union corruption. Ultimately, however, both films are more interested in larger issues than the specifics of labor. They address themselves to the nature of freedom in an increasingly repressive society and it is not surprising, as we shall see, that both are reactions to the HUAC hearings and the Hollywood blacklist.

—20—

THE INDIVIDUAL AND
SOCIETY: DARKER VIEWS OF
THE POSTWAR WORLD

Barbara Deming's *Running Away from Myself*, a fascinating study of America's image in forties movies, begins and ends with a vision of hell. The typical heroes of the decade are "products of a deep crisis of faith" and "each mourns a vision of happiness which eludes him." It is a nightmare vision which "falters in any gesture of promise," but as Deming points out, this bleak portrait is largely subconscious, operating beneath the surface of the films. It is discernible only when a number of films are taken as a whole and a general pattern emerges: "From such a series of instances one can deduce a plight more general, sensed by the public (and the public-minded filmmakers)—a condition that transcends the literal situation dramatized in any single film."[1]

However, some films of the late forties did explore this crisis between the individual and society more self-consciously, presenting a complex, dark vision of postwar America intentionally, without a lot of the subterfuge of movie conventions which set up a problem only to handily resolve it. Even Capra's highly optimistic *It's a Wonderful Life* (1946) has a harrowing nightmare sequence which nullifies both the existence of the hero and the way of life he so valued. Its hero, George Bailey (Jimmy Stewart), despairs that any good or satisfaction can come of his life in Bedford Falls and finally resolves to kill himself. John Garfield's Charlie Davis in *Body and Soul* and Joe Morse in *Force of Evil* (1949) both demonstrate a willingness devoid of moral principles to attain success and power, while Chaplin's title character in *Monsieur Verdoux* (1947) is so brutalized by life that he takes up a career as a

Bluebeard, amorally applying sound business practice to the art of wife murder. Society is not so much corrupt as corrupting, tainting anyone who does not resist it.

All of these films are serious comments on life in modern America, yet they move beyond the conventions of the problem film genre. None of them look at a particular problem or pay much attention to social institutions. Nor are their conclusions easily reached or without qualification, since society itself, not the individual who reflects it, is the real force of evil. Even though there is a strong political philosophy at work in them all, they are not strictly social problem films. They are instead films which exhibit a political purpose without treating a limited social situation or problem.

The best of the social problem genre—*I Am a Fugitive from a Chain Gang, Grapes of Wrath, Dead End, You Only Live Once*—not only focus on a specific problem but also see that problem as a paradigm of a larger condition. But except perhaps for Capra's *Deeds–Smith–Doe* trilogy, no problem films create political viewpoints in isolation from a particular issue. As long as such issues remain at the core of the films' politics, then their view is limited to specific reformism. Their function is to present a problem that calls for circumscribed change rather than to call into question some of the deeper values at the foundation of society. The late forties films discussed in this chapter were important steps toward freeing social and political themes from the narrow reformist confines of the problem film genre and defining new film approaches to political concerns.

It's a Wonderful Life

It's a Wonderful Life is supreme Capra, where his desperation and his faith reach their extremes and finally find a satisfying resolution. The film in many ways parallels the trilogy, charting the progress of its ingenuous hero through a series of events in which his natural virtue and intelligence show up the cynical monopoly capitalist. Like Doe and the others, the hero experiences a major crisis of faith and seriously questions man's goodness before his faith is renewed by all the friends and common people who rally around him. But there are several significant differences between *It's a Wonderful Life* and its predecessors, most importantly the greater distance the later film goes toward final despair before resurrecting the hero. There is little doubt that George Bailey would have gone through with his suicide plans if not for divine intervention in the form of guardian angel Clarence Oddbody (Henry Travers). Through Clarence's extraterrestrial powers, George is brought back to his senses, but not before he has traveled through the film's version of hell in which his very existence is negated. Life denied now appears valuable to George and all the mundane and frustrating things in it are wonderful when compared to nonexistence.

Another very significant difference between this and earlier Capra films is that the drama is played out in the small town rather than the big city. George is not the naive hick visiting Babylon and becoming an important force for moral right, but just a small-town boy who stays a small-town boy. The heart of Capra's populism, small-town life is here the center of the film instead of an abstract force for good in the alien big city. By zeroing in on George's dissatisfaction with life in Bedford Falls, Capra is putting his own beliefs to a severe test, dramatizing with a tough-minded candor his doubts and questions about the validity of his sacred populist ethic.

Capra imbues the basic fable structure of the film with strong political overtones and an urgent sense of drama, both of which elevate the film from a simple fantasy to a moving testimony of the director's ethos. The whole film is built around George's crisis, beginning with the prayers of family and friends to help George in his hour of tribulation. Those prayers are answered by God, who reviews the case for the benefit of apprentice angel Clarence in a series of flashbacks. These encapsulate the key events of George's life leading to the situation that now finds him poised to jump off the bridge to his icy death. Clarence's briefing on George is a catalogue of an apparently average small-town life with an inordinate amount of bad luck thrown in. George is a dreamer who wants to "shake off the dust of this crummy little town" and see the world, go to the university, build skyscrapers and bridges. Instead he must acquiesce to all the routine things he hoped to avoid— work at his father's rundown business, Bailey Building and Loan; marriage to Mary (Donna Reed), the girl down the street; raising a family in a drafty old house with a stair bannister knob that keeps coming off as a reminder of his disappointed hopes. While his peers go off to school and big careers in the city and then to the war overseas (brother Harry even wins the Congressional Medal), George sticks it out in little old Bedford Falls.

George remains home through bad luck and his sense of duty. Each time he is ready to make his big escape, something happens which forces him to choose between his own goals and the Bailey Building and Loan: his father's death on the eve of George's departure for college leaves the firm open to takeover by the town's venal capitalist, Potter (Lionel Barrymore), unless George stays on to run things; when brother Harry returns from college he can't take over the company from George because he's married into a bigger job in Buffalo; on his way out of town on his honeymoon George must use up all his funds to circumvent a run on the Building and Loan.

The Bailey Building and Loan, however, represents far more than family responsibility; it represents a moral and political obligation to the whole town. Through it, George is preserving the human, populist values of traditional small-town life against the encroachments of Potter's monopoly capitalism. George is the one alternative to banker Potter in Bedford Falls, the champion of individual home ownership and small capitalism: without the Building and Loan's Bailey Park subdivision of clean new homes, the townspeople would be forced to live in Potter's high-rent slum tenements; without George's loans on character instead of collateral, people like Mr. Martini would never get the chance to open their own businesses and would be forced to work for one of Potter's companies. George is the ultimate good neighbor, using the Building and Loan to help the townspeople realize their own goals and to protect them all from the self-serving greed of Potter.

George's problem is that he does not appreciate his worth and views himself a failure who never fulfilled his dreams. Through his increasing despondency, the film questions the validity of his life. But the same flashbacks that catalogue his sense of failure also indicate his accomplishments. It is then up to George to recognize—or up to Clarence to point out to George—the importance of his life. So when George blurts out that he wishes he'd never been born, Clarence accommodates his wish and George enters a frightening, macabre nightmare as the angel shows him what life in Bedford Falls would have been like without him. This sequence is the most powerful in the film, as George retraces his steps through the town back to the many townspeople whose lives he has touched. It is the reverse of the previous flashback; in it all the responsibilities he undertook and all the good he accomplished have been left undone. Mr. Gower (H. B. Warner), the druggist he prevented from filling the wrong prescription, is now a down-and-out rummy; his brother was killed in the childhood accident George saved him from; his mother (Beulah Bondi) is a lonely old woman running a boarding house; and Mary is a spinster librarian with thick glasses and hair in a bun. Most dramatically, Bedford Falls the small-town haven has become Pottersville, a garish strip of neon-lit bars and clubs full of brusque, unfriendly people.

George's confusion and disorientation are played up by Capra's energetic direction. Jimmy Stewart's panic-stricken, near-hysterical expression as the full truth dawns on him is intercut with subjective, impressionistic views of Pottersville at night, of close friends who don't recognize George, of Mary, the woman who has known him so intimately all his life, recoiling at his desperate attempts to make contact with her. The nightmare is a denial not just of George Bailey's existence but of everything he represents. A world based on family and community has been raped by the forces of greed, progress, and cynicism. It is a horrifying vision of the corruption at the core of modern society run rampant, unchecked by the forces of good.

Of course, it is not too late to reverse the vision, as it is only Clarence's spell that has induced it. When Clarence frees him of the nightmare, George has far greater appreciation for what is normal. Bedford Falls, his family, and "the good old Bailey Building and Loan" take on a new and wonderful hue. The miraculous reversal so strained in *Smith* and *Doe* here springs naturally from the main plot device of the deus ex machina, and just as the nightmare vision is far more frightening than anything mounted by Taylor and Norton, so the resolution can be far more optimistic and sentimental than anything in the entire Capra canon. The one extreme serves to set the other up with everyone in the town dropping in with the money shortfall that had prompted George's crisis. Even the sheriff and bank examiner who were waiting to take him to jail contribute to the fund. Harry arrives with his Congressional Medal in time to toast "the richest man in town—my brother," and the bells on the Christmas tree jingle as an indication that Clarence has earned his wings. Capra pulls out every stop and yet every element of the scene is in place, each one having been carefully established within the structure of the film. It is "the happy ending to end happy endings"[2] and in it Capra finally reconciles the thematic conflicts he never quite resolved in his earlier films. George has learned his simple but elemental lesson that "no man is poor who has a friend" and all his dreams and ambitions are seen to be secondary to his one great achievement: he has remained true to his principles, having resisted Potter's temptations and opted for family and community values. His earlier frustrations are now placed in a new perspective where being ordinary is elevated to a virtue and life in Bedford Falls indeed proves to be wonderful.

Still the film has its problems, particularly in Lionel Barrymore's Potter. Whereas Edward Arnold's villain displayed a vitality and charm that made him that much more dangerous, Barrymore's Potter is a caricature of Scrooge—old, wizened, and crippled. He is too facile a foil to pit against George and their battle thus becomes a cardboard allegory between good and evil. Furthermore, the impact George has on the town is too great to be credible. The fact that he and he alone has made all the difference between Bedford Falls and Pottersville again points up Capra's mistrust of the little people and his belief in their need for a leader. Of course, the extremity of George's influence is necessary to set up the extremity of the nightmare and the ending. So, while the fable taxes credibility, it does not violate its dramatic integrity. Together the nightmare and the happy ending add up to a hard-won assertion of Capra's faith.

Body and Soul, Force of Evil

On the surface, *Body and Soul* and *Force of Evil* are fairly standard social problem films. The form is familiar (the exposé of corruption within our society) and so is the plotline (a tough guy hero rises from poverty to success outside the law and then, prompted by a young ingenue, decides to go straight). But screenwriter Abraham Polonsky gives both dramas a depth and ambiguity untypical of Hollywood. The protagonists' involvement in crime is not just the stuff of gangster melodrama, but the basis for a study of the nature of greed, of how personal acquisitiveness is generated and then exploited by social institutions. As such, the films are a combination of Marx and Freud, of Formula convention and rhythmic street poetry.

Part of Polonsky's strength is in his criticism of capitalism through character study rather than polemics. While there are still social victims and victimizers, all the people in a Polonsky film are the product of their society. In effect there is no distinction between society and individual since social values are what makes up the individual. The struggle between the two thus becomes a personal one, full of complexities. No one remains uncontaminated by the American emphasis on success and getting the good things out of life at any cost.

In seeking wealth, the heroes of each film sell out themselves and those closest to them. The central drama revolves around their immersion in corruption and their gradual realization of their own guilt. Polonsky structures both films to emphasize the theme of moral awakening by having his heroes recall the events that led to their downfalls. In *Body and Soul*, this is achieved through a flashback technique, with the bulk of the film taking place in the memory of boxer Charlie Davis as he awaits what is to be his last fight, a fight he has agreed to throw in order to retire wealthy. *Force of Evil* is narrated by Joe Morse in the past tense. He comments on his own actions with an awareness born after the fact, so that the film traces how and why he ended up where he did. This presentation of events by hindsight allows the stress in each film to fall on motive, linking the hero's own guilt with that of the society around him.

While the theme and structure of the two films are parallel, there are some essential differences. *Body and Soul* is very much a product of Depression thinking, hinging on the environmentalist premise that Charlie's corruption is the product of a slum childhood. Joe Morse is much more a postwar hero, an affluent lawyer who has already achieved success and now wants more money. In *Force of Evil*, sociological factors are placed within a larger psychomythological framework. Whereas Charlie's destructive drive is almost exclusively determined by economic want, Joe is provoked by the evil within himself, within every person in the film, and within all of society.

Charlie, fed by his hatred of the slums and his mother's desire that he make something of himself, finds that the only escape route the slum provides is through the boxing ring. But because the sport is controlled by mobsters, the only way to achieve his ambition is to become part of the mob. Through his affiliation with boxing czar Roberts (Lloyd Gough), Charlie becomes the champ and is inevitably corrupted by the brutality of the sport and its overlords. Polonsky's script plays up the economic imagery to emphasize Charlie's function as a "money machine," ever greedy for more money at the expense of his personal integrity, family, and friends. The more successful he is, the more isolated he becomes, carefully manipulated by Roberts to fulfill his potential as an investment property. A montage reveals Charlie as a lonely champ, pummeling opponents, accepting bulky envelopes from Roberts, and relentlessly partying with a blonde fortune-hunter. The money machine must discard any meaningful human experiences outside the bounds of a narrow economic function.

Throughout the film Polonsky equates corruption with death. Just as Charlie is morally deadened by his experiences, so others around him are literally killed. First Shorty (Joseph Pevney), Charlie's initial partner and best friend, and then Ben (Canada Lee), his faithful trainer, lose their lives because of Roberts. Both men represent positive values and try to save Charlie from himself and the mob. Roberts is almost Polonsky's angel of death, providing a commentary on the subject by continually reminding Charlie that "everybody dies. Ben—Shorty—even you."

It is Ben's death that prods Charlie into analyzing what he has become. When he refuses to throw the big fight, Charlie finally stands up for himself and boxing is, for once, not just an economic enterprise but a means of self-assertion. Afterwards, Charlie defiantly spits back Robert's threats to him: "What are you gonna do, kill me? . . . Everybody dies." And indeed there is every reason to believe that Roberts will have his vengeful way with Charlie, but the moral triumph still goes to the hero. Free of Roberts and his own greed, he is, however briefly, his own man, a resurrected human being capable of loving Peg (Lilli Palmer), his deserted fiancée, once more.

Joe Morse is quite different from Charlie, who is unwittingly caught up in a situation he doesn't understand and who recognizes his guilt only long after he has committed the sin. An educated, articulate lawyer, Joe is aware of his guilt and willingly becomes part of Tucker's money machine. His narrative commentary thus traces a far more complex pattern of guilt than that found in *Body and Soul*. Joe defends his actions by pointing out that everyone is in his own way corrupt. This is an important rationalization; throughout the film, Joe seeks to make everyone around him equally guilty. This theme of universal guilt, muted in *Body and Soul*, is given full play in *Force of Evil*. Each representative of good turns out in some way to be just as tainted as his counterpart on the side of evil: not only gangster mouthpiece Joe, but his morally righteous older brother Leo (Thomas Gomez); not just Tucker's amoral wife Edna (Marie Windsor), but also Leo's pure-looking stenographer Doris (Beatrice Pearson); and not just Tucker and his underworld organization but also unseen Special Prosecutor Hall and the police.

The double-edged guilt motif is most evident in Joe's Cain-and-Abel relationship with Leo. Leo sacrificed his own ambitions to be a lawyer in order to put Joe through law school and now Joe feels guilty because in return he has become involved in crime. Leo for his part feels guilty because he provided the education that led to Joe's criminality. With this as the basis of their relationship, each tries to clear his own conscience by forcing the guilt on the other. Joe seeks to make amends but at the same time implicate his brother by bringing Leo's little numbers parlor into Tucker's corporation. But Leo's moral righteousness prohibits him from joining the mob. He insists he is just a businessman— "I do my business honest and respectable"—even though, as Joe points out, he is already corrupt. Taking in thousands a week by stealing secretaries' thirty-five-dollar paychecks is as immoral as Tucker's reaping millions: "You lost a crooked peanut stand. Now you can open up on Fifth Avenue." To Polonsky, Leo is representative of the modern American,[3] a typical small businessman who hides his guilt behind a presumed ethical basis while blaming the big corporations for all financial corruption. So what Leo is really doing is forcing Joe to force him into Tucker's mob, keeping his own hands clean and making Joe the guilty party. Joe protests, "Why are you doing this to me? I'm trying to save you. Do you want to make me feel guilty?" to which Leo angrily retorts, "You *are* guilty!"

They are both guilty, for no matter how he evades it, Leo is still responsible for his own fate, just as Joe, by forcing Leo into the corporation, is responsible for putting him in the vulnerable position that eventuates in his murder. Leo never faces up to his guilt, but his death finally compels Joe to accept his share of the responsibility. He informs on Tucker and goes searching for Leo's body, which he finds by the East River beneath a towering suspension bridge. As he descends from his "fine office in the clouds" to the dirty base of the bridge, he recites a litany of guilt and of commitment to action:

> Down, down, down. It was like going down to the bottom of the world—to find my brother. Like a dirty rag nobody wanted. I felt I'd killed him . . . because if a man can live so long and have his whole life come out like rubbish, then something was horribly wrong . . . and I decided to help.

As in *Body and Soul*, lust for money brings death and destruction and, like Charlie Davis, Joe finally accepts his guilt and acts to free himself. But where we sense that Charlie's redemption is going to lead to his death, Joe's seems more optimistic. Even though the mob could get him just as easily as it got Leo—and if it doesn't then Joe faces imprisonment and disbarment—the finale stresses the heroics without reference to the price Joe must pay. This optimism contradicts the claustrophobic bleakness of the rest of the film and has been excused by Polonsky as "partly a cop-out"[4] to placate the censor. What is perhaps more significant is the hero's movement toward self-recognition, the stripping away of his success and rationalizations to face the truth about himself and the values by which he has lived.

The guilt drama is mirrored on a smaller scale in Joe's relation to Doris. All sweetness and innocence on the surface, she also has the same evil lurking within her. First, because Leo has been kind to her, she continues working for him even though she knows he's involved in the numbers racket, telling herself it's a legitimate lottery. Then, she is attracted to Joe and while repulsing him is forcing him to seduce her. Joe points this out to her while at the same time trying to tempt her: "you squirm for me to do something wicked to you—make a pass for you, bowl you over, sweep you off and take the childishness out of you and give you . . . money and sin. That's real wickedness."

Beyond the immediate characters of the drama, dominating all events and people, are the larger forces of the society, the underworld and the law. The numbers racket, like boxing in *Body and Soul*, is a microcosm of modern capitalism and Tucker (Roy Roberts) the industrial magnate. Business success requires optimum control, so Tucker seeks to monopolize the numbers game and, in so doing, must destroy smaller businessmen like Leo and exploit the talents of professionals like Joe. The law enforcers, like everyone else, are suspect. From the protagonists' perspective, they are as much a threat as Tucker and his cohorts, arresting Leo and Doris and bugging Joe's phone. Compounding the metaphor of crime as a legitimate business is the rather dubious rela-

tionship between Tucker and the authorities. Though Special Prosecutor Hall has mounted a crusade against crime, Tucker can still have
Joe negotiate with government officials to legalize the numbers racket.
Through all the intricate events of the narrative, the law appears as just
another part of the sordid urban inferno.

Much of the power of Polonsky's vision is the product of his language. His combination of street jargon and rhythmic poetry is basic
to establishing mood, delineating character, and communicating meaning. *Force of Evil*'s sense of infectious corruption is summarized perfectly when Joe tells us, "I could feel money spreading in the air like
perfume. Tucker opened his pocket and I dived right in." In *Body and
Soul*, one of Roberts's opening lines—"It's all addition and subtraction.
The rest is conversation"—is a précis of the character's direct, single-
minded nature, and a summary of the precedence money takes over
everything else. Charlie and Peg's relationship is delicately implied when
she recites Blake's "The Tyger" to him—"What Immortal hand or eye
Dare frame thy fearful symmetry?" "What's symmetry?" queries Joe;
"Well built," responds Peg, adding a goodnight kiss for punctuation.
Her cultural and aesthetic refinement is what holds him in awe and it
is his virility, his instinctive animalism, that attracts her. In *Force of
Evil*, Joe Morse pinpoints the root of his problem—"I didn't have the
strength to resist corruption, but I was strong enough to fight for a piece
of it."

Despite their literary quality neither fails as film. The direction uses
the screenplay to create a vibrant and often compelling visual drama.
Robert Rossen and James Wong Howe's use of space, light, and composition in *Body and Soul* creates a *Film-Noir* world of dank pool halls
and gyms, of offices full of foreboding shadows and cigarette smoke, of
luxury apartments where the bright light only serves to reveal the emptiness and enticement of material success. A particularly effective visual
motif is a crane shot from above of Charlie lying flat on his back, as if
pinned under the weight of his conscience. The dramatic tension and
excitement of the final match (will Charlie fight back and if so, when?)
is created mainly by the cinematography (with Howe and camera on
roller skates) and the rhythmic cutting of the fight in closeup and medium long shot with reaction shots of the various characters concerned
with the outcome.

Polonsky's own direction of *Force of Evil* sets up a kind of dialectic
between image and sound, so that the highly literary narration functions within a cinematic framework. Joe Morse's commentary sometimes
serves as a complement to the action, explaining the motives behind it,
and at other times as a contrast to the picture, highlighting the hypocrisy or ambivalence of an action. The opening long shots from above

of crowded New York streets, of bustling skyscraper lobbies where Joe moves among the throngs of people, are accompanied by Joe's voice-over explanation of the numbers game, how all the people are involved in this illicit racket to get rich and how he in particular will become a millionaire on the next draw. Both the general corruption of the modern metropolis and the particular corruption of Joe Morse are thereby established, as well as the implication of how the former serves as an excuse for the latter. This concept is realized not through any literal explanation, for Joe has not yet achieved that awareness, but through the implication springing from the particular juxtaposition of image and sound. In opposition to the opening are the final shots and voice-over. Joe now recognizes his own personal guilt as something he himself is responsible for in isolation from the general social evil. While he explains this we see him alone on a deserted, grey Wall Street, no longer moving among the crowd and on his way up to his office but running down ever lower "to the bottom of the world" and the body of Leo, his guilt objectified. Here, the literal relation of word to picture illustrates Joe's new awareness and his understanding of what his actions mean.

Polonsky, in these two films, creates a remarkably critical portrait of postwar America, using crime-genre conventions to explore the gulf between the success ethic and social responsibility. His viewpoint and technique, especially in the second film, are very sophisticated and well in advance of their time. In its fusion of psychology and social commentary, *Force of Evil* is a precursor of the political cinema which would emerge in the sixties. Like Capra, Polonsky presents a cohesive vision of the relationship between individual behavior and political values. But Polonsky does not yearn for a more humane populist past. Instead, he argues for the need to assert humanity, no matter how futile the gesture, against the urban, economic corruption of the present. His conclusion may not be as emotionally inspiring as Capra's but it is certainly intellectually tougher. His is a guarded optimism that the Joe Morses will make their stand no matter what the price and Polonsky's own experience with the blacklist is a testimony to his own loyalty to such principles.

Monsieur Verdoux

With *Modern Times* and *The Great Dictator*, Chaplin's Tramp reached the end of his career. Trekking down the road had become a paradox since in the first film the road could lead nowhere and in the second fascism reached out everywhere. But although the Tramp has been forced out of existence, Chaplin offers us at the end of *Dictator* the idealistic hope of all men united changing the world. Seven years later, however, in *Monsieur Verdoux* Chaplin comes to quite a different conclusion, despairing that there is no hope or idealism left in the world. It is the darkest, most daring film to come out of Hollywood during the studios' prime period.

In *Verdoux*, the Tramp is not killed off by society but, worse, is transformed by it into its own image. Verdoux is the reverse of the Tramp, the ultimate rebel as the ultimate conformist. The maladjusted Charlie is now the super-adjusted, super-bourgeois businessman. The baggy pants and scruffy demeanor are replaced by elegant suits and careful coiffure. No longer clumsy in social situations, the new Charlie is a bluebeard who earns his living by marrying and murdering wealthy women for their fortunes. Whereas the Tramp was basically defensive in his relationship with authority, Verdoux manipulates the law, being apprehended only when he voluntarily turns himself in to a squad of police who have bungled his arrest.

Though the roots of Charlie's personality have been perverted by Verdoux and the Tramp's natural instincts transformed into cold-blooded business practice, many surface similarities remain. Verdoux exudes the same old charm and combination of physical grace and awkwardness (his seductive lunge at Mme. Grosnay sends him tumbling off the couch, yet he doesn't upset the teacup he is holding) and, at least until his final disillusionment, the same survival instinct. The Tramp's belief in the value of love and self-sacrifice is also upheld by Verdoux who claims that he murders only to support his invalid wife (*his* blind flower girl) and son. But there is an essential difference which colors everything: the Tramp is innocent, innately unable to adapt to society's demands, while Verdoux is corrupt, exploiting his natural qualities to fulfill the bourgeois dream that is inaccessible to Charlie. Nevertheless, Charlie and the Gamin could bring life into their ramshackle waterfront shack. Verdoux, despite his protestations of love for his family, never seems to stay home for more than a day and proudly displays the deed of ownership for his country home as if it were a badge of fulfillment. The Tramp has always been able to create his own world outside society, while Verdoux is a mirror image of society. Even more so than in Polonsky's films, society has flowed into the individual and, as Robert Warshow described it, the opposition between the two

> is now an internal struggle, full of ambiguities and contradictions; it is man himself who is corrupt, both as individual and as society, and Verdoux's problem is to make some working order out of the conflicting needs of his own personality. When he makes his decision, it is as much a decision about his own nature as about the nature of society.[5]

Verdoux is in his own way a victim of the same social forces that buffeted Charlie around in *Modern Times* and *The Great Dictator*. His perverted conformity is the outcome of industrialization, depression, and war. His sensibility has been deadened by thirty years in a bank ("I was a bank clerk once, by existence a monotonous rhythm—day in and day out counting other people's money") and his moral judgment thrown awry when the bank fires him during an economic slump ("I have brains . . . and for thirty-five years I used them honestly and after that nobody wanted them. So I was forced to go into business for myself"). Like Charlie, the assembly line has driven him mad and, when it has no further use for him, he simply applies its principles in their most logical extreme. Since it is a ruthless world, Verdoux argues, "one must be ruthless to cope with it." Criminality is the only possible stance in a criminal society and wife-killing is no more evil than the wars created for profit. When it is pointed out that "other people don't do business that way," Verdoux glibly replies, "That's the history of many a big business. Wars, conflict—it's all business. One murder makes a villain, millions a hero. Numbers sanctify. . . ."

The society Verdoux moves in is a bleak wasteland. After years of destruction (a montage of headlines announces "Stock Crash," "Banks Fail," "Riots," "Crisis in Europe," "Nazis Bomb Spanish Loyalists"), its inhabitants are emotionally deadened. The Bluebeard's wives are repugnant spinsters or snobbish socialites. Lydia (Margaret Hoffman) is a wizened hag who disdains Verdoux's attempts at poetry and romanticism and Mme. Grosnay (Isabel Elsom) a vain widow who succumbs to Verdoux only when he has sufficiently flattered her ego. The only people who exhibit the Tramp's old life force are in some way compromised. Verdoux's real wife (Mady Correll) is hardly a presence in the film, an invalid who dies at the onset of the Depression. A more vital figure is Annabella Bonheur, the one bogus wife Verdoux does not succeed in murdering. However, if Annabella is fully alive, she is, in the person of blustery, loud-mouthed Martha Raye, thoroughly obnoxious. Our attitude toward her is crystallized in the hilarious sequence where she unwittingly thwarts Verdoux's carefully laid plan to drown her in the middle of a lake (à la Clyde Griffith). As she looks over the side of the boat for a fish, she blurts out, "I see one. It's a monster. Oh no, it's me." Annabella may be plucky but she is totally lacking the Tramp's grace and sensibility and we can't help hoping that Verdoux will succeed in his plans.

The Girl (Marilyn Nash) does exhibit much of the Tramp's fineness of spirit. Verdoux finds her on the streets, dressed in a shabby raincoat and just released from jail, imprisoned because, like Charlie with the flower girl, she has committed a crime for love, sacrificing herself to support her invalid husband. Despite her husband's recent death and the privation which has now led her to prostitution, she truly believes in the beauty of love. But, like Verdoux, she ends up corrupted, living off the ill-gotten wealth of a munitions manufacturer ("Ah, that's the business I should have been in," muses Verdoux). Survival and purity of the spirit have become irreconcilable.

Verdoux loses his will to survive when he realizes what he has become, that in fact he has not survived. After the ruin of his fortune and the death of his wife and child, he comes to recognize the sordid nature both of his acquisitive life and of society. He had always justified his ruthlessness by claiming that it was done on behalf of his family, and now without them, he is forced to question his action. A new, disillusioned Verdoux recalls his career as "a numbed confusion. A nightmare in which I lived in a half dream world. Horrible world. Now I've awakened. I wonder if that world ever existed." Even though he's fully capable of escaping, he surrenders to the police and certain death.

Since Verdoux is the embodiment of society, society is committing suicide by executing him: "Upon leaving this spark of earthly existence, I have this to say. I shall see you all very soon, very soon!" This is the pinnacle of cynicism—society has consumed man and will consume itself. The final shot is Chaplin's version of the Apocalypse. Verdoux, like the Tramp, walks away from the camera, proud and undaunted. Only this time, the road ends at the guillotine.

Although the overall conception of the film and the Verdoux character are brilliant, the film has many flaws and demonstrates the main creative problem Chaplin the director faced when he tried to use sound. His silent films had depended on pantomime. The delicate silent interplay between the Tramp and other characters was captured in simple medium shots with a minimum of editing to interrupt the timing or break up the space. However, when his characters began to talk to one another, a whole new set of dramatic requirements was introduced and the simple medium shots and minimal editing produced a static effect in which much of the comic and dramatic tension is lost. The static effect was accentuated by Chaplin's increasing reliance on language. The curtain speech in *The Great Dictator* proved to be an omen of Chaplin's future course. Many sequences in *Verdoux*, especially those between Verdoux and the Girl, consist of long passages of dialogue that contain very little dramatic subtext. The literal meaning of Chaplin's words carries the full weight of the scene and those words are often embarrassingly florid ("Despair is a narcotic that lulls the mind into indifference," philosophizes Verdoux).

Still, regardless of these failings, even Chaplin's weak films are often startlingly effective. When Chaplin uses language in a comic context,

Verdoux is very good. The scene where he seduces Mme. Grosnay over the flowershop telephone, rhapsodizing on her beauty while concentrating his look on a swooning salesgirl, is marvelous. Although the final trial scenes have a slightly self-indulgent edge, they are also powerful because the message functions within a seriocomic framework, the irony of the condemned condemning his condemners. Here, the tension between Verdoux's situation and his comic putdowns of the moralistic reporters and priest ("May God have mercy on your soul." "Why not? after all, it belongs to Him"), between his impending death and his assertion of life (asked if he'd like some rum before he dies, he at first refuses and then changes his mind, "I've never tasted rum"), raises the film to the old Chaplin level.

One can't help admiring Chaplin for his daring in *Verdoux*, even when the execution fails to match the film's conception. For Chaplin to express such a corrosive view of capitalism just as America was entering a period of repression merits much respect. No other Hollywood film, not even *I Am a Fugitive* or *You Only Live Once*, makes such a frontal attack on the values of modern society and Chaplin suffered duly for this transgression. Middle America was already scandalized at his private life and nonconformist political views. He now underwent what amounted to an inquisition at the press conference for *Monsieur Verdoux*. Such reporters as James Fay of the *Catholic War Veterans* demanded that Chaplin explain why he'd never become an American citizen, why he'd never voted, and why he continued to support a "known Communist" such as Hanns Eisler.[6] *Monsieur Verdoux* was seen as one more damning piece of evidence as the reporters pressed Chaplin to prove his loyalty to America.

Perhaps as a result, in his next film, *Limelight* (1952), Chaplin avoided any sociopolitical stands. Still, the film met with protests and pickets; soon after, Chaplin was forced into exile. Just as his films dramatized the natural antagonism between the individual and society, so now the filmmaker himself was impelled to live out the Tramp's role as outcast, turning his back on America and taking up residence in Europe.

Much of *Verdoux*'s power rests in its relationship to the Chaplin oeuvre. Its comment on how the Tramp has finally evolved is its most damning statement and it concludes Chaplin's comic saga of man entering the twentieth century and being completely reshaped by it. In his first films, the Tramp is a free spirit wandering the countryside and sleeping in parks, stealing and begging what he needs. But with the spread of industrialization and subsequent institutional control, the Tramp could no longer function. Charlie's story then is basically that of a nineteenth-century man caught in the twentieth century. John Belton summarizes Chaplin's social viewpoint as a "dialectic between nine-teenth-century Victorian and twentieth-century modern sensibilities, equating the struggle between the individual and the state with the struggle between Old World and New World values—the term 'Old World' working both a geographical and a temporal sense."[7]

But if Chaplin preferred the old world he did not yearn for a return to a lost age of innocence. Nor was he offering a revolutionary pipe dream of a workers' utopia. An artist and a political anarchist, Chaplin simply pointed out the paradoxes within society and man with a profound comic insight.

—21—

HUAC AND THE END
OF AN ERA

The Blacklist

Conservative elements have always attacked liberalism by associating it with the extreme left, seeing in many progressive social welfare programs the dangerous seeds of communism. Throughout the thirties, enemies of New Deal liberalism conducted a campaign to so discredit Roosevelt, but the overall viability of the New Deal's programs and the immense personal appeal of the President overrode such attacks. Then, with Roosevelt's death and the advent of the Cold War, this right-wing thesis found a sympathetic audience. Given a veneer of credibility by international events (the imperialist postures of Stalin, the rise of Red China) and a series of domestic spy scandals (especially the case involving New Dealer Alger Hiss), the "Red scare" snowballed into a major political movement. First the House Un-American Activities Committee in the late forties and then Senator Joseph McCarthy in the early fifties aroused the public to the "danger" in its midst. Any form of social protest became suspect—to have signed an antifascist petition or merely to have been in the presence of a "known" radical was enough to have many people fired from their jobs, slandered and ostracized by the community. All major institutions, from the federal government to the universities, the Army, and the mass media, came under severe scrutiny. In many industries there existed illegal blacklists of supposed Communists who were considered unemployable. That the Red-hunters could never find proof of a substantial Communist threat to the United States and that the American Communist Party was a completely legal political organization until the Communist Control Act of 1954 were irrelevant.

Among the earliest targets of HUAC was the movie industry, an industry with a high public profile and therefore a source of maximum publicity for the Committee and its work. The Hollywood blacklist is now almost as big a legend as the stars and movies of the period. It is a sorry tale of political repression, of individuals unfairly tormented and careers often ruined, of an industry which far too readily surrendered any semblance of its political independence. The initial hearings were called for October 1947 as an "investigation of Communism in motion pictures," but the tone of the proceedings quickly established that the Committee was not so much interested in the subversive content of movies as in the political affiliations and activities of the people who made the movies.

At first, the industry protested. Nineteen of the forty-one witnesses subpoenaed declared their intention to be "unfriendly" and refused to answer questions concerning their political beliefs. A group of Hollywood liberals, including Bogart, Bacall, Danny Kaye, John Huston, Gene Kelly, and William Wyler formed the Committee for the First Amendment, while Eric Johnston, prestigious president of the Motion Picture Association of America, defended the movies' right to freedom of speech.

The hearings quickly dashed liberal hopes. Friendly witnesses such as Jack Warner, L. B. Mayer, Walt Disney, Leo McCarey, Sam Wood, Robert Taylor, Adolphe Menjou, Ronald Reagan, George Murphy, and Gary Cooper were allowed, as *Daily Variety* reported, to "read prepared statements, use notes and ramble widely in offering testimony of strong nature without supporting evidence."[1] The "unfriendlies," on the other hand, were prohibited in all but two cases from making statements so that their protests had to be shouted out over Chairman Parnell Thomas's rulings. The spectacle of the "unfriendly" witnesses vociferously challenging the Committee's legal authority and their refusal to answer any questions boomeranged, creating much adverse publicity. After calling only eleven of the unfriendlies, the Committee abruptly called off the hearings and charged ten of the eleven—the Hollywood Ten—with contempt of Congress. Parnell Thomas ended the hearings by warning the industry to "set about immediately to clean its own house and not wait for public opinion to do so."[2]

Protest quickly gave way to expediency as industry personnel began to worry about their careers. The Committee for the First Amendment disintegrated, with such luminaries as Bogart and Bacall referring to their participation as a "mistake."[3] Within a month, industry heads held the infamous summit meeting at the Waldorf Astoria and issued the "Waldorf Statement," a tacit agreement to form a blacklist: the industry would not reemploy the Ten or any other members of a party advocating the overthrow of the United States government. Eric Johnston declared:

> We are frank to recognize that such a policy involves dangers and risks. There is the danger of hurting innocent people. There is the risk of creating an atmosphere of fear. Creative work at its best cannot be carried on in an atmosphere of fear. We will guard against this danger, this risk, this fear.[4]

But of course, just such an atmosphere was created. In 1950, the Supreme Court upheld the contempt charges against the Hollywood Ten, sending them to prison for a year and paving the way for a new set of HUAC hearings in 1951. This time there was no pretense of investigating Communist propaganda in the movies. Nor was there any protest.

The victim of the blacklist was caught, no matter what course of action he took, in an impossible dilemma. Merely being named at the hearings set off a relentless chain of events even though membership in the Party or signing an antifascist petition represented no transgression of the law. Once named, the individual was automatically labeled as suspect and found himself on the blacklist. Since the individual had done nothing illegal his accusers required no documented evidence of his transgression and he had no legal recourse to defend himself. When actually called before HUAC, the accused had but two choices, neither of them particularly palatable. First, he could cooperate, confessing to left-wing political affiliations and naming any people engaged in similar activities. By so doing, the individual generally cleared himself and saved his career, but he also lent validity to the Committee and helped perpetuate the investigation by supplying more names and forcing more individuals to face the same predicament. The other alternative was to defy the Committee and thus destroy one's career. The witness could refuse to testify under the First Amendment and face a jail sentence for contempt or he could invoke the Fifth Amendment, refusing to testify on the grounds of self-incrimination. The latter tactic failed to save the witness from blacklisting since, in Representative Morgan M. Moulder's words, any "refusal to testify so consistently leaves a strong inference that you are still an ardent follower of the Communist Party and its purpose."[5] Either way, then, whether confessing to a "crime" that was no crime or refusing to confess on the basis of constitutional rights, the individual was "guilty" and yet without legal recourse.

Over two hundred individuals within the movie industry were named by HUAC,[6] and countless others were judged by the studios and pressure groups as "guilty" by association. Many submitted to the Committee's demands and to other clearance procedures (such as studio loyalty tests) in order to salvage their careers, while many others refused to yield and paid the price. Virtually everyone else within the industry proceeded with extreme caution lest they grant the Committee or any right-wing zealot the slightest grounds for criticism. The very last thing those still employed dared do was stand up for their former coworkers, since such action would only blacklist them to the same limbo.

Movies and Communism: From *Mission to Moscow* to *Big Jim McLain*

Not surprisingly, the 1947 Committee and its successors failed to establish that Communist propaganda had ever been injected into the Hollywood film. A thorough study undertaken by Dorothy Jones[7] failed to uncover any fragments of Marxism in the movies and even Robert Vaughn, himself an anti-Communist, concedes in his book *Only Victims*:

> At no time during the Thomas, Wood, or subsequent investigations of Hollywood film content was the Committee ever able to establish conclusively that Communist Party dogma managed to find its way to the American people via the American screen.[8]

As we have discussed, Hollywood throughout the thirties had taken a strong anti-Communist line, viciously caricaturing leftists as villainous agitators or lazy, cowardly bums. About the only examples of Marxist propaganda the Committee members or witnesses were able to unearth were preposterous: single lines of dialogue as innocuous as "Share and share alike—that's democracy"—spoken by down-and-out college roommates who decide to pool their resources in *Tender Comrade* (1943, written by Dalton Trumbo). Clifford Odets' *None but the Lonely Heart* (1944) was damned by Mrs. Lela Rogers (Ginger's mother) because, among other reasons, the *Hollywood Reporter* had said that it was "moody and somber throughout in the Russian manner."[9]

The main basis for HUAC's claims was the series of wartime propaganda films that glorified America's Russian allies. And even here the Committee failed to unearth any real threat: Ayn Rand felt MGM's *Song of Russia* was propagandistic because it presented Russia in a positive light by showing Soviet children laughing and playing. That these films were the expression of the official foreign policy of the time was no defense, since that policy, the product of Roosevelt's "Communist-influenced" New Deal, was itself suspect. In fact, when Jack Warner took the stand, the Committee members were less interested in the film *Mission to Moscow* than in getting Warner to incriminate FDR by admitting that the President personally requested the movie be made.

Mission to Moscow was the only film that could really be said to conform to the official Communist line. While the other wartime films about Russia set out to improve the Russian image in America, *Mission* also took a direct look at the internal policies of the Soviet Union. Based on Ambassador Joseph Davies' book, the film dramatizes Davies' experiences in Russia during the late thirties, where FDR had sent him to assess the Soviets' willingness to fight. In the film, Davies (Walter Huston) first learns that we're all alike, that Soviets are no different from Americans. A factory foreman explains that he has worked hard and studied to get ahead and that the factory operates on a capitalist-like profit motive system to ensure "the most good for the most people." Davies replies, "It's the same in our country." Also, Mrs. Davies upon visiting a cosmetic factory, inquires, "Isn't this against Soviet principles?" to which she is answered, "Women all over the world like to look feminine. Beauty is no luxury." Then, the ambassador comes to his most important discovery—that the purge trials and secret police repression are necessities in a country threatened by sabotage. He does not even mind his own embassy being bugged since he has nothing to hide: "Perhaps counterespionage is a matter of self-preservation."

The film's main thrust is to demonstrate how truly antifascist the Soviets are, and how those aligned against them are pro-Nazi. The Nazi-Soviet pact is justified as a stalling tactic, a means of buying time to prepare for a war Stalin knew was inevitable all along. Internal sabotage is pinned on the Nazis. At the purge trials, Davies learns that Trotsky, along with Bukharin and Radek, was involved with the Germans and Japanese in a plot to overthrow the government. The film naively accepts the Stalinist version of the trials as gospel, something that even the real Davies had trouble believing.[10] Stalin (Mannart Kippen) himself is portrayed as a wise, affable grandfather figure, who along with Roosevelt and Churchill is the only world leader to foresee the dangers of Nazi Germany. Yet, when Davies returns to America and tries to arouse support for Russia, he is confronted with the wrath of isolationists who see no danger in Hitler ("We got a coupla' oceans, ain't we?") but are violently opposed to Stalin. The film thus attacks anti-Communists and isolationists as profascists. Though the Warners could hardly be accused of Bolshevism and *Mission* would never have been made if not for the war cause, any film which supported Stalin was wide open for attack. To paraphrase Alistair Cooke, the film was judged in one era for what it represented in another.

As ever, hypersensitive to such controversy and "advised" by Chairman Thomas to produce films which attack communism, the studios readily complied with an entire cycle of anti-Red pictures. Just as the wartime propaganda films had been a complete reversal in attitude from the thirties anti-Communist movies, so the postwar cycle performed a political flip-flop from the war pictures. Within weeks of the 1947 hearings, MGM released its 1939 anti-Communist satire, *Ninotchka*, in which cold commissar Greta Garbo is seduced by captivating capitalist Melvyn Douglas. Then, in May 1948, Twentieth Century-Fox released *Iron Curtain*. The other studios soon followed suit. Except for the modest success of *Iron Curtain* (it was number two at the New York box office for the month of May[11]), none of these films were particularly popular. Yet despite cool public response, Hollywood relentlessly pursued the anti-Communist theme and when it appeared to be waning throughout 1950–51, the second HUAC hearings produced another, even greater, flurry of movie Red-baiting. Dorothy Jones estimates that there were between thirty-five and forty films released between 1948 and 1954 attacking communism and the Soviet Union.[12] This perseverence with a political issue in the face of poor box office is unprecedented in Hollywood history and indicates the degree of paranoia felt by the studios during the period.

The cycle itself followed the tradition of the World War II features, translating the ideological conflict between capitalism and communism into the most simplistic form of morality play. As Pauline Kael, among others, has pointed out, if we were not told that the villains were Communists, we could easily mistake them for Nazis:

> the filmgoer who saw the anti-Nazi films of ten years ago will have no trouble recognizing the characters, just as ten years ago he could have detected (under the Nazi black shirts) psychopathic killers, trigger-happy cattle rustlers, and the screen villain of earliest vintage —the man who will foreclose the mortgage if he doesn't get the girl. The Soviet creatures of the night are direct descendents of the early film archetype, the bad man.[13]

Again, the films closely conform to genre conventions, the majority of them indistinguishable from *Confessions of a Nazi Spy*. Films such as *Iron Curtain, Walk a Crooked Mile* (1948), *I Was a Communist for the FBI* (1951), *Walk East on Beacon* (1952), and *Big Jim McLain* (1952) are generally shot in the same documentary style, with the same authoritative narrator who tells us that this is based on a real case, and the familiar plot of the investigator-hero uncovering a scheme by nefarious foreigners to overthrow the country. The other most common story line, seen in *Sofia* (1948), *The Red Danube* (1949), *Never Let Me Go*

(1953), *Man on a Tightrope* (1953), and *Night People* (1954), is borrowed from *Escape* (1940) and dramatizes the attempts of the protagonists to flee from repressive Iron Curtain countries to the freedom of America. One genre which the World War II propagandists had failed to use was science fiction. In *Red Planet Mars* (1952), both the Martians and God help destroy the atheistic Soviet regime.

Like the Nazis, the Communists are condemned on character traits more than ideology. Party members are almost always severely disturbed—some are blood-hungry killers (Arnold in *I Married a Communist* [also known as *The Woman on Pier 13*], 1949); others are mad scientists (*Whip Hand*, 1951); the women, if not nymphomaniacs (Mollie in *The Red Menace*, 1949, and Christine in *I Married a Communist*), are frigid and repressed (*Walk East on Beacon*). One of the most dramatically deranged Communists is Yvonne (Betty Lou Gerson) in *The Red Menace*, who bursts forth in a demented tirade about the revolution when questioned by authorities. The leaders are either hysterical fanatics like Vanning in *I Married a Communist* or shysters. Generally the Party elite live, as Karel Reisz points out, "in large, luxurious flats with suspect modernistic furniture (but the larder is always a photographic darkroom) and large libraries, eat off silver plates and openly look forward to the age of caviar for the commissar."[14] As one character in *Walk East on Beacon* enthuses, "Someday we won't have to worry about dough. A commissar gets everything for free—*everything*!"

Just as Hollywood never dealt with the fascist ideology, so the political and economic principles of communism are never really explicated. They receive token expression in crudely distilled comments and speeches. "Man is state—state is man. Someone upstairs says something and that's that," intones a Party intellectual in *I Married a Communist*.

The Communist Party doesn't seem to stand *for* anything, only *against* sacred American principles such as God, motherhood, and true love. It is continually in conflict with members of the Catholic Church, including a priest in *I Was a Communist*, a cardinal in *Guilty of Treason* (1949), and a Mother Superior in *The Red Danube*. In *My Son John* (1952), John Jefferson (Robert Walker) betrays both God and his mother when he swears on the Bible that he is not a Communist, while Mollie, an amoral floozie in *The Red Menace*, turns her back on Father O'Leary for the truth "as laid down by Marx, Engels, Lenin, and Stalin." In other films, the Party boss is continually warning romantically inclined members: "Love! Why don't you call it what it is—emotion!" (*I Married a Communist*). According to Karel Reisz, "The following lines of dialogue occur with minor variations in four of the films:

PARTY GIRL: (In love and therefore deviating) **Don't worry about**
                       my private life.
PARTY BOSS: You *have* no private life."[15]

Nor is human life very sacred to the Communists. Party members are
expendable, expected to give themselves up to the police in order to
protect more important compatriots. In *Iron Curtain*, one imprisoned
unfortunate is consoled: "Don't be too unhappy, Keith. We'll name a
city after you when we take over." The faithful are even expected to
kill those close to them when the leaders so demand: a brother is ordered to murder his sister in *Whip Hand* and a husband his wife in
Conspirator (1950). Whole sections of the population are equally dis-
pensable. In *Whip Hand*, the "Commies" talk of germ warfare, and in
Big Jim McLain, they plan to poison the waterfront as a strike tactic.
In the latter film, John Wayne, with his customary political insight,
explains to a spy the difference between Americans and Communists:

> I wanted to hit you one punch, just one full-thrown right hand. But
> now I can't do it. Because you're too small. That's the difference be-
> tween you and us, I guess. We don't hit the little guy. We believe in
> fair play and all that sort of thing.

If the Soviet Union represents the evils of totalitarianism, of course,
America is the land of freedom and goodness. But though our society
is basically sound, the films warn that it is still vulnerable and locate
the source of that vulnerability in America's innocence. The country is
so free and open that people have become too trusting, taking everyone,
including the Communists, at their word. Idealistic dupes are seduced
into the Party ranks by phony front organizations such as the antifascist
group in *I Was a Communist for the FBI* which really raises funds for
Party activities. Blacks, Jews, and other minorities are lured into the
Party through its platform of racial equality only to discover that the
leaders are in fact vicious racists seeking new members to manipulate
in their quest for world power. A student who has won a trip to Russia
returns home brainwashed in *Big Jim McLain* while, to John Jefferson,
communism is like a contagious disease: he begins attending meetings
for intellectual stimulation and before he knows it he's being enticed
into spying for the Party.

When the innocents discover the truth (the cabbie in *Walk East on
Beacon* describes it as "like waking up married to a woman you hate"),
they soon realize that the Communists are much more ruthless than
expected and will kill anyone who tries to desert. Such a fate befalls the
protagonists in *I Married a Communist* and *My Son John*, as well as

minor characters in *The Red Menace. I Was a Communist for the FBI* even implies that this is what happened to such important figures as Trotsky and Masaryk. Many other innocents choose suicide either to avoid corruption (the ballerina in *The Red Danube*) or to free themselves from the living death of Party membership (the Jewish poet in *The Red Menace* and the army officer in *Conspirator*). So great is their sin that the only way ex-Communists can redeem themselves is through martyrdom. These films echo the common sentiment of "innocence betrayed" propounded by such writers as Leslie Fiedler, who saw the liberals of the New Deal as culpable because they had allowed themselves to be used by the Communists. Just as the liberals have been betrayed, so they have betrayed their countrymen. FDR, under the influence of New Deal "Reds" like Alger Hiss, "sold us out" at Yalta.

To combat any further chance of betrayal, the films offer a vigilant antiintellectualism. In films such as *My Son John* and *Big Jim McLain*, the parents of the fallen youths argue for a return to the old values. John's father (Dean Jagger) is meant to represent the ideal American: a Legionnaire, staunch churchgoer, and small-town schoolteacher who gives lessons in "simple down-to-earth" morality and Americanism. He scorns his son's university education, his important Washington job, and his relations with intellectuals and professors. Mr. Jefferson relies on the Bible and patriotic platitudes for enlightenment and mistrusts any open debate which deviates from these narrow principles. In short, the heroic American patriarch is a right-wing bigot who frequently bursts into song: "If you don't like your Uncle Sammy / Then go back to your home o'er the sea." Mr. Lester, the father in *Big Jim McLain*, reveres the values of hard work and religious faith which have allowed him to "retire on my pension and live free in the sun." He too sees his son's communism as a repudiation of America and God.

Like HUAC, these films rely on their own internal logic which betrays a tendency toward the very totalitarianism that they are supposedly combatting. Any of the beliefs and freedoms which fail to conform precisely to the values of the American right are held up as suspect, as the means by which the Communists infiltrate and poison the country. So, although America is glorified as the land of freedom where everyone can speak and think for himself, the threat of communism is simultaneously located in that very exercise of free thought. This logic is succinctly captured in *Big Jim McLain*. After he breaks up the Communist spy ring, Big Jim does not take the criminals to court where they would be tried as spies under normal procedures, but subpoenas them to appear before HUAC. By thus misrepresenting HUAC's role, the film is able to attack Constitutional freedom. The Communists are guilty of espionage, but by invoking the Fifth Amendment, they elude the Committee's investigations and go free to continue their evil work. By conforming to the principles of the Constitution, HUAC cannot do justice to the traitors and the country remains unprotected. According to McLain, America's freedom is both glorious and dangerous: "There are a lot of wonderful things written into our Constitution that were meant for honest, decent citizens. I resent the fact that it can be used and abused by the very people who want to destroy it." In short, to preserve our freedom we must relinquish it. Loyalty to motherhood and HUAC must be as absolute as loyalty to the Party.

HUAC and the Social Problem Filmmaker

The problem film did not really disappear after the 1947 hearings. As we have seen, films that dealt with race and politics continued to be made. While the case of the Hollywood Ten was making its way through the courts, some liberal opposition remained alive and a handful of films seriously questioned the basic tenets of American society. *All the King's Men* and *The Lawless* analyze the nature of political and social repression while *Monsieur Verdoux* and *Force of Evil* argue that corruption, greed, and murder are the basis of western society. *Monsieur Verdoux* and Chaplin were attacked bitterly in the press and the movie was boycotted by various right-wing groups. The other three films were accepted without controversy. But in 1950, the Hollywood Ten were finally convicted and sentenced, clearing the way for the second HUAC hearings in 1951. By 1952, none of the directors of the above films were free to work in the United States: Chaplin had been forced into exile; Losey, Rossen, and Polonsky were blacklisted. Losey and Chaplin never worked in America again and Polonsky did not direct another film until 1969 (*Tell Them Willie Boy Was Here*). Only Rossen, who after a term on the blacklist acquiesced to HUAC, was able to return to filmmaking in America during the fifties.

A number of films made by those who came under political scrutiny bear an interesting if indirect relationship with the Committee. Subsequent to their cooperative appearances before HUAC, Budd Schulberg and Elia Kazan made *On the Waterfront* and Edward Dmytryk *The Caine Mutiny* (1954). Both films were major studio productions with major stars; both films tacitly justified the filmmakers' stand before the Committee. On the opposite side of the issue, Herbert Biberman, Paul Jarrico, and Michael Wilson's *Salt of the Earth* and the exiled Chaplin's *A King in New York* (1957) were produced outside Hollywood and in defiance of HUAC and the studios.

On the Waterfront is a defense of the act of informing. Terry's heroic testimony to the police and subsequent rejection by the dockers can be seen to parallel Schulberg and Kazan's case: they broke from the iron-handed Communist Party, testified against it as a threat to America, and now must suffer the ostracism of their colleagues. The parallel is not, however, entirely accurate. Terry risks his life to voluntarily testify against those involved in criminal offenses—his is purely an act of moral conscience. Schulberg and Kazan's testimony was not voluntary, not altruistic, and not against criminals. Indeed, Kazan initially refused to cooperate and it was only under the threat of contempt charges and blacklist that he agreed to implicate others. Ironically, there is one scene in the film where Terry is placed in Kazan's shoes. Threatened with unemployment, ostracism, and violence, Terry is ordered to spy on the church meeting. In this instance, though it more accurately parallels Kazan's position, Terry's informing is condemned because it perpetuates the mob's evil.[16]

Edward Dmytryk was the only one of the Hollywood Ten who reversed his opposition to the Committee after he was imprisoned. Although *The Caine Mutiny* is not as personal as *Waterfront*, based as it is on a famous novel and play, its drama still mirrors Dmytryk's predicament. The film sets up a situation where rebellion seems justified, only to prove that conformity is a higher value. The first part of the film convincingly demonstrates Captain Queeg's (Humphrey Bogart) cowardice and incompetence and presents the mutiny as the only way to save the ship during a typhoon. The film then executes a complete turnabout: the defense lawyer (Jose Ferrer) who has proven Queeg's incompetence now attacks the crew for not supporting Queeg when he really needed them. Yet at no time have the men failed in their duties and responsibilities; it is only their captain, too paranoid to command the ship adequately, who has failed. The crew's sin is that they have not followed and loved a leader who has been completely contemptuous of them and would have led them to their deaths.

The mutiny is ultimately blamed on an intellectual writer and officer who has cunningly manipulated events for his own selfish ends. Keefer (Fred MacMurray) is the left-wing figure who has duped the naive liberals, Merrick (Van Johnson) and Keith (Robert Francis), into rebelling against authority. So the film ends by telling us to remain loyal to social authority, no matter how inept and destructive it may appear, and to be wary of those who would have you rebel, no matter how legitimate they may seem.

Both *Waterfront* and *Caine* were major box-office successes in 1954, whereas neither *Salt of the Earth* nor *A King in New York* ever received widespread distribution. The latter two films had to be made outside Hollywood—*Salt* was produced and distributed independently and *King* filmed entirely in England. *Salt* then met with an industrywide boycott while Chaplin, after having both *Monsieur Verdoux* and *Limelight* (1952) greeted with animosity and picket lines, did not even try to release *A King in New York* in America until 1973.

Though *Salt* may not directly confront the issues of the blacklist, its very existence is an extraordinary assault on HUAC. Biberman, Jarrico, and Wilson were attempting to show that films could be produced beyond the blacklist. On the other hand, HUAC itself is a major plot element in *King*. A clumsily conceived film, *King* nevertheless makes a brave attempt to expose the idiocy and dangers of the Committee. The deposed King Shahdov (Chaplin) innocently befriends a homeless young schoolboy, Rupert (Michael Chaplin), but because the youth's parents are being held by HUAC under contempt charges, the King is smeared by association. At first calmly dismissing the slander ("A Royal Communist! Ha!"), he is soon caught up in the prevailing atmosphere of paranoia. Called before HUAC, Shahdov accidentally becomes entangled in a fire hose, rushes into the hearing trailing the hose behind him, and as a result is cited for contempt. Then the scene disintegrates into chaos with the fire hose suddenly dousing the Committee members, an appropriate but not terribly funny dampening of the Committee's hot air.

It is Rupert who makes the film's most direct statements on HUAC. The boy is an impassioned "free thinker" who at the slightest provocation launches into heavy-handed harangues on political repression in America. He essentially echoes Chaplin's viewpoints, making prominent reference to how passports are used as a political weapon to limit one's freedom of travel. (It was when his reentry visa was revoked during a trans-Atlantic voyage in 1952 that Chaplin began life as an exile.) The boy asserts that he mistrusts all forms of government and admits to being a Communist only because "I'm so sick and tired of people asking me if I'm this, if I'm that, so then if it pleases everybody, I'm a Communist."

Rupert is also a surrogate Tramp figure. Often referred to as a "little fellow," he is seen wandering the streets cold and alone and later wearing the king's oversized, baggy pajamas. Though he is more articulate (and also more obnoxious and far less enchanting) than the Tramp, his espousal of free speech parallels Charlie's freedom of spirit. However, in the America of the fifties, the Tramp does not have the pluck to carry on. Rupert begins defiantly—"Make me give names. Make a snivelling stool pigeon out of me. Brainwash me! But you can't." But by the end he has been brainwashed, reduced to a snivelling stool pigeon, naming his parents' associates in order to save his mother and father from jail. At the school where Shahdov bids him farewell, a subdued Rupert is led into the waiting room and quietly sobs while the Headmaster speaks for him: "Of course we still have our moods and doubts, don't we Rupert? And I keep telling him he has nothing to worry about. We consider Rupert a hero and a real patriot. We're all very proud of him here." Rupert cannot opt out like the Tramp and hit the road. He cannot even visit Shahdov in Europe because of "complications." The youth, who has been held up as the hope for the future, has been destroyed. Shahdov, the older Tramp figure, is able to turn his back on a hopeless society and flee to Europe, offering the token reassurance that the hysteria will soon pass.

The Decline of the Problem Film

HUAC has often been blamed for the drop in political subject matter in Hollywood films during the fifties. Dorothy Jones has carefully charted the shifts in film content between 1947 and 1954. From a high of 28 percent of Hollywood's product that dealt with "social themes and psychological problems" in 1947, the percentage diminished to 9.2 percent in 1954.[17] Ms. Jones suggests that this decrease in problem pictures was one of the Committee's chief aims:

> the writer cannot but question to what extent the attack made by the House Committee on Un-American Activities on the content of Hollywood films was the result of a fear (also reflected in earlier Congressional inquiries) that motion pictures—the most popular medium of our time—were beginning to devote themselves seriously to an exploration of some of the social, economic and political problems of our time.[18]

After the harassment he suffered at the hands of HUAC, Jack Warner broke with the old image of the "socially conscious studio." Eric Johnston now complained:

> We'll have no more *Grapes of Wrath*. We'll have no more *Tobacco Roads*. We'll have no more films that show the seamy side of American life. We'll have no more pictures that deal with labor strikes. We'll have no more pictures that show the banker as villain.[19]

Certainly HUAC created an environment in which it was difficult to hold political viewpoints at all critical of the establishment, but the fact that problem films did continue to reach the screens belies Jones's assertion of HUAC's influence on film content. The problem film continued its analyses of issues in the standard format we have delineated throughout this book. Matters of race, juvenile delinquency, prison conditions, political corruption, big business were dramatized throughout the fifties as conflicts between shysters and liberal redeemers, between victims and victimizers. Certainly there were no radical critiques on the scale of *Monsieur Verdoux* or *Force of Evil*, but on the whole, the politics of the genre had always come under severe scrutiny, which is why HUAC had quickly given up looking for subversive content in movies to concentrate on the political affiliations of industry personnel. There was no need for HUAC to control politics in movies since the politics were already inoffensive.

Still, the number of these films did decline and, more importantly, the dramatic urgency characteristic of the genre throughout the thirties and forties was for the most part lacking in the fifties. If this cannot be traced directly to HUAC, it can be traced to a new cultural temper of which HUAC was an ingredient. McCarthyism signaled the end of the era of social idealism that had so permeated the Depression and post-war years and had given the problem film genre its vitality. Eisenhower and affluence relegated social concerns to a position that was secondary to matters of personal identity. The forties hero whose social rebellion was in the end reduced to a personal neurosis now lost the social context for his disaffection and became a "rebel without a cause."

The prototypes for the fifties hero were Marlon Brando and James Dean, whose delinquency has no ready environmental roots. There are no slums or criminal role models leading them astray. When asked what he's rebelling against in *The Wild One* (1954), Brando taunts, "Whadda ya got?" Dean's conflict is not with social authority but with parental authority and by extension the middle-class way of life. He clumsily seeks to win his father's love in *East of Eden* (1955) and re-bels against his father's ineffectuality in *Rebel Without a Cause* (1955). In that the Dean and Brando personae are expressions of the middle-class alienation of the fifties, the films question the prevailing values of their time. But the power of these films lies in their personal drama of identity crisis, not their social analysis in the tradition of the Depression and postwar message pictures.

With social consciousness no longer a dominant cultural motif, so-cially conscious films dwindled in number and in relevancy. There were still several outstanding problem pictures made (Kazan's *A Face in the Crowd*, 1957, and *Wild River*, 1960; Sidney Lumet's *Twelve Angry Men*, 1957), but the genre as a whole had lost its connection with the central cultural concerns of the time. The previous two decades were filled with problem films which were among the most important pictures of their time. These films functioned within a cultural context where social concerns were vital to popular thought, whereas the fifties exam-ples of the genre operated on the edge of what was considered cultur-ally important.

The late sixties saw a revival of Hollywood social concern, but the most important aspect of this revival was not the renewal of the social problem film but the infusion of an explicitly antisocial subtext that the Formula had previously prohibited. With the breakdown in the structure of the old studio industry and the Code, new film narrative techniques and a broader range of subject matter and viewpoints created a new approach to film and a new perspective in movie politics. Films began to operate beyond the conventions of the genre, no longer viewing social themes in terms of "problems" to be identified, isolated, and resolved. Social values, not social problems, were the chief concern. Antisocial attitudes became standard, permeating almost all of the films as a natural subtext to the action.

It is instructive to compare *Bonnie and Clyde* (1967) to *You Only Live Once* (1937) and *They Live by Night* (1947). All three essentially treat the same story of doomed outlaw lovers on the run, but the earlier pictures are problem films, definitely establishing a causal relationship between the protagonists' criminality and society. On the surface, their concern is social reform. Their broader political viewpoints must be played out beneath the genre's conventions. *Bonnie and Clyde*, on the other hand, operates separately from the problem film and does not have to view society as a self-enclosed mechanism suffering from a few problems that can be resolved by applications of moral integrity. Instead it is a grotesque comedy providing an overview of violence and crime in America. Society is not a dominant plot element and there are no ready-made social reasons for the heroes' careers of robbery and murder. It is the fact of their criminality and how their violence is a vicarious but double-edged thrill for the audience that are central to the film. *Bonnie and Clyde* comments on society by using movie violence itself as a means of questioning the violence in America, rather than by making society itself the subject of the film. Society and politics are part of a whole universe and value system, and in looking at that universe politics inevitably enters into it.

The traditional problem film does continue to exist as well (sometimes with notable success, as with *Norma Rae* and *The China Syndrome*, both 1979), but as a genre it has never regained the impact it had in the thirties and forties. Perhaps where it has functioned best is on television. In miniseries such as *Roots* (1977) and *Holocaust* (1978) and in regular series such as *The Defenders*, *Lou Grant*, and *The White Shadow*, specific issues are dramatized within highly formulized conventions. Like the studio products of old Hollywood, television programming reaches a mass audience and is part of everyone's cultural fabric so that these programs are important conveyors of political and social attitudes. Although these problem series probably fulfill the role of the old Hollywood problem film, only rarely do they match the dramatic power or aesthetic quality of the best of their precursors. The Hollywood problem film in its prime could still excite with its passions despite all the moderating subterfuges of the Formula. The balance it drew between social outrage and social pacification was often very fine and the images it established of the individual's relation to social institutions are of lasting value.

CONCLUSION:
SULLIVAN'S TRAVELS—
HOLLYWOOD GOES SLUMMING

SULLIVAN: How can you talk about musicals at a time like this with the world committing suicide, with corpses piling up in the streets, with grim death gargling at you from every corner, with people slaughtered like sheep . . .

EXECUTIVE: Maybe they'd like to forget that.

John L. Sullivan is an archetype of the socially conscious person who works for political change in an idealistic effort to improve the conditions of the world but in the process expiates his guilt feelings for his own affluence in such a world. Through the figure of Sullivan and his comic quest for honesty as a political film director, Preston Sturges raises many of the issues surrounding the role of the Hollywood social problem movie. Sturges toys with Sullivan's idealism and guilt and with Hollywood's social concern until he resolves the whole question of social commitment with a justification of "pure entertainment" over political didacticism.

Sullivan's "travels" are his field trips into the "real world" to research poverty first hand. Dressed as a hobo, he moves through the Hoovervilles, alleyways, and freightyards of the land. Throughout the first half of the film, Sullivan is strictly a tourist, followed closely by a rambunctious entourage of press corps and medical staff. But in the second half, the great John L. Sullivan finally gets his wish to become one of the common men: presumed dead by the public and studio, all proof of identification lost and suffering temporary amnesia, Sullivan ends up as just another convict doing six years hard labor on a Southern chain gang. Once he is truly part of the "real world," Sullivan comes to appreciate real suffering.

What Sullivan discovers from his experience is that society cannot be changed and that social inequities are the natural state of affairs: the poor don't want any help and the well-meaning rich are powerless to make changes anyway. Sullivan in the first half finds it impossible to get away from his natural place as the rich movie director, always winding up back in Hollywood. Yet in the second half, once he does manage to make his real identity known to authorities, he quite readily escapes the unnatural world of the chain gang: "They don't send big picture directors to a place like this." Sullivan ponders Sturges's major point: "Maybe there's a Universal Law that says 'Stay put. As you are so you shall remain.' Maybe that's why tramps are always in trouble. They don't vote, they don't pay taxes. They're trying to break a natural law."

Certainly the poor are unreceptive to Sullivan's attempts to help them. When he queries a couple of freight-car tramps about their feelings on the "present labor situation," they get up in disgust and move to another freight car. And when he tries to give away some money (one thousand dollars in five-dollar bills, "in return for what they gave me"), Sullivan is brutally beaten and robbed by a greedy old tramp. Concern and philanthropy are meaningless gestures because they go against the Universal Law, the law that in essence justifies the good fortunes of some men without having to account for the misery of others.

If social change is impossible, then problem films are irrelevant. However, Sullivan does learn that there is a place for escapism. Shackled with the rest of the chain gang, he is marched off to a poor Negro church where they join the congregation for a Sunday night picture show. Captivated by the antics of Walt Disney's Pluto, the downtrodden audience bursts into joyful, uncontrollable laughter. Sullivan too joins in ("Am I laughing?" he shouts to his neighbor in happy amazement) and the experience makes him realize that movies need not be profound social commentaries to serve a worthwhile purpose. Sullivan now respects escapism as a profound, even religious experience which provides a few moments of happiness and relief from bitter reality. This realization nullifies the need for social significance as well as providing an idealistic rationale for pure entertainment. Sullivan explains to his producers why he will not make "Oh Brother": "There's a lot to be said for making people laugh. Did you know that's all some people have? It isn't much but it's better than nothing in this cockeyed caravan." If people do not want messages, then escapism is a valid outlet for idealism, and if five-dollar handouts do little good, then the Universal Law overrides any feelings of guilt. Sullivan can go back contentedly to making "Ants in Their Pants of 1939."

Sturges here focuses on a common reaction to politics in the arts: social action is useless and social drama is spurned in favor of entertainment that has no significance beyond its function as amusement and diversion. But the equation is loaded, based on the assumption that social idealism and entertainment are mutually exclusive. Sturges does not concede that a genuinely concerned film can be both didactic and also compelling human drama that appeals to a mass audience. The best films of the genre necessarily satisfy all the requirements of film narrative, couching their politics in terms of dramatic conflict. They are good because of their quality as film, not because of or in spite of their political content. The content is at the service of the entertainment movie, making it axiomatic that the problem film entertains as much as it teaches and transforms.

One need only look at Sturges's own work, especially *Sullivan's Travels*. In it Sturges uses satire and knockabout farce to make a serious political comment. The rest of his films, from *The Great McGinty* (1940) through to *Hail the Conquering Hero* (1944) are neither trivial fluff nor heavyhanded drama but pungent, inventive social satires that make people laugh while they make their point. The self-appointed champion of escapism was ironically one of Hollywood's most unconventional and thought-provoking directors. Sturges not only thumbed his nose at the movie community's liberal pretensions but also at some of the Formula's most sacred precepts: motherhood, patriotism, small-town America, Horatio Algerism, and even the Virgin Birth.

In *Sullivan's Travels* Sturges also questions the integrity of the problem film and its ability to accurately reflect the conditions it seeks to portray. Through Sullivan's voyage of self-discovery, Sturges satirizes Hollywood social consciousness and the efforts of the rich, isolated movie community to deal with anything but entertainment fantasies. The distance between Hollywood and the Depression is parodied in one particularly clever scene. To catch a freight, Sullivan is outfitted as a tramp by the studio costume department, has his butler phone for the freight train's departure time, and is then chauffeured right into the yard in his big limousine. Social problem stereotypes also receive sarcastic treatment. The opening film-within-a-film parodies the pretentiousness of the genre, showing a bum and a yard boss thrashing away at one another on a moving train until they both fall to their deaths. "Capital and labor destroy one another," intones Sullivan. Sturges extends *I Am a Fugitive*'s chain-gang brutalities into a ridiculous ritual whereby every time the naive Sullivan opens his mouth in protest, the warden pummels him in response. His reward for acting as a typical movie benefactor distributing the money is to be beaten and robbed.

Sullivan in the end concedes that he is incapable of making an honest picture of social reality—"I haven't suffered enough"—and to persevere with the project would be hypocritical. The distance between the movie stereotypes and social reality is too great for the genre to attain the high purpose Sullivan claimed for it in the opening scene. When Sullivan is a bum confronted by a cop in the rail yard, it is not a case of capital and labor in symbolic conflict but of one man who is confused and unfortunate being harassed by another who is doing his job. Sturges thus concludes not only that it is politically useless to make problem films, but it is also impossible to capture any social "truth" in such an artificial, conventionalized genre format.

Sturges here pinpoints a major limitation of political cinema. Because its priorities are dramatic conflict and entertainment values, the problem film must make its politics subservient. Social concerns are translated through the Formula into a fictional conflict lasting from ninety minutes to two hours and in the process the politics are redefined by the requirements of the medium into something removed from their original state. We have illustrated throughout the book how the film conventions are the most significant factor in determining a film's interpretation of social reality, by and large imposing a conservative political view on most problem films. While this appears to have been an unconscious process in most cases, many filmmakers did purposely refine the relation between Formula conventions and politics to articulate a more self-conscious social viewpoint. Capra, Ford in *Grapes of Wrath*, the best of the Warners' exposés all remain faithful in their fashion to Formula conventions and yet still come close to achieving what Sullivan concludes is impossible.

Still other films (or sometimes even scenes within conventional films) present different, often subversive political viewpoints by moving slightly beyond the Formula and upsetting audience expectations. The pessimistic fadeout of *I Am a Fugitive* and Verdoux's triumphant refusal to repent his crimes deny the affirmative resolution of the Happy Ending, leaving questions unanswered and social structures open for criticism. Other deviations likewise discomfort and provoke the audience toward a more radical conclusion: the documentary look of the Hooverville camp in *Grapes of Wrath* drives home the need for change throughout the midwest whereas the back-lot Hooverville in *A Man's Castle* rationalizes the living conditions of the unemployed as acceptable; King Vidor's Eisenstein-like climactic montage in *Our Daily Bread* emphasizes a communal identity over the individual hero who normally resolves the crisis; Fritz Lang's unorthodox camera and editing techniques manipulate viewpoint in *Fury* and *You Only Live Once* to highlight audience responsibility for the social injustice on the screen; Abraham Polonsky's use of narration and visual motifs within the conventional story lines of *Body and Soul* and *Force of Evil* creates a far more complex and critical view of American capitalism than normal. The dramatic experiences of these films differ from those of the Formula and as a result so do their politics. If a film cannot argue with the kind of documentary thoroughness or intellectual authority of the print medium, it can still make its point on an experiential level. The audience emotionally experiences the human ramifications of the issue and comes to a personally felt understanding of it.

Sullivan would still maintain that these films do not fulfill their ultimate purpose because they fail to effect any change in the social situations they dramatize. Except for examples of isolated reforms—in chain-gang regulations after *Fugitive*, in mental health institutions after *The Snake Pit*—Sullivan is correct: there is no direct relationship between the problem film and social change. Indeed, as we have noted throughout the book, the movies picked up on concerns that were already prevalent and reflected processes that were already happening rather than initiating changes. Hollywood expressed a great deal of concern over social inequities; it was offended by all forms of persecution, upset over widespread unemployment and fascist atrocities. But just as this concern rarely burst the tight bonds of conventional narrative in the movies, so in the political arenas of society at large it rarely extended into an all-out critique of basic American institutions. In the pre-Roosevelt years, the movies were at their most cynical and despairing because the populace itself was in a state of turmoil. Correspondingly, during the New Deal honeymoon and the war, they were at their most optimistic and patriotic. The problem film, then, is part of a larger cultural process and cannot by itself fundamentally alter social attitudes or inspire social action unless society is predisposed to such change. What the genre can do is reinforce values, pick up on popular attitudes and give them a recognizable cultural shape for the public to more readily embrace. Only if society is open to, indeed undergoing, change do the movies contribute to the process by promulgating prevalent attitudes which are already bringing about the change. The movies are but one of many cultural, social, and political variables which both contribute to and are influenced by the process of social evolution.

A key component in this process is the public itself. It is hardly the victim of a bread-and-circuses media conspiracy to keep it appeased and complacent, but is centrally involved in feeding its preoccupations back to the movies through the barometer of the box office. Despite

Sullivan's assertions to the contrary, regular attendance sustained the problem film and indicated the public's approval. The films reflected largely what the public wanted, and what it wanted, paradoxically, was messages remarkably similar to Sullivan's Universal Law. The problem film is removed from standard entertainment only by its surface conventions of social realism. Through repetition of the same Formula, the genre as a whole served as a formulized ritual to assuage extreme political disaffection, to absorb the extensive reforms and developments of the Depression and war, and to reinforce the establishmentarian values encapsulated in the Formula. Nearly every film we have discussed repeats with minor variations the same pattern: arouse indignation over some facet of contemporary life, carefully qualifying any criticism so that it can in the end be reduced to simple causes, to a villain whose removal rectifies the situation. Allusions to the genuine concerns of the audience play up antisocial feelings only to exorcise them on safe targets contained within a dramatic rather than social context. The effect is cathartic, purging us for the time being of anxieties and guilts over the state of the world.

The genre then accurately reflects the liberal concerns of its time; its limitations were very much the limitations of its audience and era. Like Sullivan, the public was driven by a combination of idealism and guilt over the state of the world and the problem film was an important means of venting both. As Michael Wood has written, Hollywood's liberalism, like middle-class American liberalism in general, was undoubtedly "all too timid and discreet and all too quickly exhausted."[1] But the problem film exhibits a genuine compassion over social inequities. Just as there's a lot to be said for making people laugh, so there's a lot to be said for the social problem film. If social progress is measured by the inch, then some of the more stirring moments from these films and the overall, compromised thrust of the genre as a whole helped to keep us moving a little further along, John L. Sullivan to the contrary.

Notes

Introduction

1. Mae D. Huettig, *Economic Control of the Motion Picture Industry* (Philadelphia: University of Pennsylvania Press, 1944), p. 81.

2. Ibid., p. 69.

3. Robin Wood, *Howard Hawks* (London: Martin Secker & Warburg, 1968), p. 8.

4. Roy Armes, *Film and Reality: An Historical Survey* (Harmondsworth, Middlesex: Penguin Books, 1974), pp. 141–142.

5. Martha Wolfenstein and Nathan Leites, *Movies: A Psychological Study* (New York: Atheneum, 1970), p. 25.

6. This and subsequent quotes are from the Production Code, reprinted in Ruth Inglis, *Freedom of the Movies* (Chicago: University of Chicago Press, 1947), pp. 205–219.

7. Lillian Ross, *Picture* (New York: Avon Books, 1969), p. 169.

8. Ibid., p. 25.

9. Gilbert Seldes, quoted in Huettig, p. 9.

10. Lewis Jacobs, *The Rise of the American Film* (New York: Teachers College Press, 1967), pp. 164–165.

1. Prototypes: Gangsters, Fallen Women, and Convicts

1. Richard Griffith, *The Film Till Now* (London: Spring Books, 1967), p. 433.

2. Andrew Bergman, *We're in the Money* (New York: Harper Colophon Books, 1972), pp. 7–10.

3. Lewis Jacobs, *The Rise of the American Film* (New York: Teachers College Press, 1967), p. 276.

4. Robert Warshow, "The Gangster as Tragic Hero," *The Immediate Experience* (New York: Atheneum, 1972), pp. 127–133.

5. Michael Goodwin and Naomi Wise, "An Interview with Howard Hawks," *Take One*, Vol. 3, No. 8, p. 19.

6. Bergman, p. 54.

7. Robin Wood, "Venus de Marlene," *Film Comment*, March–April 1978, p. 63.

8. Chain gangs became a somewhat popular cause after the appearance of Robert E. Burns' *I Am a Fugitive from a Georgia Chain Gang* as a serial in *True Detective Mysteries* from January to June 1931 and the publication of John L. Spivak's passionate exposé, *On the Chain Gang*, in 1932. See William Stott, *Documentary Expression and Thirties America* (New York: Oxford University Press, 1973), pp. 33–35, 41–45.

2. The Shysters

1. Andrew Bergman, *We're in the Money* (New York: Harper Colophon Books, 1972), p. 19.

2. Arthur M. Schlesinger, Jr., *The Crisis of the Old Order* (Boston: Houghton Mifflin, 1956), p. 245.

3. Caroline Bird, *The Invisible Scar* (New York: David McKay Co., 1969), p. 112.

4. Robert Bendiner, *Just Around the Corner* (New York: Harper & Row, 1967), p. 3.

5. Lewis Milestone on directing *The Front Page*: "I made them talk even faster than they had in the play; I don't think anybody has made a picture as fast-talking as that" (quoted in Charles Higham and Joel Greenberg, *The Celluloid Muse* [New York: Signet Books, 1972], p. 177). Howard Hawks on directing the remake, *His Girl Friday* (1940): "the characters spoke so fast that the characters kept stepping on each other's lines" (quoted in Andrew Sarris, ed., *Interviews with Film Directors* [New York: Avon Books, 1970], p. 238).

6. Hecht and MacArthur, *The Front Page* (New York: Covici-Friede, 1928), p. 40.

7. Ibid., p. 129.

8. Richard Griffith, *The Film Till Now* (London: Spring Books, 1967), p. 442.

3. The Populists—Or, Who's Afraid of the Big Bad Wolf?

1. Robert S. Lynd and Helen Merrell Lynd, *Middletown in Transition* (New York: Harcourt, Brace & Co., 1937), p. 493.

2. Frederick Lewis Allen, *Since Yesterday* (New York: Harper & Row, 1972), p. 55.

3. Caroline Bird, *The Invisible Scar* (New York: David McKay Co., 1969), pp. 76–78.

4. Frank Capra, *The Name Above the Title* (New York: Bantam Books, 1972), p. 154.

5. Richard Schickel, *The Disney Version* (New York: Avon Books, 1969), p. 129.

6. *New York Times*, April 20, 1934, 17:1.

7. William E. Leuchtenberg, *Franklin D. Roosevelt and the New Deal, 1932–1940* (New York: Harper & Row, 1963), p. 2.

8. Edward Robb Ellis, *A Nation in Torment* (New York: Coward McCann, 1970), p. 127.

9. Lewis Jacobs, *The Rise of the American Film* (New York: Teachers College Press, 1967), p. 521.

10. Quoted in Richard Schickel, *The Men Who Made the Movies* (New York: Atheneum, 1975), p. 143.

11. Raymond Durgnat, "King Vidor," *Film Comment* (July–August, 1973), p. 31.

12. According to C. B. Baldwin, one of the chief administrators of a New Deal program experimenting in rural communities, such communities met with limited success:

> . . . you take people out of a highly competitive situation and try to set up a Utopian society, you're gonna have some difficulty . . . Although they were happy and more secure than they'd ever been in their lives, they were lookin' forward to gettin' out and ownin' their own land (quoted in Studs Terkel, *Hard Times* [New York: Pantheon Books, 1970], p. 230).

13. See Irving Bernstein, *The Lean Years* (Boston: Houghton Mifflin Co., 1960), pp. 323, 421.

14. Quoted in Richard Hofstadter, *The American Political Tradition* (New York: Alfred A. Knopf, 1968), p. 325.

15. Theodore Saluotos, "Introduction," in Theodore Saluotos, ed., *Populism: Reaction or Reform?* (Holt, Rinehart & Winston, 1968), pp. 2–3.

4. Desperation—Hollywood Turns to the Right

1. Quoted in Arthur M. Schlesinger, Jr., *The Crisis of the Old Order* (Boston: Houghton Mifflin, 1956), p. 268.

2. William E. Leuchtenberg, *Franklin D. Roosevelt and the New Deal, 1932–1940* (New York: Harper & Row, 1963), p. 26.

3. Studs Terkel, *Hard Times* (New York: Pantheon Books, 1970), p. 34.

4. Bernard Rosenberg and Harry Silverstein, *The Real Tinsel* (London: Macmillan & Co., 1970), p. 90.

5. Bosley Crowther, *Hollywood Rajah* (New York: Dell Publishing, 1960), pp. 205, 206.

6. Rosenberg and Silverstein, p. 87.

7. Samuel I. Rosenman, ed., *The Public Papers and Addresses of Franklin D. Roosevelt* (New York: Random House, 1938), Volume II, pp. 14–15.

8. William E. Leuchtenberg, "The New Deal and the Analogue to War," in *Change and Continuity in Twentieth-Century America*, ed. John Braeman, Robert H. Bremner, Everett Walters (Columbus: Ohio State University Press, 1964), p. 114.

9. Both quoted in Edward Robb Ellis, *A Nation in Torment* (New York: Coward McCann, 1970), p. 341.

10. William Troy, "Prayers for a President," *The New Republic*, Dec. 26, 1934, p. 750.

11. Andrew Bergman, *We're in the Money* (New York: Harper Colophon Books, 1972), p. 119.

12. Upton Sinclair, "The Movies and Political Propaganda," in *Movies on Trial*, ed. William J. Perlman (New York: Macmillan Co., 1936), pp. 189–195; also cited in Leo Rosten, *Hollywood: The Movie Colony, the Movie Makers* (New York: Harcourt Brace & Co., 1941), pp. 135–138.

5. From Despair to Recovery: Warner Brothers and FDR

1. Quoted in William Manchester, "Rock Bottom in America," *New York*, August 5, 1974, p. 24.

2. Quoted in Irving Bernstein, *The Lean Years* (Boston: Houghton Mifflin Co., 1960), p. 440.

3. Russell Campbell, "Warners Revisited," *Velvet Light Trap*, No. 2, p. 26.

4. "Woman's Angle," *Variety*, November 22, 1932 (cited in Campbell, p. 25).

5. Charles Higham, "When Muni Wore Chains and Bogart Wore a Black Hood," *New York Sunday Times*, July 1, 1973, p. 9.

6. Jack Warner, *My First Hundred Years in Hollywood* (New York: Random House, 1965), p. 208.

7. Ibid., p. 216.

8. Russell Campbell, "Warners, the Depression, and FDR," *Velvet Light Trap*, No. 4, p. 34.

9. Ibid., p. 35.

10. Mark Roth, "Some Warners Musicals and the Spirit of the New Deal," *Velvet Light Trap*, No. 1, p. 20.

11. Arthur M. Schlesinger, Jr., *The Politics of Upheaval* (Boston: Houghton Mifflin, 1960), p. 2.

12. Irving Lerner, "The March of the Movies," *New Theatre*, January 1934, p. 13.

13. *Variety*, April 24, 1934.

6. Unemployment—Doing Your Part

1. According to the National Industrial Conference Board. Cited by Frederick Lewis Allen, *Since Yesterday* (New York: Harper & Row, 1972), p. 266.

2. Geoffrey Perrett, *Days of Sadness, Years of Triumph* (Baltimore: Penguin Books, 1974), pp. 69, 11.

3. The title of an article by A. Wayne McMillen, published in *Survey*, September 1932, p. 389.

4. William Troy, "Forgotten Children," *The Nation*, October 18, 1933, p. 458.

5. *Time*, March 4, 1935, p. 16.

6. Raymond Durgnat, *The Crazy Mirror* (London: Faber & Faber, 1969), pp. 124–125.

7. Hollywood and the Worker

1. See John Cogley, *Report on Blacklisting: Volume I—The Movies* (Fund for the Republic, Inc., 1956), pp. 57–59; and Dalton Trumbo, *Additional Dialogue* (New York: Bantam Books, 1972), pp. 1–2.

2. Edward Robb Ellis, *A Nation in Torment* (New York: Coward McCann, 1970), p. 382.

3. Jack Warner, *My First Hundred Years in Hollywood* (New York: Random House, 1965), pp. 12–13.

4. Richard Schickel, The Disney Version (New York: Avon Books, 1969), pp. 214–215.

5. From a report in the New York *Daily News*, 1925: "We saw thousands of women and children literally starving to death. We found hundreds of destitute families living in crudely constructed bare-board shacks. They had been evicted from their homes by the coal companies. We unearthed a system of despotic tyranny reminiscent of Czar-ridden Siberia at its worst. We found police brutality and industrial slavery" (quoted in Irving Bernstein, *The Lean Years* [Boston: Houghton Mifflin Co., 1960], pp. 130–131.

6. The description in the screenplay quoted by Joel Faith and Louis Norden, "Hollywood's *Riffraff*," *New Theatre*, 1935, p. 6.

7. This could be seen as an attack on the CIO's attempt to break away from the conservative AFL and formulate a more active unionism. The conflict between the two factions was reaching its peak in 1935, the year of the films' release.

8. Albert Maltz, "Coal Diggers of 1935," *New Theatre*, April 1935.

9. Quoted in screenplay, Faith and Norden, p. 6.

10. Ibid., p. 7.

11. Otis Ferguson, *The Film Criticism of Otis Ferguson*, Robert Wilson, ed. (Philadelphia: Temple University Press, 1971), p. 358.

12. *New York Times*, July 5, 1941, 14:2.

13. Theodore Huff, *Charlie Chaplin* (New York: Henry Schuman, 1951), p. 256.

14. Raymond Durgnat, *The Crazy Mirror* (London: Faber & Faber, 1969), pp. 81–82.

15. Gerald Mast, *The Comic Mind* (Indianapolis: Bobbs-Merrill Co., 1973), p. 114.

8. Rural Problems

1. Richard Pells, *Radical Visions and American Dreams* (New York: Harper Torchbooks, 1974), p. 72.

2. The screenwriter, Paul Green, had dealt with Southern tenant farming in his successful play, *The House of Connally*, produced a year earlier by the Group Theatre. In it, the croppers emerged as symbols of a new social order which supplants the decadence of the old South. In *Cabin*, one can discern the same sympathy for the tenants compromised by Hollywood's enforced neutrality.

3. Michael Mok in *The Nation* noted ironically that the first three rows at the film's New York premiere were reserved for the Officers of the Chase National Bank: "By an odd coincidence it is also one of the Eastern institutions, along with the Irving and Manufacturer's Trust company and the National City and Central Hanover banks, which control the Western land companies that tractored the Joads, and thousands like them, off their farms . . . and [was] about to wax still richer from the profits of a dramatization of the agonies of those unfortunately shiftless and stupid people" (*The Nation*, February 3, 1940, p. 127).

4. See George Bluestone, *Novels into Films* (Baltimore: Johns Hopkins University Press, 1957), p. 160.

5. Rebecca Pulliam, "The Grapes of Wrath," *Velvet Light Trap*, No. 2, p. 7.

6. See Bluestone for a thorough discussion of these changes.

7. Ibid., p. 161.

8. Erskine Caldwell, *Tobacco Road* (New York: Signet Books, 1970), p. 60.

9. Ibid., p. 102.

9. The Juvenile Delinquent and Society

1. *New York Times*, July 3, 1939, 10:5.

2. By 1944, another Irish priest, Father O'Malley (Bing Crosby), had no problems getting the local toughies to play baseball and sing in the church choir. In *Going My Way*, class tensions are dissipated the moment the good Father croons "Swingin' on a Star."

3. *New York Times*, November 21, 1938, 14:4.

4. See Mike Wilmington, "Nicholas Ray: The Years at RKO," *Velvet Light Trap*, No. 10, pp. 50–51.

5. *New York Times*, April 8, 1949, 31:3.

10. The Ex-Con and Society

1. Edward Anderson, *Thieves Like Us* (New York: Avon Books, 1974), p. 167.

2. Quoted in Joe Morella and Edward Z. Epstein, *Rebels* (New York: Citadel Press, 1971), p. 12.

3. Quoted in *Rebels*, p. 17.

4. Lang's description quoted in Peter Bogdanovich, *Fritz Lang in America* (New York: Praeger Film Library, 1967), p. 39.

5. Quoted in Charles Higham and Joel Greenberg, *The Celluloid Muse* (New York: Signet Books, 1972), p. 121.

11. Different Problems, Same Solutions

1. Karyn Kay, "Happy Days Are Here Again . . . *Massacre*," *Velvet Light Trap*, No. 4, p. 42.

2. Robert Gessner, "*Massacre* in Hollywood," *New Theatre*, March 1934, pp. 16–17.

3. This sequence was repeated almost word for word, shot for shot, in Warners' *They Drive by Night* (1940), with Ida Lupino trying to pin the blame on trucker George Raft.

12. Native Fascists—Lynching and Legions

1. MGM bought the film rights to the novel in late 1935 but the project was quickly dropped. Initial news releases announced that Will Hays of the

Production Code Administration had banned the film for fear of international complications and the displeasure of the Republican Party. Mark Schorer, in his biography of Lewis (*Sinclair Lewis* [New York: McGraw-Hill, 1961], pages 615–616), neither confirms nor denies that MGM acted on the advice or orders of the Hays office. Lewis did however make lengthy statements to the press expressing shock at such a blow to free expression.

2. Arthur M. Schlesinger, Jr., *The Politics of Upheaval* (Boston: Houghton Mifflin, 1960), p. 436.

3. Robert L. Zangrando, "The NAACP and a Federal Anti-Lynching Bill, 1934–1940," *The Negro in Depression and War*, Bernard Sternsher, ed. (Chicago: Quadrangle Books, 1969), p. 183.

4. Ibid., p. 185.

5. U.S. Bureau of Statistics, *Historical Statistics of the U.S., Colonial Times to 1957* (Washington, D.C.: 1960), p. 218; cited in Zangrando, p. 192.

6. Zangrando, p. 187.

7. A point made by Paul Jensen, *The Cinema of Fritz Lang* (New York: A. S. Barnes & Co., 1969), pp. 118–119.

8. *The Nation*, June 24, 1936, p. 821.

9. Fritz Lang interview in Peter Bogdanovich, *Fritz Lang in America* (New York: Praeger Film Library, 1967), p. 28.

10. According to Walter White's testimony before the Senate Judiciary Subcommittee in 1934, of the 5,053 lynchings between 1882 and 1934, 3,543 victims were black (cited in Zangrando, p. 183).

11. Fritz Lang interview in Charles Higham and Joel Greenberg, *The Celluloid Muse* (New York: Signet Books, 1972), p. 119.

12. Lang in Bogdanovich, p. 32. *Cabin in the Cotton*, made four years before *Fury*, contains a brief sequence which partially fulfills Lang's requirements. It shows Southern landowners hunting down and lynching a cropper who has murdered one of the planters. In effect, the hanged man is both guilty and the victim of social discrimination. Although Marvin, the film's hero, registers shock at the lynching, both he and the audience quickly forget the issue in the ensuing excitement about the store fire. The lynching appears as just one of the many evils and serves to balance the wrongs committed by both sides and to provide Marvin with another lever to force Norwood to join the co-op. By resolving the cropper–planter strife, the filmmakers automatically put an end to the lynching problem.

13. David M. Chalmers, *Hooded Americanism* (New York: Doubleday & Co., 1965), pp. 308–309.

14. Raymond Gram Swing, *Forerunners of American Fascism* (New York: J. Messner Inc., 1935).

15. Chalmers, p. 310.

16. Ibid., pp. 309–310.

13. Frank Capra's Super-Shysters and Little People

1. This and subsequent quotes from Frank Capra, *The Name Above the Title* (New York: Bantam Books, 1972).

2. *You Can't Take it with You*, although thematically linked to Capra's other social films, is structurally separate from the trilogy.

3. Leland A. Poague, *The Cinema of Frank Capra: An Approach to Film Comedy* (New York: A. S. Barnes & Co., 1975), p. 196.

4. Donald C. Willis, *The Films of Frank Capra* (Metuchen, N.J.: Scarecrow Press, 1974), p. 108.

5. Quoted in *American Film Criticism*, ed. Stanley K. Kauffmann, with Bruce Henstell (New York: Liveright, 1972), p. 380.

6. Gerald Mast, *The Comic Mind* (Indianapolis: Bobbs-Merrill Co., 1973), p. 262.

7. Capra, p. 339.

14. More Plutocrats and Would-Be Dictators

1. T. Harry Williams, *Huey Long* (New York: Bantam Books, 1970), pp. 5–7.

2. William Manchester, *The Glory and the Dream* (New York: Bantam Books, 1975), p. 231.

3. Quoted in Tony Thomas, *The Films of Gene Kelly* (New York: Citadel Press, 1974), p. 36.

4. Arthur M. Schlesinger, Jr., *The Politics of Upheaval* (Boston: Houghton Mifflin, 1960), p. 84.

5. Ibid., p. 88.

15. International Fascism—From Pacifism to War

1. Frederick Lewis Allen, *Only Yesterday* (New York: Harper & Row, 1957), p. 32.

2. William E. Leuchtenberg and the Editors of *Life*, *The New Deal and Global War* (New York: Time–Life Books, 1964), p. 91.

3. Frederick Lewis Allen, *Since Yesterday* (New York: Harper & Row, 1972), p. 257.

4. Richard R. Lingeman, *Don't You Know There's a War On?* (New York: G. P. Putnam's Sons, 1970), p. 191.

5. *Time*, September 14, 1936, pp. 28, 30.

6. *New York Times*, June 19, 1937, 20:2.

7. Folke Isaksson and Leif Furhammer, *Politics and Film* (New York: Praeger Publishers, 1971), p. 49.

8. Harold Clurman, *The Fervent Years* (New York: Hill & Wang, 1957), p. 187.

9. Otis Ferguson in *The New Republic*: "There is achieved a deadly dumb level of shameless hokum out of which anything true or decent rises for a second only to confound itself. When it comes to what *Blockade* has to say for Spain to the common bewildered man, identification has been so smoothly rubbed out that to protest its content, as some of our hair-trigger Catholic friends are already naively doing, is to give away the fact of a deep and abounding ignorance, or of a stinking guilty conscience, and very probably both" (*The New Republic*, June 29, 1938, pp. 222–223).

10. *The Nation*, July 9, 1938, pp. 38–40.

11. John Howard Lawson, *Film: The Creative Process* (New York: Hill & Wang, 1964), p. 127.

12. James Agee, *Agee on Film* (New York: McDowell, Obolensky, 1958), p. 47.

13. Ibid., p. 46.

14. Ibid., p. 49.

15. *New York Times*, November 18, 1935, 19:6.

16. John Belton, "Souls Made Great by Love and Adversity: Frank Borzage," *Focus*, No. 9, Spring–Summer 1973, pp. 17–18.

17. Aaron Latham, *Crazy Sundays* (New York: Viking Press, 1971), p. 133.

18. *The Letters of F. Scott Fitzgerald*, ed. Andrew Turnbull (New York: Charles Scribner's Sons, 1966), pp. 565–566; see also Latham, p. 142, and F. Scott Fitzgerald, *Three Comrades* (New York: Popular Library, 1978), p. 232.

19. *Time*, June 6, 1938, pp. 41–42.

20. Jack Warner, *My First Hundred Years in Hollywood* (New York: Random House, 1965), p. 249.

21. Charles Higham, *Warner Brothers* (New York: Charles Scribner's Sons, 1975), pp. 139–140.

22. Ibid., p. 141; for further details see also Jack Warner, p. 262.

23. David Chierichetti, *Hollywood Director: The Career of Mitchell Liesen* (New York: Curtis Books, 1974), p. 147.

24. Charles Higham and Joel Greenberg, *The Celluloid Muse* (New York: Signet Books, 1972), p. 123.

25. Quoted in Lingeman, *Don't You Know There's a War On?*, p. 172.

26. Charles Chaplin, *My Autobiography* (Harmondsworth, Middlesex, England: Penguin Books, 1973), pp. 387–388, 392.

27. Ibid., pp. 387–388.

28. *Time*, August 7, 1939, p. 24.

29. Quoted in Lewis Jacobs, "World War II and the American Film," in *The Movies: An American Idiom*, Arthur F. McClure, ed. (Fairleigh Dickinson University Press, 1971), p. 164.

30. Dorothy Jones in Lingeman, p. 205.

31. Joe Morella, Edward Z. Epstein, and John Griggs, *The Films of World War II* (Secaucus, N.J.: Citadel Press, 1973), p. 59.

32. Francois Truffaut, *Hitchcock by Truffaut* (London: Panther Books, 1969), p. 184.

33. Mel Gussow, *Don't Say Yes Until I Finish Talking* (New York: Pocket Books, 1972), pp. 109–110.

16. Readjustment—"Nervous from the Service"

1. Barbara Deming, *Running Away from Myself* (New York: Grossman Publishers, 1969), p. 53.

2. Ibid.

17. The Minorities

1. Alvah Bessie, *Inquisition in Eden* (Berlin: Seven Seas Publishers, 1967), p. 96.

2. Herbert F. Margolis, "The Hollywood Scene: The American Minority Problem," *Penguin Film Review*, No. 5, p. 83.

3. James Agee, *Agee on Film* (New York: McDowell, Obolensky, 1958), p. 270.

4. Quoted by Penelope Houston in "Mr. Deeds and Willie Stark," *Sight and Sound*, November 1950, p. 285.

5. Joe Morella and Edward Z. Epstein, *Rebels: The Rebel Hero in Films* (New York: Citadel Press, 1971), p. 32.

6. Lawrence D. Reddick, "Educational Programs for the Improvement of Race Relations: Motion Pictures, Radio, the Press and Libraries," *Journal of Negro Education*, 13, Summer 1944, p. 369; Peter Noble, *The Negro in Films* (London: Skelton-Robinson, 1948); Sterling A. Brown, "Negro Characters as Seen by White Authors," cited in Thomas H. Cripps, "The Death of Rastus: Negroes in American Films Since 1945," in Arthur F. McClure, ed., *The Movies: An American Idiom* (Fairleigh Dickinson University Press, 1971); Edward Mapp, *Blacks in American Films: Today and Yesterday* (Metuchen, N.J.: Scarecrow Press, 1972); Donald Bogle, *Toms, Coons, Mulattoes, Mammies, and Bucks: An Interpretive History of Blacks in American Films* (New York: Viking Press, 1973).

7. Bogle, pp. 17–18.

8. King Vidor, *A Tree Is a Tree* (New York: Harcourt, Brace & Co., 1953), p. 175.

9. Manny Farber, *Negative Space* (New York: Praeger Publishers, 1971), pp. 68–69.

10. Bogle, p. 152.

11. Mel Gussow, *Don't Say Yes Until I Finish Talking* (New York: Pocket Books, 1972), p. 139.

12. With the studios' vehement opposition, for it was a threat both to their monopoly of American production and to the blacklist. See Herbert Biberman's account in *Salt of the Earth: The Story of a Film* (Boston: Beacon Press, 1965).

13. Ibid., p. 69.

14. Tom Milne, *Losey on Losey* (London: Secker & Warburg, 1967), p. 7.

18. More Neuroses—Alcoholism and Insanity

1. For a thorough discussion on the film's politics and its alterations to Sinclair's novel see Joe Mansfield, "Upton Sinclair's *The Wet Parade*," *Velvet Light Trap*, No. 18, Spring 1978, pp. 24–26.

2. Quoted in Charles Higham and Joel Greenberg, *The Celluloid Muse* (New York: Signet Books, 1972), p. 282.

3. Axel Madsen, *Billy Wilder* (London: Secker & Warburg, 1968), p. 68.

4. Shirley O'Hara, *The New Republic*, Feb. 24, 1947, p. 39.

5. Mel Gussow, *Don't Say Yes Until I Finish Talking* (New York: Pocket Books, 1972), p. 142.

6. Francis Farmer, *Will There Really Be a Morning?* (New York: G. P. Putnam's Sons, 1972), p. 9.

19. Postwar Labor Problems

1. Richard R. Lingeman, *Don't You Know There's a War On?* (New York: G. P. Putnam's Sons, 1970), p. 187.
2. Lindsay Anderson, "The Last Sequence of *On the Waterfront*," *Sight and Sound*, Jan.–March, 1955, pp. 127–130; Robert Hughes, "*On the Waterfront*: A Defense and Some Letters," *Sight and Sound*, Spring 1955, pp. 214–215.
3. Quoted in Michel Ciment, *Kazan on Kazan* (London: Secker & Warburg, 1973), p. 108.

20. The Individual and Society: Darker Views of the Postwar World

1. Barbara Deming, *Running Away from Myself* (New York: Grossman Publishers, 1969), p. 6.
2. Donald C. Willis, *The Films of Frank Capra* (Metuchen, N.J.: Scarecrow Press, 1974), p. 78.
3. Polonsky to Eric Sherman and Martin Rubin, *The Director's Event* (New York: New American Library, 1972), p. 25.
4. Ibid., p. 23.
5. Robert Warshow, *The Immediate Experience* (New York: Atheneum, 1972), p. 211.
6. "Charlie Chaplin's *Monsieur Verdoux* Press Conference," *Film Comment*, Winter 1969, pp. 34–43.
7. John Belton, "*A King in New York*," *Velvet Light Trap*, No. 11, Winter 1974, p. 52.

21. HUAC and the End of an Era

1. *Daily Variety*, quoted in John Cutts and Penelope Houston, "Blacklisted," *Sight and Sound*, Summer 1957, p. 16.
2. Quoted in Cutts and Houston, p. 17.
3. Quoted in John Cogley, *Blacklisting: Volume I: The Movies* (Fund for the Republic, Inc., 1956), p. 5.
4. Quoted in Cogley, p. 22.
5. Quoted in Robert Vaughn, *Only Victims* (New York: G. P. Putnam's Sons, 1972), p. 138.
6. Murray Kempton, *Part of Our Time* (New York: Dell Publishing Co., 1967), p. 208. Also see Cogley, p. 100.
7. Dorothy Jones, "Communism and the Movies: A Study of Film Content," in Cogley, pp. 196–233.
8. Robert Vaughn, *Only Victims*, p. 176.
9. Alvah Bessie, *Inquisition in Eden* (Berlin: Seven Seas Publishers, 1967), p. 226.
10. Charles Higham, *Warner Brothers* (New York: Charles Scribner's Sons, 1975), p. 163.
11. *Variety*, August 18, 1947, p. 11. Cited by Harry Wasserman, "Ideo-

logical Gunfight at the RKO Corral: Notes on Howard Hughes' *I Married a Communist*," *Velvet Light Trap*, No. 11, Winter 1974, p. 9.

12. Jones, in Cogley, p. 215.

13. Pauline Kael, "Morality Plays Left and Right," *I Lost It at the Movies* (New York: Bantam Books, 1966), p. 288.

14. Karel Reisz, "Hollywood's Anti-Red Boomerang," *Sight and Sound*, January 1953, p. 134.

15. Ibid.

16. See Roger Tailleur, "Elia Kazan and the House Un-American Activities Committee," *Film Comment*, Fall 1966, pp. 43–58 for a thorough discussion of this point.

17. Jones, in Cogley, p. 232.

18. Ibid.

19. Quoted in Murray Schumach, *The Face on the Cutting Room Floor* (New York: William Morrow & Co., 1964), p. 139.

Conclusion: Sullivan's Travels—Hollywood Goes Slumming

1. Michael Wood, *America in the Movies* (New York: Basic Books, 1975), p. 129.

Selected Bibliography

Books and Articles

In addition to the specific articles listed below, we made thorough use of film reviews and discussions in the following journals:

Action
Cahiers du Cinema (English)
Cineaste
Cinema (American)
Cinema (English)
Close Up
Common Weal
Experimental Cinema
Film
Films (quarterly published 1939–40)
Film Comment
Film Culture
Films and Filming
Film Heritage
Film Journal
Film/Literature Quarterly
Film Quarterly
Films in Review
Film Society Review
Focus on Film

Harpers Magazine
Life
Movie
The Nation
New Masses
The New Republic
New Theatre
New York Film Bulletin
New York Times
Penguin Film Review
Saturday Review (English)
Saturday Review of Literature
Screen
Sequence
Sight and Sound
Take One
Theatre Arts
Time
Variety
Velvet Light Trap

Aaron, Daniel. *Writers on the Left*. New York: Harcourt, Brace & World, Inc., 1961.

Aaron, Daniel and Bendiner, Robert, eds. *The Strenuous Decade: A Social and Intellectual Record of the 1930s*. Garden City, N.Y.: Doubleday & Co., Anchor Books, 1970.

Agee, James. *Agee on Film*. New York: McDowell, Obolensky, 1958.

Allen, Frederick Lewis. *Only Yesterday*. New York: Harper and Row, Publishers, 1957.

———. *Since Yesterday*. Perennial Library. New York: Harper & Row, 1972.

Alloway, Lawrence. *Violent America: The Movies 1946–1964*. New York: Museum of Modern Art, 1971.

Alpert, Hollis. *The Dreams and the Dreamers*. New York: Macmillan Co., 1962.

Anderson, Edward. *Thieves Like Us*. New York: Avon Books, 1974.

Anderson, Lindsay. "The Last Sequence of *On the Waterfront*," *Sight and Sound*, January–March, 1955, pp. 127–130.

———. "John Ford: A Monograph." *Cinema*, Spring 1971, pp. 20–36.

Anstey, Edgar et al., eds. *Shots in the Dark*. London: Allen Wingate, 1951.

Bardeche, Maurice and Brasillach, Robert. *The History of Motion Pictures*. New York: Arno Press and the *New York Times*, 1938.

Baxter, John. *Hollywood in the Thirties*. New York: Paperback Library, 1970.

———. *The Cinema of John Ford*. New York: A. S. Barnes and Co., 1971.

Bazin, Andre. *What Is Cinema?* 2 vols. Translated and edited by Hugh Gray. Berkeley and Los Angeles: University of California Press, 1967.

Behlmer, Rudy. *Memo from David O. Selznick*. New York: Avon Books, 1973.

Belton, John. "*A King in New York*." *Velvet Light Trap*, No. 11, pp. 50–53.

———. "Souls Made Great by Love and Adversity: Frank Borzage." *Focus*, No. 9, Spring–Summer, 1973, pp. 16–22.

Bendiner, Robert. *Just Around the Corner: A Highly Selective History of the Thirties*. New York: Harper & Row, Publishers, 1967.

Bentley, Eric, ed. *Thirty Years of Treason*. New York: Viking Press, 1971.

Bergman, Andrew. *We're in the Money: Depression America and Its Films*. New York: Harper Colophon Books, 1972.

Bernstein, Irving. *The Lean Years*. Boston: Houghton Mifflin Co., 1960.

———. *The Turbulent Years*. Boston: Houghton Mifflin Co., 1970.

Bessie, Alvah. *Inquisition in Eden*. Berlin: Seven Seas Publishers, 1967.

Biberman, Herbert. *Salt of the Earth: The Story of a Film*. Boston: Beacon Press, 1965.

Bird, Caroline. *The Invisible Scar: The Great Depression and What It Did to American Life, From Then Until Now*. New York: David McKay Co., 1969.

Bluestone, George. *Novels into Films*. Baltimore: Johns Hopkins University Press, 1957.

Bogdanovich, Peter. *Fritz Lang in America*. New York: Praeger Film Library, 1967.

———. "The Dore Schary–Stanley Kramer Syndrome." *New York Film Bulletin*, Series One: Numbers 12, 13, 14, pp. 12–14.

Bogle, Donald. *Toms, Coons, Mulattoes, Mammies, and Bucks: An Interpretive History of Blacks in American Films*. New York: Viking Press, 1973.

Braeman, John, Bremner, Robert H., and Walters, Everett, eds. *Change and Continuity in Twentieth-Century America*. Columbus: Ohio State University Press, 1964.

Braudy, Leo. *Jean Renoir*. Garden City, N.Y.: Doubleday & Co., 1972.

Brenton, Guy. "Two Adaptations: *All the King's Men* and *Force of Evil*." *Sequence*, No. 12, Autumn 1950, pp. 33–36.

Brown, Geoff. *"The Struggle." Sight and Sound*, Winter 1974–75, p. 59.

Brown, J. A. C. *Techniques of Persuasion: From Propaganda to Brainwashing*. Harmondsworth, Middlesex: Penguin Books, 1971.

Budd, Michael. "Notes on Preston Sturges and America." *Film Society Review*, January 1968, pp. 22–26.

Byron, Stuart and Rubin, Martin L. "Elia Kazan Interview." *Movie: Elia Kazan*, Winter 1971/72, pp. 1–13.

Caldwell, Erskine. *Tobacco Road*. New York: Signet Books, 1970.

Campbell, Marilyn. "RKO's Fallen Women, 1930–1933." *Velvet Light Trap*, No. 10, pp. 13–16.

Campbell, Russell. "Warner Brothers in the Thirties: Some Tentative Notes." *Velvet Light Trap*. No. 1, pp. 2–4.

———. *"I Am a Fugitive from a Chain Gang." Velvet Light Trap*, No. 1, pp. 17–20.

———. "Warners Revisited." *Velvet Light Trap*, No. 2, p. 26.

———. "Warners, the Depression, and FDR." *Velvet Light Trap*, No. 4, pp. 34–38.

Canham, Kingsley. "Polonsky: Back into the Light." *Film*, No. 58, Spring 1970, pp. 12–15.

Capra, Frank. *The Name Above the Title*. New York: Bantam Books, 1972.

Chalmers, David M. *Hooded Americanism: The First Century of the Ku Klux Klan 1865–1965*. Garden City, N.Y.: Doubleday & Co., 1965.

Chaplin, Charles. *My Autobiography*. Harmondsworth, Middlesex: Penguin Books, 1973.

Ciment, Michael. *Kazan on Kazan*. London: Secker & Warburg, 1973.

Clurman, Harold. *The Fervent Years*. New York: Hill & Wang, 1957.

Cogley, John. *Report on Blacklisting: 1. The Movies*. Fund for the Republic, Inc., 1956.

Cook, Fred J. *The Nightmare Decade: The Life and Times of Senator Joe McCarthy*. New York: Random House, 1971.

Cook, Jim and Canham, Kingsley. "An Interview with Abraham Polonsky." *Screen*, Summer 1970, pp. 57–73.

Cooke, Alistair. *A Generation on Trial: The U.S.A. vs. Alger Hiss*. New York: Alfred A. Knopf, 1950.

———, ed. *Garbo and the Night Watchmen*. London: Secker & Warburg, 1971.

Corliss, Richard, ed. "The Hollywood Screenwriter." *Film Comment*, Winter 1970–71.

———. *Talking Pictures: Screenwriters in the American Cinema 1927–1973*. Woodstock, N.Y.: Overlook Press, 1974.

Cotes, Peter and Niklaus, Thelma. *The Little Fellow: The Life and Work of Charles Spencer Chaplin*. New York: Citadel Press, 1965.

Crowther, Bosley. *The Lion's Share*. New York: E. P. Dutton, 1957.

———. *Hollywood Rajah*. New York: Dell Publishing Co., 1960.

Dale, Edgar. *How to Appreciate Motion Pictures*. New York: Macmillan Co., 1935.

Dalton, Elizabeth. "Women at Work: Warners in the Thirties." *Velvet Light Trap*, No. 6, pp. 15–20.

Davis, John. "Notes on Warner Brothers Foreign Policy." *Velvet Light Trap*, No. 4, pp. 23–33.

Degenfelder, E. Pauline. "The Film Adaptation of Faulkner's *Intruder in the Dust*." *Film/Literature Quarterly*, Vol. 1, No. 2, April 1973, pp. 138–148.

Deming, Barbara. *Running Away from Myself: A Dream Portrait of America Drawn from the Films of the 40's*. New York: Grossman Publishers, 1969.

Dorr, John. "Griffith's Talkies." *Take One*, Vol. 3, No. 8, pp. 8–12.

Dowdy, Andrew. *Movies Are Better Than Ever: Wide-Screen Memories of the Fifties*. New York: William Morrow & Co., 1973.

Drinkwater, John. *The Life and Adventures of Carl Laemmle*. New York: G. P. Putnam's Sons, 1931.

Dunne, John Gregory. *The Studio*. New York: Farrar, Straus & Giroux, 1968.

Durgnat, Raymond. *The Crazy Mirror: Hollywood Comedy and the American Image*. London: Faber & Faber, 1969.

———. "King Vidor." *Film Comment*, Part One: July–August, 1973, pp. 10–49; Part Two: September–October 1973, pp. 16–51.

Dyer, Peter John. "The Murderers Among Us." *Films and Filming*, December 1958, pp. 13–15, 32–33.

———. "American Youth in Uproar." *Films and Filming*, September 1959, pp. 10–12, 32–33.

Ellis, Edward Robb. *A Nation in Torment: The Great American Depression 1929–1939*. New York: Coward, McCann, 1970.

Esnault, Phillipe. "Cinema and Politics." *Cineaste*, Vol. III, No. 3, Winter 1969–70, pp. 4–11.

Faith, Joel and Norden, Louis. "Hollywood's *Riffraff*." *New Theatre*. 1935, pp. 6–7, 33.

Farber, Manny. *Negative Space*. New York: Praeger Publishers, 1971.

Farrell, James T. "The Language of Hollywood." *Saturday Review of Literature*, August 5, 1944, pp. 29–32.

Ferguson, Otis. *The Film Criticism of Otis Ferguson*. Robert Wilson, ed. Philadelphia: Temple University Press, 1971.

Fox, Julian. "A Crack in the Dream: An Aspect of Hollywood in the Hungry Thirties." *Films and Filming*, Part One: August 1972, pp. 34–40; Part Two: September 1972, pp. 30–36.

———. "A Man's World: William Wellman." *Films and Filming*, Part One: March 1973, pp. 32–40.

French, Philip. *The Movie Moguls*. Harmondsworth, Middlesex: Penguin Books, 1969.

French, Warren. *Filmguide to The Grapes of Wrath*. Bloomington: Indiana University Press, 1973.

Froug, William. *The Screenwriter Looks at the Screenwriter*. New York: Macmillan Co., 1972.

Gans, Herbert J. "The Rise of the Problem Film: An Analysis of Changes in Hollywood Films and the American Audience." *Social Problems*, No. 11, Spring 1964, pp. 327–336.

Gassner, John and Nichols, Dudley, eds. *Twenty Best Film Plays*. New York: Crown Publishers, 1943.

———. *Best Film Plays 1943–1945*. New York: Crown Publishers, 1945.

Geduld, Harry, ed. *Filmmakers on Filmmaking*. Bloomington: Indiana University Press, 1967.

Gelman, Howard. "John Garfield: Hollywood was the Dead End." *Velvet Light Trap*, No. 7, pp. 16–20.

Gessner, Robert. "*Massacre* in Hollywood." *New Theatre*, March 1934, pp. 16–17.

Gish, Lillian. *The Movies, Mr. Griffith and Me*. New York: Avon Books, 1970.

Goodman, Ezra. *The Fifty Year Decline and Fall of Hollywood*. New York: Simon & Schuster, 1961.

Goodwin, Michael and Wise, Naomi. "An Interview with Howard Hawks." *Take One*, Vol. 3, No. 8, pp. 19–25.

Gow, Gordon. *Hollywood in the Fifties*. New York: A. S. Barnes & Co., 1971.

Greene, Graham. *The Pleasure Dome*. London: Secker & Warburg, 1972.

Grierson, John. *Grierson on Documentary*. Forsyth Hardy, ed. New York: Harcourt, Brace & Co., 1947.

Griffith, Richard. *Samuel Goldwyn: The Producer and His Films*. New York: Museum of Modern Art Film Library, 1956.

————. *The Movie Stars*. Garden City, N.Y.: Doubleday & Co., 1970.

Griffith, Richard and Mayer, Arthur. *The Movies*. New York: Bonanza Books, 1957.

Guild, Leo. *Zanuck: Hollywood's Last Tycoon*. Los Angeles: Holloway House Publishing Co., 1970.

Gussow, Mel. *Don't Say Yes Until I Finish Talking: A Biography of Darryl F. Zanuck*. New York: Pocket Books, 1972.

Handel, Leo A. *Hollywood Looks at Its Audience*. Urbana: University of Illinois Press, 1950.

Handzo, Stephen. "Under Capracorn." *Film Comment*, November–December 1972, pp. 8–14.

Hanson, Curtis Lee. "William Wellman: A Memorable Visit with an Elder Statesman." *Cinema*, July 1966, pp. 20–32.

Hecht, Ben and MacArthur, Charles. *The Front Page*. New York: Covici-Friede, 1928.

Hickey, Terry. "Accusations Against Charles Chaplin for Political and Moral Offenses." *Sight and Sound*, Vol. 5, No. 4, Winter 1969, pp. 44–55.

Higham, Charles. *Hollywood at Sunset*. New York: Saturday Review Press, ·1972.

————. "When Muni Wore Chains and Bogart Wore a Black Hood." *New York Sunday Times*, July 1, 1973, Section 2, pp. 9, 17.

————. *Warner Brothers*. New York: Charles Scribner's Sons, 1975.

Higham, Charles and Greenberg, Joel. *The Celluloid Muse: Hollywood Directors Speak*. New York: Signet Books, 1972.

————. *Hollywood in the Forties*. New York: Paperback Library, 1970.

Hillier, Jim. "Out of the 40's." *Movie: Elia Kazan*, Winter 1971–72, pp. 14–16.

Himelstein, Morgan Y. *Drama Was a Weapon: The Left-Wing Theatre in New York 1929–1941*. New Brunswick, N.J.: Rutgers University Press, 1963.

Hofstadter, Richard. *The American Political Tradition*. New York: Alfred A. Knopf, 1968.

Houston, Penelope. "Mr. Deeds and Willie Stark." *Sight and Sound*, November 1950, pp. 276–279, 285.

————. "Kramer and Company." *Sight and Sound*, July–September 1952, pp. 20–23, 48.

————. "Rebels Without Causes." *Sight and Sound*, Spring 1956, pp. 178–181.

————. "Preston Sturges." *Sight and Sound*, Summer 1965, pp. 130–134.

Houston, Penelope and John Cutts. "Blacklisted." *Sight and Sound*, Summer, 1957, pp. 15–19, 53.

Huettig, Mae D. *Economic Control of the Motion Picture Industry*. Philadelphia: University of Pennsylvania Press, 1944.

Huff, Theodore. *Charlie Chaplin*. New York: Henry Schuman, 1951.

Hughes, Robert. "*On the Waterfront*: A Defense." *Sight and Sound*, Spring 1955, pp. 214–215.

————, ed. *Film: Book 2, Films of Peace and War*. New York: Grove Press, 1962.

Inglis, Ruth. *Freedom of the Movies*. Chicago: University of Chicago Press, 1947.

Isaksson, Folke and Furhammar, Leif. *Politics and Film*. New York: Praeger Publishers, 1971.

Jacobs, Lewis. *The Rise of the American Film*. New York: Teachers College Press, 1967.

Jarvie, I. C. *Movies and Society*. New York: Basic Books, 1970.

Jensen, Paul M. *The Cinema of Fritz Lang*. New York: A. S. Barnes and Co., 1969.

Jobes, Gertrude. *Motion Picture Empire*. Hamden, Conn.: Archon Books, 1966.

Kael, Pauline. *I Lost It at the Movies*. New York: Bantam Books, 1966.

————. *Kiss Kiss Bang Bang*. Boston: Little, Brown & Co., 1968.

Kahn, Gordon. *Hollywood on Trial*. New York: Boni and Gaer, 1948.

Kanfer, Stefan. *A Journal of the Plague Years*. New York: Atheneum, 1973.

Kantor, Bernard R., Blacker, Irwin R., and Kramer, Anne, eds. *Directors at Work: Interviews with American Film-Makers*. New York: Funk & Wagnalls, 1970.

Kauffmann, Stanley K., with Henstell, Bruce, ed. *American Film Criticism*. New York: Liveright, 1972.

Kaufman, George S. and Ryskind, Morrie. *Of Thee I Sing*. New York: Alfred A. Knopf, 1933.

Kay, Karyn. "Happy Days Are Here Again . . . *Massacre*." *Velvet Light Trap*, No. 4, pp. 39–43.

Kempton, Murray. *Part of Our Time*. New York: Dell Publishing Co., 1967.

Kitses, Jim. "A Structural Analysis of Elia Kazan." *Cinema*, Winter 1972–73, pp. 25–36.

Knight, Arthur. *The Liveliest Art*. New York: Macmillan Co., 1957.

Kraft, Hy. *On My Way to the Theatre*. New York: Macmillan Co., 1971.

Kramer, Stanley. "The Independent Producer: Requires Energy, Brains and —Luck." *Films in Review*, March 1951, pp. 1–4, 47.

————. "Politics, Social Comment and My Emotions." *Films and Filming*, June 1960, pp. 7–8, 33.

————. "Sending Myself the Message." *Films and Filming*, February 1964, pp. 7–8.

Kuhns, William. *Movies in America*. Dayton, Ohio: Pflaum/Standard, 1972.

Lambert, Gavin. "Fritz Lang's America." *Sight and Sound*, Summer 1955, pp. 14–16.

Lasky, Jesse, with Don Weldon. *I Blow My Own Horn*. Garden City, N.Y.: Doubleday & Co., 1957.

Latham, Aaron. *Crazy Sundays*. New York: Viking Press, 1971.

Lawson, John Howard. *The Theory and Technique of Playwrighting and Screenwriting*. New York: G. P. Putnam's Sons, 1949.

————. *Film in the Battle of Ideas*. New York: Masses & Mainstream, 1953.

————. *Film: The Creative Process*. New York: Hill & Wang, 1964.

————. "Comments on Blacklisting and *Blockade*." *Film Culture*, Fall 1970, pp. 16–20.

Leahy, James. *The Cinema of Joseph Losey*. New York: A. S. Barnes & Co., 1967.

Lerner, Irving. "The March of the Movies." *New Theatre*, January 1934, p. 13.

————. "The March of the Movies." *New Theatre*, February 1934, pp. 20–21.

Leroy, Mervyn, as told to Alyce Canfield. *It Takes More Than Talent*. New York: Alfred A. Knopf, 1953.

Leroy, Mervyn. *Take One*. New York: Hawthorn Books, 1974.

Leuchtenburg, William E. *Franklin D. Roosevelt and the New Deal, 1932–1940*. New York: Harper & Row, 1963.

————, ed. *Franklin D. Roosevelt*. New York: Hill & Wang, 1967.

Leuchtenburg, William E. and the Editors of *Life*. *The New Deal and Global War*. New York: Time-Life Books, 1964.

Linden, George W. *Reflections of the Screen*. Belmont, Calif.: Wadsworth Publishing Co., 1970.

Lingeman, Richard R. *Don't You Know There's a War On?: The American Home Front 1941–1945*. New York: G. P. Putnam's Sons, 1970.

Lipset, Seymour Martin. *Political Man: The Social Bases of Politics*. Garden City, N.Y.: Doubleday & Co., Anchor Books, 1963.

Lynd, Robert S. and Lynd, Helen Merrell. *Middletown in Transition*. New York: Harcourt, Brace & Co., 1937.

MacCann, Richard Dyer, ed. *Films and Society*. New York: Charles Scribner's Sons, 1964.

MacDonald, Dwight. *Dwight MacDonald on Movies*. Englewood Cliffs, N.J.: Prentice-Hall, 1969.

Maltz, Albert. "Coal Diggers of 1935." *New Theatre*, April 1935.

Manchester, William. *The Glory and the Dream*. New York: Bantam Books, 1975.

Manvell, Roger. *Film*. Harmondsworth, Middlesex: Penguin Books, 1946.

————. *Film and the Public*. Harmondsworth, Middlesex: Penguin Books, 1955.

Mapp, Edward. *Blacks in American Films: Today and Yesterday*. Metuchen, N.J.: Scarecrow Press, 1972.

Marcus, Robert D. and Burner, David. *America Since 1945*. New York: St. Martin's Press, 1972.

Margolis, Herbert F. "The Hollywood Scene: The American Minority Problem." *Penguin Film Review*, No. 5, pp. 82–85.

Marion, Frances. *Off with Their Heads*. New York: Macmillan Co., 1972.

Mast, Gerald. *A Short History of the Movies*. New York: Bobbs-Merrill Co., Pegasus, 1971.

————. *The Comic Mind: Comedy and the Movies*. Indianapolis/New York: Bobbs-Merrill Company, Inc., 1973.

McCaffrey, Donald W. *Four Great Comedians*. New York: A. S. Barnes and Co., 1968.

————, ed. *Focus on Chaplin*. Englewood Cliffs, N.J.: Prentice-Hall, Inc., 1971.

McClure, Arthur F., ed. *The Movies: An American Idiom*. Madison, N.J.: Fairleigh Dickinson University Press, 1971.

McGilligan, Patrick. "James Cagney: The Actor as Auteur." *Velvet Light Trap*, No. 7, pp. 3–15.

Miller, Don. "Rowland Brown: He Socked a Supervisor." *Focus on Film*, No. 7, Summer 1971, pp. 43–52.

————. *"B" Movies*. New York: Curtis Books, 1973.

Milne, Tom. *Losey on Losey*. London: Secker & Warburg, 1967.

Mok, Michael. "Slumming with Zanuck." *The Nation*, February 3, 1940, pp. 137–138.

Montagu, Ivor. *With Eisenstein in Hollywood*. New York: International Publishers, 1969.

Morella, Joe and Epstein, Edward Z. *Rebels: The Rebel Hero in Films*. New York: Citadel Press, 1971.

Morella, Joe, Epstein, Edward Z., Griggs, John. *The Films of World War II*. Secaucus, N.J.: Citadel Press, 1973.

Morin, Edgar. *The Stars*. New York: Grove Press, 1960.

Morison, Samuel Eliot. *Oxford History of the American People*. New York: Oxford University Press, 1965.

Morton, Eustice. "Additional Dialogue: Scribblers in Hollywood." *Theatre Arts Monthly*, Vol. XXI, No. 6, June 1937, pp. 443–452.

Nash, Alanna. "An Exclusive Centennial Salute: Remembering D. W. Griffith." *Take One*, Vol. 4, No. 7, pp. 8–28.

Nathan, Robert. *One More Spring*. New York: Alfred A. Knopf, 1933.

Navasky, Victor. "To Name or Not to Name: The Hollywood Ten Recalled." *New York Times Magazine*, March 25, 1973, pp. 34–35, 110–112, 118–121.

Noames, Jean-Louis. "Lessons Learned in Combat: An Interview with Robert Rossen." *Cahiers du Cinema in English*, January 1967, pp. 202–229.

Noble, Peter. *The Negro in Films*. London: Skelton Robinson, 1948.

Nye, Russell. *The Unembarrassed Muse*. New York: Dial Press, 1970.

Pechter, William S. *Twenty-Four Frames a Second*. New York: Harper & Row, 1971.

Pells, Richard. *Radical Visions and American Dreams*. New York: Harper Torchbooks, 1974.

Perrett, Geoffrey. *Days of Sadness, Years of Triumph*, Baltimore: Penguin Books, 1974.

Petrie, Graham. "Alternatives to Auteurs." *Film Quarterly*. Spring 1973, pp. 27–35.

Pines, Jim. *Blacks in the Cinema*. London: Education Department, British Film Institute, June 1971.

Platt, David. "From Palmer Raids to Vigilantes." *New Theatre*, October 1934.

Poague, Leland A. *The Cinema of Frank Capra: An Approach to Film Comedy*. New York: A. S. Barnes & Co., 1975.

Polonsky, Abraham. "How the Blacklist Worked in Hollywood." *Film Culture*, Fall 1970, pp. 41–48.

Potamkin, H. A. "The Year of the Eclipse." *Close-Up*, Vol. X, No. 1, March 1933, pp. 30–39.

Powdermaker, Hortense. *Hollywood: The Dream Factory.* Boston: Little, Brown & Co., 1951.

Pulliam, Rebecca. "The Grapes of Wrath." *Velvet Light Trap*, No. 2, pp. 3–7.

Randall, Richard S. *Censorship of the Movies.* Madison: University of Wisconsin Press, 1968.

Reisz, Karel. "Milestone and War." *Sequence*, No. 14, New Year 1952, pp. 12–16.

———. "Hollywood's Anti-Red Boomerang." *Sight and Sound,* January 1953, pp. 132–137, 148.

Richards, Jeffrey. *Visions of Yesterday.* London: Routledge & Kegan Paul, 1973.

Robinson, David. *Hollywood in the Twenties.* New York: A. S. Barnes & Co., 1968.

Robson, E. W. and M. M. *The Film Answers Back.* London: John Lane, The Bodley Head, 1947.

Rosenberg, Bernard and Silverstein, Harry. *The Real Tinsel.* London: Macmillan & Co., 1970.

Ross, Lillian. *Picture.* New York: Avon Books. 1969.

Rosten, Leo. *Hollywood: The Movie Colony, the Movie Makers.* New York: Harcourt, Brace & Co., 1941.

Roth, Mark. "Some Warners Musicals and the Spirit of the New Deal." *Velvet Light Trap*, No. 1. pp. 20–25.

Rotha, Paul. *Celluloid: The Film Today.* London: Longmans, Green & Co., 1931.

———. *Rotha on the Film.* Fair Lawn, N.J.: Essential Books, 1958.

Rotha, Paul and Griffith, Richard. *The Film till Now.* London: Spring Books, 1967.

Salemson, Harold J. "Mr. Capra's Short Cuts to Utopia." *Penguin Film Review*, September 1948, pp. 25–34.

Saluotos, Theodore, ed. *Populism: Reaction or Reform?* Holt, Rinehart & Winston, 1968.

Sarris, Andrew. *The American Cinema.* New York: E. P. Dutton, 1968.

———, ed. *Interviews with Film Directors.* New York: Avon Books, 1970.

———. "Preston Sturges in the Thirties." *Film Comment.* Winter 1970–71, pp. 80–85.

Schary, Dore, as told to Charles Palmer. *Case History of a Movie.* New York: Random House, 1950.

Scherle, Victor and Levy, William Turner. *The Films of Frank Capra.* Secaucus, N.J.: Citadel Press, 1977.

Schickel, Richard. *The Stars.* New York: Dial Press, 1962.

———. *Movies.* New York: Basic Books, 1964.

———. *The Disney Version.* New York: Avon Books, 1969.

Schlesinger, Arthur M., Jr. *The Crisis of the Old Order.* Boston: Houghton Mifflin Co., 1956.

———. *The Politics of Upheaval.* Boston: Houghton Mifflin Co., 1960.

Schumach, Murray. *The Face on the Cutting Room Floor.* New York: William Morrow & Co., 1964.

Seldes, Gilbert. *The Great Audience.* New York: Viking Press, 1951.

———. *The Public Arts.* New York: Simon & Schuster, 1956.

Sennett, Ted. *Warner Brothers Presents.* New Rochelle, N.Y.: Arlington House, 1971.

Shales, Tom, et al. *The American Film Heritage*. Washington, D.C.: Acropolis Books, American Film Institute Publication, 1972.

Sherman, Eric and Rubin, Martin. *The Director's Event*. New York: New American Library, 1972.

Simon, Rita James. *As We Saw the Thirties*. Urbana: University of Illinois Press, 1967.

Sklar, Robert. *Movie-Made America: A Social History of American Movies*. New York: Random House, 1975.

Smith, John M. "Three Liberal Films." *Movie: Elia Kazan*, Winter 1971–72, pp. 19–21.

Solomon, Stanley J. *The Film Idea*. New York: Harcourt Brace Jovanovich, 1972.

Springer, John. "Sylvia Sidney: Says Being an Actress Has Meant More than Being a Star." *Films in Review*, December 1965, pp. 6–16.

Steinbeck, John. *The Grapes of Wrath*. New York: Bantam Books, 1972.

Stott, William. *Documentary Expression and Thirties America*. New York: Oxford University Press, 1973.

Swindell, Larry. *Body and Soul: The Story of John Garfield*. New York: William Morrow & Co., 1975.

Tailleur, Roger. "Elia Kazan and the House Un-American Activities Committee." *Film Comment*, Fall 1966, pp. 43–58.

Taylor, Winchell. "Secret Movie Censors." *The Nation*, July 9, 1938, pp. 38–40.

Terkel, Studs. *Hard Times: An Oral History of the Great Depression*. New York: Pantheon Books, 1970.

Thomas, Bob. *King Cohn*. New York: G. P. Putnam's Sons, 1967.

———. *Thalberg: Life and Legend*. Garden City, N.Y.: Doubleday and Co., 1969.

Thomson, David. *Movie Man*. New York: Stein & Day, 1967.

Time-Life Books. *This Fabulous Century: Volume 4, 1930–1940*. New York: Time-Life Books, 1969.

Toffler, Alvin. *The Culture Consumers*. New York: St. Martin's Press, 1964.

Trumbo, Dalton. *Additional Dialogue*. Helen Manfull, ed. New York: Bantam Books, 1972.

———. "The Time of the Toad." *Film Culture*, Fall 1970, pp. 31–41.

Tyler, Parker. *Magic and Myth of the Movies*. New York: Henry Holt & Co., 1947.

———. *The Three Faces of the Film*. New York: Thomas Yoseloff, 1960.

———. *The Hollywood Hallucination*. New York: Simon & Schuster, 1970.

Ursini, James. *Preston Sturges: An American Dreamer*. New York: Curtis Books, 1973.

Vaughn, Robert. *Only Victims*. New York: G. P. Putnam's Sons, 1972.

Vidor, King. "Rubber-Stamp Movies." *The New Theatre*, September 1934, pp. 11–12.

———. *A Tree Is a Tree*. New York: Harcourt, Brace & Co., 1953.

———. *King Vidor on Filmmaking*. New York: David McKay Co., 1972.

Warner, Jack, with Dean Jennings. *My First Hundred Years in Hollywood*. New York: Random House, 1965.

Warshow, Robert. *The Immediate Experience*. New York: Atheneum, 1972.

Wasserman, Harry. "Ideological Gunfight at the RKO Corral: Notes on Howard Hughes' *I Married a Communist*." *Velvet Light Trap*, No. 11, pp. 7–11.

Watts, Richard, Jr. "Hollywood Sees Pink." *New Theatre*, November 1934, pp. 14–15, 34.

Wecter, Dixon. *The Age of the Great Depression: 1929–1941*. A History of American Life. Volume XIII. New York: Macmillan Co., 1948.

White, David Manning and Averson, Richard, ed. *Sight, Sound and Society.* Boston: Beacon Press, 1968.

———. *The Celluloid Weapon*. Boston: Beacon Press, 1972.

Willis, Donald C. *The Films of Frank Capra*. Metuchen, N.J.: Scarecrow Press, 1974.

Wilmington, Michael. "Nicholas Ray: The Years at RKO." *Velvet Light Trap*, No. 10, pp. 46–53.

Winnington, Richard. *Drawn and Quartered*. London: Saturn Press, 1948.

Wolfenstein, Martha and Leites, Nathan. *Movies: A Psychological Study.* New York: Atheneum, 1970.

Wood, Michael. *America in the Movies, or "Santa Maria, It Had Slipped My Mind."* New York: Basic Books, 1975.

Wood, Robin. "Ideology, Genre, Auteur." *Film Comment*, January–February 1977, pp. 46–51.

———. "Venus de Marlene." *Film Comment*, March–April 1978.

Zangrando, Robert L. "The NAACP and a Federal Anti-Lynching Bill, 1934–1940" in *The Negro in Depression and War*. Bernard Sternsher, ed. Chicago: Quadrangle Books, 1969.

Zanuck, Darryl F. "Do Writers Know Hollywood?" *Saturday Review of Literature*. October 30, 1943, pp. 12–13.

———. "Darryl Zanuck Answers Elmer Rice." *Saturday Review of Literature*. April 22, 1944, pp. 17–18.

Zierold, Norman. *The Moguls*. New York: Avon Books, 1972.

Zukor, Adolph, with Dale Kramer. *The Public Is Never Wrong*. New York: G. P. Putnam's Sons, 1953.

Selected Filmography

The following are the credits of the social problem films discussed in this book. We have omitted other kinds of films which are alluded to—some gangster films, pacifist films, war films—because we have tried to restrict our selection to those films which bear directly on the social problem genre.

All the King's Men. November 1949. Columbia
> DIRECTOR: Robert Rossen; Screenplay: Robert Rossen from the novel by Robert Penn Warren; Producer: Robert Rossen.
> CAST: Broderick Crawford, John Ireland, Mercedes McCambridge, Joanne Dru.

An American Madness. July 1932. Columbia
> DIRECTOR: Frank Capra; Screenplay: Robert Riskin.
> CAST: Walter Huston, Pat O'Brien, Gavin Gordon, Constance Cummings.

An American Romance. October 1944. MGM
> DIRECTOR: King Vidor; Screenplay: Louis Adamic, Herbert Dalmas, William Ludwig, story, King Vidor; Producer: King Vidor.
> CAST: Brian Donlevy, Ann Richards, Walter Abel, Horace McNally.

Angels Wash Their Faces. September 1939. Warners
> DIRECTOR: Ray Enright; Screenplay: Robert Buckner, Michael Fessier, Niven Busch.
> CAST: Ann Sheridan, Ronald Reagan, the Dead End Kids, Eduardo Cianneli.

Angels with Dirty Faces. November 1938. Warners
> DIRECTOR: Michael Curtiz; Screenplay: John Wexley, Warren Duff, story, Rowland Brown; Producer: Samuel Bischoff.
> CAST: James Cagney, Pat O'Brien, Ann Sheridan, Humphrey Bogart, the Dead End Kids.

Are We Civilized? June 1934. Raspin Productions
> DIRECTOR-PRODUCER: Edwin Carewe; Screenplay: Harold Sherman.
> CAST: William Farnum, Anita Louise.

Arise My Love. November 1940. Paramount
>DIRECTOR: Mitchell Leisen; Screenplay: Charles Brackett, Billy Wilder; Producer: Arthur Hornblow, Jr.
>CAST: Claudette Colbert, Ray Milland, Walter Abel, Dennis O'Keefe.

Arrowsmith. December 1931. United Artists
>DIRECTOR: John Ford; Screenplay: Sidney Howard from the Sinclair Lewis novel; Producer: Samuel Goldwyn.
>CAST: Ronald Colman, Helen Hayes, Richard Bennett, Myrna Loy.

Back Street. July 1932. Universal
>DIRECTOR: John M. Stahl; Screenplay: Gladys Lehman from the Fanny Hurst novel.
>CAST: Irene Dunne, John Boles, George Meeker, Zasu Pitts.

Bad Day at Black Rock. January 1955. MGM
>DIRECTOR: John Sturges; Screenplay: Millard Kaufman, story, Howard Kreslin; Producer: Dore Schary.
>CAST: Spencer Tracy, Robert Ryan, Ernest Borgnine, Lee Marvin.

Beast of the City. March 1932. MGM (Cosmopolitan Pictures)
>DIRECTOR: Charles Brabin; Screenplay: W. R. Burnett, John Lee Mahin.
>CAST: Walter Huston, Wallace Ford, Jean Harlow, Jean Hersholt, J. Carroll Naish.

Bed of Roses. July 1933. RKO
>DIRECTOR: Gregory La Cava; Screenplay: Wanda Tuchock, dialogue, Gregory La Cava, Eugene Thackerey; Producer: Pandro S. Berman.
>CAST: Constance Bennett, Joel McCrea, Pert Kelton.

The Best Years of Our Lives. November 1946. RKO
>DIRECTOR: William Wyler; Screenplay: Robert E. Sherwood, story, Mackinley Kantor; Producer: Samuel Goldwyn.
>CAST: Fredric March, Dana Andrews, Harold Russell, Myrna Loy, Teresa Wright, Virginia Mayo, Cathy O'Donnell, Hoagy Carmichael.

The Big House. June 1930. MGM
>DIRECTOR: George Hill; Story and Dialogue: Frances Marion, additional dialogue, Joe Farnham, Martin Flavin; Producer: Irving Thalberg.
>CAST: Wallace Beery, Chester Morris, Robert Montgomery, Lewis Stone.

Big Jim McLain. September 1952. Warners
>DIRECTOR: Edward Ludwig; Screenplay: James Edward Grant, story, Richard English; Producer: Robert Fellows.
>CAST: John Wayne, Nancy Olson, James Arness, Alan Napier, Hans Conreid.

Black Fury. April 1935. Warners
>DIRECTOR: Michael Curtiz; Screenplay: Abem Finkel, Carl Erickson from a story by Judge M. A. Musmanno.
>CAST: Paul Muni, Karen Morley, John Qualen, J. Carroll Naish, Barton MacLane.

Black Legion. January 1937. Warners
>DIRECTOR: Archie Mayo; Screenplay: Abem Finkel, William Wister Haines, story, Robert Lord; Producer: Robert Lord.
>CAST: Humphrey Bogart, Dick Foran, Erin O'Brien-Moore, Ann Sheridan, Joseph Sawyer.

Blessed Event. August 1932. Warners
    DIRECTOR: Roy Del Ruth; Screenplay: Howard Green.
    CAST: Lee Tracy, Mary Brian, Allen Jenkins, Ned Sparks.

Blockade. June 1938. United Artists
    DIRECTOR: William Dieterle; Screenplay: John Howard Lawson; Producer: Walter Wanger.
    CAST: Henry Fonda, Madeleine Carroll, Leo Carillo, Vladimir Sokoloff.

Blonde Venus. September 1932. Paramount
    DIRECTOR: Josef Von Sternberg; Screenplay: Jules Furthman, S. K. Lauren.
    CAST: Marlene Dietrich, Herbert Marshall, Cary Grant, Dickie Moore.

Blondie Johnson. March 1933. Warners
    DIRECTOR: Ray Enright; Screenplay: Earl Baldwin.
    CAST: Joan Blondell, Wayne Morris, Sterling Holloway.

Blood Money. November 1933. United Artists
    DIRECTOR: Rowland Brown; Screenplay: Rowland Brown, Hal Long.
    CAST: George Bancroft, Judith Anderson, Frances Dee, Chick Chandler.

Body and Soul. August 1947. United Artists (Enterprise Studios)
    DIRECTOR: Robert Rossen; Screenplay: Abraham Polonsky; Producer: Bob Roberts.
    CAST: John Garfield, Lilli Palmer, Anne Revere, William Conrad, Canada Lee, Lloyd Gough, Joseph Pevney.

Bordertown. January 1935. Warners
    DIRECTOR: Archie Mayo; Screenplay: Laird Doyle, Wallace Smith, story, Robert Lord; Producer: Robert Lord.
    CAST: Paul Muni, Bette Davis, Margaret Lindsay, Eugene Pallette, Robert Barrat.

Born to Love. April 1931. RKO
    DIRECTOR: Paul L. Stein; Screenplay: Ernest Pascal.
    CAST: Constance Bennett, Joel McCrea, Paul Cavanaugh.

Born Yesterday. November 1950. Columbia
    DIRECTOR: George Cukor; Screenplay: Albert Mannheimer from the play by Garson Kanin; Producer: S. Sylvan Simon.
    CAST: Judy Holliday, William Holden, Broderick Crawford.

Boy of the Streets. December 1937. Monogram
    DIRECTOR: William Nigh; Screenplay: Gilson Brown, Scott Darling, story, Rowland Brown; Producer: George E. Kahn.
    CAST: Jackie Cooper, Marjorie Main.

Boy Slaves. February 1939. RKO
    DIRECTOR-PRODUCER: P. J. Wolfson; Screenplay: Albert Bein, Ben Orkow.
    CAST: Anne Shirley, Roger Daniel, Alan Baxter.

Boys Town. September 1938. MGM
    DIRECTOR: Norman Taurog; Screenplay: Dore Schary, John Meehan, story, Dore Schary, Eleanor Griffin; Producer: John W. Considine, Jr.
    CAST: Spencer Tracy, Mickey Rooney, Henry Hull, Bobs Watson, Sidney Miller.

Bright Victory. July 1951. Universal
    DIRECTOR: Mark Robson; Screenplay-Producer: Robert Buckner.
    CAST: Arthur Kennedy, James Edwards, Peggy Dow, Will Geer.

Cabin in the Cotton. October 1932. Warners
    DIRECTOR: Michael Curtiz; Screenplay: Paul Green; Producer: Hal B. Wallis.
    CAST: Richard Barthelmess, Bette Davis, Henry B. Walthall, Berton Churchill.

The Caine Mutiny. September 1954. Columbia
    DIRECTOR: Edward Dmytryk; Screenplay: Stanley Roberts from the novel by Herman Wouk; Producer: Stanley Kramer.
    CAST: Humphrey Bogart, Jose Ferrer, Van Johnson, Fred MacMurray.

Castle on the Hudson. February 1940. Warners
    DIRECTOR: Anatole Litvak; Screenplay: Seton I. Miller, Brown Holmes, Courtney Terrett; Producer: Samuel Bischoff.
    CAST: John Garfield, Ann Sheridan.

Christopher Strong. March 1933. RKO
    DIRECTOR: Dorothy Arzner; Producer: Pandro S. Berman.
    CAST: Katharine Hepburn, Colin Clive.

The Citadel. October 1938. MGM
    DIRECTOR: King Vidor; Screenplay: Ian Dalrymple, Frank Wead, Elizabeth Hill from the novel by A. J. Cronin; Producer: Victor Saville.
    CAST: Robert Donat, Rosalind Russell, Ralph Richardson, Rex Harrison.

Citizen Kane. September 1941. RKO
    DIRECTOR: Orson Welles; Screenplay: Herman Mankiewicz, Orson Welles; Producer: Orson Welles.
    CAST: Orson Welles, Joseph Cotton, Dorothy Comingore, Everett Sloane.

City Across the River. May 1949. Universal
    DIRECTOR-PRODUCER: Maxwell Shane; Screenplay: Maxwell Shane, Dennis Cooper from the novel *The Amboy Dukes* by Irving Shulman.
    CAST: Stephen McNally, Thelma Ritter, Jeff Corey.

Common Clay. August 1930. Fox
    DIRECTOR-PRODUCER: Victor Fleming; Screenplay: Jules Furthman.
    CAST: Constance Bennett, Lew Ayres.

Confessions of a Nazi Spy. May 1939. Warners
    DIRECTOR: Anatole Litvak; Screenplay: Milton Krims, John Wexley.
    CAST: Edward G. Robinson, George Sanders, Paul Lukas, Francis Lederer.

Confidential Agent. November 1945. Warners
    DIRECTOR: Herman Shumlin; Screenplay-Producer: Robert Buckner from a novel by Graham Greene.
    CAST: Charles Boyer, Lauren Bacall, Katina Paxinou, Peter Lorre.

The Conquerors. November 1932. RKO
    DIRECTOR: William Wellman; Screenplay: Robert Lord, story, Howard Estabrook; Producer: David O. Selznick.
    CAST: Richard Dix, Ann Harding, Guy Kibbee.

Conspirator. February 1950. MGM
>DIRECTOR: Victor Saville; Screenplay: Sally Benson, Garard Fairlie; Producer: Arthur Hornblow, Jr.
>CAST: Robert Taylor, Elizabeth Taylor.

Counsellor-at-Law. December 1933. Universal
>DIRECTOR: William Wyler; Screenplay: Elmer Rice from his play.
>CAST: John Barrymore, Bebe Daniels, Doris Kenyon, Melvyn Douglas.

Crime School. May 1938. Warners
>DIRECTOR: Lewis Seiler; Screenplay: Vincent Sherman, Crane Wilbur, story, Crane Wilbur; Producer: Bryan Foy.
>CAST: Humphrey Bogart, Gale Page, the Dead End Kids.

Criminal Code. January 1931. Columbia
>DIRECTOR: Howard Hawks; Screenplay: Seton I. Miller, Fred Niblo, Jr.; Producer: Harry Cohn.
>CAST: Walter Huston, Phillips Holmes, Constance Cummings.

Crossfire. August 1947. RKO
>DIRECTOR: Edward Dmytryk; Screenplay: John Paxton from a novel by Richard Brooks; Producer: Adrian Scott.
>CAST: Robert Ryan, Robert Young, Robert Mitchum, Sam Levene.

The Crowd. February 1928. MGM
>DIRECTOR: King Vidor; Screenplay: King Vidor, John V. A. Weaver, Harry Behn; Producer: Irving Thalberg.
>CAST: James Murray, Eleanor Boardman, Bert Roach.

The Dark Horse. June 1932. Warners
>DIRECTOR: Alfred A. Green; Screenplay: Joseph Jackson, Wilson Mizner, story, Melville Crossman (pseud. of Darryl F. Zanuck); Producer: Raymond Griffith.
>CAST: Warren William, Bette Davis, Guy Kibbee.

Dead End. August 1937. United Artists
>DIRECTOR: William Wyler, Screenplay: Lillian Hellman from the play by Sidney Kingsley; Producer: Samuel Goldwyn.
>CAST: Sylvia Sidney, Joel McCrea, Humphrey Bogart, Wendy Barrie, Claire Trevor, Allen Jenkins, Marjorie Main, the Dead End Kids— Billy Halop, Huntz Hall, Bobby Jordan, Leo Gorcey, Gabriel Dell, Bernard Punsley.

The Devil and Miss Jones. April 1940. RKO
>DIRECTOR: Sam Wood; Screenplay: Norman Krasna; Producer: Frank Ross.
>CAST: Jean Arthur, Robert Cummings, Charles Coburn, Spring Byington.

The Devil Is a Sissy. September 1936. MGM
>DIRECTOR: W. S. Van Dyke; Screenplay: Richard Schayer, John Lee Mahin, story, Rowland Brown; Producer: Frank Davis.
>CAST: Freddie Bartholomew, Jackie Cooper, Mickey Rooney, Ian Hunter.

Dr. Ehrlich's Magic Bullet. March 1940. Warners
>DIRECTOR: William Dieterle; Screenplay: John Huston, Heinz Herald, Norman Burnside; Producer: Wolfgang Reinhardt.
>CAST: Edward G. Robinson, Ruth Gordon, Otto Kruger, Donald Crisp.

A Doctor's Diary. January 1937. Paramount
> DIRECTOR: Charles Vidor; Screenplay: David Boehm, story, Samuel Ornitz, Joseph Anthony; Producer: B. P. Shulberg.
> CAST: George Bancroft, Helen Burgess.

Dust Be My Destiny. September 1939. Warners
> DIRECTOR: Lewis Seiler; Screenplay: Robert Rossen; Producer: Hal Wallis.
> CAST: John Garfield, Priscilla Lane, Alan Hale, Frank McHugh, Henry Armetta, Charley Grapewin, Billy Halop.

The Easiest Way. March 1931. MGM
> DIRECTOR: Jack Conway; Screenplay: Edith Ellis.
> CAST: Constance Bennett, Adolphe Menjou, Robert Montgomery.

East of Eden. April 1955. Warners
> DIRECTOR: Elia Kazan; Screenplay: Paul Osborn from the John Steinbeck novel; Producer: Elia Kazan.
> CAST: James Dean, Raymond Massey, Julie Harris, Jo Van Fleet.

Easy Living. July 1937. Paramount
> DIRECTOR: Mitchell Leisen; Screenplay: Preston Sturges, story, Vera Caspary; Producer: Arthur Hornblow, Jr.
> CAST: Jean Arthur, Edward Arnold, Ray Milland, Luis Alberni, Franklin Pangborn, William Demarest.

Edge of the City. January 1957. MGM
> DIRECTOR: Martin Ritt; Screenplay: Robert Alan Aurthur; Producer: David Susskind.
> CAST: Sidney Poitier, John Cassavettes, Jack Warden, Ruby Dee.

Escape. November 1940. MGM
> DIRECTOR-PRODUCER: Mervyn Leroy; Screenplay: Arch Oboler, Marguerite Roberts.
> CAST: Norma Shearer, Robert Taylor, Conrad Veidt, Nazimova, Felix Bressart.

Faithless. November 1932. MGM
> DIRECTOR: Harry Beaumont; Screenplay: Carey Wilson, story, Mildred Cram.
> CAST: Tallulah Bankhead, Robert Montgomery.

The Fallen Sparrow. 1943. RKO
> DIRECTOR: Richard Wallace; Screenplay: Warren Duff; Producer: Robert Fellows.
> CAST: John Garfield, Maureen O'Hara, Walter Slezak.

Five Star Final. September 1931. Warners
> DIRECTOR: Mervyn Leroy; Screenplay: Byron Morgan, Robert Lord.
> CAST: Edward G. Robinson, Aline MacMahon, Boris Karloff, H. B. Warner.

Flowing Gold. August 1940. Warners
> DIRECTOR: Alfred E. Green; Screenplay: Kenneth Gamet, story, Rex Beach; Producer: William Jacobs.
> CAST: John Garfield, Pat O'Brien, Frances Farmer, Raymond Walburn.

Footlight Parade. September 1933. Warners
> DIRECTOR: Lloyd Bacon; Screenplay: Manuel Seff, James Seymour.
> CAST: James Cagney, Joan Blondell, Ruby Keeler, Dick Powell, Guy Kibbee.

For Whom the Bell Tolls. July 1943. Paramount
> DIRECTOR: Sam Wood; Screenplay: Dudley Nichols from the Ernest Hemingway novel; Producer: Sam Wood.
> CAST: Gary Cooper, Ingrid Bergman, Katina Paxinou, Akim Tamiroff.

Force of Evil. December 1949. MGM (Enterprise Studios)
> DIRECTOR-SCREENPLAY: Abraham Polonsky from the novel *Tucker's People* by Ira Wolfert; Producer: Bob Roberts.
> CAST: John Garfield, Thomas Gomez, Beatrice Pearson, Roy Roberts.

Foreign Correspondent. August 1940. United Artists
> DIRECTOR: Alfred Hitchcock; Screenplay: Charles Bennett, Joan Harrison; Producer: Walter Wanger.
> CAST: Joel McCrea, Laraine Day, Herbert Marshall, George Sanders.

Four Daughters. 1938. Warners
> DIRECTOR: Michael Curtiz; Screenplay: Julius Epstein, Lenore Coffee from a story by Fanny Hurst; Producer: Benjamin Glazer and Hal B. Wallis.
> CAST: John Garfield, Priscilla Lane, Claude Rains, Jeffrey Lynn, Frank McHugh, Lola Lane, Rosemary Lane, Gale Page.

Four Sons. June 1940. Fox
> DIRECTOR: Archie Mayo; Screenplay: John Howard Lawson from the play by I. A. R. Wylie; Producer: Darryl F. Zanuck.
> CAST: Don Ameche, Alan Curtis, Eugenie Leontovitch.

From This Day Forward. March 1946. RKO
> DIRECTOR: John Berry; Screenplay: Hugo Butler, adaptation, Garson Kanin, from the novel by Thomas Bell; Producer: William Pereira.
> CAST: Mark Stevens, Joan Fontaine, Henry Morgan, Rosemary Decamp.

The Front Page. March 1931. United Artists
> DIRECTOR: Lewis Milestone; Screenplay: Bartlett Cormack, Charles Lederer from the play by Ben Hecht and Charles MacArthur; Producer: Howard Hughes.
> CAST: Pat O'Brien, Adolphe Menjou, Mary Brian, George E. Stone, Edward Everett Horton.

Fury. May 1936. MGM
> DIRECTOR: Fritz Lang; Screenplay: Fritz Lang, Bartlett Cormack, story, Norman Krasna; Producer: Joseph L. Mankiewicz.
> CAST: Spencer Tracy, Sylvia Sidney, Walter Brennan, Edward Ellis, Bruce Cabot, Walter Abel.

Gabriel over the White House. April 1933. MGM (Cosmopolitan Pictures)
> DIRECTOR: Gregory La Cava; Screenplay: Carey Wilson, Bertram Block; Producer: Walter Wanger.
> CAST: Walter Huston, Karen Morley, Franchot Tone, David Landau, Mischa Auer, C. Henry Gordon.

The General Died at Dawn. September 1936. Paramount
> DIRECTOR: Lewis Milestone; Screenplay: Clifford Odets; Producer: William LeBaron.
> CAST: Gary Cooper, Madeleine Carroll, Akim Tamiroff, Porter Hall, Dudley Digges, William Frawley.

Gentleman's Agreement. November 1947. Fox
> DIRECTOR: Elia Kazan; Screenplay: Moss Hart from a novel by

Laura Z. Hobson; Producer: Darryl F. Zanuck.
Cast: Gregory Peck, Dorothy McGuire, John Garfield, Celeste Holm, Anne Revere, Sam Jaffe.

Gentlemen Are Born. November 1934. Warners
Director: Alfred E. Green; Screenplay: Eugene Solow, Robert Lee Johnson, story, Robert Lee Johnson.
Cast: Franchot Tone, Dick Foran, Margaret Lindsay, Ann Dvorak, Robert Light, Ross Alexander.

Golddiggers of 1933. May 1933. Warners
Director: Mervyn Leroy; Screenplay: Erwin Gelsey, James Seymour, Dialogue, David Boehm, Ben Markson.
Cast: Warren William, Joan Blondell, Ruby Keeler, Dick Powell, Ginger Rogers, Aline MacMahon, Guy Kibbee.

Golden Harvest. November 1933. Paramount
Director: Ralph Murphy; Screenplay: Casey Robinson, story, Nina Wilcox Putnam; Producer: Charles S. Rogers.
Cast: Richard Arlen, Chester Morris, Genevieve Tobin.

The Grapes of Wrath. January 1940. Fox
Director: John Ford; Screenplay: Nunnally Johnson from the novel by John Steinbeck; Producer: Darryl F. Zanuck.
Cast: Henry Fonda, Jane Darwell, Russell Simpson, Charley Grapewin, John Carradine, John Qualen, Grant Mitchell, Ward Bond.

The Great Dictator. October 1940. United Artists
Director-Screenplay-Producer: Charles Chaplin.
Cast: Charles Chaplin, Jack Oakie, Paulette Goddard, Reginald Gardiner, Henry Daniell, Billy Gilbert, Maurice Moscovich.

The Great O'Malley. February 1937. Warners
Director: William Dieterle; Screenplay: Milton Krims, Tom Reed; Producer: Harry Joe Brown.
Cast: Pat O'Brien, Ann Sheridan, Humphrey Bogart, Sybil Jason.

Guilty of Treason. December 1949. Eagle Lion
Director: Felix Feist; Screenplay: Emmet Lavery; Producer: Jack Wrather, Robert Golden.
Cast: Charles Bickford, Paul Kelly, Bonita Granville.

Hallelujah! August 1929. MGM
Director: King Vidor; Screenplay: Wanda Tuchock, treatment, Richard Schaver; Producer: Irving Thalberg.
Cast: Daniel Haynes, Nina Mae McKinney, William Fountaine, Victoria Spivey.

Hallelujah, I'm a Bum. January 1933. United Artists
Director: Lewis Milestone; Screenplay: S. N. Behrman, story, Ben Hecht.
Cast: Al Jolson, Madge Evans, Harry Langdon, Frank Morgan.

Hearts in Dixie. March 1929. Fox
Director-Producer: Paul Sloane; Screenplay: Walter Weems.
Cast: Clarence Muse, Stepin Fetchit, Mildred Washington.

Hell's Highway. September 1932. RKO
Director: Rowland Brown; Screenplay: Samuel Ornitz, Robert Tasker, Rowland Brown; Producer: David Selznick.
Cast: Richard Dix, Tom Brown, Rochelle Hudson, C. Henry Gordon.

Hell's Kitchen. July 1939. Warners
Director: Lewis Seiler, E. A. Dupont; Screenplay: Crane Wilbur,

Fred Niblo, Jr.; Producer: Bryan Foy, Mark Hellinger.

CAST: Ronald Reagan, Margaret Lindsay.

Heroes for Sale. July 1933. Warners

DIRECTOR: William Wellman; Screenplay: Robert Lord, Wilson Mizner.

CAST: Richard Barthelmess, Loretta Young, Robert Barrat, Aline MacMahon, Grant Mitchell, Berton Churchill, Gordon Westcott.

The Hitler Gang. April 1944. Paramount

DIRECTOR: John Farrow; Screenplay: Frances Goodrich, Albert Hackett; Producer: B. G. DeSylva, Joseph Sistrom.

CAST: Robert Watson, Roman Bohnen.

Hitler's Children. March 1943. RKO

DIRECTOR: Edward Dmytryk; Screenplay: Emmet Lavery; Producer: Edward A. Golden.

CAST: Tim Holt, Bonita Granville, Kent Smith, Otto Kruger.

Holiday. June 1938. Columbia

DIRECTOR: George Cukor; Screenplay: Donald Ogden Stewart, Sidney Buchman from the Philip Barry play; Producer: Everett Riskin.

CAST: Cary Grant, Katharine Hepburn, Lew Ayres, Edward Everett Horton, Doris Nolan.

Home of the Brave. July 1949. United Artists

DIRECTOR: Mark Robson; Screenplay: Carl Foreman; Producer: Stanley Kramer.

CAST: James Edwards, Lloyd Bridges, Jeff Corey, Frank Lovejoy, Douglas Dick, Steve Brodie.

How Green Was My Valley. December 1941. Fox

DIRECTOR: John Ford; Screenplay: Philip Dunne from a novel by Richard Llewellyn; Producer: Darryl F. Zanuck.

CAST: Roddy McDowell, Walter Pidgeon, Maureen O'Hara, Donald Crisp, Sara Allgood, Anna Lee.

I Am a Fugitive from a Chain Gang. October 1932. Warners

DIRECTOR: Mervyn Leroy; Screenplay: Edward S. Green, Brown Holmes from a story by Robert E. Burns; Producer: Darryl F. Zanuck.

CAST: Paul Muni, Helen Vinson, Glenda Farrell, Allen Jenkins, David Landau, Preston Foster, Edward Ellis.

I Believed in You. March 1934. Fox

DIRECTOR: Irving Cummings; Screenplay: William Conselman.

CAST: Rosemary Ames, Victor Jory, John Boles.

I Married a Communist (aka *The Woman on Pier 13*). October 1949. RKO

DIRECTOR: Robert Stevenson; Screenplay: Charles Grayson, Robert Hardy Andrews, story, George W. George, George F. Slavin; Producer: Jack J. Gross.

CAST: Laraine Day, Robert Ryan, Thomas Gomez.

I Was a Communist for the FBI. May 1951. Warners

DIRECTOR: Gordon Douglas; Screenplay: Crane Wilbur; Producer: Bryan Foy.

CAST: Frank Lovejoy, Dorothy Hart, Philip Carey, Konstantin Shayne.

Imitation of Life. November 1934. Universal

DIRECTOR: John M. Stahl; Screenplay: William Hurlbut from the Fannie Hurst novel; Producer: Carl Laemmle, Jr.

CAST: Claudette Colbert, Warren William, Ned Sparks, Louise Beavers, Fredi Washington.

Intruder in the Dust. October 1949. MGM

DIRECTOR-PRODUCER: Clarence Brown; Screenplay: Ben Maddow from the novel by William Faulkner.

CAST: Juano Hernandez, Claude Jarman, Jr., David Brian, Will Geer, Elizabeth Patterson, Charles Kemper, Porter Hall.

The Iron Curtain. May 1948. Fox

DIRECTOR: William Wellman; Screenplay: Milton Krims, based on the personal story of Igor Gouzenko; Producer: Sol C. Siegel.

CAST: Dana Andrews, Gene Tierney, June Havoc.

Is My Face Red? June 1932. RKO

DIRECTOR: William Seiter; Screenplay: Casey Robinson, Ben Markson; Producer: David O. Selznick.

CAST: Ricardo Cortez, Helen Twelvetrees, Robert Armstrong, Zasu Pitts.

It's a Wonderful Life. December 1946. RKO-Liberty

DIRECTOR-PRODUCER: Frank Capra; Screenplay: Frances Goodrich, Albert Hackett, Frank Capra.

CAST: James Stewart, Donna Reed, Lionel Barrymore, Henry Travers, Beulah Bondi, Ward Bond, H. B. Warner.

The Jackie Robinson Story. May 1950. Eagle Lion

DIRECTOR: Alfred E. Green; Screenplay: Lawrence Taylor, Arthur Mann; Producer: Mort Briskin.

CAST: Jackie Robinson, Ruby Dee, Louise Beavers.

The Joe Louis Story. September 1953. United Artists

DIRECTOR: Robert Gordon; Screenplay: Robert Sylvester; Producer: Sterling Silliphant.

CAST: Coley Wallace, Paul Stewart, James Edwards.

John Meade's Woman. February 1937. Paramount

DIRECTOR: Richard Wallace; Screenplay: Vincent Lawrence, Herman Mankiewicz, story, John Bright, Robert Tasker; Producer: B. P. Schulberg.

CAST: Edward Arnold, Francine Larrimore, Gail Patrick, George Bancroft.

Keeper of the Flame. December 1942. MGM

DIRECTOR: George Cukor; Screenplay: Donald Ogden Stewart; Producer: Victor Saville.

CAST: Spencer Tracy, Katharine Hepburn, Richard Whorf.

A King in New York. Released in England, 1957; released in the U.S., 1972. Archway

DIRECTOR-SCREENPLAY-PRODUCER: Charles Chaplin.

CAST: Charles Chaplin, Michael Chaplin, Dawn Addams.

King's Row. December 1941. Warners

DIRECTOR: Sam Wood; Screenplay: Casey Robinson; Producer: Hal Wallis, David Lewis.

CAST: Robert Cummings, Betty Field, Ann Sheridan, Ronald Reagan, Charles Coburn, Claude Rains.

Knock on Any Door. April 1949. Columbia

DIRECTOR: Nicholas Ray; Screenplay: Daniel Taradash and John Monks, Jr. from a novel by Willard Motley; Producer: Robert Lord.

CAST: Humphrey Bogart, John Derek, George Macready.

Ladies of the Big House. January 1932. Paramount
DIRECTOR: Marion Gering; Screenplay: Louis Weitkenzorn, additional dialogue, William Slavens McNutt, Grover Jones, from the play by Ernest Booth.
CAST: Sylvia Sidney, Gene Raymond.

The Last Flight. August 1931. Warners
DIRECTOR: William Dieterle; Screenplay: John Monk Saunders from his novel, *Single Lady*.
CAST: Richard Barthelmess, Johnny Mack Brown, Helen Chandler, David Manners.

The Last Mile. August 1932. World Wide
DIRECTOR: Sam Bischoff; Screenplay: Seton I. Miller from the play by John Wexley.
CAST: Howard Phillips, Preston Foster.

The Last Train from Madrid. June 1937. Paramount
DIRECTOR: James Hogan; Screenplay: Louis Stevens, Robert Wyler, story Paul Hervey Fox, Elsie Fox; Producer: George N. Arthur.
CAST: Dorothy Lamour, Lew Ayres, Gilbert Roland, Karen Morley.

The Lawless. July 1950. Paramount
DIRECTOR: Joseph Losey; Screenplay: Geoffrey Homes (pseud. for Daniel Mainwaring); Producer: William H. Pines and William C. Thomas.
CAST: Macdonald Carey, Gail Russell, Lee Patrick, John Sands.

Lawyer Man. December 1932. Warners
DIRECTOR: William Dieterle; Screenplay: Rian James, James Seymour from the novel by Max Trell.
CAST: William Powell, Joan Blondell, Allen Jenkins, David Landau.

Legion of Terror. November 1936. Columbia
DIRECTOR: C. C. Coleman, Jr.; Screenplay: Bert Grante.
CAST: Bruce Cabot, Marguerite Churchill.

The Life of Emile Zola. July 1937. Warners
DIRECTOR: William Dieterle; Screenplay: Norman Reilly Raine, Heinz Herald, Geza Hercaeg; Producer: Hal B. Wallis.
CAST: Paul Muni, Joseph Schildkraut, Gale Sondergaard, Louis Calhern.

Lifeboat. January 1944. Fox
DIRECTOR: Alfred Hitchcock; Screenplay: Jo Swerling from a story by John Steinbeck; Producer: Kenneth Macgowan.
CAST: Tallullah Bankhead, William Bendix, Canada Lee, John Hodiak, Walter Slezak, Hume Cronyn.

Little Caesar. November 1930. Warners
DIRECTOR: Mervyn Leroy; Screenplay: Francis Edward Faragoh from the novel by W. R. Burnett.
CAST: Edward G. Robinson, Douglas Fairbanks, Jr., Glenda Farrell.

Little Man, What Now? June 1934. Universal
DIRECTOR: Frank Borzage; Screenplay: William Anthony McGuire; Producer: Carl Laemmle, Jr.
CAST: Margaret Sullavan, Douglass Montgomery, Alan Hale, Alan Mowbray.

Little Tough Guy. July 1938. Universal
DIRECTOR: Harold Young; Screenplay: Gilson Brown, Brenda Weisberg; Producer: Kenneth Goldsmith.

CAST: Billy Halop, Huntz Hall, Gabriel Dell.

Little Tough Guys in Society. November 1938. Universal
DIRECTOR: Erle C. Kenton; Screenplay: Edward Eliscu, Mortimer Offner; Producer: Max H. Golden.
CAST: Mischa Auer, Mary Boland, Edward Everett Horton, Jackie Searle.

Looking Forward. June 1933. MGM
DIRECTOR: Clarence Brown; Screenplay: Bess Meredyth from the play *Service* by C. L. Anthony (pseud. for Dorothy Gladys Smith); Producer: Clarence Brown.
CAST: Lionel Barrymore, Lewis Stone.

Lost Boundaries. August 1949. Four Continents
DIRECTOR: Alfred Werker; Screenplay: Charles Palmer, Virginia Shaler, Eugene Ling; Producer: Louis de Rochemont.
CAST: Mel Ferrer, Beatrice Pearson, Susan Douglas, Richard Hylton, Leigh Whipper, Canada Lee.

The Lost Weekend. November 1945. Paramount
DIRECTOR: Billy Wilder; Screenplay: Billy Wilder, Charles Brackett from a novel by Charles R. Jackson; Producer: Charles Brackett.
CAST: Ray Milland, Jane Wyman, Howard Da Silva, Philip Terry.

The Male Animal. April 1942. Warners
DIRECTOR: Elliot Nugent; Screenplay: Julius J. and Philip G. Epstein from the play by James Thurber and Elliot Nugent; Producer: Hal B. Wallis, Wolfgang Reinhardt.
CAST: Henry Fonda, Olivia de Havilland, Jack Carson.

Man Hunt. June 1941. Fox
DIRECTOR: Fritz Lang; Screenplay: Dudley Nichols from the novel by Geoffrey Household; Producer: Kenneth Macgowan.
CAST: Walter Pidgeon, Joan Bennett, George Sanders, John Carradine.

The Man I Married. August 1940. Fox
DIRECTOR: Irving Pichel; Screenplay: Oliver H. P. Garrett; Producer: Darryl F. Zanuck.
CAST: Joan Bennett, Francis Lederer.

Man on a Tightrope. May 1953. Fox
DIRECTOR: Elia Kazan; Screenplay: Robert E. Sherwood; Producer: Robert L. Jacks.
CAST: Fredric March, Terry Moore, Gloria Grahame.

Manpower. August 1941. Warners
DIRECTOR: Raoul Walsh; Screenplay: Richard Macaulay, Jerry Wald; Producer: Hal B. Wallis, Mark Hellinger.
CAST: Edward G. Robinson, George Raft, Marlene Dietrich.

A Man's Castle. November 1933. Columbia
DIRECTOR: Frank Borzage; Screenplay: Jo Swerling from the play by Lawrence Hazard.
CAST: Spencer Tracy, Loretta Young, Walter Connolly, Glenda Farrell.

The Man Who Dared. September 1933. Fox
DIRECTOR: Hamilton McFadden; Screenplay: Dudley Nichols, Lamar Trotti.
CAST: Preston Foster, Zita Johann.

Mary Burns, Fugitive. November 1935. Paramount
    DIRECTOR: William K. Howard; Screenplay: Gene Towne, Graham Baker; Producer: Walter Wanger.
    CAST: Sylvia Sidney, Melvyn Douglas, Alan Baxter.

Massacre. January 1934. Warners
    DIRECTOR: Alan Crosland; Screenplay: Ralph Block, Sheridan Gibney from the story by Robert Gessner.
    CAST: Richard Barthelmess, Ann Dvorak, Dudley Digges, Sidney Toler.

Mayor of Hell. July 1933. Warners
    DIRECTOR: Archie Mayo; Screenplay: Edward Chodorov.
    CAST: James Cagney, Frankie Darrow, Dudley Digges, Allen Jenkins, Madge Evans, Arthur Byron.

Meet John Doe. May 1941. Warners
    DIRECTOR-PRODUCER: Frank Capra; Screenplay: Robert Riskin.
    CAST: Gary Cooper, Barbara Stanwyck, Walter Brennan, Edward Arnold, James Gleason.

The Men. September 1950. United Artists
    DIRECTOR: Fred Zinneman; Screenplay: Carl Foreman; Producer: Stanley Kramer.
    CAST: Marlon Brando, Teresa Wright, Everett Sloane, Jack Webb.

Men in White. March 1934. MGM
    DIRECTOR: Richard Boleslavsky; Screenplay: Waldeman Young from the play by Sidney Kingsley; Producer: Monta Bell.
    CAST: Clark Gable, Myrna Loy, Jean Hersholt.

Mission to Moscow. May 1943. Warners
    DIRECTOR: Michael Curtiz; Screenplay: Howard Koch from the book by Ambassador Joseph Davies; Producer: Robert Buckner.
    CAST: Walter Huston, Ann Harding, Oscar Homolka, George Tobias.

Mr. Deeds Goes to Town. March 1936. Columbia
    DIRECTOR-PRODUCER: Frank Capra; Screenplay: Robert Riskin from a story by Clarence Buddington Kelland.
    CAST: Gary Cooper, Jean Arthur, Lionel Stander, Douglas Dumbrille, George Bancroft, John Wray.

Modern Hero. April 1934. Warners
    DIRECTOR: G. W. Pabst; Screenplay: Gene Markey, Kathryn Scola from the novel by Louis Bromfield.
    CAST: Richard Barthelmess, Jean Muir, Marjorie Rambeau.

Modern Times. February 1936. United Artists
    DIRECTOR-SCREENPLAY-PRODUCER: Charles Chaplin.
    CAST: Charles Chaplin, Paulette Goddard.

Monsieur Verdoux. October 1947. United Artists
    DIRECTOR-SCREENPLAY-PRODUCER: Charles Chaplin.
    CAST: Charles Chaplin, Martha Raye, Mady Correll, Marilyn Nash.

Moonlight and Pretzels. August 1933. Universal
    DIRECTOR: Karl Freund, Monte Brice; Screenplay: Monte Brice, Sig Herzig, story, Monte Brice, Arthur Jarrett.
    CAST: Leo Carrillo, Mary Brian.

The More the Merrier. April 1943. Columbia
    DIRECTOR-PRODUCER: George Stevens; Screenplay: Robert Russell, Frank Ross, Richard Flournoy, Lewis R. Foster.
    CAST: Jean Arthur, Joel McCrea, Charles Coburn.

The Mortal Storm. June 1940. MGM
DIRECTOR: Frank Borzage; Screenplay: Claudine West, Anderson Ellis, George Froeschel.
CAST: Margaret Sullavan, James Stewart, Robert Young, Frank Morgan, Robert Stack.

The Mouthpiece. April 1932. Warners
DIRECTOR: James Flood, Elliot Nugent; Screenplay: Joseph Jackson, Earl Baldwin.
CAST: Warren William, Guy Kibbee, Bette Davis, Aline MacMahon, Sidney Fox.

My Man and I. August 1952. MGM
DIRECTOR: William Wellman; Screenplay: John Fante, Jack Leonard; Producer: Stephen Ames.
CAST: Shelley Winters, Ricardo Montalban.

My Man Godfrey. September 1936. Universal
DIRECTOR-PRODUCER: Gregory La Cava; Screenplay: Eric Hatch, Morrie Ryskind.
CAST: William Powell, Carole Lombard, Gail Patrick, Alice Brady, Eugene Pallette, Alan Mowbray, Mischa Auer.

My Six Convicts. March 1952. Columbia
DIRECTOR: Hugo Fregonese; Screenplay: Michael Blankfort from the book by Donald Powell Wilson; Producer: Stanley Kramer.
CAST: Millard Mitchell, Gilbert Roland.

My Son John. March 1952. Paramount
DIRECTOR-PRODUCER: Leo McCarey; Screenplay: Myles Connelly, Leo McCarey.
CAST: Robert Walker, Dean Jagger, Helen Hayes, Van Heflin.

Never Let Me Go. May 1953. MGM
DIRECTOR: Delmer Daves; Screenplay: Ronald Millar, George Froeschel from the novel by Roger Bax; Producer: Clarence Brown.
CAST: Clark Gable, Gene Tierney.

Night People. March 1954. MGM
DIRECTOR-PRODUCER-SCREENPLAY: Nunnally Johnson from a story by Jed Harris and Thomas Reed.
CAST: Gregory Peck, Broderick Crawford, Anita Bjork.

Ninotchka. November 1939. MGM
DIRECTOR-PRODUCER: Ernst Lubitsch; Screenplay: Charles Brackett, Billy Wilder, Walter Reisch, story, Melchoir Lengyel.
CAST: Greta Garbo, Melvyn Douglas.

No Way Out. October 1950. Fox
DIRECTOR: Joseph L. Mankiewicz; Screenplay: Joseph L. Mankiewicz, Lesser Samuels; Producer: Darryl F. Zanuck.
CAST: Sidney Poitier, Richard Widmark, Stephen McNally, Linda Darnell.

Numbered Men. June 1930. Warners
DIRECTOR: Mervyn Leroy; Screenplay: Al Cohn, Henry McCarthy from a play by Dwight Taylor.
CAST: Conrad Nagel, Bernice Claire.

Objective Burma! February 1945. Warners
DIRECTOR: Raoul Walsh; Screenplay: Lester Cole, Ronald MacDougall, story, Alvah Bessie; Producer: Jerry Wald.
CAST: Errol Flynn, George Tobias.

Oil for the Lamps of China. April 1935. Warners
> DIRECTOR: Mervyn Leroy; Screenplay: Laird Doyle from the novel by Alice Hobart; Producer: Robert Lord.
> CAST: Pat O'Brien, Josephine Hutchinson, Jean Muir, Lyle Talbot, Arthur Byron, Donald Crisp.

On the Waterfront. October 1954. Columbia
> DIRECTOR: Elia Kazan; Screenplay: Budd Schulberg; Producer: Sam Spiegl.
> CAST: Marlon Brando, Eve Marie Saint, Karl Malden, Lee J. Cobb, Rod Steiger.

One Hundred Men and a Girl. September 1937. Universal
> DIRECTOR: Henry Koster; Screenplay: Bruce Manning, Charles Kenyon, story, Hans Kraly; Producer: Joe Pasternak, Charles R. Rogers.
> CAST: Deanna Durbin, Adolphe Menjou, Eugene Pallette, Leopold Stokowski.

One More Spring. February 1935. Fox
> DIRECTOR: Henry King; Screenplay: Edwin Burke from the novel by Robert Nathan; Producer: Winfield R. Sheehan.
> CAST: Warner Baxter, Janet Gaynor, Walter King.

One Third of a Nation. February 1939. Paramount
> DIRECTOR: Dudley Murphy; Screenplay: Oliver H. P. Garrett; Producer: Harold Orlob, Dudley Murphy.
> CAST: Sylvia Sidney, Leif Erickson, Sidney Lumet.

Our Daily Bread. August 1934. United Artists
> DIRECTOR-PRODUCER-STORY: King Vidor; Adaptation: Elizabeth Hill.
> CAST: Tom Keene, Karen Morley, John Qualen, Barbara Pepper.

The Ox-Bow Incident. May 1943. Fox
> DIRECTOR: William Wellman; Screenplay: Lamar Trotti from the novel by Walter Van Tilberg Clark; Producer: Lamar Trotti.
> CAST: Henry Fonda, Henry Morgan, Dana Andrews, Anthony Quinn, Leigh Whipper, Jane Darwell, William Eythe, Frank Conroy.

Panama Flo. January 1932. RKO
> DIRECTOR: Ralph Murphy; Story and adaptation: Garrett Fort; Producer: Charles R. Rogers.
> CAST: Helen Twelvetrees, Robert Armstrong, Charles Bickford.

The Phantom President. September 1932. Paramount
> DIRECTOR: Norman Taurog; Screenplay: Walter de Leon, Harlan Thompson.
> CAST: George M. Cohan, Claudette Colbert, Jimmy Durante.

Pilot Number Five. June 1943. MGM
> DIRECTOR: George Sidney; Screenplay: David Hertz; Producer: B. P. Fineman.
> CAST: Franchot Tone, Gene Kelly, Marsha Hunt, Howard Freeman.

Pinky. November 1949. Fox
> DIRECTOR: Elia Kazan; Screenplay: Philip Dunne, Dudley Nichols, from the novel *Quality* by Cid Ricketts Sumner; Producer: Darryl F. Zanuck.
> CAST: Jeanne Crain, Ethel Waters, William Lundigan, Ethel Barrymore.

The Power and the Glory. October 1933. Fox
> DIRECTOR: William K. Howard; Screenplay: Preston Sturges; Producer: Jesse Lasky.
> CAST: Spencer Tracy, Colleen Moore, Ralph Morgan, Helen Vinson.

The President Vanishes. November 1934. Paramount
>DIRECTOR: William Wellman; Screenplay: Carey Wilson, Cedric Worth; Producer: Walter Wanger.
>CAST: Arthur Byron, Janet Beecher, Osgood Perkins, Andy Devine, Edward Arnold, Rosalind Russell, Edward Ellis.

The President's Mystery. September 1936. Republic
>DIRECTOR: Phil Rosen; Screenplay: Nathaniel West, Lester Cole, based on "The President's Mystery" propounded by Franklin D. Roosevelt and solved by Rupert Hughes, Samuel Hopkins Adams, Anthony Abbot (pseud. of Fulton Oursler), Rita Weiman, S. S. Van Dine (pesud. of Willard Huntington Wright) and John Erskine; Producer: Nat Levine.
>CAST: Henry Wilcoxen, Betty Furness, Sidney Blackmer.

Pride of the Marines. September 1945. Warners
>DIRECTOR: Delmar Daves; Screenplay: Albert Maltz; Producer: Jerry Wald.
>CAST: John Garfield, Eleanor Parker, Dane Clark, Rosemary De Camp.

Private Worlds. March 1935. Paramount
>DIRECTOR: Gregory La Cava; Screenplay: Lynn Starling from the novel by Phyllis Bottome; Producer: Walter Wanger.
>CAST: Claudette Colbert, Charles Boyer, Joel McCrea, Joan Bennett.

Public Enemy. May 1931. Warners
>DIRECTOR: William Wellman; Screenplay: Kubec Glasmon, John Bright, adaptation, Harvey Thew.
>CAST: James Cagney, Jean Harlow, Mae Clarke, Edward Woods, Murray Kinnell.

Quick Millions. May 1931. Fox
>DIRECTOR: Rowland Brown; Dialogue: C. Terrett, R. Brown, John Wray, scenario, Courtney Terrett, Rowland Brown.
>CAST: Spencer Tracy, Marguerite Churchill, George Raft, Sally Eilers.

Rebel Without a Cause. October 1955. Warners
>DIRECTOR: Nicholas Ray; Screenplay: Stewart Stern, adaptation, Irving Shulman, story Nicholas Ray; Producer: Davis Weisbart.
>CAST: James Dean, Natalie Wood, Sal Mineo, Jim Backus, Ann Doran.

The Red Danube. October 1949. MGM
>DIRECTOR: George Sidney; Screenplay: Gina Kaus, Arthur Wimperis from a novel by Bruce Marshall; Producer: Carey Wilson.
>CAST: Ethel Barrymore, Walter Pidgeon, Peter Lawford, Angela Lansbury, Janet Leigh.

The Red Menace. August 1949. Republic
>DIRECTOR: R. G. Springsteen; Screenplay: Albert DeMond, Gerald Geraghty; Producer: Herbert J. Yates.
>CAST: Robert Rockwell, Hanne Axman.

Red Planet Mars. May 1952. United Artists
>DIRECTOR: Harry Horner; Screenplay: John L. Balderston, Anthony Veiller; Producer: Anthony Veiller.
>CAST: Peter Graves, Andrea King.

Red Salute. September 1935. United Artists
>DIRECTOR: Sidney Lanfield; Screenplay: Humphrey Pearson, Manuel Seff; Producer: Edward Small.

CAST: Barbara Stanwyck, Robert Young, Cliff Edwards.

Riffraff. December 1935. MGM

DIRECTOR: J. Walter Ruben; Screenplay: Frances Marion, H. W. Hanemann, Anita Loos; Producer: Irving Thalberg.

CAST: Spencer Tracy, Jean Harlow, Una Merkel, Joseph Calleia, J. Farrell MacDonald, Paul Hurst, Mickey Rooney.

Right Cross. October 1950. MGM

DIRECTOR: John Sturges; Screenplay: Charles Schnee; Producer: Armand Deutsch.

CAST: June Allyson, Dick Powell, Ricardo Montalban, Lionel Barrymore.

Rockabye. December 1932. RKO

DIRECTOR: George Cukor; Screenplay: Allen Wood, Eddie Moran; Producer: David O. Selznick.

CAST: Constance Bennett, Joel McCrea.

The St. Louis Kid. November 1934. Warners

DIRECTOR: Ray Enright; Screenplay: Warren Dugg, Seton I. Miller, Frederick Hazlitt Brennan; Producer: Samuel Bischoff.

CAST: James Cagney, Patricia Ellis, Allen Jenkins.

Salt of the Earth. August 1954. Independent Productions Corp.

DIRECTOR: Herbert Biberman; Screenplay: Michael Wilson; Producer: Paul Jarrico.

CAST: Juan Chacon, Rosaura Revueltas, Will Geer.

Scandal for Sale. April 1932. Universal

DIRECTOR: Russell Mack; Story: Emil Gauvreau, Adaptation and dialogue Ralph Graves.

CAST: Charles Bickford, Rose Hobart, Pat O'Brien.

Scandal Sheet. February 1931. Paramount

DIRECTOR: John Cromwell; Screenplay: Vincent Lawrence, Max Marcin.

CAST: George Bancroft, Clive Brook, Kay Francis.

The Searching Wind. August 1946. Paramount

DIRECTOR: William Dieterle; Screenplay: Lillian Hellman, from her own play; Producer: Hal Wallis.

CAST: Robert Young, Sylvia Sidney, Ann Richards, Dudley Digges, Douglas Dick.

The Secret Six. April 1931. MGM Cosmopolitan

DIRECTOR: George Hill; Screenplay: Frances Marion.

CAST: Wallace Beery, Lewis Stone, Jean Harlow, Johnny Mack Brown, Clark Gable.

Sergeant York. September 1941. Warners

DIRECTOR: Howard Hawks; Screenplay: Abem Finkel, Harry Chandler, Howard Koch, John Huston; Producer: Hal Wallis, Jesse Lasky.

CAST: Gary Cooper, Walter Brennan, George Tobias.

She Loved a Fireman. December 1937. Warners

DIRECTOR: John Farrow; Screenplay: Carlton Sand, Morton Grant; Producer: Bryan Foy.

CAST: Dick Foran, Ann Sheridan.

Slim. June 1937. Warners

DIRECTOR: Ray Enright; Screenplay: William Wister Haines; Producer: Hal Wallis.

CAST: Henry Fonda, Pat O'Brien, Margaret Lindsay, Stuart Erwin.

The Smash-Up. March 1947. Universal
> DIRECTOR: Stuart Heisler; Screenplay: John Howard Lawson, story, Dorothy Parker, Frank Cavett; Producer: Walter Wanger.
> CAST: Susan Hayward, Lee Bowman, Marsha Hunt, Eddie Albert.

The Snake Pit. November 1948. Fox
> DIRECTOR: Anatole Litvak; Screenplay: Frank Partos, Millen Brand from the novel by Mary Jane Ward; Producer: Anatole Litvak, Robert Bassler.
> CAST: Olivia de Havilland, Mark Stevens, Leo Genn, Betsy Blair.

Sofia. August 1948. Film Classics
> DIRECTOR: John Reinhardt; Screenplay: Frederick Stephani; Producer: Robert R. Presnell, Sr., John Reinhardt.
> CAST: Gene Raymond, Sigrid Gurie.

The Southerner. August 1945. United Artists
> DIRECTOR-SCREENPLAY: Jean Renoir; Producer: Robert Hakim, David L. Loew.
> CAST: Zachary Scott, Betty Field, J. Carroll Naish, Beulah Bondi, Percy Kilbride, Charles Kemper.

Spellbound. December 1945. United Artists
> DIRECTOR: Alfred Hitchcock; Screenplay: Ben Hecht, adaptation, Angus McPhail; Producer: David O. Selznick.
> CAST: Gregory Peck, Ingrid Bergman, Leo G. Carroll, Jean Aker, Rhonda Fleming.

Stand Up and Cheer. March 1934. Fox
> DIRECTOR: Hamilton McFadden; Screenplay: Lew Brown, Will Rogers, Phil Klein, Ralph Spence; Producer: Winfield Sheehan.
> CAST: Warner Baxter, Shirley Temple, Madge Evans, Arthur Byron, John Boles, Stepin Fetchit.

Steel Against the Sky. December 1941. Warners
> DIRECTOR: A. Edward Sutherland; Screenplay: Paul Gerard Smith, story, Maurice Hanline, Jesse Lasky, Jr.; Producer: Edmund Grainger.
> CAST: Lloyd Nolan, Alexis Smith.

Street Scene. August 1931. United Artists
> DIRECTOR: King Vidor; Screenplay: Elmer Rice from his own play; Producer: Samuel Goldwyn.
> CAST: Sylvia Sidney, William Collier, Jr., Estelle Taylor, David Landau, Max Montor, Beulah Bondi, John Qualen.

The Struggle. December 1931. United Artists
> DIRECTOR: D. W. Griffith; Screenplay: Anita Loos, John Emerson.
> CAST: Hal Skelly, Zita Johann.

Sullivan's Travels. December 1941. Paramount
> DIRECTOR-SCREENWRITER: Preston Sturges; Producer: Paul Jones.
> CAST: Joel McCrea, Veronica Lake, William Demarest, Robert Warwick, Franklin Pangborn, Porter Hall, Robert Greig, Eric Blore.

Susan Lennox: Her Rise and Fall. October 1931. MGM
> DIRECTOR-PRODUCER: Robert Z. Leonard; Adaptation Wanda Tuchock from the novel by David Graham Phillips, dialogue Zelda Sears and Edith Fitzgerald.
> CAST: Greta Garbo, Clark Gable.

The Talk of the Town. August 1942. Columbia
> DIRECTOR-PRODUCER: George Stevens; Screenplay: Sidney Buchman, Irwin Shaw, story, Sydney Harmon.

CAST: Ronald Colman, Cary Grant, Jean Arthur, Edgar Buchanan, Rex Ingram, Glenda Farrell.

Taxi. January 1932. Warners

DIRECTOR: Roy Del Ruth; Screenplay: John Bright, Kubec Glasmon.

CAST: James Cagney, Loretta Young, David Landau, Guy Kibbee.

They Drive by Night. August 1940. Warners

DIRECTOR: Raoul Walsh; Screenplay: Jerry Wald, Richard Macauley, from a novel by A. I. Bezzerides; Producer: Mark Hellinger.

CAST: George Raft, Ann Sheridan, Humphrey Bogart, Ida Lupino, Roscoe Karns, Alan Hale.

They Live by Night. June 1948. RKO

DIRECTOR: Nicholas Ray; Screenplay: Charles Schnee from the novel *Thieves Like Us* by Edward Anderson; Producer: John Houseman.

CAST: Farley Granger, Cathy O'Connell, Howard Da Silva, Jay C. Flippen.

They Made Me a Criminal. January 1939. Warners

DIRECTOR: Busby Berkeley; Screenplay: Sig Herzig; Producer: Benjamin Glazer.

CAST: John Garfield, Claude Rains, the Dead End Kids, Gloria Dickson.

They Won't Forget. October 1937. Warners

DIRECTOR-PRODUCER: Mervyn Leroy; Screenplay: Robert Rossen, Aben Kandel from the book *Death in the Deep South* by Ward Greene.

CAST: Claude Rains, Lana Turner, Allyn Joslyn, Edward Norris, Clinton Rosemond.

This Day and Age. August 1933. Paramount

DIRECTOR-PRODUCER: Cecil B. DeMille; Screenplay: Bartlett Cormack.

CAST: Charles Bickford, Richard Cromwell.

Three Comrades. June 1938. MGM

DIRECTOR: Frank Borzage; Screenplay: F. Scott Fitzgerald, Edward Paramore; Producer: Joseph L. Mankiewicz.

CAST: Margaret Sullavan, Robert Taylor, Robert Young, Franchot Tone, Lionel Atwill, Henry Hull.

Tiger Shark. September 1932. Warners

DIRECTOR: Howard Hawks; Screenplay: Wells Root.

CAST: Edward G. Robinson, Richard Arlen, Zita Johann.

Till the End of Time. June 1946. RKO

DIRECTOR: Edward Dmytryk; Screenplay: Allen Rivkin; Producer: Dore Schary.

CAST: Dorothy McGuire, Guy Madison, Robert Mitchum.

Tobacco Road. March 1941. Fox

DIRECTOR: John Ford; Screenplay: Nunnally Johnson from the novel by Erskine Caldwell and play by James Kirkland; Producer: Darryl F. Zanuck.

CAST: Charley Grapewin, Marjorie Rambeau, William Tracy, Elizabeth Patterson, Gene Tierney, Dana Andrews, Ward Bond.

Tomorrow the World. December 1944. United Artists

DIRECTOR: Leslie Fenten; Screenplay: Ring Lardner, Jr., Leopold Atlas; Producer: Lester Cowan.

CAST: Fredric March, Bette Field, Skip Homeier.

Truck Busters. February 1943. Warners
>   DIRECTOR: B. Reeves Eason; Screenplay: Robert E. Kent, Raymond L. Schrock.
>   CAST: Richard Travis, Virginia Christine.

Twenty Thousand Years in Sing Sing. January 1933. Warners
>   DIRECTOR: Michael Curtiz; Screenplay: Courtney Terrett, Robert Lord, Wilson Mizner, Brown Holmes, based on the book by Warden Lewis E. Lawes; Producer: Raymond Griffith.
>   CAST: Spencer Tracy, Bette Davis, Lyle Talbot, Arthur Byron, Grant Mitchell.

Walk a Crooked Mile. September 1948. Columbia
>   DIRECTOR: Gordon Douglas; Screenplay: George Bruce, story, Bertram Millhauser; Producer: Grant Whytock.
>   CAST: Louis Hayward, Dennis O'Keefe.

Walk East on Beacon. March 1952. Columbia
>   DIRECTOR: Alfred Werker; Screenplay: Leo Rosten, additional writing Virginia Shaler, Leonard Heidman, Emmett Murphy, suggested by "The Crime of the Century" by J. Edgar Hoover from *The Reader's Digest*; Producer: Louis de Rochemont.
>   CAST: George Murphy, Finlay Currie.

Washington Masquerade. July 1932. MGM
>   DIRECTOR: Charles Brabin; Screenplay: John Meehan, Samuel Blythe.
>   CAST: Lionel Barrymore, Karen Morley, C. Henry Gordon.

Washington Merry-Go-Round. September 1932. Columbia
>   DIRECTOR: James Cruze; Screenplay: Jo Swerling, story, Maxwell Anderson; Producer: Walter Wanger.
>   CAST: Lee Tracy, Alan Dinehart.

Watch on the Rhine. September 1943. Warners
>   DIRECTOR: Herman Shumlin; Screenplay: Dashiell Hammett from the play by Lillian Hellman; Producer: Hal Wallis.
>   CAST: Paul Lukas, Bette Davis, Geraldine Fitzgerald, George Coulouris, Beulah Bondi.

The Well. September 1951. United Artists
>   DIRECTOR: Leo Popkin; Russell Rouse; Screenplay and Producer: Russell Rouse, Clarence Greene.
>   CAST: Richard Rober, Maidie Norman.

The Wet Parade. March 1932. MGM
>   DIRECTOR: Victor Fleming; Screenplay: John Lee Mahin from the novel by Upton Sinclair.
>   CAST: Walter Huston, Robert Young, Jimmy Durante, Lewis Stone, Neil Hamilton.

The Whip Hand. October 1951. RKO
>   DIRECTOR: William Cameron Menzies; Screenplay: George Bricker, Frank L. Moss; Producer: Lewis Rachmil.
>   CAST: Carla Baldenda, Elliot Reid, Raymond Burr.

The Whistle at Eaton Falls. August 1951. Columbia
>   DIRECTOR: Robert Siodmak; Screenplay: Lemist Esler, Virginia Shaler; Producer: Louis de Rochemont.
>   CAST: Lloyd Bridges, Dorothy Gish, Murray Hamilton, Russell Hardie.

White Bondage. June 1937. Warners
> DIRECTOR: Nick Grinde; Screenplay: Antony Coldeway.
> CAST: Jean Muir, Gordon Oliver, Harry Davenport.

Wild Boys of the Road. September 1933. Warners
> DIRECTOR: William Wellman; Screenplay: Earl Baldwin, story, Daniel O'Hearn.
> CAST: Frankie Darro, Edwin Phillips, Dorothy Coonan, Grant Mitchell, Robert Barratt, Charley Grapewin.

The Wild One. January 1954. Columbia
> DIRECTOR: Laszlo Benedek; Screenplay: John Paxton, story, Frank Rooney; Producer: Stanley Kramer.
> CAST: Marlon Brando, Mary Murphy, Robert Keith, Lee Marvin.

Wilson. August 1944. Fox
> DIRECTOR: Henry King; Screenplay: Lamar Trotti; Producer: Darryl F. Zanuck.
> CAST: Alexander Knox, Geraldine Fitzgerald, Sir Cedric Hardwicke, Charles Coburn.

Wings for the Eagle. July 1942. Warners
> DIRECTOR: Lloyd Bacon; Screenplay: Byron Morgan, B. H. Orkow, additional dialogue, Richard Macaulay; Producer: Robert Lord.
> CAST: Ann Sheridan, Dennis Morgan, Jack Carson.

The Working Man. April 1933. Warners
> DIRECTOR: John Adolfi; Screenplay: Charles Kenyon, Maude T. Howell; Producer: Lucien Hubbard.
> CAST: George Arliss, Bette Davis.

The World Changes. September 1933. Warners
> DIRECTOR: Mervyn Leroy; Screenplay: Edward Chodorov, story, Sheridan Gibney.
> CAST: Paul Muni, Mary Astor, Aline MacMahon, Guy Kibbee, Margaret Lindsay, Jean Muir.

A Yank in the R.A.F. October 1941. Fox
> DIRECTOR: Henry King; Screenplay: Darrell Ware, Karl Turnberg, story, Melville Crossman (pseud. of Darryl F. Zanuck); Producer: Louis F. Edleman.
> CAST: Tyrone Power, Betty Grable.

You and Me. June 1938. Paramount
> DIRECTOR-PRODUCER: Fritz Lang; Screenplay: Virginia Van Upp, story Norman Krasna.
> CAST: Sylvia Sidney, George Raft, Robert Cummings, Harry Carey, Barton Maclane, Roscoe Karns.

You Can't Take It with You. September 1938. Columbia
> DIRECTOR-PRODUCER: Frank Capra; Screenplay: Robert Riskin from the play by George S. Kaufman and Moss Hart.
> CAST: James Stewart, Jean Arthur, Lionel Barrymore, Edward Arnold, Spring Byington, Donald Meek, Mischa Auer.

You Only Live Once. January 1937. United Artists
> DIRECTOR: Fritz Lang; Screenplay: Gene Towne, Graham Baker; Producer: Walter Wanger.
> CAST: Henry Fonda, Sylvia Sidney, Barton MacLane, William Gargan.

Index

Across the Pacific, 220
Action in the North Atlantic, 221, 237, 239
Adventures of Robin Hood, The, 147
Agee, James, 208, 238
Air Force, 153, 220, 237
Al Capone, 154
Alcoholism, 10, 228, 257–259
Alexander, Ross, 95
Allen, Robert, 36
All Quiet on the Western Front, 201
All the King's Men, 193, 195–197, 293
Allyson, June, 253
Altman, Robert, 154
Ameche, Don, 213
American Madness, An, 48–50, 98, 233
American Romance, An, 262–263
Anderson, Edward, 146–147, 153
Anderson, Judith, 18
Anderson, Lindsay, 266
Andrews, Dana, 133, 231
Angels Wash Their Faces, 144
Angels with Dirty Faces, 136, 141–143
À Nous La Liberté, 117
Anticommunism, 104–105, 172, 242, 262, 284–288; in the Hollywood film, 75–77, 203, 208–209, 211, 289–293; effect of on the problem film, 293–297
Anti-Semitism, 171, 191, 211, 215–217, 233, 235–242
Are We Civilized?, 208–209
Arise My Love, 214
Arliss, George, 51
Arms, Russell, 222
Arnold, Edward, 102, 125, 183, 185, 187, 272
Arrowsmith, 156
Arthur, Jean, 112, 182
Asch, Sholem, 238
As the Earth Turns, 58

Atwill, Lionel, 210
Auer, Mischa, 69, 99
Ayres, Lew, 21

Baby Face Nelson, 154
Back Street, 21
Bad Day at Black Rock, 253
Badlands, 154
Bainter, Fay, 222
Baldwin, C. B., 309
Ballyhoo (magazine), 36
Bancroft, George, 18, 43
Bandit King, 10
Bank Defaulter, 10
Bank failures, 49
Bankhead, Tallulah, 23, 24
Barrat, Robert, 75, 161
Barrie, Wendy, 140
Barrymore, Ethel, 249
Barrymore, John, 31–32, 76, 236
Barrymore, Lionel, 55, 102, 270, 272
Barthelmess, Richard, 52, 76, 84, 122, 158
Bartholomew, Freddie, 138
Bataan, 221, 245
Baxter, Warner, 87, 96
Beast of the City, 66–67, 71
Beauty for Sale, 45
Beavers, Louise, 245
Beery, Wallace, 17, 27
Beggar on Horseback, 11
Beloved, 58
Belton, John, 282
Bendiner, Robert, 40
Bennett, Constance, 21, 22
Bergman, Andrew, 23, 35
Bergman, Ingrid, 260
Berkeley, Busby, 83
Bessie, Alvah, 237
Best Years of Our Lives, The, 230–233

Biberman, Herbert, 254–255, 267, 293, 295, 316
Bickford, Charles, 43, 67
Big business: as portrayed by Hollywood, 47–52, 55–56, 180–181, 185–187, 193–194, 198, 201; populist attitudes toward, 47; and the New Deal, 64
Big Heat, The, 154
Big House, The, 26–28
Big Jim McLain, 289, 291–293
Birth of a Nation, The, 242
Black Fury, 105–109, 113, 264
Black Legion (organization), 175–178
Black Legion, 82, 109–110, 113, 166, 175–178
Blacklisting, 267, 285–287, 293–295
Blair, Betsy, 260
Blessed Event, 31, 42
Blockade, 205–207, 223, 314
Blondell, Joan, 33, 82, 83
Blonde Venus, 22, 24–25
Blondie Johnson, 82
Blood Money, 18
Blood on the Sun, 220
Bluestone, George, 131
Boardman, Eleanor, 59
Body and Soul, 238, 268, 273–278, 304
Bogart, Humphrey, 8, 109, 114, 137, 139, 145, 153, 177, 220, 285, 294
Bogle, Donald, 242
Bondi, Beulah, 271
Bonnie and Clyde, 154, 298
Bonus March, 56, 78–79
Boom Town, 114
Bordertown, 158, 161–162, 253
Born to Love, 21
Born Yesterday, 197–199
Borzage, Frank, 54, 96–97, 209–212
Bottom of the Bottle, The, 259
Bow, Clara, 10
Boyer, Charles, 208
Boy Slaves, 138
Boys of the Streets, 139
Boys Town, 136, 143–144, 236
Brady, Alice, 99
Brando, Marlon, 145, 231, 265–266, 297
Brandon, Henry, 110
Breaking Point, The, 242
Breen, Joseph, 211
Brennan, Walter, 182
Brian, David, 174, 250
Brick Foxhole, The (novel), 239
Bridges, Lloyd, 246, 263
Bright Victory, 231, 252
Brisbane, Arthur, 40
Brodie, Steve, 245
Broken Arrow, 252
Broken Lullaby, 201

"Brother, Can You Spare a Dime?" 79, 83
Broun, Heywood, 40
Browder, Earl, 72
Brown, Rowland, 18–19
Bullets or Ballots, 135
Bureau of Motion Pictures of the Office of War Information, 263
Burglar Bill, 10
Butch Cassidy and the Sundance Kid, 154
Byron, Arthur, 29, 73

Cabin in the Cotton, 82, 122–124, 133–134, 311, 313
Cabot, Bruce, 178
Cagney, James, 3, 8, 17, 18, 86, 93, 114, 135, 136, 142–143, 153, 235
Caine Mutiny, The, 293–294
Caldwell, Erskine, 132–133
Calleia, Joseph, 108
Campbell, Russell, 80, 86, 87
Capone, Al, 67
Capra, Frank, 2, 48–50, 57, 61, 98, 102, 166–167, 179–190, 198, 268–273, 278, 303
Carey, MacDonald, 175
Carillo, Leo, 206
Carnegie, Andrew, 17
Carradine, John, 129
Carroll, Madeleine, 204, 206
Carter, Ben, 245
Casablanca, 220
Case of Sergeant Grischa, The, 201
Castle on the Hudson, 28
Catholic War Veterans (newspaper), 282
Cavanagh, Paul, 21
Censorship, 20
Cermak, Anton, 87
Chacon, Juan, 254
Chain gangs, 308; as portrayed by Hollywood, 19, 26–27, 29–30, 79–81, 301–303
Chalmers, David, 177
Chaney, Lon, Jr., 244
Chaplin, Charles, 7, 11, 114–120, 215–218, 237, 268, 278–283, 293, 295
Chaplin, Michael, 295
China: invasion by Japanese, 203
China, 220
China Syndrome, The, 298
Christopher Strong, 21
Churchill, Berton, 122
Citadel, The, 155–158
Citizen Kane, 193–195
City Across the River, 145
Civilian Conservation Corps (CCC), 72, 91
Clair, Rene, 117, 120
Clark, Dane, 237
Clarke, Mae, 18
Clive, Colin, 21
Cobb, Lee J., 264

Coburn, Charles, 112
Coffee, Lenore, 147
Cohan, George M., 38, 40
Cohn, Harry, 2
Colbert, Claudette, 214
Collier, William, Jr., 236
Collins, Ray, 194
Colman, Ronald, 156, 173
Columbia Pictures, 1, 2, 138
Come Fill My Cup, 259
Committee for the First Amendment, 285
Common Clay, 21
Communist Control Act, 285
Communist Party, 65, 72, 105, 205, 284, 286–288, 294; in the Hollywood film, 111, 118, 120, 288, 290–293, 295
Confessions of a Nazi Spy, 212–213, 219, 289
Confidential Agent, 208
Conklin, Chester, 54, 117
Conquerors, The, 51
Conspirator, 291–292
Coogan, Jackie, 119
Cook, Donald, 17
Cooke, Alistair, 288
Cool Hand Luke, 154
Coolidge, Calvin, 10, 37, 38
Cooper, Gary, 98, 181, 182, 184, 204, 208, 215, 285
Cooper, Jackie, 139
Cooperative farms, 61–63, 124–125, 130, 309
Corey, Jeff, 231
Correll, Mady, 280
Cortez, Ricardo, 42
Cosmopolitan Pictures, 71, 87
Cotton, Joseph, 194
Coughlin, Father, 65, 72, 165, 190
Counsellor-at-Law, 76, 236
Crain, Jeanne, 247–248
Crash Dive, 245
Crawford, Broderick, 193, 197
Crime School, 137
Criminal Code, 27
Crisp, Donald, 111
Crooked Banker, 10
Crosby, Bing, 312
Crossfire, 233, 235, 238–239
Crowd, The, 11, 58–61
Crowther, Bosley, 71, 114, 138
Cruze, James, 11
Cry Havoc, 220
Cummings, Robert, 259
Curtis, Alan, 213

Daily Variety (newspaper), 285
Daniell, Henry, 216
Dark Horse, The, 31, 36–39

Darnell, Linda, 251
Darro, Frankie, 92, 93, 136
Darwell, Jane, 126
Da Silva, Buddy, 258
Da Silva, Howard, 153, 258
Daughter of Shanghai, 203
Davies, Joseph, 288
Davis, Bette, 3, 37, 161
Dawn Patrol, The, 201
Dead End (film), 111, 113, 136–143, 145, 269
Dead End (play), 139
"Dead End Kids," 136–138, 141–144, 147–148
Dean, James, 145, 154, 297
Defenders, The (television series), 298
Defiant Ones, The, 252
DeHavilland, Olivia, 260
DeMille, Cecil B., 10, 67–69, 137
Deming, Barbara, 227–228, 268
Democratic Party, 37, 39, 77, 84
Dennis, Lawrence, 165
Denny, Reginald, 206
Derek, John, 145
De Rochement, Louis, 262
Desperate Encounter, A, 10
Devil and Miss Jones, The, 111–113
Devil Is a Sissy, The, 138–139
Dick, Douglas, 222
Dickson, Gloria, 148
Dieterle, William, 201, 207, 223
Dietrich, Marlene, 22, 24
Digges, Dudley, 136, 159, 223
Dinehart, Alan, 55
Dingle, Charles, 173
Disney, Walt, 51, 105, 285
Dix, Richard, 29
Dmytryk, Edward, 293, 294
Dr. Ehrlich's Magic Bullet, 156
Doctor's Diary, A, 155
Dog's Life, A, 116
Donat, Robert, 156
Donlevy, Brian, 262
Doughgirls, 222
Douglas, Melvyn, 236, 289
Dow, Peggy, 231
Dragon Seed, 221
Dru, Joanne, 197
Dumbrille, Douglas, 101
Dunne, Irene, 21
Durbin, Deanna, 102
Durgnat, Raymond, 62, 101, 117
Dust Be My Destiny, 148–151, 227

Earth and High Heaven, 238
Easiest Way, The, 22
East of Eden, 297
East River (book), 238

Easy Rider, 154

Easy Street, 116

Economic breakdown: as portrayed by Hollywood, 21–22, 35, 48–51, 54, 56; populist interpretation of, 46–47

Edge of Darkness, 221

Edge of the City, 252

Edwards, James, 231, 245

Eisenstein, Sergei, 4, 62, 303

Ellis, Edward, 73, 176

Elsom, Isabel, 280

End Poverty in California (EPIC), 77

Epstein, Julius, 147

Erikson, Leif, 144

Escape, 213, 290

Evans, Walker, 121

Ex-Convict, The, 10–11

Ex-convicts: discrimination against (as portrayed by Hollywood), 10, 135, 149–152, 160

Exiled to Shanghai, 203

Face in the Crowd, A, 297

Factories in the Field (book), 172

Fairbanks, Douglas, 17

Faithless, 22–23

Fallen Sparrow, The, 208

Family: effect of the Depression on, 21, 24; sanctity of, 22, 25

Farber, Manny, 247

Farmer, Francis, 261

Farmers, *see* Rural life

Farm Security Administration (FSA): photographs, 121, 128

Farnum, William, 208

Farrell, Glenda, 80

Fascism, *see* International fascism; Native fascism

Fay, James, 282

Federal Bureau of Investigation (FBI), 72, 212, 267

Federal Theater Project, 144

Feminism, 25

Ferguson, Otis, 112, 314

Ferrer, Jose, 294

Ferrer, Mel, 247

Fetchit, Stepin, 243

Fiedler, Leslie, 292

Field, Betty, 219, 259

Fields, W. C., 8

Film Noir, 8

Fitzgerald, F. Scott, 210–211

Five Star Final, 42–44

Flight for Freedom, 220

Flippen, Jay C., 153

Flowing Gold, 114

Flynn, Errol, 8, 147, 237

Focus (book), 238

Fonda, Henry, 113, 126, 149, 173, 206

Fontaine, Joan, 233

Footlight Parade, 86–87

Foran, Dick, 95, 110

Force of Evil, 268, 273–278, 293, 297, 304

Ford, John, 111–112, 126, 130, 132–133, 250, 303

Foreign Correspondent, 214

"Forgotten Man": as Depression symbol, 79; as portrayed by Hollywood, 83–87, 92, 95–96, 99–100, 160, 223, 228

For Whom the Bell Tolls, 207–208

Four Daughters, 147

Four Sons, 213–214

Fox, Sidney, 33

Francis, Robert, 294

Franco, Francisco, 205, 208

Frank, Leo, 171

Freeman, Howard, 192

From This Day Forward, 233–234

Front Page, The (film), 31, 41–43, 308

Front Page, The (play), 42

Fury, 165–173, 304

Gable, Clark, 3, 42, 114, 157

Gabriel Over the White House, 68–73, 187, 201–202

Gangsters: as portrayed by Hollywood, 17–20, 22–23, 28, 31, 41–42, 69–70, 135, 140, 142–143, 147, 153–154, 276–277; as cultural heroes, 146

Garbo, Greta, 22, 289

Garfield, John, 28, 114, 144, 147–151, 153, 208, 220, 227–229, 238, 240–241, 268

Gargan, William, 150

Gaynor, Janet, 96

General Died at Dawn, The, 203–206

Genn, Leo, 260

Genre film, x, 3–4, 16

Gentleman's Agreement, 235, 238–241, 248

Gentlemen Are Born, 94–95

German-American Bund, 212–213

Gerson, Betty Lou, 290

Gessner, Robert, 160–161

Gilbert, John, 15

Giroux, Robert, 168

Gleason, James, 182, 183

G-Men, 135

Goddard, Paulette, 118, 218

God Is My Co-Pilot, 220

Go for Broke, 253

Going My Way, 312

Golddiggers of 1933, 82–83, 86

Golden Harvest, 125

Gold Rush, The, 11

Goldwyn, Samuel, 111, 136, 139, 141, 230, 238

Gomez, Thomas, 275

Gone with the Wind, 242
Good Earth, The, 203
Gorcey, Leo, 144
Gordon, C. Henry, 55, 70, 155
Gough, Lloyd, 274
Granger, Farley, 153
Grant, Cary, 24, 102, 173, 220
Granville, Bonita, 219
Grapes of Wrath, The (film), 122, 125–134, 172, 269, 296, 303, 311
Grapes of Wrath, The (novel), 121, 126–127, 130–132
Grapewin, Charley, 133
Great Dictator, The, 215–218, 220, 237, 278, 280–281
Great McGinty, The, 302
Great O'Malley, The, 147
Greed, 11
Green, Harry, 235
Green, Paul, 311
Greenleaf, Raymond, 197
Griffith, D. W., 209, 242, 257
Griffith, Richard, 45
Guess Who's Coming to Dinner? 252
Guilty of Treason, 290
Guthrie, Woody, xi, 121, 146–147

Hail the Conquering Hero, 302
Hall, Huntz, 144
Hall, Porter, 204
Hallelujah! 58, 242–243
Hallelujah, I'm a Bum, 53–54
Halop, Billy, 140
Hangmen Also Die, 221
Harburg, E. Y., 79, 87, 88
Harlow, Jean, 106
Hart, Moss, 241
Havoc, June, 240
Hawks, Howard, 19, 201, 308
Hayes, Helen, 156
Haynes, Daniel, 59, 243
Hays Office, 16, 25, 211, 312–313
Hayward, Susan, 259
Hearst, William Randolph, 65, 71, 193–194
Hearts of Dixie, 242–243
Hecht, Ben and MacArthur, Charles, 41
Hellman, Lillian, 223
Hell's Highway, 19, 27–29, 244
Hell's Kitchen, 137–138
Henry, Thomas R., 78
Hepburn, Katharine, 21, 191
Hernandez, Juano, 174, 250
Heroes for Sale, 50, 75–76, 84–86, 88, 92, 94, 98, 158, 160
Hersholt, Jean, 157
Higham, Charles, 212–213
High Noon, x
His Girl Friday, 308

Hiss, Alger, 284, 292
Hitchcock, Alfred, 214, 221, 260
Hitler, Adolf, 68, 70, 179, 187, 190, 193, 194, 208, 211, 213–216, 220, 222, 288
Hitler Gang, The, 220
Hitler's Children, 219
Hoboes: as portrayed by Hollywood, 53–55
Hoffman, Margaret, 280
Hohl, Arthur, 159
Holden, William, 198
Holiday, 102
Holliday, Judy, 198
Hollywood Formula, xi, 2–8, 11, 15, 17, 34, 35, 62, 64, 81, 82, 114, 145, 149, 151–152, 172, 180, 193, 256; reactionary implications of, 71; and the social problem film, 88, 299, 303–305
Hollywood Reporter (newspaper), 77, 287
Hollywood Ten, 285, 293, 294
Holocaust (television show), 298
Holt, Tim, 219
Homeier, Skip, 219
Home of the Brave, 231, 233, 242, 245–247
Homes, Geoffrey, 255
Hooded Americanism, 177
Hoover, Herbert, 36, 39–40, 48–50, 53, 57, 69, 72, 84
Hoovervilles, 36, 54; as portrayed by Hollywood, 96, 128–129, 131, 172, 303
House of Connally, The (play), 311
House Un-American Activities Committee (HUAC), 242, 267, 284–289, 292–297
Howard, William K., 52
Howard-Wheeler Indian Rights Bill, 161
Howe, James Wong, 277
How Green Was My Valley, 111–113
Hughes, Robert, 266
Hull, Henry, 210
Hunt, Marsha, 192
Hurley, Patrick J., 65
Hurst, Paul, 107
Huston, Walter, 48, 67, 69, 71, 288
Hylton, Richard, 248

I Am a Fugitive from a Chain Gang, 26–27, 29–30, 79–83, 84, 86, 88, 92, 147–148, 151, 244, 269, 282, 302–304
I Believed in You, 105
I'd Rather Be Right (play), 40
I'll Cry Tomorrow, 259
I Married a Communist, 290–291
Imitation of Life, 245
Ingram, Rex, 245
Insanity, *see* Mental illness
International fascism, xi, 57, 113, 189, 190–193, 200, 202–223, 290, 304
International Settlement, 203
Intruder in the Dust, 174–175, 250–251

Ireland, John, 196
Iron Curtain, 289, 291
Is My Face Red?, 42, 44
Isolationism, 201–203, 205, 207, 215, 218, 220, 222–223, 288
It Can't Happen Here (novel), 165, 187, 312–313
It's a Wonderful Life, 268–273
It's Tough to Be Famous, 45
I Was a Communist for the FBI, 289–292

Jackie Robinson Story, The, 252
Jackson, Charles, 258
Jacobs, Lewis, 10, 17, 58
Jaffe, Sam, 241
Jagger, Dean, 292
Jail Bird, The, 10
Japanese War Bride, 253
Jarman, Claude, Jr., 174, 250
Jarrico, Paul, 254, 293, 295
Jenkins, Allen, 29
Jennings, DeWitt, 97
Jesse James, 147
Jim Thorpe—All-American, 253
Joe Louis Story, The, 252
Joe Smith, American, 221
John Meade's Woman, 125
Johnson, Nunnally, 126, 132
Johnson, Van, 294
Johnston, Eric, 285–286, 296
Jolson, Al, 53
Jones, Dorothy, 287, 289, 296
Jordan, Bobby, 138
Journalism: trends during the thirties, 40; as portrayed by Hollywood, 40–45, 151, 170, 174–175, 194–195, 255
Journey's End, 201
Juarez, x
Juvenile delinquency: as portrayed by Hollywood, 135–145

Kael, Pauline, 289
Karloff, Boris, 42
Kay, Karyn, 160–161
Kazan, Elia, 265–266, 293–294, 297
Keene, Tom, 62
Keeper of the Flame, 190–192, 221
Kelly, Gene, 192, 285
Kemper, Charles, 134
Kennedy, Arthur, 231
Kibbee, Guy, 33, 37
Kid, The, 116, 119
Killers, The, 154
King, Walter, 96
King in New York, A, 293–296
Kingsley, Sidney, 139
Kings Row, 259–260
Kippen, Mannert, 288

Kirkland, James, 132
Kiss Me Deadly, 154
Kiss of Death, 153
Knock on Any Door, 145, 154
Knox, Alexander, 222
Kohler, Fred, 75
Kramer, Stanley, 242
Krims, Milton, 212
Kuhn, Fritz, 213

Labor unions, *see* Unionism
La Cava, Gregory, 98, 102
Ladd, Alan, 220
Ladies of the Big House, 27
Lady in the Dark, 259
Laissez-faire, 36, 50, 53, 63, 64, 65, 100–101
Landau, David, 32
Lane, Charles, 182
Lane, Priscilla, 148
Lang, Fritz, 117, 120, 149–154, 167–172, 214–215, 304, 313
Langdon, Harry, 54
Lange, Dorothea, 121
Last Flight, The, 201
Last Mile, The, 27
Last Train from Madrid, The, 205
Latham, Aaron, 210
Laurents, Arthur, 242
Lawless, The, 174–175, 253–256, 293
Lawson, John Howard, 206–207
Lawyer Man, 31–35, 57
League of Nations, 200, 222
Lederer, Francis, 213
Lee, Canada, 274
Lee, Russell, 121
Legal profession: as portrayed by Hollywood, 32–35, 76
Legion of Terror, 166, 175, 177–178
Leiber, Fritz, 156
Leisen, Mitchell, 214
Let Us Now Praise Famous Men (book), 121
Leuchtenberg, William E., 53, 66, 72, 201
Levene, Sam, 237, 238, 239
Levin, Meyer, 186
Lewis, Sinclair, 165, 187, 313
Liberty (magazine), 101
Life (film), 116
Lifeboat, 221
Life of Emile Zola, The, x, 236
Life of Jimmy Dolan, The, 58
Light, Robert, 95
Limelight, 282, 295
Lindsay, Margaret, 95, 113, 161
Lippmann, Walter, 40
Little Caesar, 16–17
Little Man, What Now?, 75–76, 97–98, 105, 209–210
Little Tough Guys, 144

Little Tough Guys in Society, 144
Lodge, Henry Cabot, 200
Lombard, Carole, 99
Long, Huey, 65, 72, 165, 187, 190–193
Looking Forward, 87
Los Angeles *Times*, 105
Losey, Joseph, 255, 293
Lost Boundaries, 247–249
Lost Weekend, The, 257–259
Lou Grant (television series), 298
Love Is a Racket, 45
Lovejoy, Frank, 246
Loy, Myrna, 157, 230
Lubitsch, Ernst, 10, 201
Lucky Jordan, 220
Lukas, Paul, 213, 220
Lumet, Sidney, 144, 297
Lupino, Ida, 312
Lynd, Robert and Helen M., 46–47

M, 172
McCarey, Leo, 285
McCarthy, Joseph, xi, 199, 284
McCarthyism, xi, 297
McCrea, Joel, ix, 21, 139, 214
MacDonald, J. Farrell, 106
McGuire, Dorothy, 232, 240
McHugh, Frank, 86
McKinney, Nina Mae, 243, 249
MacLane, Barton, 108, 150
MacMahon, Aline, 86
MacMurray, Fred, 294
McNally, Stephen, 251, 262
McWilliams, Carey, 172
Madison, Guy, 232
Main, Marjorie, 140
Mainwaring, Daniel, 255
Malden, Karl, 264
Male Animal, The, 221
Maltz, Albert, 106–108
Man Hunt, 214–215
Man I Married, The, 213
Mankiewicz, Joseph L., 210–211
Man on a Tightrope, 290
Manpower, 114
Man's Castle, A, 53–54, 96–97, 303
Man Who Dared, The, 87
March, Fredric, 219, 230, 233, 257
Marvin, Lee, 154
Marx Brothers, x, 8
Mary Burns, Fugitive, 147
Massacre, 82, 158–162, 253
Mast, Gerald, 187
Mayer, Louis B., 2, 7, 77, 171, 210–211, 212, 285
Mayo, Virginia, 232
Mayor of Hell, 136–137, 159, 235

Medical profession: as portrayed by Hollywood, 155–158
Meeker, George, 98
Meet John Doe, 48, 166, 180–185, 187–190, 196, 198, 269, 272
Men, The, 231
Men in White, 155, 157
Menjou, Adolphe, 23, 31, 41, 285
Mental illness, 228, 259–261
Merriam, Frank, 77
Metro-Goldwyn-Mayer (MGM), 1, 5–6, 7, 66, 105, 114, 136, 138–139, 143–144, 155, 169, 212, 238, 257, 287, 312–313
Metropolis, 117
Middletown in Transition (book), 46
Milestone, Lewis, 201, 203, 206, 308
Milland, Ray, 257
Miller, Arthur, 238
Miller, Dorie, 245
Miller, Sidney, 236
Miser's Fate, 10
Miser's Hoard, The, 10
Mission to Moscow, 221, 288
Mr. Deeds Goes to Town, 48, 98–101, 180–185, 269
Mr. Lucky, 220
Mr. Smith Goes to Washington, 48, 49, 57, 166, 180–188, 269, 272
Mrs. Miniver, 221, 222
Mitchell, Grant, 50, 130
Modern Hero, A, 52
Modern Times, 114–120, 216, 278, 280
Mok, Michael, 311
Monogram Pictures, 139
Monsieur Verdoux, 268, 279–282, 293, 295, 297, 303
Montalban, Ricardo, 253
Montgomery, Douglass, 76, 97
Montgomery, Robert, 23, 24
Montor, Max, 76
Moonlight and Pretzels, 87
More the Merrier, The, 222
Morgan, Frank, 211
Morley, Karen, 56, 107
Morris, Chester, 27
Mortal Storm, The, 209, 211–213, 236–237
Motion Picture Association of America, 285
Moulder, Rep. Morgan M., 286
Mouthpiece, The, 31–35, 57
Mowbray, Alan, 97
Muni, Paul, x, 18, 27, 51, 80, 105, 156, 158
Murray, James, 59
Muse, Clarence, 243
Mussolini, Benito, 65, 72
My Man and I, 253
My Man Godfrey, 98–101
My Son John, 290–292

Naish, J. Carroll, 106, 134
Nash, Marilyn, 280
Nathan, Robert, 96
Nation, The (magazine), 74, 169, 207, 311
National Labor Relations Board, 104
National Recovery Administration (NRA), 87, 91, 94
Native fascism: as portrayed by Hollywood, 66, 68–71, 73–74, 110, 165–167, 172, 175–178, 180–181, 186–198
Nazi Party, 97, 172, 208–214, 217, 219–221, 237, 288–290
Nazism, 176, 193, 208, 210–211, 213
Neal, Claude, 166
Need of Gold, The, 10
Never Let Me Go, 289
New Deal, xi, 16, 46, 63, 64, 72, 104, 304; as portrayed by Warner Brothers, 84, 86, 91–92, 94–95, 109, 155, 158–161; and the Hollywood film, 88, 98, 101–102, 141; economic policies, 91–92; agricultural policies, 125, 309; foreign policy, 200–202; as target of the right wing, 284, 288, 292
"New Deal and the Analogue of War, The," 75
New Republic (magazine), 314
New York *Times*, 52, 145
Nichols, Dudley, 207
Night People, 290
Ninotchka, 289
Nolan, Doris, 102
None But the Lonely Heart, 287
Norma Rae, 298
Norris, Edward, 170
North Star, 221
No Way Out, 251–252
Nugent, Frank, 144, 205
Numbered Men, 27
Nye, Sen. Gerald P., 202, 215

Objective Burma, 237
O'Brien, Pat, 41, 110, 113, 114, 142
Odets, Clifford, xi, 203–206, 287
O'Donnell, Cathy, 153, 230
Of Mice and Men, 244
Of Thee I Sing (play), 36–37
Oil for the Lamps of China, 110–111, 203
O'Neal, Frederick, 249
100 Men and a Girl, 101–102
One More Spring, 96
One Third of a Nation, 144
Only Victims (book), 287
On the Waterfront, 264–267, 293–294
Our Daily Bread, 58–59, 61–63, 98, 122, 124–125, 133, 303
Ox-Bow Incident, The, 172–174, 244

Pacifism, 201–202, 208, 215, 222
Pallette, Eugene, 99, 101, 102
Palmer, Lilli, 274
Panama Flo, 22
Paramount Pictures Corporation, 1, 5–6, 24, 253, 258
Parker, Eleanor, 229
Passage to Marseilles, 153, 220
Patman Bill, 78–79
Patrick, Gail, 99
Pearson, Beatrice, 247, 275
Pearson, Drew, 36, 40, 78
Peck, Gregory, 240, 260
Pelley, William Dudley, 165, 176
Pells, Richard, 121
Penn, Arthur, 154
Perrett, Geoffrey, 91
Personal History, 207, 214, 223
Pevney, Joseph, 274
Phantom President, The, 38–40
Phillips, Edwin, 93
Picture, (book), 7
Pidgeon, Walter, 112, 214
Pilgrim, The, 116
Pilot Number Five, 190, 192, 221
Pinky, 247–250
Poitier, Sidney, 251–252
Politician, The, 10
Politicians: public image of during the Depression, 36, 39; as portrayed by Hollywood, 37–40, 55–57, 69, 73, 170–171, 186, 192–198
Polonsky, Abraham, 273–279, 293, 304
Poole, Charles, 175, 177–178
Populism: ideology, 46–47; in the Hollywood film, 47–64, 88, 92, 98–103, 112, 122, 126–127, 130, 133–134, 141, 167–168, 181, 183–185, 187–188, 233, 262, 270–271, 278
Porter, Edwin S., 242
Powell, William, 31–32, 99
Power, Tyrone, 147
Power and the Glory, The, 52, 75–76, 105
President's Mystery, The, 101–102
President Vanishes, The, 73–74, 165, 175–176, 180–181, 201–202
"Pretty Boy Floyd," 146
Pride of the Marines, 227, 229–230, 237, 257
Prince, William, 237
Prisons: as portrayed by Hollywood, 26–30, 119, 136
Private Worlds, 259
Production Code, xi, 6, 135, 298
Prohibition, 70, 257
Prostitution: as portrayed by Hollywood, 20, 22–24, 34, 52, 140
Pryor, Thomas, 145

Public Enemy, 16–17, 19, 135
Purple Heart, The, 220

Qualen, John, 63, 107, 126
Quick Millions, 16, 18

Racism, 228, 233; and the American Indian, 158–161, 252–253; and the Chicano, 158, 161–162, 174, 253–256; as motivation for lynching, 171, 174–175; and the American Negro, 171, 174, 191, 233, 241–252; and the Japanese, 220, 253
Radical Visions and American Dreams, 121
Raft, George, 8, 114, 152, 312
Rains, Claude, 148, 170, 186
Rand, Ayn, 287
Ray, Nicholas, 153–154
Raye, Martha, 280
Raymond, Gene, 27
Reagan, Ronald, 259, 285
Rebel Without a Cause, 154, 297
Red Danube, The, 289–290, 292
Red Menace, The, 290, 292
Red Planet Mars, 290
Reed, Carol, 156
Reed, Sen. David A., 65, 66
Reed, Donna, 270
Reformatories: as portrayed by Hollywood, 135–138, 143–144
Reformatory, 138
Reisz, Karel, 290
"Remember My Forgotten Man" (song), 83, 87
Renoir, Jean, 133–134
Republican Party, 37, 48, 57, 77, 84, 101, 313
Republic Pictures, 101
Revere, Anne, 238, 241
Rice, Elmer, 76–77, 236
Richards, Addison, 125
Richardson, Ralph, 156
Riefenstahl, Leni, 68
Riffraff, 105–109, 113, 264
Right Cross, 253
Rios, Lalo, 174
Rise of the American Film, The, 10
Riskin, Robert, 48
RKO Radio Pictures Inc., 1, 138, 238
Road to Life, The, 92
Road to War, The (book), 201
Roberts, Roy, 276
Robinson, Edward G., 17, 42, 114, 135, 156, 212
Rockabye, 21
Rodgers, Richard and Hart, Lorenz, 38, 53
Rogers, Ginger, 259, 287
Rogers, Mrs. Lela, 287

Rogers, Will, 40
Rooney, Mickey, 139, 143
Roosevelt, Franklin D., xi, 15, 20, 39–40, 48, 50, 64, 65, 73, 74, 84, 101, 144, 165, 190; as portrayed by Hollywood, 71–72, 85–87, 92, 94, 130, 231; economic policies, 91; foreign policy, 202–203, 212, 218; as target of the right wing, 284, 287–288, 292
Roots (television show), 298
Rosemund, Clinton, 171
Ross, Lillian, 7
Rossen, Robert, 193, 196, 277, 293
Roth, Mark, 86
Running Away from Myself, 268
Rural life: as portrayed by Hollywood, 57–58, 61, 122–134; during the Depression, 63, 121–122, 124–125, 133, 134
Russell, Gail, 254
Russell, Harold, 230
Russell, Rosalind, 220
Ryan, Robert, 238

Saboteur, 221
Sahara, 221, 245
St. Louis Kid, The, 114
Salt of the Earth, 253–256, 264–267, 293–295, 316
Salvation Hunters, The, 11
Sanders, George, 213, 214
Sarvis, David, 267
Savage, The, 253
Scandal for Sale, 43
Scandal Sheet, 43
Scarface, 16–17, 19
Schlesinger, Arthur, Jr., 36, 87, 194
Schorer, Mark, 313
Schulberg, Budd, 265, 293–294
Scott, Zachary, 134
Screen Cartoonists Guild, 105
Screen Playwrights, 104
Screenwriters Guild, 104
Screwball comedy, 3, 8, 102
Searching Wind, The, 222–223
"Secret Movie Censors" (article), 207
Secret Six, The, 16–17, 42, 44, 66–67, 166
Seldes, Gilbert, 9
Sergeant York, 215
Service (play), 87
Shaft, 252
Shanghai, 203
Shanghai Express, 203
Shanghai Madness, 203
She Loved a Fireman, 114
Sheridan, Ann, 8
Sidney, Sylvia, 27, 111, 140, 144, 149, 152, 168, 222, 236

Sight and Sound (magazine), 266
Simpson, Russell, 122
Since You Went Away, 222
Sinclair, Upton, 9, 77, 257, 316
Sitting Bull, 253
Skelly, Hal, 257
Slim, 113–114
Slum environment: as portrayed by Hollywood, 111, 116, 135–136, 138–145, 149
Small Black Room, The, 259
Smash-Up, 259
Smith, "General" Art, 165
Smith, Gerald L. K., 190
Snake Pit, The, 260–261, 304
Sofia, 289
Song of Russia, 221, 287
So Proudly We Hail, 220
Southerner, The, 133–134
Spanish Civil War, 202, 205–208
Spellbound, 260
Spencer, Kenneth, 245
Spivey, Victoria, 243
Stack, Robert, 211
Stalin, Joseph, 284, 289, 290
Stand Up and Cheer, 87–88
Stanwyck, Barbara, 182–183
Star Is Born, A, 257
Stars Look Down, The, 156
State Fair, 58, 134
State's Attorney, 31–35
Steel Against the Sky, 114
Steinbeck, John, xi, 121, 122, 126, 130–132, 172
Stevens, Mark, 233
Stewart, James, 57, 184–185, 211, 268, 271
Stokowski, Leopold, 101, 102
Stone, George E., 42
Stone, Lewis, 17
Story of G.I. Joe, The, 221
Story of Louis Pasteur, The, 156
Stranger's Return, The 58
Street Scene, 58, 76, 111, 236, 238
Street with No Name, The, 153
Strikes: as portrayed by Hollywood, 75–76, 105–113, 118, 120, 140–141, 254–255, 263–265, 267; during the Depression, 104–105, 107–108, 129; during the forties, 262
Strudwick, Sheppard, 197
Struggle, The, 257
Studio system, xi, 1–4, 11, 298, 316
Sturges, Preston, ix, 52, 300–303
Sugarland Express, 154
Sullavan, Margaret, 75, 98, 209, 211
Sullivan, Mark, 40
Sullivan's Travels, ix, 300–305
Susan Lennox: Her Fall and Rise, 22

Sweet Sweetback's Baadasssss Song, 252
Swing, Raymond Gram, 176

Talking pictures, 15–16, 20
Talk of the Town, 172–174, 221
Tamiroff, Akim, 203
Taxi, 114
Taylor, Robert, 209, 285
Taylor, Winchell, 207
Television, xi, 4, 9, 298
Tell Them Willie Boy Was Here, 293
Temple, Shirley, x, 8, 88
Tender Comrade, 287
They Drive by Night, 8, 114, 312
They Live by Night, 153–154, 298
They Made Me a Criminal, 143–144, 148
They Won't Forget, 82, 166–167, 169–173, 244
Thieves Like Us (film), 154
Thieves Like Us (novel), 146, 153
This Day and Age, 67–68, 137, 166, 167, 235
This Land Is Mine, 221
Thomas, Parnell, 285, 289
Three Comrades, 209–212
Three Little Pigs, The, 51
Three Stripes in the Sun, 253
Tiger Shark, 114
Till the End of Time, 231–233, 237
Time (magazine), 96, 211, 218
Tobacco Road (film), 132–133, 296
Tobacco Road (novel), 132–133
Tobacco Road (play), 132
Tobias, George, 221
To Have and Have Not, 220
Toler, Sidney, 159
Tomorrow the World, 219
Tone, Franchot, 94, 192, 209
Toomey, Regis, 188
Townsend, Dr. Francis E., 165
Tracy, Lee, 31, 42, 55
Tracy, Spencer, 18, 27, 52, 53, 97, 106, 114, 143, 168, 191
Travers, Henry, 269
Trevor, Claire, 140
Triple Trouble, 116
Triumph of the Will, 68, 70
Troy, William, 74, 93
Truck Busters, 114
Trumbo, Dalton, 287
Turner, Lana, 170
Turrou, Leon, 212
Twelve Angry Men, 297
Twelvetrees, Helen, 22, 32
Twentieth Century-Fox, 1, 87, 205, 215, 238, 289
20,000 Years in Sing Sing, 27–29
Tyler, Tom, 174

Uncle Tom's Cabin (film), 242
Under My Skin, 241
Unemployment: as portrayed by Hollywood, 22, 35, 48, 53–54, 61, 69, 70, 91–101, 103, 114, 118, 233–234, 304; during the Depression, 78, 91, 105; during World War II, 190
Unionism: during the Depression, 104, 172; as portrayed by Hollywood, 105–109, 111–112, 114, 262–267; during the forties, 262
United Artists, 1, 216
Universal Pictures, 1, 87, 144

Vanity Fair (magazine), 65, 66
Variety (newspaper), 81, 88
Vaughn, Robert, 287
Veterans, *see* World War II
Vidor, King, 11, 58–63, 124–125, 156, 243, 253, 262–263, 303
Vigilantism: as portrayed by Hollywood, 66, 67–68, 165–178; in the thirties, 166; causes of, 171
Vinson, Helen, 80
Viva Zapata! x
Von Sternberg, Josef, 11, 24, 203
Von Stroheim, Erich, 11

Wagner Act, 104
Wagner-Costigan Bill, 166
"Waldorf Statement," 286
Walk a Crooked Mile, 289
Walk East on Beacon, 289, 291
Walker, Robert, 290
Walk in the Sun, A, 221, 237
Walk the Proud Land, 253
Wallis, Hal, 81
Wall Street: stock market crash of 1929, 23, 49–51
Wanger, Walter, 71–72, 74, 205, 207, 214
War Activities Committee, 219
War Against Mrs. Hadley, The, 222
War Labor Board, 263
Warner, H. B., 271
Warner, Jack, 2, 105, 237, 285, 296; relationship w. Franklin Delano Roosevelt, 84, 212, 288
Warner Brothers, x, 1, 5–6, 79, 81–84, 87, 92, 94–97, 105, 108–110, 113, 114, 136–137, 141, 143–144, 147–148, 158, 160–161, 169, 212–213, 215, 221, 235, 288, 303, 312
Warshow, Robert, 18, 279
Washington, Fredi, 245
Washington Masquerade, 55–57, 180
Washington Merry-Go-Round (book), 36

Washington Merry-Go-Round (film), 55–56, 180
Washington *Star*, 78
Watch on the Rhine, 220
Waters, Ethel, 249–250
Watson, Bobs, 143
Watson, Minor, 141
Watson, Robert, 220
Wayne, John, 291
Well, The, 252
Welles, Orson, 193
Wellman, William, 92, 94, 97
"We're in the Money" (song), 83
"We're out of the Red" (song), 88
West, Mae, 25
West of Shanghai, 203
Wet Parade, The, 257, 316
We Were Strangers, 241
Wheeler, Sen. Burton K., 202
Whip Hand, 290–291
Whipper, Leigh, 244
Whistle at Eaton Falls, 262–264
White Bondage, 125
White Feather, 253
White Heat, 153
White Shadow, The (television series), 298
Whorf, Richard, 192
Widmark, Richard, 153, 251
Wilcoxen, Henry, 102
Wild Boys of the Road, 82, 92–94, 97
Wilder, Billy, 257–259
Wild One, The, 297
Wild River, 297
William, Warren, 31–32, 37
Williams, Bill, 231
Willis, Donald C., 185
Will There Really Be a Morning? 261
Wilson, Carey, 71, 74
Wilson, Michael, 253, 293, 295
Wilson, Woodrow, 9, 222
Wilson, 222–223
Winchell, Walter, 40
Windsor, Marie, 275
Wings for the Eagle, 114, 221
Winston, Archer, 148
Wood, Michael, 305
Wood, Robin, 25
Working Man, The, 51
Works Progress Administration (WPA), 91, 101
World Changes, The, 51
World War I, 9, 21, 116, 215; American reaction to, 200–201, 203
World War II, 76, 190, 200, 204, 262, 304; in Hollywood films, 114, 153, 172, 190–192, 208, 219–223, 237, 244; American reaction to, 227; veterans' readjustment after

World War II (*cont.*)
  (as portrayed by Hollywood), 227–234;
   pro-Soviet propaganda during, 287–289
Worth, Cedric, 74
Wray, John, 100
Wright, Theresa, 231, 232
Wyler, William, 230, 285
Wyman, Jane, 258

Yank in the RAF, A, 214
You and Me, 151–153

You Can't Take It with You, 102, 180–182,
  185, 313
You Have Seen Their Faces (book), 121
Young, Loretta, 53, 85
Young, Robert, 209, 211, 222, 239
You Only Live Once, 149–153, 168, 169,
  269, 282, 298, 304

Zanuck, Darryl F., 2, 81, 132, 215, 223, 238,
  250, 261
Zukor, Adolph, 208